Christianity in Korea

Christianity in Korea

Edited by
**Robert E. Buswell Jr.
and Timothy S. Lee**

University of Hawai'i Press • Honolulu

Library of Congress Cataloging-in-Publication Data

Christianity in Korea / edited by Robert E. Buswell Jr. and Timothy S. Lee.
  p. cm.
Includes bibliographical references and index.
ISBN-13: 978-0-8248-2912-4 (hardcover : alk. paper)
ISBN-13: 978-0-8248-3206-3 (pbk : alk. paper)
1. Christianity—Korea. I. Buswell, Robert E. II. Lee, Timothy S.
BR1325.C525 2005
275.19—dc22   2005015747

Designed by the University of Hawai'i Press production staff

Contents

Acknowledgments

The research that led to this volume has been made possible by the Luce Program in Korean Christianity at the University of California, Los Angeles, a research initiative made possible by an extremely generous multiyear grant from the Henry Luce Foundation. When we first approached the Luce Foundation regarding this program, UCLA already offered the most exhaustive coverage of Korean Buddhism, Confucianism, and folk religion of any university in the country. But we had not as yet been able to offer a single course on Korean Christianity and had no faculty who specialized in this field. UCLA has the largest enrollments of Korean American students in the United States: some 3,300 students, or nearly 10 percent of our entire student body, the total enrollments of many liberal arts colleges. A substantial majority of these students have been raised as Christians, and scores of Korean American students participate actively in Bible study groups and Christian fellowships on campus. Despite their keen interest, however, there were no courses available to them on the Korean Christian tradition. Offering courses on Korean Christianity would help to strengthen our Korean American students' identities as both Korean and Christian and would give us a start in rebuilding our coverage of the Christian tradition as a whole on campus. Given UCLA's demographics, change was clearly in order.

Luce funding has enabled UCLA to sponsor a Distinguished Visiting Professor of Korean Christianity each year since 2000, an annual postdoctoral fellow, and one graduate fellowship. In addition, the Luce support has allowed UCLA to sponsor a series of research conferences on the tradition, of which this volume is one result. I am especially grateful to Dr. Terrill Lautz, vice president of the Luce Foundation, and Ms. Helena Kolenda, Luce's program officer, for their enthusiastic support in bringing this program to fruition. UCLA has also benefited greatly from the help and support we have received from several colleagues in starting our program, including Ambassador James Laney (Emory University) and professors Samuel Moffett and Sang Hyun Lee (Princeton Theological Seminary). I also would like to express my personal gratitude to Professor Gi-Wook Shin, our erstwhile colleague, who typically gave freely of his time and energy to help build UCLA's programs in Korean Studies. Special thanks go to Professor John Duncan, current director of the Center for Korean Studies, who has never wavered in his support for our efforts. Ms. Eileen Sir, assistant director of the Center for Korean Studies since its inception, has been typically indefatigable and efficient in handling all the myriad administrative details involved in running such a complex program; all of us in Korean Studies at UCLA owe her an immense debt of gratitude for her help these many years in building our programs. In bringing the volume to fruition, we also benefited from the careful reading given the manuscript by the two anonymous readers for the University of Hawai'i Press, who offered several valuable suggestions for revisions. Finally, I would also like to express my appreciation to all the scholars who have visited UCLA as Luce professors, postdoctoral fellows, and colloquia participants; they have helped to create a critical mass on campus for research and teaching on Korean Christianity. But I am especially grateful to my coeditor, Tim Lee, who was our Luce postdoctoral fellow in 2001–2002; without his enthusiasm, vision, and plain hard work, this volume would not have been possible.

ROBERT E. BUSWELL JR.
University of California, Los Angeles

Introduction

Robert E. Buswell Jr. and Timothy S. Lee

Anyone who has visited the South Korean capital of Seoul will have noticed the myriad church steeples that dominate the cityscape, especially at night when the crosses atop them light up in red or white neon. The prevalence of these steeples in Seoul—as in other cities and towns across the southern half of the Korean peninsula—speaks to the ubiquity of Christianity in modern South Korea. For understanding modern Korean culture, society, and politics, the importance of Christianity cannot be underestimated. It may be somewhat of an exaggeration to claim that Christianity is to modern Korea what Buddhism was to the Silla and Koryŏ dynasties, or Confucianism to the Chosŏn; but it is certainly not an overstatement to say that a modern South Korea without Christianity is hardly conceivable. The mere fact that at the end of the twentieth century more than 25 percent of South Koreans identify themselves as Protestants or Catholics attests to Christianity's wide-ranging influence.

As was the case with Buddhism and Confucianism, interaction between Christianity and Korea has been reciprocal. Christianity made major contributions to the shaping of modern Korea. Protestants articulated a viable religious faith that also promised economic prosperity and social relevance in an increasingly secular modern world. Christian missionaries were the first to bring Western-style higher education and health care to Korea, and Christianity became synonymous with progress and modernity. Korean Christian leaders were also at the vanguard of the independence movement against Japanese colonial occupation, and still today are among the most vocal and articulate exponents of democratization. Minjung Theology, or theology for the masses, has been extremely influential in contemporary Korean philosophical, social, and religious thought, spawning similar movements even in rival religions.

Just as Christianity helped to shape a modern Korea, so too have Koreans contributed to the formation of a global Christianity. This growing international presence for Korean Christianity is attested by the fact that in

1

1999, for example, the Korean Protestant churches commissioned more missionaries than did any other national church except the United States. More than twelve thousand Korean missionaries are active around the world, with their efforts focused in Southeast Asia, Central Asia, Russia, and Latin America. Korean Christians are also engaged in widespread elee-mosynary activities both domestically and internationally, spearheading recently, for example, the famine relief drive in North Korea.

Given these premises, it stands to reason that an adequate understanding of both modern Korean society and global Christianity requires consideration of Korean Christianity in its unique national context. Such an understanding of Korean Christianity, however, has been hard to come by in the West. For one thing, in the last quarter-century, only a handful of volumes relating to Korean Christianity have been published in Western languages; and what little research has been done on the tradition has typically occurred in the context of Christian seminaries and theological schools, rather than in research universities. More books exist from earlier periods, but nearly all of them treat Christianity in Korea from a missiological perspective, neglecting the specifically Korean context of the religion. This volume seeks to take an important step toward remedying the deficiency in both Korean Studies and Christian Studies. We believe that it provides the most comprehensive treatment of Korean Christianity to date in a Western language. And it is comprehensive at several different levels. For one thing, the chapters were written in the hopes of attracting both neophytes and specialists to the study of Korean Christianity. Neophytes will find in James H. Grayson's lucid overview chapter the background necessary to launch into the more specialized chapters that follow. Specialists will appreciate the multi- and interdisciplinary perspectives the volume offers in its seventeen chapters. Presented here are at least four disciplinary approaches: history (Cho Kwang, Sung-Deuk Oak, Wi Jo Kang, Jacqueline Pak, Yi Mahn-yol, Gari Ledyard, Donald Clark, and Chong Bum Kim), sociology (Byung-suh Kim, Paul Yunsik Chang, Kelly Chong), theology (Anselm Min and Wonil Kim), and comparative religion (Kangnam Oh). In addition, three of the chapters straddle disciplinary boundaries—Donald Baker and Timothy S. Lee bridge history and sociology, and James Grayson bridges history and theology. The volume is also noteworthy in that its contributors hail from four different countries—South Korea, Britain, Canada, and the United States—illustrating how global both Korean Studies and Korean Christianity have become. Differences in romanization and terminology reflect an author's preference.

Volumes on Korean Christianity published in both Korea and the West have tended to focus upon one or the other of the two major Christian communions in Korea—Catholicism and Protestantism—usually to the exclusion of the other. This volume, admittedly, cannot claim to provide even treatment of these communions, since most of its chapters focus on Protestantism. Nevertheless, two of the chapters (Cho and Ledyard) deal exclusively with Korean Catholicism and at least half of another (Baker) is devoted to the same subject. A mea culpa is also in order for another lacuna: coverage of the Korean Orthodox Church. The Orthodox Church arrived in Korea in 1899 from Russia, but because of setbacks it suffered during the Russo-Japanese War (1904–1905), the Russian Revolution (1917), and the Japanese colonial period (1910–1945), the church never effloresced in Korea as did the other two communions; at the end of the twentieth century, it was barely surviving, with only a few thousand adherents. As a result, the Orthodox Church has remained more or less invisible in the historiography of Korean Christianity. We regret that we are here able only to make a point of this neglect, in the hope that enterprising scholars will soon take it upon themselves to redress it.

Other than that omission, this volume includes a comprehensive overview of the tradition and specific chapters that cover all periods of the Korean Christian church—from the late Chosŏn dynasty to the last decade of the twentieth century—and hits many of the key issues in the history and life of the church, from church growth to domestic politics, Evangelical dominance, *minjung* theology, Korean apocalyptic thought, interreligious dialogue, and the role of women in building the church. We hope the reader will find this volume to be a worthy guide in better understanding Christianity, Korea, and Christianity in Korea.

PART ONE
Overview

CHAPTER 1

A Quarter-Millennium of Christianity in Korea

James Huntley Grayson

In this volume, various chapters consider a range of historical issues in the overall story of Christianity in Korea. To understand this history, why it took the shape that it did, we have to understand what the Christians of Korea believed, for it is these beliefs that in one way or another impelled their actions.

Ecclesiastical History and *Kairos*

We cannot reduce the story of Korean Christians down to simple social, economic, and political motivations. Profound beliefs motivated their actions. The twentieth-century German theologian Paul Tillich, who came to intellectual maturity in the aftermath of the First World War and later became an American citizen, developed the idea of *kairos*, the Greek word for "fulfilled time," as a hermeneutical tool for understanding Christian history. Tillich used this concept to describe the critical nature of the times in which he lived and the challenges the church faced with the rise of Nazism in Germany set against the ultimate *kairos*, Christ.[1] I will use the term *kairos* in that sense, that the history of the growth and spread of Christianity in Korea must be understood in terms of the challenges the Christians perceived that they faced, and that these challenges were essentially issues of faith, issues arising from the beliefs they held. In this chapter, I divide Korean Christian history into five periods, or eras of *kairos*:

1. The Catholic encounter with Korean culture (late eighteenth century). Christianity in its Roman Catholic and Protestant forms is a monotheistic religion with strong views on idolatry. The very first Korean Catholics, who had accepted monotheism as a refreshing alternative to the nontheistic concepts of Neo-Confucianism, experienced a clash of values over the performance of ancestral rituals. Were they memorial rituals

expressing deep feelings of filial piety, or were they idolatrous rites addressed to spirits other than God?

2. The nineteenth-century persecution of the Roman Catholic Church (early to late nineteenth century). Despite the continued clash of values and the regularization of the persecution of the church, the next generation of Catholics held firmly to their beliefs. Beliefs in the equality of all men and women under the fatherhood of God and the hope of a better life in paradise enabled the church to spread widely among the lowest orders of Korean society.

3. The Protestant encounter with Korean culture (late nineteenth to early twentieth centuries). In its first stage of encounter with Korean culture, Protestantism experienced the same clash of values as had Catholicism. However, the weakened state of the central government and the search by young progressive nationalists for new values and new means to revitalize their nation led to the rapid acceptance of Protestant Christianity. Cessation of persecution enabled Catholicism to grow quietly.

4. The Christian reaction to the loss of Korean nationhood (mid-twentieth century). The association of Protestantism with restorative nationalism led to clashes with the Japanese colonial government over independence, religious worship in schools, and ultimately over attendance at worship at State Shintō shrines. The final issue raised the question of idolatry. In this period, Catholicism continued within its mental "ghetto," the result of a century of persecution.

5. The Christian reaction to communism, national division, and industrialization (mid- to late twentieth century). The challenge to Christianity in this most recent era has been whether the church should concentrate on institutional expansion ("Church Growth") or whether it should be more deeply involved in the social and political issues of the day. Is faith simply a personal matter, or does it have social, political, and economic ramifications?[2]

Initial Missionary Probes

The history of Christianity in Korea is prefaced by a period of initial missionary endeavors, attempts made in the late sixteenth century and early seventeenth century by Catholics in Japan, China, and the Philippines to reach the population of the Hermit Kingdom. Following a level of success with many of the feudal daimyō of Japan, Jesuit missionaries in about 1567 began to think of promoting missions in Korea. Among the first was Father Gaspar Vilela, who drew up plans for a Jesuit mission but died in 1572 before he could implement them. As a result of the invasion of Korea by Hideyoshi in 1594, many Koreans had been taken back to Japan as slaves;

there they became Christians through the work of Catholic missionaries in Nagasaki and other major cities. In 1596, Father Louis Fröes reported that there were three hundred Koreans under instruction in Nagasaki. It is significant that when the Tokugawa shogunate suppressed Catholicism in the early 1600s, thirteen (6 percent) of the 205 martyrs were Koreans. Among these martyrs was "Vincent" Kwŏn, who had made several attempts to evangelize Korea between 1614 and 1626. In the Philippines, a Dominican missionary, Father Juan de Domingo, in 1611 and 1616 attempted unsuccessfully to enter Korea.

Thoughts of a Korean mission were not confined to foreign missionaries alone. In China, a Catholic minister of state, Xu Guangqi, requested permission from the emperor in 1620 and in 1621 to go to Korea with the covert intention of undertaking proselytizing work. A missionary in China, Father Antonio de Sainte-Marie, tried to enter Korea in 1650 but failed in his attempt. The head of the Jesuit mission, Joannes Adam Schall von Bell, who knew the Korean crown prince Sohyŏn, a hostage at the Manchu court, hoped that when Sohyŏn became king he would permit the open propagation of Christianity. Unfortunately, the prince died before his father.

Although attempts to enter Korea to conduct missionary work were unsuccessful, many Korean scholars were aware of the teaching of the Catholic Church through pamphlets written by Jesuit missionaries—such as the *Tianzhu shiyi* (The True Teaching of the Lord of Heaven) by Matteo Ricci—or by direct contact with missionaries in China. The scholar Yi Sugwang's collected works, the *Chibong yusŏl*, show that he had knowledge about the Catholic Church and its doctrines. Chŏng Tuwŏn met Father João Rodrígues in China, receiving several scientific works translated into Chinese. Although such scholars were aware of Catholicism, they appeared to have had no interest in it.[3]

Era One: Institutional Beginnings, 1777–1801

The history of the Christian community in Korea dates to 1777, when young Confucian scholars formed a group to study the Jesuit tracts. However, it was not until 1784 that one of their number, Yi Sŭnghun, accompanied his father to Beijing, made contact with the priests there, was baptized, and upon his return to Korea evangelized his friends. The first characteristic to note about the Korean church is that from the beginning it was self-evangelized. In 1785 the government, learning of the spread of this strange creed forbidding the performance of the *chesa* rites (the Confucian ancestral ceremony) because they were perceived to be idolatrous, issued an edict suppressing Catholicism. In the following year, another edict banning the importation of Catholic works was issued. Most of the early Catholics were highly educated, coming from either the aristocratic class or the *chungin* (middle bureaucratic class). The first martyrdom occurred in 1786 when Kim Pŏmu, a government interpreter, died as a result of torture undergone during his incarceration. Social pressure also caused many to fall away when parents threatened suicide. Yet many early Catholics did not give in. In 1791 two cousins, Kwŏn Sangyŏn and Yun Chich'ung, were executed for not performing the *chesa* rites and for burning their ancestral tablets. They were the first martyrs executed for belief in Catholicism. Thus was set the pattern for the persecutions that were to typify Catholic history in the nineteenth century.[4]

From the 1790s onward we hear less about aristocratic Catholics and more about believers drawn from the middle and lower classes. The first Catholic missionary, a Chinese priest, Father Zhou Wenmo, arrived in 1795 but had to seek refuge in the home of an aristocratic lady, Kang Wansuk. When Father Zhou arrived, there were some four thousand believers; by the turn of the century believers numbered ten thousand. The growth of the sect caused grave concern in certain circles. With the sudden death of the tolerant King Chŏngjo in 1800, the constraints against the open persecution of the church were removed. As King Sunjo was a boy, his grandmother ruled as queen regent in his stead. Under her regency the Sinyu persecution began, the first great persecution of the nineteenth century.

Era Two: Persecution and Martyrdom, 1801–1871

The second critical era of Christian history began with the Sinyu persecution of 1801, marking the end of the church of the scholar aristocrats and the beginning of an underground, persecuted church of the people. Part of the ferocity of this persecution was due to a letter written by Hwang Sayŏng in which he appealed for a Western navy and army to protect the fledgling church. In the eyes of the government, Catholicism both endangered the moral fabric of society by its refusal to perform the *chesa* rites and raised the question of the political subordination of the nation. In the Sinyu persecution, many of the early key leaders were executed. Until the middle of the second decade of the nineteenth century there were no further persecutions on a national scale, although local suppressions occurred continuously during the years 1811 to 1814. The Ŭrhae persecution of 1815 was followed twelve years later by the Chŏnghae persecution of 1827. Then came another quiet period of twelve years, followed by the fourth major persecution in 1839, the Kihae persecution. At that time, the discovery of French missionaries raised fears of the subversion of the state by foreign powers. Although there was a smaller persecution in 1846, the next major national persecution, the Great Persecution, did not occur until 1866; it lasted for five years, until 1871. This suppression of Catholicism was triggered by Russian attempts to seize part of Korean national territory in 1866; it was fanned by the appearance of a French fleet off the Korean coast in the same year, attempts to desecrate the tomb of the father of the prince regent in 1868, and the appearance of an American fleet in Korean waters in 1871. The periodicity of these persecutions shows the authorities' concern for the subversion of traditional social mores and fears of the loss of national sovereignty, and also points to the significant extent to which the church had taken root.

With the death of Father Zhou in 1801, there was no clerical oversight of the Christian community until 1831, when Korea was created a Vicariate Apostolic, but the missionary bishop died before reaching Korea. A Chinese priest, Liu Fangzhi, did enter Korea in 1831; he was joined in 1836 by Father Pierre Philibert Maubant and in 1837 by Father Jacques Honoré Chastan and Bishop Laurent Marie Joseph Imbert. The persecuted Korean church had thus survived for a generation without priestly supervision. In 1834, church membership had trebled to nine thousand, the same level of membership as in the 1790s. Hopes for a quiet period of growth were smashed by the Kihae persecution of 1839 with the execution of all the French clergy. Again, there was no clerical supervision until the arrival of Bishop Jean Joseph Ferréol and Father Marie Antoine Nicolas Daveluy in 1845. The execution of the first Korean ordinand in 1846 deprived the fledgling church of its first native priest, and the bishop's death from exhaustion in 1853 further weakened it. Bishop Siméon François Berneux reported in 1857 that church membership numbered over fifteen thousand, five times its size in the early 1800s. This is remarkable considering both the persecution and the lack of clerical supervision for nearly fifty years. These advances dramatically changed in the Great Persecution of 1866–1871, when the prince regent tried to eradicate once and for all the pernicious influences of the strange doctrines of Catholicism. Nine French clergy and some eight thousand believers were executed—that is, half of the membership of the church suffered martyrdom. Although heavily persecuted, the Catholic Church showed that it had the resilience to withstand severe persecution, the ability to manage its own affairs, and the strength to grow in spite of the lack of clerical supervision.[5]

Era Three: Cultural Clash or Cultural Encounter? 1871–1910

ROMAN CATHOLICISM

From 1871, the formal persecution of the Church ceased. The most striking characteristic of Catholicism in the period following the cessation of persecution is the emergence of a Catholic ghetto mentality among the ecclesiastical leadership and the average Catholic. This outlook led to a focus on institutional growth with little concern for social outreach and little awareness of the historical events taking place around them. For Catholics, cessation of persecution meant a period of quiet rebuilding. In 1876, five years after the end of the Great Persecution, two priests were able to return to Korea; they were joined in 1877 by Bishop Félix Clair Ridel. Although the bishop was deported in 1878 and a priest in 1879, by 1881 the government had ceased to harass priests, a result of Korea's attempts to establish diplomatic relations with the Western powers. The stability that had been achieved is reflected in the continued institutional growth of the church. In 1882, there were 12,500 believers, an increase in the six years since end of the Great Persecution of 5,500 persons or 44 percent. By 1910, the number of adherents had grown to 73,000, a 500 percent increase over 1882. By 1900 there were ten Korean priests; ten years later there were fifteen, and fifty-six foreign clergy. The history of the martyrs of the church was recognized with the erection of "martyrium," memorial churches to the martyrs such as the Yakhyŏn Church, erected in 1893 on a hill above the execution ground outside the Sŏsomun or Little West Gate, and the Cathedral of St. Mary, dedicated in 1898 and built on the site of the home of Kim Pŏmu, the first Korean martyr. Unlike Protestant churches, the Catholic Church, lacking a policy of social outreach, did not build modern schools or hospitals but concentrated on those things that strengthened the church's spiritual life.[6]

THE ADVENT OF PROTESTANT CHRISTIANITY

Like Catholic history, there had been some initial missionary probes made by Karl Friederich August Gützlaff, who explored the Manchurian and Korean west coasts in 1832, by Robert Jermain Thomas, who was aboard the American trading vessel the *General Sherman* in September 1866 when it ventured up the Taedong River to P'yŏngyang, and by Alexander Williamson, who visited the customs barrier between Manchuria and Korea in 1867. None of these attempts had any long-lasting effect on Korea. The first Protestant missionary to have an impact was John Ross of the United Presbyterian Church of Scotland Manchurian mission, who translated the New Testament into Korean using as a team of translators a group of Korean merchants in Manchuria. In 1882, the first portions of his translation of the New Testament were printed and circulated, with the entire New Testament translated, bound, and distributed as a single volume in 1887. Ross's converts were responsible for the establishment of Christian communities in northwestern Korea, in the capital, and in the communities along the northern bank of the Yalu River, nominally Korean territory. Ross believed that Christianity was spread best by convinced converts rather than by foreign missionaries. The existence of Protestant communities in Korea before foreign missionaries arrived is an eloquent testimonial to Ross's conviction. Protestantism in Korea, like Catholicism, was self-evangelized from the beginning—evangelism through the distribution of scripture. The Ross translation introduced key theological terms that are still in use, such as Hananim (Ruler of Heaven) for God.

From the mid-1880s, foreign missionaries began to arrive, including Horace N. Allen of the Northern Presbyterian Church in 1884 and Horace G. Underwood of the Northern Presbyterian mission and Henry G. Appenzeller of the Northern Methodist mission in 1885, followed almost immediately by several other missionaries. By the end of the ninth decade of the nineteenth century, a foreign-mission enterprise that could build on the foundations laid by the earliest converts was well under way. By the end of the 1880s, several of modern Korea's major institutions had been established such as three Western-style medical institutions, Paejae Boys' High School, and Ewha Girls' High School. At the same time, the Religious Tract Society for the distribution of scriptures and religious materials was created as well as the Tri-Lingual Press, the first Western-style publishing house.

The 1890s saw growth in the numbers of converts and the creation of Christian literature, including dictionaries, manuals of the Korean language, and translations of devotional works, such as *Pilgrim's Progress*. At the same time the way to create an independent church institution was also much debated. In the early 1890s, John L. Nevius, a Presbyterian missionary in Shantung, China, was invited to explain to the Korea missionaries his methods for creating a self-propagating, self-governing, and self-supporting church; this method became the universally accepted policy of Protestant missions in Korea.

In the decade preceding the annexation of Korea by Japan in 1910, church membership grew significantly; this growth is often attributed to the Great Revival of 1907 in P'yŏngyang, the effect of which quickly spread everywhere in the peninsula and into Manchuria. Although the event has to be seen against the background of the political uncertainties of the time, it can not be gainsaid that this revival unleashed the spiritual energy for the evangelization of the nation by the Koreans themselves. By 1910, 1 percent of the population adhered to the Protestant church. The Japanese Protestant church today, which has a longer history, has not equaled this achievement.

One important effect of the missionaries' social outreach was the work done by Korean Christians. Many schools in Korea today claim a Christian, but not a mission, foundation as a result of their efforts in this decade. Much of the success of the Protestant churches in the first twenty-five years after the arrival of the missionaries reflected the association of Christianity with the "progressive" West and the emphasis that the first generation of missionaries placed on the responsibility of local Christians for the growth and support of their churches. Kenneth Wells in *New God/New Nation: Protestants and Self-Reconstruction Nationalism in Korea* stresses the importance of the mixture of religious faith and nationalism at a time when the nation was facing a political crisis.

In 1910, the institutional church was well established—the first seminaries had been founded, the first seminary graduates had graduated, and the first Korean ministers had been ordained. In 1908 all Protestant missionaries, except the High Church Anglicans, had devised a comity agreement that divided the peninsula into mission spheres, avoiding competition so that there would be only one denomination in one area. A vote taken at the same time to create a United Church of Christ in Korea was rejected by the supporting denominations in North America. None the less, the comity agreement, the use of a single translation of the Bible, a common hymnal, and other pan-denominational activities helped to create a sense of a common Protestant Christianity.[7]

Era Four: Colonial Subjugation, 1910–1945

THE ROMAN CATHOLIC EXPERIENCE

The annexation of Korea in 1910 by Japan began another critical period for the Christian church—how both to remain faithful as Christians and retain a sense of Korean nationality in the absence of a Korean state. The Catholic response in this period was much the same as in the third period—to focus on institutional growth and individual spiritual development. Reflecting the numerical growth of the church, two Vicariates Apostolic were created in 1911—in Seoul and Taegu—and a third in Wŏnsan in 1920. In 1920 there were 292 churches and 90,000 communicants; by 1932 the number had increased to 323 churches with 110,000 communicants who were served by 141 priests of whom 55 were Koreans. By the early 1940s there were 183,000 communicants served by 308 priests of whom 139 were Koreans. This is fourteen times the size of the church in 1882. In spite of these increases, however, Catholics represented only 0.05 percent of the national population, which compares unfavorably with Protestant statistics of the same period. Min Kyongsuk concluded that the Catholic Church continued to divorce itself from the mainstream of Korean society, to maintain a kind of ghetto mentality toward the world outside the church itself. Moreover, such scholars point out that most converts were from the dispossessed sectors of society. As there were no Catholic institutions of higher education until 1932, the church had little appeal to the intellectual classes.[8]

Until the last five years of Japanese rule, the church led a very quiet life. There are two reasons for this fact. First, the Vatican had signed a concordat with the Japanese government in May 1936 in which it accepted the Japanese government's statement that State Shintō rites were patriotic rites and not idolatrous rituals. While giving the Roman Catholic Church in the Japanese empire a legal framework for religious activities, the concordat constrained any criticisms of the colonial regime. Second, the church leadership in Korea would have remembered the sufferings of the first century of the church and would have feared the onset of another persecution. Consequently, unlike the Protestant case, there was no Catholic reaction against these rites until the arrest of a priest in 1944. This passive acquiescence in the participation in a "pagan" rite is one indication that during this period the church had not yet outgrown its ghetto mentality. Yet the church was not unaffected by Japanese government policy, in particular attempts to "purify" it of foreign influences by creating a "Japanese" Catholic Church in Korea with the appointment of Japanese priests as bishops. Further measures that infringed on the independence of the church were taken, such as the forced induction of clergy into the military and the desecration of churches as military barracks. Thus, even in a quiet mode, the church could not avoid conflict with the colonial regime.[9]

THE PROTESTANT EXPERIENCE

The Protestant experience in this period was different. Membership grew, and the churches became engaged in social and political activities. In 1914, there were 196,000 adherents or 1.1 percent of the population. By the end of Japanese rule in 1945, there were about 740,000 Protestant Christians, or over 3 percent of the population. This growth was paralleled by the involvement of Protestant Christians in the society around them. Four events can be taken to symbolize this sociopolitical engagement: the conspiracy trial of 1912, conflict over "patriotic" schools, involvement in the March First Movement of 1919, and the Shintō Shrine Controversy.

In 1912, 124 people were accused of attempting to assassinate the Japanese governor-general, Terauchi Masatake; 98 of them were Christians, a sign that the colonial regime feared that Christians represented an organized group challenging their domination of Korea. Eventually all but 6 of the alleged conspirators were acquitted for lack of sufficient evidence. More important, the trial had the effect of creating a link in the popular imagination between Korean nationalism and Christianity. In Korea, imperialism was Japanese, not Western.

A further conflict with the Protestant community arose when the colonial government tried to impose its own system of "patriotic" schools on the Korean nation. In addition to mission-founded high schools and colleges such as Sungsil College (Union Christian College) in P'yŏngyang,

Ewha Woman's College and Yŏnhŭi College (Chosen Christian College) in Seoul, Korean Christians also had founded high schools and other educational institutions. In 1915, the colonial government announced regulations that required the use of Japanese as the national language and forbade both religious instruction and worship in private schools. Causing consternation among the mission and Korean Christian communities, this issue became one of the principal reasons for Christian involvement in the Korean Independence Movement.

The March First Movement of 1919, which effectively created the sense of modern Korean nationhood, was largely the work of Korean religious leaders. Thirty-three people, sixteen of whom were Protestants, signed the Declaration of Independence. The principal influence of the Protestant signers on the character of the movement was the insistence on nonviolence. The Japanese harshly suppressed the movement, persecuting Christians in particular. Churches were burned by Japanese troops, many Christians were executed, and in one spectacular incident villagers were herded into a local church, which was then set alight. In spite of a Japanese news blackout, these events became known because a few missionaries went to China and cabled their mission boards at home; these boards in turn lobbied Western governments to condemn Japanese brutality. Christian involvement in the organization of the movement, Christian suffering in the movement, and foreign Christian condemnation of Japanese brutality showed that Christianity was not an agent of imperialism; instead, it was linked with Korean nationalism in the minds of both the Japanese and the Koreans.

After the suppression of the March First Movement, two strands of Protestant Christianity emerged, a theologically liberal and socially active strand and a theologically conservative strand concerned with purely church affairs. In the 1920s, a quiet time when great numerical gains in church membership were made, the more conservative party began to dominate. At the same time, the control of the Japanese government by xenophobic groups led to an emphasis on a Shintō nationalism that focused on the citizens' participation in rites conducted at State Shintō shrines. When the Chōsen Shintō shrine was built in 1925 as the central shrine for Japan's colony, the stage was set for a conflict with the church for the next twenty years. Although attendance at Shintō rituals were said to be a patriotic rather than a religious act, for Korean Christians performance of the rituals was offensive to them as Koreans and idolatrous to them as Christians. In the end, the colonial regime forced the General Assembly of the Presbyterian Church in 1938 to pass a resolution that shrine worship did not contravene Christian faith; this resolution was followed shortly afterward by similar statements from all other churches and church organizations.

Between 1938 and 1945, about two thousand Protestants were arrested for noncompliance, and as many as fifty people died as martyrs as a result of incarceration and torture. Missionaries were deported for their refusal to support the shrine edicts, while at the same time the Presbyterian missions closed their schools rather than concede on this issue. Methodists, on the other hand, turned their schools over to Korean control, which often meant compliance with government regulations. As with the Catholic Church, the Japanese authorities attempted to Japanize the churches by merging them with their Japanese equivalents and controlling the content of worship by forbidding the reading of the Old Testament or the Revelation of St. John the Divine because of the prophetic revelation of God's condemnation of the powers of this world. Churches were closed and their property sold off; on one occasion the property was made into a Shintō shrine. During the final months of colonial rule, the Japanese regime forced through a union of all Protestant denominations. These actions demonstrated both the fear and scorn with which the authorities held the Christian churches and further confirmed a link between Korean nationalism and Christianity. Although the Shintō Shrine Controversy demonstrated the tenacity of Christians in the face of political oppression, their movement was principally religious, not political.[10]

Era Five: Divided Nation/Industrial Nation, 1945–

THE ROMAN CATHOLIC EXPERIENCE

In the decades following the defeat of Japan and the collapse of the colonial regime in 1945, the Christian community had to contend with two major issues in its next period of *kairos*—the division of the nation and its rapid industrialization and urbanization. With the division of the nation, two different policies toward the practice of religion were implemented. The Communist regime in North Korea saw religion as the opiate of the people and determined to control all expressions of religion contrary to state policy. A year before the outbreak of the Korean War, the northern regime arrested and imprisoned Bishop Bonifatius Sauer and the monks of Tŏgwŏn Benedictine Abbey and confiscated the Catholic agricultural college, which was renamed for Kim Ilsŏng. Many parishes became inactive because priests had been arrested in such numbers. Bishop Hong Yongho of P'yŏngyang was imprisoned after sending a letter of protest to Kim Ilsŏng. After the Korean War, little was heard of North Korean Catholics until the government announced in the late 1980s that they had built a Catholic church for open worship.

In southern Korea, there was a more laissez-faire attitude toward religion, with no legal or bureaucratic impediments placed in the way of

Catholic evangelism. However, with the outbreak of the Korean War, the northern army took into custody and later killed numbers of priests, monks, and nuns, and took others to P'yŏngyang for interrogation. When hostilities ceased in 1953, Catholics in south Korea numbered 166,000 or 90 percent of all Korean Catholics in 1945.

In the decade following the Korean War, Catholicism experienced a period of great growth. The six dioceses of 1953 had become fourteen dioceses in 1963 with 575,000 adherents. The Vatican created the first ecclesiastical hierarchy in 1962 with the three archdioceses of Seoul, Taegu, and Kwangju. Two tertiary-level colleges were founded at this time, Hyosŏng College in Taegu and Sŏgang College in Seoul. From 1963 to 1974 there was continued growth in membership; communicants had risen to over one million people representing some 2.5 percent of the population. More important, Catholic social outreach was greater than at any time in the past; notably, the church involved itself in movements for the welfare of industrial workers in Korea's rapidly changing society. This stance reflects the roots of the church in the poorer sector of society and stands as a condemnation of Protestant concern with Church Growth. Institutional outreach is indicated by the foundation of nine church-related universities and sixty-eight schools.

An important part of the consciousness of modern Korean Catholics is the memory of the thousands of people who died for their faith. When Pope John Paul II went to Korea in 1984 for the bicentennial celebrations of Korean Catholicism, he canonized 103 martyrs of the Korean church, including 10 French priests, as saints of the church, the largest number of saints canonized at any one time. As part of the preparations for its bicentennial, the church built several martyrium—in particular the Chŏltu-san (Beheading Hill) Church (1967) and the Saenamt'o Church (1984)—and erected a memorial in Little West Gate park.

Catholic missiologists single out the Korean church as having had the most rapid numerical growth among the world's Catholic churches over the past twenty-five years, a trend that began at some time in the late 1950s or early 1960s. There are two principal reasons for this sudden change: the dramatic increase in the size of the Protestant churches and the Second Vatican Council (1962–1965). The high visibility of a sister form of Christianity removed the stigma surrounding Christian belief. The liberality of the council with its openness to other religions and its Christian ecumenical emphasis changed the theology of the Korean church and its attitudes toward other Christian churches. Donald Baker points out two other factors, namely, the increasing Koreanization or localization of the clergy and the increasing urbanization of the membership of the church.[11] By the 1960s, Korean Catholicism had joined both the mainstream of

Korean society and the mainstream of Korean Christianity. In 1994, the Roman Catholic Church in Korea reported that it had a membership of 3,209,494 adherents. The 1995 National Household Census statistics, however, revealed 2,950,730 self-identified Catholics. There were 2,174 priests, three archdioceses, sixteen dioceses, and 947 churches. Catholics are now 6.6 percent of the population, the same percentage as Protestants in the 1960s.[12]

THE PROTESTANT EXPERIENCE

Following liberation from Japanese rule, the Protestant churches faced three problems: different policies north and south regarding religion, questions of complicity in Japanese rule by church leaders, and the legacy of the Japanese-imposed church union.

In North Korea, the Soviet zone of influence, Christians formed political parties including the Christian Social Democratic Party and the Christian Liberal Party; these were soon suppressed. Another conflict arose in 1946 when Christian leaders wanted to commemorate the uprising of March 1, 1919, seen by the regime as a bourgeois movement. Christians again clashed with the Communist authorities over the holding of elections for the People's Assembly on a Sunday, which ran counter to the strong sabbatarian views of many Korean Christians. Control or suppression of the Christian community in the north was important not only because Christians represented a different voice on social and political matters, but also because of the size of the Christian community. At this time, the center of Christianity in Korea was in the north, not the south, an irony of history considering the current size of the Christian church in South Korea. Objections made to government policy by the Joint Presbytery of the still-unified Protestant church were countered by the authorities with the formation of the Federation of Christians, which all church officers were required by law to join. All those who refused to join were arrested for belonging to an illegal organization; churches were confiscated and put to secular uses; many Christians fled to the south, while those who remained in the north were rounded up shortly before the onset of the Korean War and executed en masse.

Little was heard about the state of Protestantism in the north until the mid-1980s when it was announced that a hymnal and a translation of the New Testament had been published in 1983 and a translation of the Old Testament in 1984. In the late 1980s, delegations of North American and European churches reported taking part in worship in the homes of individual Christians. In 1988, the government of North Korea announced that it had built and opened a new Roman Catholic and a new Protestant church for use by the respective religious communities. Subsequently, officials designated as leaders of the Christian community in North Korea have met with various Western and South Korean church leaders to discuss national unification. However, the church organizations in North Korea are not freely formed associations but the creatures of the government, their representatives being government-approved personnel.

In southern Korea, the laissez-faire policy of the American military government left the church free to handle its own affairs. Two issues emerged: the continuation of the Japanese-created unified church and the question of complicity with the Japanese colonial regime. By late 1945 a bloc of Methodists had bolted from the union church to recreate the Methodist church structure, effectively dissolving it. Conflicts over attendance at Shintō rituals and the perversion of scripture were more difficult to resolve. In 1947, accusations were made that those who wanted the union to continue had collaborated with the Japanese. The Presbyterians were similarly split with a group leaving the Presbytery to form the Koryŏ Group. This group, claiming descent from those Christians who had made a covenant against shrine worship, took a hard line against any one who had attended a shrine ritual. This split is one of the most significant events in Korean church history and indicates the extent to which theology has determined the course of the church's history.

The 1950s were a time of repairing the material damage done to churches and church-related institutions, as well as providing various social services to a war-ravaged population. Housing, transportation for refugees, emergency medical aid, distribution of clothing and food, and the establishment of orphanages were all undertaken in the immediate postwar period, heavily supported by foreign church mission bodies. Mission support was provided for the maintenance of Yonsei University, Severance Hospital, and Ehwa Womans University. The church continued to grow in numbers throughout the 1950s, but the percentage of Christians within the national population remained at about 3 percent.

The rapid growth of the church started in the 1960s when Church Growth caught the attention of the clergy and laity. The 1960s saw a doubling of the size of the membership of the Protestant churches until they represented more than 6 percent of the population, roughly 1,900,000 adherents. From that point, reached at some time in the late 1960s, the church grew phenomenally until by the year 1995 the National Household Census showed that nearly 20 percent of the population self-identified themselves as Protestant Christians.

The 1960s also saw greater social and evangelistic outreach in projects for prostitutes and laborers, foreign mission work by Korean ministers, provision of relief supplies to foreign nations, and the establishment of a nationwide radio network, the Christian Broadcasting System. Support for education and higher education continued unabated. At the end of the twentieth century, there were 31 universities and 225 schools that had a Protestant Christian connection.

Throughout the 1970s, Christian political movements pressing for a more democratically based, representative system of government emerged, constituting the reemergence of the liberal, politically active strand of Protestantism that had lain virtually dormant since the 1920s. It is important to note that it was liberal laymen and laywomen, not the leadership of the Protestant churches, who called for the restoration of democracy and for justice and fairness in dealings with workers. The petition of 1973 demanding the repeal of the Yusin Constitution entrenching Pak Chŏnghŭi in power is seen as the beginning of this movement. Many of these Christians were imprisoned and tortured for their opinions. For nearly twenty years, the political opposition to undemocratic government came largely from the Christian community.

One of the major social conflicts of the 1970s through to the 1990s was for greater legal equality for women, a battle effectively between Christian laywomen on the one hand and conservative men and the Yudo-hoe (Confucian Association) on the other hand. The most prominent leader in this fight was the Methodist laywoman Yi T'aeyŏng (Lee Tai-young), who founded the Korean Legal Aid Center for Family Relations and who was deeply involved with every revision of the Family Law from 1979 to the 1990s.

Although Protestantism is criticized for lacking accommodation to Korean culture, maintaining unnecessary Western cultural attributes, this criticism is only partly true. There also has been significant accommodation, an obvious example being the Protestant approach to Confucian ancestral rites. Centuries of Confucian influence on society stressing filial piety and its ritual expression through the performance of the ancestral or *chesa* ceremonies created within Korean Christians the need to ritually express filiality, while their Christian beliefs gave them a fear about participating in any rituals that could be considered to be idolatrous. From the beginning of Protestant missions, Christians placed great emphasis on the fifth of the Ten Commandments to honor one's father and mother as a way of reflecting their innate attitude of filial piety. Consequently, from the late 1890s, Christianized ancestral memorial rituals have been performed; these, in varying formats, have now found their way into the books of liturgy of virtually every Protestant denomination. These rites, called *ch'udo yebae* (service of recollection), are different from the Confucian *chesa* rites in that they are addressed to God and are normally performed only for one's immediate relatives such as parents and grandparents, although there is no formal prohibition against going further back. Nonetheless, they represent a significant degree of accommodation to the local culture of Korea.

Another indication of the localization of Christianity in Korea has been its ability to create an indigenous theology, *minjung sinhak* (theology of the people). Developed from the mid-1970s, this theology has many parallels with Latin American Liberation Theology and emphasizes how faith can give hope to the dispossessed. These theologians, arguing that God is working out universal destiny by his commitment to the poor and the oppressed, use two theological concepts, the *minjung* (the people) and *han* (enmity, grudge). *Minjung* theology proclaims that the *minjung* are the proper subject of history and that understanding history is to understand God's work in overcoming the *han* of the people. Drawing on the example of the liberation of the Hebrew slaves from Egyptian bondage, this theology argues that God's actions are a direct response to the suffering of the mass of the people.[13]

Final Observations

One important common characteristic of Korean Catholicism and Protestantism is that both forms of Christianity were initially disseminated before the arrival of foreign missionaries. This experience gave Christianity in its early stages in Korea a great strength. In both cases, early believers found the monotheistic, ethical, and social teachings of Christianity to be refreshing, and there was rapid growth in church population, even in the face of severe persecution. While the extensive martyrdoms of nineteenth-century Catholicism led to a ghetto mentality that existed into the 1960s, Protestantism from the first evinced a strong engagement with the social and political circumstances of the day. Influenced by the Second Vatican Council and the numerical success of Protestantism, Catholicism broke out of its mental ghetto and in the past three decades has exercised a major role as a social and political critic. By the final decade of the twentieth century, the Christian churches, especially the Protestant churches, had become the predominant religious fact of modern Korean history. Numerically, Christians of all groups constitute more than one-quarter of the South Korean population. Conceptually, Protestantism has exercised an extraordinary influence on the other religious traditions—in helping to create a more outward-looking attitude among Catholic Christians, by providing both a sense of competition and a model for growth that aided in the revival of Buddhism, and by being a conceptual inspiration for various non-Christian new religious movements.

NOTES

1. Paul Tillich, *Systematic Theology*, vol. 3: *Life and the Spirit: History and the Kingdom of God* (Welwyn: James Nisbet, 1964), 393–396. Tillich uses the concept of *kairos* to explain the work or presence of the Holy Spirit in human history and as a way of understanding the dynamics or self-transcending dynamics of history. He contrasts *kairos* with *chronos*, a simple chronological statement of events, by referring to *kairos* as "the right time, the time in which something can be done." In other words, a *kairos* is a point in history that must call forth a response or, as he refers to it again, a "good occasion for some action." This idea was developed out of his experience of the First World War and its aftermath, but for Tillich the concept of *kairos* is universal. He states that the "experience of *kairos* has occurred again and again in the history of the churches." It is for this reason that I thought it would be a useful tool to organize and examine the experience of Korean Christians over the past quarter millennium. Tillich goes on to remark that *kairos* is "a matter of vision" and "not an object of analysis or calculation." That is, the experience of *kairos* grows out of the spiritual understanding of Christians. I have used the term *kairos* both in a strict Tillichian sense, as a precise moment, and in a general sense to characterize a whole period of time, a way of looking back at an era to understand its historical dynamics.

2. A general survey of the history of Christianity in Korea may be found in James H. Grayson, *Korea: A Religious History*, rev. ed. (Richmond, Surrey: RoutledgeCurzon, 2002); Allen D. Clark, *A History of the Church in Korea* rev. ed. (1961; repr., Seoul: Christian Literature Society of Korea, 1971); Donald N. Clark, *Christianity in Modern Korea* (London: University Press of America, 1986); and Chai-Shin Yu, ed., *Korea and Christianity,* Studies in Korean Religions and Culture, 8 (Seoul: Korean Scholar Press, 1996).

3. The history of early attempts at Catholic mission in Korea is discussed in Juan G. Ruiz de Medina, *The Catholic Church in Korea: Its Origins from 1566–1784*, trans. John Bridges (Roma: Instituto Storico, 1991).

4. The classical resource for the study of late-eighteenth- and nineteenth-century Korean Catholicism is Charles Dallet, *Histoire de l'Église de Corée*, 2 vols. (1874; repr., Seoul: Royal Asiatic Society, Korea Branch, 1975), which is based upon documents used in the process of the beatification of the Korean martyrs. An accessible hagiography of the nineteenth-century martyrs produced for the Korean Catholic bicentennial is Changseok Thaddeus Kim, *Lives of 103 Martyr Saints of Korea* (Seoul: Catholic Publishing House, 1984).

5. As above, Dallet is the classical resource for this period. A summary of the history of the period may be found in Grayson, *Korea: A Religious History*, and in Chai-Shin Yu, ed., *The Founding of the Catholic Tradition in Korea* (Seoul: Myung Hwa, 1996).

6. General surveys of this period may be found in a publication by the Bicentennial Episcopal Commission of the Roman Catholic Church titled *The Catholic Church in Korea* (Seoul, 1984); in Grayson, *Korea: A Religious History*; and in Yu, *The Founding of the Catholic Tradition in Korea*.

7. The classical source for the study of the Protestant Church in this period is Lak-Geoon George Paik, *The History of Protestant Missions in Korea: 1832–1910* (1927; repr., Seoul: Yonsei University Press, 1970). A general survey may be found in Grayson, *Korea: A Religious History*, and in Clark, *A History of the Church in Korea*. The modern classic study of the effect of the relationship between nationalism, concepts of national development, and Protestant Christianity in Korea is Kenneth M. Wells, *New God, New Nation: Protestantism and Self-Reconstruction Nationalism in Korea, 1896–1937* (Honolulu: University of Hawai'i Press, 1990).

8. Anselm K. S. Min, *Findings of Content Analysis: The Spiritual Ethos of Korean Catholicism*, in *Catholic Socio-Religious Survey of Korea*, Luke J. Im, project director, et al., 2 pts. (Seoul: Social Research Institute, Sŏgang University, 1971, 1972), pt. 1, 7, 88–92, 102–104.

9. Information on this period is discussed in Hongyŏl Yu, *Han'guk Ch'ŏnju kyohoe-sa* [A History of the Korean Catholic Church] (Seoul: Kat'ollik Ch'ulp'an-sa, 1964).

10. Surveys of the history of this period may be found in Clark, *A History of the Church in Korea*; in Clark, *Christianity in Modern Korea*; and in James H. Grayson, *Early Buddhism and Christianity in Korea: A Study in the Emplantation of Religion* (Leiden: E. J. Brill, 1985). A study of the reaction to the requirement to attend State Shintō shrine rituals is in James H. Grayson, "The Shintō Shrine Conflict and Protestant Martyrs in Korea, 1938–1945," *Missiology* 29 no. 3 (2001).

11. Donald Baker, "From Pottery to Politics: The Transformation of Korean Catholicism," in *Religion and Society in Contemporary Korea*, ed. Lewis R. Lancaster and Richard K. Payne, Korea Research Monograph, 24 (Berkeley: Institute of East Asian Studies, University of California, 1997), 159–216.

12. Recent studies of the modern Korean Catholic Church include Baker, "From Pottery to Politics"; William E. Biernatzki, Luke J. Im, and Anselm K. Min, *Korean Catholicism in the 1970s: A Christian Community Comes of Age* (Mary-knoll, N.Y.: Orbis, 1975); and Im et al., *Catholic Socio-Religious Survey of Korea*. A general survey may be found in Bicentennial Episcopal Commission, *The Catholic Church in Korea*.

13. General surveys of the history of the Protestant Church in the modern period may be found in Clark, *A History of the Church in Korea*; Clark, *Christianity in Modern Korea*; idem, "History and Religion in Modern Korea: The Case of Protestant Christianity," in *Religion and Society in Contemporary Korea*, ed. Lewis R. Lancaster and Richard K. Payne; and Grayson, *Korea: A Religious History*.

Reflections on the relationship between Protestant Christianity and Korean culture are discussed in James H. Grayson, "Cultural Encounter: Korean Protestant-ism and Other Religious Traditions," *International Bulletin of Missionary Research* 25 no. 2 (2001); and idem, "Dynamic Complementarity: Korean Confucianism and Christianity," in *Religion and the Transformations of Capitalism: Comparative Approaches*, ed. Richard H. Roberts (London: Routledge, 1995).

A discussion of *minjung* theology may be found in Jürgen Moltmann, ed., *Minjung: Theologie des Volkes Gottes in Südkorea* (Neukirchen-Vlyun: Neukirchener Verlag, 1984), and in David Kwang-sun Suh, *The Korean Minjung in Christ* (Hong

Kong: Christian Conference of Asia, Commission on Theological Concerns, 1991). Essays on the rapid growth of Protestant Christianity may be found in Bong Rin Ro and Marlin L. Nelson Ro, eds., *Korean Church Growth Explosion* (Seoul: Word of Life Press, 1983). Information on Christianity in contemporary North Korea is in Han'guk kidokkyo yŏksa yŏn'gu-so [The Institute of Korean Church History Studies], *Puk Han kyohoe-sa* [North Korean Church History] (Seoul: Han'guk Kidokkyo Yŏksa Yŏn'gu-so, 1995). Essays comparing Christianity in Korea and Japan are contained in Mark R. Mullins and Richard Fox Young, eds., *Perspectives on Christianity in Korea and Japan: The Gospel and Culture in East Asia* (Lewiston, N.Y.: Edwin Mellen, 1995).

PART TWO

The Beginnings of Christianity in Korea

CHAPTER 2

Human Relations as Expressed in Vernacular Catholic Writings of the Late Chosŏn Dynasty

Cho Kwang
Translated by Timothy S. Lee

Catholicism began to be disseminated in earnest in East Asia with the arrival of Francis Xavier in Japan in 1549 and especially with the arrival of Matteo Ricci in Beijing in 1601. In Beijing, Catholic missionaries published tracts and other doctrinal literature in Chinese to promote their religion, and these Sinitic writings made their way into Korea via Korean envoys.[1] From these writings, many Koreans discovered a new worldview, one that posed an alternative to the Neo-Confucian orthodoxy of late Chosŏn society. And, as is well known, it is through the study of these writings that a group of Koreans—first mostly from the elite *yangban* class but later also from the lower classes—took the initiative to form an indigenous Catholic community in Korea.

Inasmuch as literary Chinese was the preserve of the *yangban* elite and all but inaccessible to the vast majority of the populace, Sinitic Catholic writings were often translated into the Korean vernacular, or *ŏnmun* (later more commonly known as *han'gŭl*). In time, these translations inspired the converts to compose their own vernacular tracts and catechisms. Thus, by the early nineteenth century, a significant body of vernacular Catholic writings came into being.

The Catholic faith began in Korea in 1784, largely on the initiative of a group of *yangban* disillusioned with the Neo-Confucian orthodoxy, whose creative energy they believed had been spent.[2] In time, for the reasons discussed in chapter 1, the Chosŏn government regarded the Catholic religion as subversive and severely suppressed the nascent Catholic community. In the course of the suppression, the government succeeded in decimating the elite leadership but not the community itself. The leadership now devolved upon the less learned, underprivileged classes, and the religion came to resemble a popular movement.

Such devolution of leadership succeeded, in part, because of the vernacular Catholic writings that enabled common Koreans easily to access teachings on a variety of topics pertaining to the Catholic community, providing guidelines for them in their life as Catholics.[3] These writings, therefore, afford an insight into the early Korean Catholic worldview and warrant a close examination. In examining these sources, this chapter focuses on the writings that treat the social dimensions of the Catholic worldview—more specifically, those that deal with human relationships involved in family, politics, and pecuniary matters.[4] There will also be a discussion about to what extent the ideals these writings espouse became actual modi vivendi of these Catholics.

The Basis for the Catholic Understanding of Human Relations

The view of human relations that prevailed in the late Chosŏn dynasty is predicated on the theory of human nature developed by the Chinese Neo-Confucian philosopher Zhu Xi (1130–1200). Zhu Xi held that human nobility and baseness, prosperity and adversity were inherent; thus, social inequality and status differences were natural. Such an inegalitarian view of human nature permeated late Chosŏn and undergirded the society's acute sense of status and hierarchy, as was reflected in such prototypical relations as that between father and son, lord and subject, husband and wife, and junior and senior.[5]

In such a milieu, values espoused by Sŏhak—broadly "Western learning" but more specifically "Roman Catholicism"—stood out sharply. Whereas Neo-Confucianism accepted human inequality as axiomatic, Catholicism affirmed the essential equality among humans before God. The vernacular Catholic writings posit that all humans, whether they believe in God or not, are created in the image of God; that the significance of human existence is superseded only by that of God; and that human nature is in some essential sense in contact with divine nature.[6] They point to the incongruity—given that all humans are created in the divine image—of humans' claiming to love God and yet not loving each other. They also argue that since all humans are descendants of Adam and Eve, they owe each other brotherly love, regardless of their individual merits or stations in life.[7] In short, in opposition to the late Chosŏn's caste-like social structure spawned by Neo-Confucianism, Catholicism emphasized human dignity, love, and reconciliation.

The Catholic Understanding of Family Ethics

Family ethics is another area in which vernacular Catholic writings evince a view that sharply contrasted with Neo-Confucian orthodoxy. Living amidst a culture that put a great store by family—the ideology of filial piety in particular—the church sought to ingratiate itself with the culture by stressing the importance of familial—especially parent-child—relationships. By doing so, the church, in part, hoped to deflect the commonly levied charge that the Catholics cared for neither father nor sovereign.

The Catholic view on the father-son relationship is treated in some depth in one of the writings known as *Sŏngch'al kwiryak* (A Brief Record of Reflection), published in 1864 by Bishop Daveluy (1818–1866). In twenty-five articles, this booklet spells out children's obligations toward their parents, urging the children's responsibility to care for their parents, readily paralleling Neo-Confucian teachings on the parent-child relationship.[8]

However, even as the writings sought to accommodate themselves to Neo-Confucian virtues, their views diverged significantly from them. One area of obvious divergence was ancestral rites. In the first half of the nineteenth century, the Catholic Church avoided speaking directly on ancestral rites—an understandable demurral given the severe hardships the church suffered when some of its members, in the late eighteenth century, ostensibly rejected those hallowed practices.[9] Even so, there was no mistaking where the church stood on the issue. For example, without directly disparaging ancestral rites, the church gnawed away at its theoretical basis by injecting God into the relation between father and son, thereby relativizing the son's filial duty toward his father and ancestors. This tack could be seen in the most important prayer book of the time, *Ch'ŏnju sŏnggyo konggwa* (A Prayer Book of the Catholic Church), which included "An Incantation for Parents," to be used as a substitute for traditional ancestral rites.[10] Such relativizing of ancestral rites contrasted significantly with traditional Neo-Confucian family ethics, which saw such rituals as a natural and necessary means of expressing filial piety.

In a similar vein, the *Brief Record,* in explaining the fourth of the Ten Commandments, placed about as much emphasis on parents' duty toward their children as vice versa. For example, it emphasized the parents' duty to provide for their children and condemned evils such as the abandonment of children in times of famine. It stressed that parents should not abuse their children or treat them angrily. It enjoined parents to look after their children's spiritual as well as physical needs. It also prohibited discriminating between sons and daughters and cautioned against midwives' neglect of newborn daughters. It proscribed the betrothal of children without their consent and denounced abusive treatment of daughters-in-law.[11]

If the church tended to de-emphasize the parent-child relationship, it emphasized the marital relationship. Indeed, it is arguable that the Catholic Church sought conscientiously to replace the father-son relation with the husband-wife relation at the center of family ethics.

In late Chosŏn, marriage was seen as a means to bond different families. The Catholic Church, in contrast, stressed marriage as a bonding of individuals—husband and wife—rather than families and stressed the significance of the couple's consent.[12] These vernacular writings moreover stress that marriage is an inviolable relationship of love. Love between husband and wife, the writings assert, is the most cherished of bonds on earth, to be prized more than the bond between friends, between patriot and his kingdom, or indeed between father and son. And insofar as marriage is consummated with God's blessing, no human being may undermine it.[13]

As a corollary, these vernacular Catholic writings urged monogamy and denounced concubinage, a widespread practice in late Chosŏn. They also opposed a person's marrying another before the death of his or her original spouse and stressed a man's, no less than a woman's, need to be faithful.[14]

The literature also countered the Confucian disparagement of women who could not bear male heirs.[15] The writings urged that even if a wife could not bear a child or bear only daughters, the husband ought not reproach her. On the other hand, from some standpoints, at least, these Catholic writings did not diverge much from their Neo-Confucian counterparts—for example, in the view that the husband needs to protect and be tolerant of his wife, since women are weaker than, if not inferior to, men.

These writings also command interest in the way they treat sibling relationships, in that they do not invest any extraordinary significance in them, treating the relationships more or less on the level of general human affection. Such an attitude, of course, differs markedly from the Confucian orientation in which siblings and near relatives were set apart from general humanity by virtue of shared ancestry and were entitled to claims of affection on their kin in ways nonrelatives were not.[16]

Moreover, while playing down the sibling relationship, the church valorized the relationship between fellow believers, terming it *kyo hyŏng*, "brothers in faith," and taught—citing views of the fourth-century church father John Chrysostom—that such a relationship is more intimate than that of biological siblings.[17]

In sum, the family ethics expressed in the vernacular Catholic writings diverged considerably from the Neo-Confucian ethics that prevailed in nineteenth-century Chosŏn. Most important, these writings indicated that in the Catholic community, the main axis of the family had shifted from the father-son relationship to that of husband and wife. Accompanying this shift was the weakening of the belief that a family's bloodline had to be maintained at all cost—to the point that ancestral rites, the hallowed ligature of Neo-Confucian family, was no longer given pride of place in family life. And marriage was regarded less as a vertical relationship in which the husband lorded over the wife but more of a horizontal one, wherein reciprocal duties and rights were emphasized.

The Catholic Understanding of Social Ethics

Human beings, of course, have relationships aside from those based solely on blood. They have relationships in larger society that encompass areas such as politics, economy, and society. Norms that regulate behavior in these kinds of relationships constitute social ethics. The early Korean Catholic Church, notwithstanding its introversive tendency, could not avoid interacting with the larger society and had to articulate a social ethic; indeed, much of the vernacular Catholic writings testify to such efforts. And as in family ethics, in social ethics, too—specifically in regard to the state, slavery, and pecuniary matters—the Catholics, these writings attest, attempted to adapt to the Korean context even as they adamantly clung to key tenets of their religion.

How should Catholics relate to the state? The vernacular Catholic writings' answer to this question may be best summarized by the biblical norm, What is Caesar's should be rendered unto Caesar. The writings premise that a king's command is God's command, that rulers have the people's interest at heart, that people properly owe their king fear and love, respect and prayer, and taxes.[18] People should fear their king because he has the power to punish the wicked and love him because he takes care of them as would a parent. People should respect the king, for his status is lofty; pray for him, since his well-being affects their well-being; and pay taxes, since money is needed if the king is to defend the kingdom. What is important in this conservative litany is the assumption that the king is a virtuous ruler whose power is legitimate and whose rule is just. A question naturally arises: what ought the Catholics do if the king lacks virtue, if he is a tyrant? The writings are silent on this issue, perhaps intentionally so, lest any such articulation add fuel to the allegation that the church was treasonous and bent on undermining the establishment.

To promote the view that the Catholic Church was loyal to the state, the vernacular writings urged Catholics to pray for the king and magistrates. Accordingly, the Ch'ŏnju sŏnggyo konggwa contains a prayer for the king and magistrates and exhorts believers to pray for the peace and prosperity of

Chosŏn, the well-being of the government, the sanctification of the people, and the elimination of evils. The writings recommended that a time be set aside for such prayers during all Sabbaths and holidays. As regards laws, the writings emphasized believers' obligation to obey them, insofar as doing so did not compromise their faith.[19]

The writings forbade evading or refusing to pay taxes, and urged the faithful to abstain from lying or employing other subterfuge to avoid paying them. Quoting Augustine of Hippo, a passage enjoined believers to pay their taxes to the king, the earthly lord.[20]

In late Chosŏn, slavery (or bond servanthood) was a widespread social institution. The Catholic Church did not repudiate this practice, although even as early as the end of the eighteenth century, some individual Catholics freed all their slaves out of their religious conviction.[21] Though conservative on slavery and servanthood, the Catholic Church did not merely subscribe to prevailing notions on the subjects: the vernacular Catholic writings show that the church attempted to inject a measure of leniency, if not compassion, into this often-exploitative relationship. It did so, for example, by forbidding the master from cruelly rebuking servants and by denouncing masters who postponed, or even skipped, paying their servants.[22]

In pecuniary matters, the vernacular Catholic writings reveal that the church taught traditional Catholic ethics, espousing essentially that one could not at the same time serve both God and Mammon and that between the two, it is much better to serve God, since God is compassionate.[23] True happiness, the church taught, lies not in wealth but in living after the example of the Lord; and wealth is best used when it is used for compassionate purposes, such as aiding the poor.[24] This kind of pecuniary ethics is exemplified in writings that explain the seventh of the Ten Commandments. Dwelling at length on just and unjust economic activities, some of the writings forbid the taking of another's property and warn against refusing or postponing the payment of debts; denounce usury in loaning money or grains and cheating in commercial dealings; and disapprove of selling falsely advertised goods and reaping profits by manipulating prices. The writings also warn against cheating when dividing profits among partners and engaging in fraudulent brokering; against demanding money when labor-for-labor arrangement is assumed and performing a given task half-heartedly; against merchants' cheating with weights and sharecroppers' falsely reporting their crop yields.[25]

The Catholic Social Ethics in Practice

It is safe to say that the above-mentioned teachings bespeak more of ideals than actual practices among the first-generation Korean Catholics. Even so, it stands to reason that at least the more devout of the believers would have been convinced of the Catholic ideals and have strived to live accordingly. Unless this is assumed, it is difficult to explain the thousands of Korean Catholics who, for the most part, quietly submitted to martyrdom during the persecutions. Evidence, in fact, indicates that the ideals had been embraced by a great many Korean Catholics, who regarded their religion as "a gospel of peace."[26] One such Catholic, Ch'oe P'ilgong, for example, was so convinced of these ideals that he opined that they underlay beliefs and actions of respectable persons everywhere. He asserts, "By and large, learned people practice Catholicism as a matter of course; and even among common Chinese [Koreans having traditionally respected the Chinese], all those with even a modicum of judgment believe in Catholicism."[27]

Moreover, it is because many Catholics shared Ch'oe's sentiments that they were able to band together to form communities based strictly on Catholic ideals. An example of such a community was one in Chŏnju, of which a French missionary in the 1880s wrote the following:

> New believers' cooperative spirits are amazing. The most outstanding virtue among them is that they show love and care for each other. Though poor in worldly goods, they live with one another sharing whatever goods they have, irrespective of their status. Examining this community, I feel as if I were in the early Christian church. In Acts of the Apostles we find that believers of the time turned all their properties in to the apostles and desired nothing but living the honest poverty of Jesus Christ and sharing in brotherly love.[28]

Conclusion

There is no doubt that the family and social ethics that vernacular Catholic writings expounded did not remain as mere ideals but were actually practiced. And by practicing them in their villages, the Catholics sought to establish a heavenly kingdom on earth, of the kind prefigured in the Gospels. And the fact that the Catholic Church managed to grow in early-nineteenth-century Korea—in spite of the severe persecutions leveled against it—shows that those ethics resonated with a significant portion of the population and may very well have affected non-Catholic popular movements that proliferated in the period. These ethics, when compared with the prevailing Neo-Confucian norms, were radical. And their radicalness, disseminated through the vernacular literature, undoubtedly stimulated the social imagination of Koreans in the late Chosŏn period—especially the oppressed Koreans' capacity to envision a new moral order.

NOTES

1. Pae Hyŏnsuk, "Chosŏn e chŏllae taehan Ch'ŏnjugyo sŏjŏk" [Catholic Writings Transmitted to Chosŏn], in *Han'guk kyohoesa nonmunjip 1* [A Collection of Works on the Korean (Catholic) Church 1] (Seoul: Han'guk Kyohoesa Yŏn'guso, 1984).

2. For a comprehensive history of the Korean Catholic history, see Yu Hongyŏl, *Han'guk kyohoe Ch'ŏnju kyohoesa* [A History of the Korean Catholic Church] (Seoul: Kat'ollik Ch'ulpansa, 1962).

3. Cho Kwang, *Chosŏn hugi ch'ŏnjugyosa yŏn'gu* [A Study of Late Chosŏn Catholic History] (Seoul: Koryŏ Taehakkyo Minjokmunhwa Yŏn'guso, 1988), 4.

4. I have written bibliographical notes on the *han'gŭl* Catholic sources used for this study. These notes were published in *Kyŏnghyang chapchi* in sixty-six installments, from July 1990 to December 1995. Among the sources especially pertinent to this study are *Chugyo yoji* [Essentials of the Lord's Teaching] written by Chŏng Yakchong; *Sŏnggyŏng chikhae* (Straight Understanding of Scriptures), originally written in Chinese but translated into *han'gŭl* about 1790; *Ch'ŏnju sŏnggyo konggwa* [Lessons on Sacred Teachings of the Heavenly Lord], which was published as woodblock prints in 1859 and served as the church's representative prayer book; and *Sŏnggyo yori mundap* [A Catechism on the Sacred Teaching], published in 1864 as a woodblock print. Also pertinent are *Sŏngch'al kwiryak* [A Brief Record of Reflection] and *Sinmyŏng ch'ohaeng* [First Journey in Divine Life] authored by Bishop Marie Nicolas Antoine Daveluy, with help from Hwang Sŏktu, published as a woodblock print in 1864; and *Sŏnggyo paek mundap* [One Hundred Questions and Answers on the Sacred Teaching], originally published in Chinese in Beijing, in 1657, and later transmitted to and widely used in Chosŏn.

5. Han Yŏngu, "Chosŏn chŏn'gi sŏngnihakpa ŭi sahoe kyŏngjae sasang" [Early Chosŏn Neo-Confucians' Socioeconomic Thought], in *Chosŏn sasangsa taegye II* [Great Lineages in Chosŏn Thought II] (Seoul: Sŏnggyun'gwan Taehakkyo Taedong Munhwa Yŏn'guwŏn, 1976), 95.

6. Daveluy, *Sinmyŏng ch'ohaeng*, bk. 2, 70a.

7. Chŏng Yakchong, *Chugyo yoji*, bk. 2, 39a.

8. Daveluy, *Sŏngch'al kwiryak,* 12b–14a.

9. Cho Kwang, "The Chosŏn Government's Measures against Catholicism," in *The Founding of Catholic Tradition in Korea* (Mississauga, Ontario: Korean and Related Studies Press, 1996).

10. *Ch'ŏnju sŏnggyo konggwa,* bk. 4, 65a.

11. Daveluy, *Sŏngch'al kwiryak*, 15a–17b.

12. *Sŏnggyŏng chikhae*, 22a–23a.

13. *Sŏnggyo yorimundap,* 12a.

14. *Sŏng'ch'al kwiryak,* 27a.

15. *Sŏnggyŏng chikhae*, bk. 2, 24b.

16. *Ch'onju sŏnggyo konggwa*, bk. 1, 26b.

17. *Sŏnggyŏng chikhae*, bk. 3, 75ab.

18. Ibid., bk. 7, 107ab.

19. Daveluy, *Sŏngch'al kwiryak,* 20a.
20. *Sŏnggyŏng chikhae,* bk. 7, 107b.
21. Cho Kwang, *Chosŏn hugi Ch'ŏnju kyosa yŏn'gu,* 108.
22. Daveluy, *Sŏngch'al kwiryak,* 20b–21a.
23. Chŏng Yakchong, *Chugyo yoji,* bk. 2, 41a.
24. *Sŏnggyŏng chikhae,* bk. 7, 44ab.
25. Daveluy, *Sŏngch'al kwiryak,* 33a.
26. *Ch'ŏnju sŏnggyo konggwa,* bk. 3, 15a.
27. This quotation is found in the records of the royal prosecutorial office of Chosŏn, *Ch'uan Kŭpkukan,* under the section, "Sahak choein Yi Kahwan tŭng" [Evil Heretic Yi Kahwan and Others] (1801). The records are kept at the Kujang-gak Archives of Seoul National University.
28. Calixte Xavier Baudounet, "Beaudounet sinbu ŭi 1889 nyŏn pogosŏ" [Father Beaudounet's 1889 Year-End Report], April 22, 1889, in *Mwit'ael munsŏ* [Documents de Mgr. Mutel], archived at Han'guk kyohoesa yŏn'guso [The Research Foundation of Korean Church History] in Seoul.

CHAPTER 3

Kollumba Kang Wansuk, an Early Catholic Activist and Martyr

Gari Ledyard

Kollumba (Columba) Kang Wansuk (1761–1801), who perished in the great anti-Catholic persecution of 1801, is well known among a small number of historians of Korean Catholicism, but not among more general scholars of Korean history or in the wider field of Korean Studies. She should be more broadly recognized, since aside from her importance as an early Catholic, she was also a remarkable woman who worked in a cause that unfolded outside the home in public space, something that was hardly imaginable for a woman in her time and probably without precedent in earlier Korean history. She had a genuine career, participated in matters of great moment for her country and church, and died as a martyr and a heroine to her fellow church members.

The beginnings of the Catholic Church in Korea must surely be one of the most singular stories in religious history.[1] In 1777, a small group of Korean scholars organized a secret seminar to study writings in Chinese relating to the teachings of Catholicism. Such books, brought back by members of diplomatic missions to China, had been known and commented upon for a century and a half, but often as strange curiosities; those who took them seriously had usually been hostile.[2] In 1784, a young man with connections to that group, which had approached the texts in a positive, critical spirit, returned to Korea after accompanying his father, a diplomat, to Peking, where he had taken religious instruction at the famous North Church (Beitang) and been baptized. He brought back a harvest of books and other information and began to baptize his friends and colleagues; soon a unique church organization was active.

Almost immediately these Catholic meetings drew the attention of alarmed Confucians, who quickly branded the new learning as unorthodoxy (*sahak*, "deviant learning," in opposition to Confucianism or *chŏnghak*, "correct learning"). Pressures began to arise within the general community of Confucian scholars, and at their prodding, soon from the government itself. By 1785 the chief Catholic figures, mainly men of prominent families who were known in government circles, were publicly known if not notorious. By 1786, the church already had its first martyr, a lesser figure, the interpreter Kim Pŏm'u. Families with members involved in the new religion came under attack, and in turn sometimes went on the attack against their own refractory member. Some of the new Catholics maintained their ground; others gave in to the pressures. But a core of believers continued their activities. The religion spread from family to family and from Seoul to outlying towns such as Yanggŭn and Yŏju in Kyŏnggi province and to a wide area of southern Ch'ungch'ŏng province around Kongju and Hongju. In 1791, a young Catholic in northern Chŏlla province refused to perform full Confucian mourning ceremonies for his deceased mother, and he and one of his relatives were executed by decapitation. Prominent Catholics in Seoul also became victims. And in Hongju, Kang Wansuk's name appeared for the first time in the records of the persecution.

The Confucian resistance to Catholicism began from a sincere conviction that any religion, philosophy, or ethics outside of Confucianism was wrong, and therefore a danger to Korean society. Koreans attracted to Catholicism were equally sincere and did not see themselves as necessarily in conflict with Confucianism. But Confucian Korea and its government became relentless and ultimately unreasoning foes, while the Catholics, under attack and weak, could only defend themselves or apostatize. By the beginning of the lunar year Sin'yu (Feb. 13, 1801–Feb. 2, 1802), twenty-one people had already been charged and lost their lives. But in Sin'yu, which I shall generally call "1801," Catholicism was officially declared to be treason, and a broad persecution was organized and ruthlessly pursued. Some 156 individuals, 29 of them women, are known to have perished.[3] This was not a matter of random slaughter, but a carefully controlled operation that went forward under the full legal and penal procedures of the state. Transcripts of testimony were made, specific charges were carefully deliberated, and executions were carried out, all with meticulous attention to law. Many records were created, and although most of them are lost, detailed summaries have survived in both officially and privately compiled works.[4]

Women in the Early Korean Church

Because the practice of Catholicism was an underground affair from the very beginning, there were no churches and, until 1795, no priest, no Mass, and apart from baptism no sacraments. These conditions continued

for most people even after the arrival of the Chinese missionary priest Zhou
Wenmo (K., Chu Munmo) in that year. Normal Catholic life as we would
understand it did not exist. What did happen—study, prayer, and discussion, and after 1795, an occasional Mass—happened in homes, usually at
night. This circumstance had important consequences for women, for anything that took place in the home was in their domain. Since public proselytization was out of the question, the religion spread from household to
household, usually along in-law family lines, and that too centrally involved
the wives and mothers, who dominated such communications.[5] Furthermore, at least until 1801, women were formally immune from the attention
of the courts and the police except in cases of treason. If they were guilty of
anything, their fathers, husbands, or adult sons had to answer for it. No police officer could enter the women's quarters of a household, so the men of
the family could even hide there without fear of arrest. This circumstance
insured that women could and did with virtual impunity serve as the mes-
sengers, letter carriers, and facilitators in connection with religious gatherings. Even in 1801 and after, with the added dimension of treason, the prosecutors tended to avoid involving women in their investigations out of
general habit and inclination; this was especially true for *sadaebu* (*sabu, sahwan*) and *yangban* women.[6] We know of many women of such background
who were Catholics in 1801 but who do not appear in government records,
although they often suffered severely because of the confiscation of their
husbands' property. Most of the twenty-nine women that we can identify
as victims of 1801 were widows or, like Kang Wansuk, otherwise single, or
were from the commoner and slave classes of Korean society. Although
Kang is said to have converted a great number of *sahwan* women, we do
not have any information as to their specific names or families. The importance of women comes out strongly in one of the central Catholic sources
for 1801, the famous *Silk Letter* (*Paekso*) of Aleksanderŭ Hwang Sayŏng
(1775–1801), which also serves to introduce Kollumba Kang Wansuk
more concretely:

> In Fourthmoon of the year Kyŏngsin (Apr. 24–May 23, 1800), after
> the registration of names in the Confraternity on Doctrine (Myŏnghoe,
> Myŏngdohoe), the members applied themselves to their spiritual work.
> Outside the confraternity as well people went into action wherever the wind
> took them. All applied themselves to the conversion of others. The effort
> increased in intensity during the autumn and the winter, producing more
> conversions with every passing day. But women made up two-thirds of these,
> and one-third were either of the common run or slaves. Among elite (*sabu*)
> men, who were fearful of the purges of the day, those who accepted the faith
> were very few. In the persecution of Ŭlmyo (1795), Kollumba gained great

distinction for her sheltering and protection of [Father Zhou], and since her talents and abilities stood out from the crowd, Father assigned her special responsibilities. Kollumba was also a very zealous manager. She converted a great many people, and the women she brought into the faith from officials' families (*sahwan*) were especially numerous. This arises from the fact that in Korean law, with the exception of cases of treason, punishments do not extend to the women of gentlemen's families (*sajok*), and for this reason they do not worry about the prohibition against our religion. Father, for his part, considered this a foundation for broad growth. He treated her with particular kindness. The general balance of strength in the church thus came to be with the women members, and as a result her own renown spread far and wide.[7]

The Early Years of Kang Wansuk

There is no disagreement in either Catholic or government sources as to the importance that Kollumba had attained in the church by 1800. Whether by the singing of her praises in the *Silk Letter* and in still other Catholic sources used by Charles Dallet for his early history of the Korean church or by the obloquy that covers her name in sources sympathetic to the persecution, it is clear that she was one of a handful of key figures in those early years.[8]

Kang Wansuk was a native of the district of Tŏksan (now part of Yesan) in southwestern Ch'ungch'ŏng province, about half way between the important provincial towns of Kongju and Hongju (now Hongsŏng). Tŏksan was one of about a dozen districts comprising what was locally known as the Naep'o region, which alongside Seoul itself was a very active area of operation for the early church. It had been proselytized by Yi Chonch'ang (1752–1801), one of the original converts and certainly the most successful in terms of his distinction in creating the Catholic community. Judging from Kang's age at death in 1801, forty-one *se*, she was probably born within the Western year 1761 or in the first month or so of 1762. The name of her father seems to be unknown.[9]

According to the *Silk Letter*, Kang was descended from a family line established by the son of a *sabu* by a concubine, a status that Antoine Daveluy called "demi-nobles."[10] The common term for this status was *pansŏ*, which might be understood as "*yangban* with one or more illegitimate (*sŏ*) male ancestors." She married into a family of the same status; this would have been the expected match and is in itself support for the *Silk Letter*'s statement.[11] In spite of these clear indications of her ancestry, some consider her an unqualified *yangban*.[12] By all indications she was not only literate but was considered among Seoul Catholics to be an expert in doctrinal matters, and she clearly had an air of authority and command. Thus, whatever her technical social status, it would not be surprising if she had been commonly perceived to be a *yangban*, and in the Korea of the early nine-teenth century, such a perception could well have been conclusive for all practical purposes. Certainly people of Kang's flawed *yangban* status would not have advertised the fact.

The date of her marriage is unknown, but her husband was a widower, and inasmuch as we know by the age of the widower's son that the first wife was living at least as late as 1774, it could have been no earlier than about 1775, when Kang was fifteen *se*, and no later than about 1781, the year be-fore her daughter Sunhŭi was born. Given that the tendency was for early marriages, the date of her marriage was probably closer to 1775. By all the accounts we have, which are partisan on Kang's side, her husband, Hong Chiyŏng, was of indifferent abilities and quite unpleasant personally.[13] Her interest in religion started after her marriage. She is said to have had an ear-lier inclination toward Buddhism along with the other women of her fam-ily, but she lost interest after she began to hear about Catholicism from one of her husband's relatives. This could not have been until about 1785, when people in the Naep'o region were beginning to hear about the newly ar-rived religion, and it could not have been later than 1791, when she was arrested during a roundup of Catholics in northern Chŏlla and southern Ch'ungch'ŏng provinces. This had been sparked by the sensational case of Yun Chich'ung (1759–1791), who was executed in that year after refusing, on Catholic grounds, to perform the proper Confucian ancestral rites fol-lowing the death of his mother.[14] At that time Kang was briefly imprisoned at the military commander's compound in Hongju, but then released.[15]

Kang's proselytizing activity began soon after her own conversion, and among her early successes were her mother-in-law and her stepson, Hong P'ilchu (1774–1801), followed by her own parents in her natal home.[16] But her efforts to convert her husband to Catholicism produced only vacillation between grudging acceptance and half-hearted refusal, and she ultimately gave up the effort. In the *Silk Letter*, Hwang Sayŏng writes:

> Only Chiyŏng had no idea whatever. When exhorted by his wife, he would
> tell her, "Yes, yes," and go along. Then wicked parties would revile him, and
> he would tell them, "Sure, sure." His wife would then scold him and he
> would break out in tears and express regret for his sins, whereupon the
> wicked friends would come back again and he would revert to his earlier
> ways. Kollumba made every effort she could, but to no effect. She knew that
> she would never be able to work things out with him.[17]

These circumstances led to her divorce, probably not too long after her detention. Although divorce was rare and a matter of great moral moment in traditional Korean society, the actual accomplishment of it was relatively informal. Kang's thoughts on it, whether from her own personal feelings or from a Catholic point of view, are unrecorded, but in any case it was not an option that she, as a woman, had. From the husband's point of view it was self-executed, and unless his own family objected or the wife's family had sufficient standing and recognition in the community that local opinion might oppose it, the arrangements were easily accomplished. She would simply be expelled from the household, and once she was removed from the official household register (*hojŏk*), she was divorced. Although Hwang Sayŏng implies that she left voluntarily, she stated in her testimony to the police interrogators in 1801 (to be sure, while under torture) that her husband had expelled her.[18] The general surmise is that following her arrest in 1791, her husband, having no disposition toward Catholicism and wishing to stay above suspicion on the part of the local police, decided to be rid of her, and in any case she wanted to go.

It is a matter of some interest that Kang's converted mother-in-law also left Hong Chiyŏng and went with Kang to live with her in Seoul. In traditional Korean lore, the relations between a wife and her mother-in-law were often seen as difficult, particularly when the wife had produced no son, as Kang had not. But Kang would seem to have turned custom on its head, converting her mother-in-law to her own religion and then leaving her husband behind and taking his mother with her. It is also possible that her husband, wary of criticism and police pressures, simply wanted all the Catholics out of his household, even if that meant expelling his own mother.

The other members of Kang's departing troupe were her stepson P'illippo Hong Mun'gap, who later in Seoul changed his name to P'ilchu, and her daughter Nusia (Lucy) Hong Sunhŭi. P'ilchu was then eighteen *se*, and as yet unmarried. At the time of the 1801 interrogations, Sunhŭi appears to have been already a young adult, although unmarried, which would put her age at anywhere from eight to ten *se* when she left Tŏksan. I will come back to her later.

The Move to Seoul

Owing to the aftershocks of the ancestral worship scandal that emerged from the prosecution of Yun Chich'ung, the affairs of the Catholics in Seoul were in some turmoil in 1791 and the years immediately following. The scandal had stirred outrage in both government and general Confucian circles and led to considerable pressures on the leaders of the Catholics, who were mostly of the *sabu* class and affiliated with the Nam'in faction. The Nam'in as a general group were part of the pressure, since the vulnerability of the Catholic Nam'in threatened to extend to them as well. Some of the most tenacious critics pushing to get the government to launch a full-scale persecution were Nam'in. And since King Chŏngjo (r. 1776–1800) had included Nam'in in his government and was personally fond of many of them, there was no lack of would-be non-Nam'in officials who had much to gain by a Nam'in fall from power. Since Chŏngjo would not think of a general purge but could not ignore the rage over the perceived threat to the ancestral rites, his reaction took the form of pressuring the Catholic leaders to apostatize (or re-apostatize, since some of them had already done so after earlier anti-Catholic incidents). This policy was more or less successful from the king's point of view, but many of the surviving Catholic leaders were heavily compromised. Some were never trusted again by either side; others, who resisted the pressure, died or suffered grievously.[19]

By the time Kang and her small family arrived in Seoul, this broadly applied pressure was already in play. It would have been risky and probably difficult for her to make attempts to contact these leaders and settle into some kind of Catholic life. Even if contact had been feasible, the idea of a woman from the country meeting with church members of that rank was probably not something those leaders were yet ready for. As far as we know from available records, relatively few women had been converted outside the families and social orbits of the early converts themselves; certainly none had yet come to prominence or public notice. Thus it is not surprising that the first known contacts that Kang made among the Seoul Catholics were with men of the professional, or *chung'in*, class. In any case exploring these contacts will throw interesting light on her acquisition of a house and on her finances in general. Her relationship with Saba (Sabas) Chi Hwang (?–1795), a *chung'in* with no official position who made his living as a physician and pharmacist, is mentioned in the *Silk Letter* narrative: "In the persecution of the year Sinhae (1791), her native village was swept up in turmoil, so she turned over her farmlands (*chŏnjang*) to her husband and, taking her children with her, went up to Seoul. There she worked with Saba Chi [Hwang] and was of great assistance to him in regard to his mission [to Peking]."[20]

The mission to Peking involved the recruitment of the first priest to serve the quickly growing Catholic community. Chi Hwang, who was an active Catholic in Seoul, would perform that mission, together with Paoro Yun Yuil (1760–1795), who had already made two other trips to Peking on church liaison matters. There is no doubt that the "great assistance" rendered by Kang had to do in part with money, devoted to a home for herself and to the operation of that home as a safe haven for Catholics taking religious instruction or participating in meetings or services—even Masses if and when the priest should arrive.

Before we can consider either Kang's finances or her religious role, we need to examine the testimony of Chi Hwang's wife, Kim Nyŏm'i. She was interrogated in 1801 as part of the investigation of Kang and others arrested at that time. The following extract from her statement is translated to reflect the insults routinely showered upon the objects of the inquiry, including pejorative suffixes for people being prosecuted and the official term "deviant learning," or *sahak*, for Catholicism. Any individual giving testimony is always referred to as "culprit" (*ŭisin*), including first-person references:

> In the winter of the year Kabin (1794), when culprit's husband (Chi) Hwang followed the embassy to China as a traveling merchant, gang members Ch'oe In'gil and Hong P'ilchu's mother—Woman Kang (Kangnyŏ)—conspired to bring in a Chinese man, the rogue surnamed Zhou. All of the money for expenses in connection with his emergence here at that time was exclusively arranged and handled by P'ilchu's mother. They hid rogue Zhou in In'gil's house. So it was that culprit went there on one occasion, and on the instructions of culprit's husband made a suit of winter clothing there for rogue Zhou. Later, rogue Zhou was moved to P'ilchu's mother's house in Ch'angdong.[21]

The source of the money that P'ilchu's mother—that is, Kang Wansuk—provided to finance this enterprise was probably dual. Some was no doubt contributed by various Seoul Catholics, although to conceal the conspiracy that group would have been a very small and select one. But Kang's contribution seems to have also been important, and whatever the size of her share, she was the person who "exclusively" held the money and paid the bills. The expenses would have been significant: traveling expenses for the two emissaries and probably a servant for a round-trip between Seoul and Peking to make the arrangements (fifty–sixty days for the China part of the trip alone, plus a stay of at least one month in Peking); the bankrolling of an inventory of trade articles for the men to take to Peking, of enough volume and quality to make their cover activity credible; then, in the winter of the following year, another round-trip for two between Seoul and Bianmen (on China's frontier with Korea),[22] north of Ŭiju, to pick up the priest and insert him safely into Korea; plus a fund for paying the necessary bribes in both Korea and China to enable the emissaries to travel safely with the embassy. And however much all that came to, it was a relatively small amount in comparison with the cost of a safe house in Seoul big enough for the living needs of Kang and her dependents (the number of which was soon increased by two female slaves and a few other Catholic women who stayed there for long periods at a time) and the accommodation of groups of visitors for religious services.

What was the source of Kang's money? It has been noted that, on her departure from Tŏksan, Kang "'turned over' her farmlands to her husband." That she was a landowner is in itself interesting; clearly her natal family had

had some resources, and these had come with her in her marriage. Yet unless the terms of the marriage agreement are known, it is impossible to know how the ownership was defined or understood, and specifically what rights Hong Chiyŏng had or was entitled to, if any. The term for "turn over" here is simply *pu*, which can have the meanings of "transfer," "assign," or "pay," but it can also mean "entrust to," with the implication that the transfer is temporary or conditional. Although one can usually rely on the terms before or after *pu* to be certain of the exact connotation, absent these the fact is that in general, *pu* means to give, pay, transfer, or hand something over to someone, and the only safe assumption is that Hong Chiyŏng ended up owning his departing wife's land. Could he have paid her for it? In the circumstances that might seem unlikely, but she certainly did have some funds when she arrived in Seoul. Or perhaps he allowed his son P'ilchu—as far as we know, his only son—to draw income from it. Apart from these possibilities, it is hard to account for Kang's evident access to money in an amount that was well beyond what was needed for simple survival in the capital city.

Whatever happened, it is clear that Kang and her stepson P'ilchu owned property in Seoul and that a significant part of her funds was spent on church activities. In addition to the house that Kang had in Ch'angdong, which would seem to have been of bigger-than-average size, P'ilchu had a house of his own in Taesadong (modern Insadong near Chongno 2-ka), from which he later moved to another one in An'guktong a few neighborhoods to the north.[23]

Father Jacobo Zhou Wenmo was successfully inserted into Korea on December 23, 1794, and arrived in Seoul early in January 1795.[24] He was hidden in the home of Mat'ia (Mathias) Ch'oe In'gil (1764–1795), an interpreter of spoken Chinese and an early convert. Presumably Zhou began learning Korean from Ch'oe at this time, and he also met with the principal Catholics of the city, among them Kang Wansuk. However, his presence in Seoul was soon detected by informers, and an order for his arrest was handed down in June. Chi Hwang, Yun Yuil, and Ch'oe In'gil were all arrested and quickly executed, and another round of persecutions and pressures began for all of the principal Catholics. But by the time the police had arrived at Ch'oe In'gil's house, Father Zhou was already gone. He had been taken to Kang's house, where he lived undetected for the next six years, almost to the time of his death.

Catechist and Church Coordinator

From the time Father Zhou arrived at Kang's house, it was his safe house, his home, his office, and his church. As a result, Kang Wansuk became his housekeeper, chief assistant, secretary, liaison officer, and above all, the person solely responsible for his personal security. In addition, he created for her the position of women's catechist (*yŏhoejang*), responsible for all matters relating to women in the church, in particular for their conversion and religious training. Although there were several male catechists, their access to Father Zhou was completely in her hands. No one else shared this power. Until the spring of 1801, although informers and police agents never stopped looking for the priest in Seoul and elsewhere, and men and women constantly visited the house for catechism lessons and religious services, no hint of Father Zhou's presence there ever got beyond a closely guarded circle of trusted church members. This secrecy can only have been accomplished through Kang's management talents and rigorous execution of her duties. The narrative of Hwang Sayŏng in his *Silk Letter* runs as follows:

> [Kollumba Kang Wansuk] was baptized in the year Ŭlmyo (1795). Father had liked her on their first meeting and had created for her a position as catechist, assigning her responsibility for managing the affairs of the female church members. During the crisis in Fifthmoon (June 17–July 15, 1795), she had taken the lead in planning his escape to safety. All by herself she handled the arrangements, hiding Father in her own house and making every possible effort for his protection, so that when policemen came to her door they went away empty-handed. When the crisis had passed, Father decided to make his residence in her house, and for six years she was his facilitator for all important church affairs. Father looked upon her with the very highest regard and trust. No other person enjoyed comparable status. Inside the house, Kollumba assisted him in all his activities and attended to his meals and clothing, in all matters deciding what was best for him. Outside, she coordinated the affairs of the church. In her administration there was never the slightest lapse. She assembled a large group of virgins and effectively trained and instructed them. They would go off separately to the homes [of believers], exhorting them to trust in the Lord. She herself traveled far and wide in the work of exhortation and conversion. She would work through the night until sunup; seldom did she take time to rest or sleep. Because of her thorough understanding of doctrine, her articulateness in speech, and her powers of argument, a very large number of people were converted. She was impressive in dealing strongly and decisively with any matter. Everyone held her in awe.... From the year Ŭlmyo on, Father always stayed in Kollumba's house, but from time to time he would make a circuit of other places, and Kollumba was the only person who had any knowledge of it. Apart from her, no one knew anything. When the [present] persecution started up, there was a certain male church member who, as he saw matters tending toward a dangerous stage, began to worry about [Father's] safety. He went out into the

countryside and sought out church members who were in hiding. He made arrangements for two places that might be appropriate, and then came back to Seoul to see Kollumba. He earnestly begged her to admit him to see the priest with a view to making a plan for him to escape to a place where he could be protected. But Kollumba said, "He already has a secure place; we must not move him yet again." The church member made repeated requests of her, but to no avail.[25]

Charles Dallet's account of these matters also benefited from the *Silk Letter* (albeit an imperfect copy of it), but he elaborates on them with the aid of other contemporary Korean sources collected and translated by French missionaries during the middle years of the nineteenth century but which are now lost. According to Dallet, Kang in 1795 had hidden Father Zhou in her woodshed for three months. Before he could be admitted into the house, her family members had to be sufficiently conditioned to the necessary secrecy and caution. Her mother-in-law in particular was seen as a problem. In a scene that anticipates hagiography, Kang tearfully began to soften her into acceptance:

"The priest has come to us at the risk of his life to save our souls, but we have done nothing to recognize his good deeds, and today he has no refuge. Unless I were stone or wood, how could I not be keenly distressed? So I'm going to dress like a man and go around the country looking for him, so that I can help him." Her mother tearfully responded, "If you do that, what will I have for support? I'll go with you then, and die with you." Kollumba said, "Venerable mother, it is such a consolation to see the level of virtue you've reached. I am certainly not afraid to offer my life to save the missionary, but in such difficult circumstances we might not be able to find him, and we would expose ourselves in vain. The Lord of Heaven, who knows all, and who penetrates the hearts of men, sees our good will, and he might permit the priest to come to us. If you assure me of your consent, your daughter's soul will find peace immediately. She will be happy, as before, and will perform for you the duties of filial piety until the day you die." ... It was there, then, that Father Zhou, protected by the Korean custom that forbids the entry of strangers into the homes of nobles, made his regular residence for three years.[26]

This account, with its obvious Korean wording and sensibility, comes from a Korean Catholic tradition that had already elevated Kang Wansuk to virtual sainthood. Although it unwittingly presents her as a skillful manipulator, it casts her deceptiveness within a plan to save the Korean church itself. In contrast to the realistic, unadorned prose of the *Silk Letter*, which was written in hiding in the midst of crisis and insecurity, the Korean narrative presented by Dallet reveals an accretion over time of elements of drama, piety, and veneration. And on a more mundane level, it raises Kang from her flawed ancestry up to genuine *yangban* status.

Various Activities

Accounts already introduced give a general idea of Kang's activities over the six-year period when Father Zhou was sheltered in her house, but for some concrete idea of her work, we have to consult the interrogations of 1801. A great many people, both men and women, mentioned her in their testimony, attesting to the broad influence that her unique access to the only priest in Korea gave her, but also to her own zeal for her work and her recognized importance. This is attested in many casual references, both by fellow church members and by interrogators. No one was unreserved in praise of her: the situation in the torture chambers of 1801 was much too tense for gratuitous hagiography. Neither was she the object of any significant criticism, except in the implicit insults of the interrogators themselves. Some did give information that was not favorable to her, but even that often shows her commanding presence and her determination to run things without mishap. In her world, even in the less pressing atmosphere between the crisis of 1795 and the cataclysm of 1801, the slightest error could end in quick death for many people. The very fact that for six years she had total success in protecting Father Zhou attests to her thoroughness and care. Even his eventual arrest occurred only after her own, and because he voluntarily surrendered himself to the authorities.

In this part of my study I will examine Kang's activities in four categories: her liaison work, her measures to protect the priest, her religious activities including her evident desire to promote virginity as a way for women to strengthen their faith, and the question of appearances in the relationship between her and Father Zhou.

Father Zhou's work pattern naturally revolved around Sundays. Sometimes he would say Mass at Kang's, other times at the separate home of Hong P'ilchu. He is known to have also held services at the homes of Hwang Sayŏng and Kim I'u, younger brother of the first Korean martyr, Kim Pŏm'u. Moving the services around was a way of decreasing traffic in and around any one site, thereby limiting suspicion. Only Kang could have arranged the details of this circuit. She also had a network of safe houses in which people could hide at times of danger[27] and a number of places where she arranged to store and hide religious books.[28] Father Zhou kept in close touch with a few important people such as his catechist-general (*ch'onghoe-jang*), Ch'oe Ch'anghyŏn (1754–1801); his catechist for doctrine (*myŏngdo hoejang*), Chŏng Yakchong (1760–1801); Hwang Sayŏng; and a few others. Kang arranged these meetings and communicated with the principals in writing. In the general statement she gave to her interrogators, she freely confessed to maintaining correspondence with a list of people who were in the top echelon of Korean Catholicism (see the following section).

Kang's greatest responsibility was to protect the security of Father Zhou. Her general approach to this task lay in restricting access to her own home. I have seen in the interrogation reports very few instances in which major figures visited her house, and this should perhaps not be surprising, since such well-known people were watched, and any visit could only throw suspicion on her and endanger the priest. Most of the visitors mentioned in the interrogations were Catholic women from middle- to low-profile families or members of her troupe of virgins—all people who had her complete trust and who often helped her by doing errands, carrying messages, and helping guests. An exception were the two ladies of the so-called defunct palace (*p'yegung*), converts whom she had catechized and made special efforts to cultivate. They were Maria Song and her daughter-in-law Maria Sin, who will come into the story below as Father Zhou's last protectors. Among the other members of her household, only her mother-in-law; her stepson, P'ilchu; and her daughter, Sunhŭi, knew the identity of the man in the room of the "outer master" (*oe sangjŏn*) and could enter it to bring him meals or for other household matters. The two female slaves, Chŏng'im and Somyŏng, were expressly forbidden to enter that room or talk about it, although in the course of time they inevitably came to know who was there. Outside female visitors who might happen to notice some male sign and who would ask about it were always given some false identity. In the interrogations I have seen him variously described as Kang's father-in-law, as "an elderly relative from the country," or as "Scholar Yi" (Yi *saengwŏn*). Sunhŭi, who of course came to know who he was, told the interrogators that the man had been identified to her as "a relative of your grandfather's generation."[29] Visitors who aroused Kang's suspicion were dropped. When Father Zhou was moved for a temporary stay in another house, the travel was always done at night. It was probably Hong P'ilchu who served as his escort on these occasions.

These precautions worked well for six years. Only at the very end, in Twelfthmoon of the lunar year 1800 (Jan. 15–Feb. 12, 1801), when clear signs of the upcoming persecution had alerted the Catholics, did Kang find it necessary to arrange a new residence for her long-time roomer. Remarkably, the new safe house was a former palace, at that time occupied only by two faithful converts, Maria Song and Maria Sin. This palace had been established for the illegitimate male survivors of Prince Sado (and therefore half brothers of lower status of Sado's royal heir, King Chŏngjo) following

his murder by King Yŏngjo.[30] The original occupants had been the late
Sado's concubine and her children. The eldest of these was Prince Ŭnŏn
(Yi In), who was the husband of Maria Song. Their son, Prince Sanggye
(Yi Tam), was the husband of Maria Sin. In 1786, Sanggye had been executed for his role in a treasonous plot, and his father Ŭnŏn had been banished to Kanghwa Island, after which their palace, which had probably been
a relatively modest establishment, was institutionally discontinued. But the
wives of the two men lived on in what then came to be known as the defunct palace. In their miserable existence, forgotten and ignored by the
world, they were introduced to Catholicism by a palace maid, who directed
them to Kang Wansuk for their training. Kang cultivated them assiduously
and gave them the rare privilege of meeting Father Zhou and being baptized by him. She had seen their isolated abode and recognized in it an ideal
place of refuge for the priest. As an added advantage, a private house that
shared a rear gate with the palace was occupied by an early convert, Antonio Hong Ingman (?–1802), one of whose daughters had married Kang's
stepson, Hong P'ilchu. Hong Ingman had met Father Zhou soon after his
arrival in Korea, and by Ingman's own description the priest was his "very
close personal friend."[31] Thus, there was every reason to believe that Father
Zhou's personal safety was assured when he was moved to this new location. Since his later arrest arose from his own personal decision to surrender
and not from any betrayal by others, we can conclude that in the matter of
his protection, Kang Wansuk's measures were successful to the very end.[32]

Kang's religious work was principally the conversion and training of
other women, in which by all accounts she was outstandingly successful.
Mentions of her instruction and explaining of religious matters are not in-
frequent in the interrogation reports relating to female church members,
but in these references there is a paucity of detail. Descriptions of the scene
are, however, interesting. The following description is from the interrogation of Agada (Agatha) Yun Chŏmhye, who was raised in a Catholic family
in the district of Yanggŭn. Wishing to avoid marriage and to live as a virgin,
she had moved to Seoul, met Kang, and soon moved into Kang's house,
where she stayed until the end.

> It has been six years now since Brother Zhou has been a hidden visitor in
> Wansuk's house. In each month there might have been six or seven,
> sometimes even ten or more holy days when the scriptures would be read
> and studied. Men and women from all over [would come for] the lectures,
> participating all together, and culprit assisted on these occasions.[33]

The presence of Father Zhou at services on the holy days (*ch'ŏmnye*)
at Kang's house is frequently remarked in the interrogations. I have not

detected in the interrogation records any word that might stand for "Mass," but it is evident that Masses were said at occasions called *sŏlpŏp ch'ŏmnye*, or "obligatory *ch'ŏmnye*." But whether it was a matter of Mass or a service of some other kind, it was Kang's role to do the talking. Father Zhou, who on some occasions stayed unseen in a side room and on others joined with the general crowd, did not apparently speak very good Korean, making Kang's interlocutory role an important element of the proceedings. One visitor testified:

> Culprit's house was very close to P'ilchu's house, and occasionally culprit would go there and study the weird books (*yosŏ* [Catholic texts]) with P'ilchu's mother. On the occasion of a *sŏlpŏp ch'ŏmnye*, the participants heard a lecture from the person called the "priest (*sinbu*) who had come from Nanking," . . . a man of about fifty, with a long face, medium-sized body, and a long beard. He had a speech defect, and it was very difficult to know what he was saying.[34]

Another defendant, who thought the priest "sounded like a person incapable of speech," said she understood very well, but only after Kang helped him in teaching the lesson.[35] Many of the other female defendants made similar remarks.[36] It seems that he really was unable to perform his ministry without an interlocutor. If a Mass was the context for Kang's explanations, she would undoubtedly have been reading from a missal, Korean and Chinese versions of which were generally available in that period.

Such testimony implies that Kang understood what Father Zhou was saying. It is unlikely that she knew much spoken Chinese, if any at all. Since his Korean seems to have been inadequate for serious conversation, their mutual understanding must have evolved slowly, through long study sessions in which they gradually worked out effective communication. On technical matters concerning the Mass and other religious subjects, Kang's background in religious reading must have been an essential element in understanding her Chinese visitor. A list of Catholic books and objects, compiled by the persecution from confiscated material from the homes of fifteen individuals, shows 164 books and 101 objects including pictures, rosaries, crucifixes, and the like.[37] Since many books were successfully hidden or destroyed during 1801, this should be taken as but a small representation of a vast collective library of Catholic literature held in homes or circulating in Seoul in the period leading up to that year. Most of the books are translations or original works in Korean, but untranslated works in Chinese are also found. Kang was a relatively well-read Catholic, and while I have found no indication that she was able to read Chinese (*hanmun*) materials, given her general intelligence and zeal it is by no means to be ruled out. It can be safely assumed that Father Zhou had brush conversations in classical Chinese with many of the better-educated Catholic men and that the instruction thus derived soon passed into the general knowledge of the Catholic community and especially to Kang Wansuk if she had not already acquired it directly.

An important element of Catholic religiosity for Korean women at that time was the maintenance of virginity. Although Kang made a special point of promoting this practice, she was by no means the only source of the idea; one of the most remarkable virgins of the early Korean Catholic Church, Nugalda (Luthgarde) Yi Yuhŭi, though born in Seoul, lived in Chŏnju, quite out of Kang's orbit.[38] Kang's faithful young friend Agada Yun conceived her desire to live as a virgin in her home district of Yanggŭn after her Catholic identity had already been forged by her parents, who however did not encourage such a vocation and were in fact quite opposed to it.[39] Thus one can conclude that the model of a virgin life for women was generally respected in the Catholic community even if some, such as Yun's parents, had residual Confucian reservations. What is truly worth note, however, is the number and variety of cases in which women responded positively to this model. In the normal expectation of the traditional Korean society of the time, a young woman of marriageable age would get married, and the family took seriously the obligation to find for her (and for the family) the best possible match. The society did not really have a concept of a respectable, single young woman. Because of hair and dress distinctions between unmarried and married women, a single female in her late teens or early twenties would be immediately spotted; people might assume she had an incurable disease or was limited mentally and was thus unmarriageable. So for women like Agada Yun Chŏmhye and Parŭbara (Barbara) Chŏng Sunmae of Yŏju, the only option was to pretend they had been married and lost their husbands at an early age. They both undid their braids, put their hair in a bun pierced with the pin traditionally worn by married women, and lived in the relative anonymity of Seoul, where they became close associates of Kang Wansuk.[40] Nugalda Yi Yuhŭi adopted a different strategy. Her family arranged for her a virgin marriage, in which her husband, Yu Chungsŏng of Chŏnju, also vowed to live a celibate life. Nugalda, in her letters to her mother, sisters, and brother in Seoul, has vivid descriptions of the emotional difficulty of maintaining such a state. The following comes from a letter to her mother:

> When I arrived at my husband's house, I easily obtained the thing that was the object of all my anxiety and the worry of all my days. I found myself with him at the ninth hour; at the tenth, both of us took a vow to keep our virginity, and for four years we have lived as brother and sister. During that

time there were some temptations—ten times or so—when we were not far
from losing everything. But thanks to the Precious Blood, which we both
invoked, we avoided the devil's ambush. I tell you this fearing that you may
have been anxious on my account.[41]

Kang herself exemplified another aspect of the chaste state. She fell into
the different category of widows. For them, Korean Confucian mores favored chastity and in particular circumstances rewarded it highly. Although
she was not technically a widow during the time of our coverage, but a divorced woman in her thirties and early forties, she could, like widows, dress
and function as an ordinary, once-married woman of her age without public notice or comment. But she still valued her chaste state and cultivated
personal purity as a religious commitment. She made particular efforts to
encourage the practice among young unmarried women, starting in her
own home with her daughter, (Hong) Sunhŭi. She found a natural constit-
uency for virginity among palace maids, who were recruited into palace service (or, if their families disapproved, arbitrarily drafted) soon after puberty,
and they were required to remain unmarried and chaste during their time of
service, which in itself was not up to them to decide. Such women became
an important part of her network. Likewise, one sees among her closer associates a fair number of widows. Both of these groups could find in their
socially accepted state a religious purpose in the conditions of their existence. No doubt for many it was a source of personal religious gratification.

In asking ourselves why virginity was sought and cultivated by respectable numbers of women, we might find an answer that also applies to the
bigger question of the attraction of the church itself. While marriage was
more a matter of fate than of choice for the average Korean woman, maintaining virginity or postmarital chastity was, at bottom, a woman's own personal decision to make. It was a way of asserting agency, defining independence. As virgins or chaste widows in Kang Wansuk's and other church
networks, they had not only a religious vocation but a life and solidarity in
an enterprise that was bigger than all of them. And if, in being faced with
the conventional gender attitudes of the society, they had the courage to
make that decision, they also usually had the strength to resist the pressures
that inevitably followed. As a practical matter, such opportunities were
available to few Korean women, but for that reason, perhaps, were all the
more prized by those who seized them.

One particular feature of the activities at Kang Wansuk's house—or
Hong P'ilchu's (Mun'gap's) house as it is often called in persecution documents, even though Hong had a separate house of his own in another part
of the city—caught the eyes of more than a few people: the mixing of the
sexes. Yi Hapkyu told the interrogators that "at the gathering of gangs at

Hong Mun'gap's house, they share the same cushions with Brother Zhou as he lectures, men and women all mixed up together."[42] However, at similar occasions in men's homes, things were different. For example, Pedŭro (Peter) Ch'oe P'ilche testified:

> (Culprit) once went at dawn with the other gentlemen to [Kim] I'u's house, where the priest had been invited from Hong Mun'gap's. For the *ch'ŏmnye* they had put up a picture of Jesus on a wall hung with drapes. Cushions and other items had been laid out and the priest was sitting there with [male] culprits. The women from Yi'u's house sat outside the window, reciting [their prayers].[43]

While it is completely believable that the Catholic men would have generally maintained the separation of sexes that was their custom, the interrogators seem to have pointedly contrasted their testimony on the segregated participation of women with the representations of the mixing of the sexes at Kang's house. Indeed, this particular theme was explicitly stated in Kang's sentence: "For six years (culprit) venerated and hosted rogue Zhou, hiding him away [in her house], where vile acts and disorderly doings soiled the eyes and ears of others."[44] This wording, putting the "vile acts and disorderly doings" in the immediate context of Father Zhou, may have carried the added intention to suggest personal impropriety on the parts of Kang and the priest themselves. Certainly some innuendoes to that effect were squeezed out of Sŏ Kyŏng'ŭi, a young widow and one of Kang's converts, who was one of the maids of Maria Song and Maria Sin at the defunct palace, both before and after Father Zhou had come there to stay for a while. She testified about matters concerning both the palace and Kang's house, where her mistresses occasionally went for discussions with Father Zhou.

> There was a man who was called "the head of the church" (*kyoju*). Brother Hong's mother shared a seat with the *kyoju* as he instructed the two ladies.[45] Culprit saw such scenes several times. Later, after culprit had returned to culprit's house after having been away, something quite unusual happened, although culprit never told anybody about it. One night, when culprit, without particularly thinking about it, opened Lady Song's door and looked in, a man suddenly jumped up and ran out to the back door of the side room. It was dark, and though culprit could not make out the figure, culprit thought it very strange. Culprit asked Lady Song about it and she thought it was just female slave Hong going out for a private moment. Later, a man's shoes were seen in the cabinet, and Lady Song again said they were just female slave Hong's shoes. On the twentieth of this month, around the second or third watch of the night (10 p.m.–2 a.m.), I heard a loud noise. I

opened the window and looked out, and there was a man coming out of
Lady Song's toilet and hurrying in the door of the side room. I went straight
to the mistress's room and asked her about it; she said, "It's dark at night, and
you didn't see things clearly. It was just the young mistress (Maria Sin) going
into the toilet."[46]

This statement, a masterpiece of suggestion and innuendo serving only
to suggest the worst about Maria Song and Zhou Wenmo, is virtually the
only topic covered in the presently available version of Sŏ Kyŏng'ŭi's testimony. She must have had a great deal to say; she had been a practicing
Catholic and had observed many Catholic activities, which were the normal
subject of inquiry in the interrogations, but we find no word of that here. It
was she who, on Fourthmoon 29 (June 10), after Kang Wansuk was in custody and Father Zhou was already dead, secretly informed the authorities
that Zhou had been at the defunct palace and that her two mistresses were
Catholics. She concluded her testimony with a general statement of apostasy, then was banished to Ungch'ŏn in southern Kyŏngsang province.
The two Marias, Song and Sin, as women married into the royal family,
were immune from questioning by civil authorities in criminal matters.
The usual manner of execution for royals was poisoning, and in this case
their cups arrived at their quarters almost immediately.

That took care of suggesting moral turpitude in Father Zhou; now the
interrogators looked to another defendant to similarly involve Kang Wansuk. The testimony was from Kim Wŏrim, a young virgin who, after the
death of her parents, found her way to Kang and grew up in her household,
sewing and working there from 1795 on.

The one they call the priest ... lived in the middle room of the upper hall.
The only people who went in there were Wansuk, her daughter, and
Tasŭra.[47] Woman Kang often went into the room alone, and whenever she
did she would immediately lock the door from the inside. Not only did she
not let anyone else in there, but when culprit might peek in through a crack
in the window, Mother Kang became terribly alarmed and turned white. She
forbade culprit on pain of death from transgressing [again]. So culprit never
actually saw much, but from a quick glance [the man] had a beard that was
half white, and a broad face. When culprit was arrested, Woman Kang
strongly ordered culprit "not to testify truthfully even if it means being
beaten to death."[48]

Kim Wŏrim also apostatized and was banished to Ulsan. As in the case
of Sŏ Kyŏng'ŭi, her information is virtually the only matter of substance in
her file. And like Sŏ, what she said was basically suggestion and innuendo.

It is impossible in evaluating such materials, with all their uncertainties, either to give them much credit or to reject them completely. They certainly cannot be ignored. Their real meaning was known only to the interrogators, who alone had complete control over their construction in the form we have them. My personal conviction, after critically reading all the testimony in the *Sahak ching'ŭi*, as well as the materials emanating from Korean Catholic sources preserved in Charles Dallet's equally partisan account in the *Histoire de l'Église de Corée*, is that more weight should be given to Kang's long and determined commitment to her religion and in particular to her strong belief in the practice of virginity and chastity. It seems to me that it would have been harder for her to compromise than for the interrogators, and that if they had really believed they had evidence of concupiscence, they would have put it in full play.

Arrest and Death

Kang Wansuk and her entire household were arrested and taken to one of Seoul's two major police stations—the so-called bandit tribunals (*p'odoch'ŏng*)—on Secondmoon 24 (Apr. 6, 1801).[49] Hwang Sayŏng says: "When she was arrested and taken before the officials, they questioned her, in six sessions of rope dislocation torture, on the movements of the priest. She neither moved nor uttered any sound or gasp. The evil underlings on either side of her said, 'This one is a god (*sin*), not a human being!' In the end her life was taken by beheading. She was forty-one *se*."[50]

The "rope dislocation" torture, called *churoe chil* (or *churi chil*) in Korean, involved tying the legs firmly together at the big toes, with a thick piece of wood inserted between the legs at the calves. Then two men, one on each side, would each loop a rope around the farther knee, then pull from opposite directions to force the knees together, causing the shin bones to bend into a bow slowly, so that they would not break, but also intensifying the pain. Then the bowed legs would be allowed, again very slowly and painfully, to return to their straight form.[51] The early hagiography of Dallet's Korean source elaborates: "The only thing they could think of in their bitterness was how to obtain her apostasy, and to this end they employed against her every torture that the most refined cruelty could invent. But always they were overcome by the supernatural endurance of their victim."[52]

We do not know for how long a period she underwent interrogation under torture. She was executed on Fifthmoon 23 (July 3), on the eighty-ninth day of her detention. If the arrest of Father Zhou could be a factor in determining that period, it might have ended on either Thirdmoon 12 or 16 (Apr. 24 or 28)—depending on which date we accept for his surrender—a much shorter period of from nineteen to twenty-three days.[53] Only apostasy, or the interrogators for their own reasons, could have stopped the torture. Since she never apostatized, we simply have no way of knowing how long she had to endure it.

The *Sahak ching'ŭi* has short summaries of four interrogations under bone dislocation torture at the bandit tribunal. At some point she was then sent to the Ministry of Punishments (Hyŏngjo) for review and sentencing. Her final statement, in which she recapitulated what she had confessed to at the bandit tribunal, was as follows, beginning with her background in Tŏksan:

> Culprit studied the deviant learning from the widow of Brother Kong. At the time of Yun Chich'ung's arrest at the governor's compound in Chŏnju in the year Sinhae (1791), culprit's name appeared among those detained and questioned. Culprit was arrested and culprit's deviant books were confiscated. Culprit's husband, disciplining culprit for not maintaining family harmony, charged culprit with wrongdoing and expelled culprit, who has not seen him since. Culprit hid Brother Zhou in culprit's house, and received from him baptism and the name Kollumba. Every seventh day during the month, when there was an obligatory holy day (*sŏlpŏp ch'ŏmnye*), [Pibianna (Vivian)] Mun Yŏng'in, Pokchŏm, and others participated.[54] Culprit maintained communication with the household of Cho Yesan and with the defunct palace in Chŏndong, and both palace maids, Sŏ and Kang, came to culprit's house to study; from the princesses' residence, the traitor's wife and a lady also came twice to culprit's house and listened to the scriptures, with culprit and Brother Zhou on adjoined cushions, and then went home. Therefore culprit too several times went to them. As for people culprit has enticed into the religion, there are culprit's daughter Sunhŭi, Chŏmhye, Pokchŏm, Wŏrim, Chŏng'im, Hyomyŏng, Nyŏn'i, Tŏg'i, [Mun] Yŏng'in, Sunmae, Tŏg'im, and Sun'i; as for people culprit has exchanged letters with, there are the households of [Chŏng] Yakchong and Yagyong, O Sŏkch'ung, and [Kwŏn] Ch'ŏlsin and his younger sister. As for Hwang Sayŏng, naturally culprit and he were close friends; with him culprit had discussions with Brother Zhou on deviant writings. In Secondmoon (Mar. 14–Apr. 12) Sayŏng wanted to find a hiding place, so culprit pointed out Nyŏn'i's house to him. Ever since culprit has studied this religion, she has believed that she will go to heaven. Therefore, even if punishments and tortures are applied to culprit, culprit will not have any regret or change of mind. That is culprit's testimony. Culprit is infected and suffused with the deviant learning. Culprit hid Rogue Zhou, violated human morality, abused customs, and befuddled and deceived the world. For these crimes, ten thousand death verdicts would still be too light a punishment.[55]

Such is the word from the torture yard. Catholic accounts of her experience there come from an utterly different conceptual universe:

> Immediately after her arrest, the judges, wanting to extract from her the secret of the priest's refuge, subjected her six times to the horrible torture of bone dislocation. Throughout these torments she remained mute and seemingly unconscious, which led the underlings looking on to say among themselves: "She's a spirit, not a woman." Far from giving the least sign of weakness, she continued her apostolate in prison, and even before the judges she constantly proclaimed the divine character of Christian religion, bringing to the support of her words proofs drawn from Confucius and others of the most celebrated philosophers. In their admiration the officials would only call her "the wise woman," or "the unmatchable woman," and would say that she took their breath away, a Korean expression that denotes the kind of stupor produced by an extraordinary shock.... Kollumba's faith triumphed no less gloriously in her maternal love. Her stepson P'illippo, who had been arrested with her but incarcerated in another prison, had appeared to weaken under torture. She heard about this, and having caught a glimpse of him from afar one day while being led from her prison to the tribunal, shouted to him in a loud voice: "Jesus is over your head. He sees you. Can you be so confused and lost? Take courage, my child, and think of the happiness of Heaven." This noble exhortation saved the soul of the young man, who, fortified by her words, received the martyr's crown several months later.[56]

It remained only to issue the notice of sentence and carry out the execution by decapitation, on Fifthmoon 23 (July 3, 1801). Seoul's execution ground was outside the Minor West Gate (Sŏsomun), through which used to pass the road that leads today from Seoul City Hall plaza out toward Sinch'on and Yŏnse University. Kang and four other women were placed in a cart and taken under guard to the execution ground. Normally in executions the clothing on the upper body was removed, presumably for the convenience of the executioner. Kang is said to have turned to the presiding officer and said, "The laws prescribe that those who are to be put to the ordeal must be stripped of their clothing, but it would be improper to treat women in this way. Advise your superior that we ask to die clothed." This was agreed to, and Kang was the first to present her head to the executioner.[57] Prior to her death she would have been required to sign her statement of sentence (kyŏranch'o), as all condemned had to do. This notice was posted at the execution ground and remained there for a period of time after the execution. Kang Wansuk's sentence reads as follows:

Statement of Sentence: Culprit studied deviant books and acknowledged
them as the true way. Therefore, even though arrested by provincial officials
in Hongju in the year Sinhae (1791), culprit neither took warning nor stood
in awe. Nor when expelled by her husband did culprit pull back to reflect.
For six years culprit venerated and accepted Rogue Zhou, hiding him away
[in her house], where vile acts and disorderly doings (ch'uhaeng nangjŏk) soiled
the eyes and ears of others. Culprit enticed family members both old and
young into the religion, made common cause with the vile and depraved of
all quarters, maintained communication with the defunct palace, and deceived
and misled people everywhere. Ten thousand death verdicts are still too light
a punishment.[58]

Kollumba Kang Wansuk, Woman of Agency

Somewhere between the outraged hostility and humiliations of the interrogators on the one side and the saintly pieties of the hagiographical tradition on the other, we have to look for the real life and deeds of Kang
Wansuk. As readers of the foregoing will be able to appreciate, the gap between those two extremes is immense, and each one is implacably one-
dimensional. Where are we to interpolate Kollumba Kang Wansuk on a
scale that forces us to begin at thuggery and allows us to end only at sainthood?

The thing that is the hardest to assess is Kang as a Catholic. The transmission of Catholicism to Korea, amazing as it was, had planted only an
imperfect and incomplete church to start with. Immediately it was besieged
by opponents on all sides and forced into an underground existence. Much
of what it genuinely did achieve has been denied to history by the fires of
1801. The martyring of some of the Korean founders, the uncertainties and
missteps of the others, and the loss of almost every book they imported,
wrote, or translated, severely impairs and limits both the human and literary
traditions that might today have helped us come to a nuanced understanding of what the communicants believed and practiced. We do have a basic
idea of how Catholic doctrine was summed up before 1801, thanks to a
catechism by Chŏng Yakchong called Chugyo yoji (The Bishop's Essentials).[59] But we know scarcely anything about Kang's understanding of
that catechism, except that she believed in the certainty of heaven, and
beyond that in the spiritual benefits of chastity and virginity. We can say
that her faith was unshakable. We know that for six years she had access to
a priest, Catholic training, the Mass, the Eucharist, and the sacrament of
penance—by all indications a level of access greater than that of any other
Korean Catholic of her time. But we still do not have any satisfactory
understanding of what that experience meant to her or how she felt it or

perceived it. The few indications that have come through suggest little of Catholic religiosity. This is an unavoidable problem in assessing all of the early Catholics, not just Kang. As an exception, when one reads the gushing expressions of faith in the letters of the teenage virgin bride Nugalda Yi Yuhŭi, naïve and unsophisticated as she was, we do at least see a recognizably Korean expression of Catholic sensibility that I have not detected in the materials concerning any other early Catholic woman. So at least we can get a rough idea of what we don't know in the case of Kang Wansuk.

But if Kang as a Catholic is somewhat of a mystery, Kang as a woman comes out more clearly and interestingly. And while her Catholic context is hard to plumb, the context of Korean society and a woman's role in it at that time are much better understood, even if we do still have much to learn. What strikes us immediately is how quickly and unerringly she moved beyond many of the restrictions that kept women in the home and out of public life. She took and accepted serious risks. She welcomed the opportunity for leadership, and used it to the fullest. She had a life in the bigger world, and made an impression in that world. Her house, rather than being the place of her sequestration from a public life, was the stage on which it was played out.

Her family background in an illegitimate *yangban* line—giving her the status of a so-called bastard yangban (*pansŏ*) or a one-name (*ilmyŏng*)— meant that like all people who bore such a handicap in the late traditional Korean society, she grew up well aware of real limitations on her prospects. For a woman, this was chiefly measured by whom she was able to marry, and her husband, not unexpectedly, was a *pansŏ* himself. If they are to get anywhere, people of such status have to be more aggressive and thick-skinned because society is predisposed to discriminate against them. Either a bold pluckiness develops, or they sink below public notice. On the other hand, such a status was still well above that of a commoner; it implied a sense of some distinguished ancestors however far back and probably conferred some modest social advantage and opportunities for education, at least to the extent then possible for a woman. By all accounts, Kang Wansuk was certainly literate in vernacular texts written in the Korean alphabet. Beyond that, a woman who participated in three-person textual seminars with a highly educated Chinese immigrant priest and an accomplished scholar of the class of Hwang Sayŏng undoubtedly had some knowledge of Chinese characters and at least some Chinese textual abilities. Such a level of literacy for a woman, if she took advantage of it, could strengthen her authority and leadership.

Kang took a risk by becoming avowedly interested in Catholicism, although in a part of Korea that early on saw a large and rapid growth of the religion, she had a lot of company. Her zeal in spreading the faith in the

Naep'o area gave her a high enough profile to get her arrested in 1791, in a period when women were still largely immune from arrest. Her challenge to her husband was more than more-docile women would have considered. It ultimately led to her husband's rejection of her and her expulsion from his household, against which, by the indications we have, she did not protest much. Since a divorced woman would not have had an easy time in the rural society in which she had grown up, Kang decided to move to the city.

Seoul at that time was hardly a metropolis on the order of Peking or Edo, but it was Korea's biggest and most important city, and it did confer a certain degree of anonymity upon its residents, making it possible for Kang to walk through the streets in the evening hours as easily as a mature widow. By 1795 she had already achieved a degree of prominence and leadership among Seoul's Catholics. As an organizer, manager, and part financier of the successful plot to introduce a Chinese priest into Korea, she became for all practical purposes a professional churchwoman and a person of some power. As Father Zhou's protector and coordinator, she was one of the most important Catholics in Seoul. As the designated catechist (hoejang) for women, she had responsibility for the organization and religious training of two-thirds of the membership of the church if we credit Hwang Sayŏng's nationwide estimate, but still a significant number even if we consider only the Seoul membership plus that of the Kyŏnggi towns of Yanggŭn and Yŏju, with which we know she had significant ties. (Kang is not known to have ever returned to her native turf in southern Ch'ungch'ŏng province.)

In short, Kang Wansuk was an independent woman with a public career. True, she had to pursue that career covertly, but her field of action extended far beyond the home, and widespread recognition of her work came from outside it. Whether she capitalized her own existence in Seoul or in some way was financially supported by the Catholic community for her important services or benefited from some combination of such circumstances, she spent her own money for things she wanted and believed in and was responsible for her own livelihood. In a religious community that had been established and dominated by sabu men, she moved unerringly to leadership at its center. She was not the first woman to die for the church in Korea (that distinction goes to either Maria Song or Maria Sin, whose cup of poison arrived the very day that they were revealed by Maid Sŏ), but her death was the most noticed. She was the undisputed leader of the twenty-nine women who in 1801 were either decapitated, beaten to death in prison, strangled, or poisoned for their faith.[60] Judging by the exuberant hagiography that developed after her death, she was a role model for later Korean Catholics.[61]

I have been unable to find in either Catholic or Confucian/government sources any clear expressions of a woman's self-consciousness on the part of Kollumba Kang Wansuk or any of her female associates. A faint suggestion of it seemed to be trying to emerge from Agada Yun Chŏmhye, when, having been taunted by an interrogator for her *pansŏ* social status, she replied, "People may call culprit a *pansŏ*, but in my person (*sin*) I am a virgin (*ch'ŏnyŏ*) who has run away from home to find a place for herself in Wansuk's house."[62] Did she mean that she had nothing to do with the status (*sin*) she was born into, while the status she had at Wansuk's was of her own choice? We can only ask the question. The vocabulary of female self-assertion was not very developed in Korea in 1801. Judging by Dallet's account of Yun, we can conclude that she helped Kang in her Catholic education activities but was much more absorbed in her personal, virginal sanctification.[63] Her life as narrated by Dallet seems very much like that of a cloistered nun. But we always have to be mindful of a possible French Catholic ethos consciously or unconsciously overlaid by Daveluy on the Korean Catholic account at its base.

Kang Wansuk's career is easier for us to assess because it played out on a churchwide scale and involved leadership and administrative responsibilities throughout the Catholic community. Indeed, I can think of no other woman in Korean history prior to the nineteenth century who played such an important public role in a movement with as many consequences for the country as the implantation on Korean soil of Christianity. On the public level, she had and was known to have power at the center of that activity. On the personal level, she created for herself that important quality, called agency, that marks women and other socially marginalized individuals who achieve the power of independent action in public space of their own choice. We must also, however, recognize that Korean Catholics, in trying to establish in their country an institution with its own worldwide hierarchical structure—in effect what we might now call a nongovernmental organization—were in fact engaged in an early phase of the battle for a civil society, one in which social, economic, religious, and other institutional relationships are allowed to legally exist, prosper, and develop without arbitrary government intervention.[64] In Kang Wansuk's time and place, such a concept was more than unthinkable; it had scarcely even been imagined. In the government's mind, the only concept available to describe it was treason, and even in the minds of the Catholic protagonists there seems to have been no sense of these wider implications of their struggle. But if we are to look for a moment when it is time for autonomous, public female social roles to develop, it will be in circumstances very much like those that emerged in Korea in the late eighteenth century.[65] And if we are to seek a model for an independent, self-directed Korean female life, we can well look to Kollumba Kang Wansuk.

NOTES

1. For the early history of Korean Catholicism, the best text is still the classic one: Charles Dallet, *Histoire de l'Église de Corée*, 2 vols. (Paris: Librairie Victor Palme, 1874). There is a Korean reprint published by Kyung-in Publishing Company for the Royal Asiatic Society, Korea Branch, Seoul, 1975. Dallet (1829–1878), who never had an opportunity to visit Korea, compiled his history on the basis of materials gathered and translated in Korea between 1855 and 1862 by Msgr. Marie Antoine Nicolas Daveluy (1818–1866) and sent by him to Paris in 1862. Daveluy, who was martyred in 1866, used sources from the Korean government, the Confucian community hostile to Catholicism, and Catholic sources collected after 1836 by himself and his colleagues of the Société des Missionaires Étrangères de Paris, including the ones used in this article, but in addition many that no longer survive. One of the most important of these was a history of the early church by Tasan Chŏng Yag'yong (1762–1836), upon which Daveluy relied for most of his coverage for that period (see Dallet, *Histoire*, 1:121). In writing his history, Dallet did more than rely on Daveluy; he frequently copied him verbatim for page after page, as can be seen by a comparison of his published pages with Daveluy's vast notes, which still survive in Paris. So although Dallet is properly responsible for the text we have, the reader should bear in mind that, at least for the period covered in this chapter, it is usually Daveluy speaking when we cite Dallet. Daveluy was an astute and critical scholar, very capable in Korean and Classical Chinese (of both of which Dallet was ignorant), who worked under extremely difficult conditions as an underground missionary. His account, though obviously intended as a resolutely Catholic version of events, is marked by a due objectivity suffused with a devout Catholic piety, with clear hagiographic tendencies. Readers may want to consult the modern Korean translation of Dallet by Ch'oe Sŏg'u and An Ŭngnyŏl: *Han'guk Ch'ŏnju kyohoesa*, 3 vols. (Seoul: Han'guk Ch'ŏnju Kyohoesa Yŏn'guso, 1980). Father Ch'oe's abundant annotations from Korean and other European source materials make his a magisterial work that no serious scholar of this subject can do without. Hereafter, the *Histoire* will be cited as "Dallet," and the Korean translation by Ch'oe and An as *HCK*. In the case of each work, all citations will be to volume 1 in each case, so the volume number is hereafter omitted in references.

A note on Christian names: In the case of Korean Christian names, it has seemed to me insensitive to render them in either English or French. I have chosen to present them as they are pronounced today by Korean Catholics. In cases where the names still don't quite come through, I add the English equivalent in parentheses, as in "Parŭbara (Barbara)." At the time Christianity was introduced into Korea from China, the common forms of Chinese Christian names were based on a generally Latinate form, which comes out clearly in the Korean forms.

2. See Don Baker, "Catholicism in a Confucian World," in *Culture and the State in Late Chosŏn Korea*, ed. JaHyun Kim Haboush and Martina Deuchler (Cambridge, Mass.: Harvard University Asia Center, 1999), 199–230.

3. These figures are derived from Han'guk Kyohoesa Yŏn'guso, comp., *Han'guk Kat'ollik Taesajŏn, purok* volume, appendixes 7.2, 1, "List of [Male] Martyrs

and Victims" (130–165), and 7.2, 2, "List of Female Martyrs and Victims" (166–177). The lists are arranged in Korean alphabetical order.

4. Chiefly *Pyŏgwi p'yŏn*, compiled by Yi Kigyŏng (1756–1819), and *Sahak ching'ŭi* (hereafter *SC*), both in reprints published by Purham munhwasa for the Han'guk Kyohoesa Yŏn'guso, Seoul, in 1978 and 1977, respectively. Both works were compiled during or just after the 1801 persecution. The copy of the *Sahak ching'ŭi* used for the reprint contains indications that it was used in (and probably compiled by) the Ministry of Punishments (Hyŏngjo) as a general reference for officials of the persecution.

5. See, in *Han'guk Kat'ollik Taesajŏn*, *purok* volume, appendix 7.3, "Diagrams of Family Relationships among the Early Church Faithful" (178–194). There are sixty-nine fascinating genealogical diagrams showing the marriage ties of the early Catholic families.

6. The general term *yangban* has very flexible application during this period. It should be distinguished from the term *sadaebu*, its abbreviation *sabu*, and its synonym *sahwan*, which all refer to the ruling class, based mainly in Seoul. Because of class instability and various strategies then common for class mobility, people who were acknowledged as *yangban* at this time cannot automatically be assumed to be of the ruling class. And as we shall see, there were even technical variations of the term *yangban* that marked specific and important gradations. I take *yangban* to mean a person who by his assumed family background, education, and Confucian lifestyle (principally, the practice of standard ancestral rituals) was seen to be of the upper classes but who was not confused with a *sabu*.

7. *Paeksŏ*, lines 20–21. The *Paeksŏ* was an extremely long letter written in the midst of the 1801 persecution by Hwang Sayŏng, one of the younger leaders of the Catholics, while he was deep in hiding in a rural town far from Seoul. It was addressed to the Catholic bishop in Peking, but it fell into the government's hands when its bearer was arrested before he could cross into China. Written on a piece of silk so that it could be sewn into the clothing of the messenger, and consisting of 13,311 very tiny Chinese characters, it stated the precarious situation of the Catholics in 1801, gave a long and interesting history of the Korean church up to that point, and appealed for European intervention to end the persecution. This latter part shocked the Korean court and was quite understandably taken as evidence validating its ruling that Catholicism had to be considered as treasonous. Hwang Sayŏng himself was soon tracked down, the last of the major *sabu* leaders to be arrested and executed (Tenthmoon 24 = Nov. 29, 1801). The original letter came to light in 1895, at the time of the dissolution of the state tribunal (Ŭigŭmbu), and was purchased by the French bishop Gustave Mutel in Seoul, who sent it as a gift to the Vatican Library, where it now resides. There are two modern editions: *Hwang Sayŏng Paeksŏ* (Seoul: Han'guk Kyohoesa Yŏn'guso, 1967), and Yamaguchi Masayuki, ed., *Kō Shiei Hakusho no kenkyū* (Tōkyō: Zenkoku shobō, 1946). Yamaguchi's edition has an especially fine and legible facsimile reproduction. Both editions number the original lines—which are very long—so that citation by line number is possible with either. In the versions of the *Silk Letter* known through Korean sources prior to 1895, such as the *Pyŏgwip'yŏn* and in the extracts found in the

"veritable records" *(sillok)* and other official sources, some passages were omitted or altered, and of course for such versions the line numbers given here will be useless.

8. Kang Wansuk is by far the most frequently mentioned woman in the *SC* notes and records of interrogations of Catholics, where she is variously called Kangnyŏ (Woman Kang), Kangmo (Mother Kang), Kangp'a (Old Grandma Kang), or Wansuk, which in a prosecutorial context was by itself demeaning since defendants and convicts were commonly referred to without the surname. Praise of her role on the Catholic side is evidenced in quotes to be later cited from the *Silk Letter*.

9. Dallet, 75, in speaking of Kang's parents, says that they "would both die in an edifying way." But as far as I can determine, he never comes back to mention or identify them in his later text. Nor does Father Ch'oe Sŏg'u *(HCK, 384)*, who always provides extra information relevant to the text when he has it, say anything to elucidate this remark.

10. *Paeksŏ*, line 65. Hwang Sayŏng uses the distinctly nontransparent term *ilmyŏng*, "one name," to identify Kang's formal social status. Fortunately, in a note for the intended readers in Beijing, which he had earlier inserted into line 8 in connection with another individual of this status, he glossed it for us: "A son or a descendant of a *sabu* by a concubine is called a 'one-name.'" The summary of Kang's interrogation at the Ministry of Punishments also applies this term to her: *SC*, 96. I have no explanation as to why the term should have this meaning.

11. Kang's husband's son, Hong P'ilchu, identified himself as a *pansŏ* in his interrogation at the Ministry of Punishments; see *SC*, 116. He also married a woman of *pansŏ* status.

12. Daveluy/Dallet generally have the notion that Kang Wansuk is a "noble," in spite of their description of her ancestry as "née ... d'une famille païenne des demi-nobles, ou, selon l'expression coréenne, des nobles bâtards" (Dallet, 74), which seems to be based on the *Silk Letter* (of which Daveluy had a copy of an expurgated text). Ch'oe Sŏg'u *(HCK, 382)*, in pondering Dallet's "demi-noble," considers a *pansŏ* interpretation but comes down in favor of *hyangban*, which in my understanding suggests a person that would be recognized in his local community as a *yangban* but probably not in Seoul. I do not think it implies any *necessary* dimension of illegitimacy, though in a given case it might. In another place *(HCK, 499,* n. 40) Ch'oe states that "it is certain that Kang Wansuk was a *yangban* lady *(puin),*" but he does not explain whence the certainty comes.

13. Dallet, 74; *HCK*, 383.

14. Dallet, 39–58; *HCK*, 333–356. See also Baker, "Catholicism," 217–220.

15. *SC*, 95–97. These are retrospective references from 1801. No 1791 provincial report on Kang seems to have survived.

16. Dallet, 74–75; *HCK*, 382–383.

17. *Paeksŏ*, lines 66–67.

18. *SC*, 97.

19. Dallet, 59–72; *HCK*, 357–373.

20. *Paeksŏ*, line 67.

21. *SC*, 363–364. In terms of today's Seoul, Ch'angdong was inside the South Gate on the southeastern side of Namdaemun-no 4-ka.

22. Dallet and many other people since have had the idea that Bianmen was on the north bank of the Yalu across from Ŭiju. Actually there was a no-man's-land fifty-two kilometers wide between the north bank and Bianmen. It was patrolled by Manchu soldiers, and Koreans had access to it only at times of diplomatic missions or designated trade fairs. This is why so much time had to go by before the Korean introducers could go up to Bianmen to meet and bring him in.

23. For Hong P'ilchu's separate homes in An'guktong and Taesadong, see *SC*, 361 and 370, respectively. In the interrogations the Ch'angdong home is referred to sometimes as Kang's and sometimes as Hong Mun'gap's (P'ilchu's). It is quite possible that the neighborhood office had the house registered under Hong's name, as the oldest male. He probably lived there for a while, but I suspect that when he got married, he moved into the Taesadong house.

24. Dallet, 71ff.; *HCK*, 378ff. According to Dallet, 70 (*HCK*, 377), Zhou Wenmo was known among Portuguese in China as Jacobo Vellozo. This should be seen in conjunction with Hwang Sayŏng's remark in the *Silk Letter* (*Paeksŏ*, lines 79–80) that he heard while he was in hiding that non-Catholic Koreans were saying that Zhou had claimed to his interrogators that he was a Westerner (*sŏyang'in*). Although it is certain that Zhou was born in China and was culturally Chinese, it would seem likely that he was of Portuguese paternity. We know that he had a long and bushy beard.

25. *Paeksŏ*, lines 67–68, 77–78.

26. Dallet, 76; *HCK*, 385–386. The "three years" is either Dallet's error or possibly a slip he inherited from Daveluy. Hwang Sayŏng's "six years" is correct; see *Paeksŏ*, lines 67–68.

27. One place that is mentioned several times is an "old hag's house" at the Yongho Garrison, a royal guard detachment. I have tried without success to find where this was. See *SC*, 71, where a defendant reports that Kang had sent Hwang Sayŏng to stay there for a while.

28. The house of Mrs. Im (Im *sosa*) was one such place. See the testimony of Nusia Yun Unhye, whose sister Chŏmhye was a semipermanent resident of Kang's house. *SC*, 93.

29. *SC*, 354.

30. On the Sado affair, see JaHyun Kim Haboush, *Heritage of Kings* (New York: Columbia University Press, 1988); and in translation by the same author, the narratives of Sado's wife in *The Memoirs of Lady Hyegyŏng* (Berkeley and Los Angeles: University of California Press, 1996).

31. *SC*, 123, 126. Hong Ingman was of *pansŏ* descent.

32. Although the relationships with the *p'yegung* definitely intensified from Twelfthmoon of the lunar year 1800 (solar Jan. 15–Feb. 12, 1801) on, the actual date of Father Zhou's move there is uncertain. It may have been as late as Secondmoon of 1801 (Mar. 15–Apr. 12). It is also possible that some of his time was spent in Hong Ingman's house close by.

33. *SC*, 109.

34. *SC*, 357.

35. *SC*, 100 (Kang Kyŏngbok). Father Zhou's efforts to speak Korean were apparently not very successful.

36. *SC*, 104 (Yuanna [Joanne?] Nyŏn'i), and 106 (Pibianna [Vivian] Mun Yŏng'in).

37. *SC*, 379–386. Although it does not necessarily follow that books with titles in Chinese characters represent texts in Chinese, some probably do, and in some cases there are explicit notes to that effect. But most of the titles (and implicitly the texts) are written in the Korean alphabet. The great majority of these books were almost certainly copies made by hand (*sabon*). Many of the books in this list had been hidden at Kang's direction in the early stages of the persecution, before her arrest.

38. See Dallet, 176–197; *HCK*, 527–555. Her given name is identified as Sun'i in *SC*, 171. Unfortunately, her legal proceedings all took place in Chŏnju, and *SC* has no interrogation summaries for her.

39. *SC*, 107–110.

40. See ibid. and 110–112.

41. Dallet, 184; *HCK*, 539.

42. *SC*, 70.

43. *SC*, 74, 76.

44. *SC*, 97.

45. Brother Hong, here Hong P'ilchu, is written with the unusual male suffix *ka* (colloquial Ch. *ge*, younger brother). In this period it was usually applied to merchants and shopkeepers; here it connotes low status for Hong.

46. *SC*, 356–357.

47. I cannot identify this Christian name. Could it be a garbled metathesis of "Theresa"? The testimony identifies her as "Mrs. Yun" (Yun *sosa*), but in an interlinear note the interrogators wonder if "Tasŭra" is not Kim (Wŏrim) herself.

48. *SC*, 349–350 (Kim Wŏrim).

49. *Paeksŏ*, line 30.

50. *Paeksŏ*, lines 68–69.

51. Dallet, Introduction, lxvi; *HCK*, 112. This comes from a general essay on the criminal justice system in Korea, based of course on materials provided by Antoine Daveluy, who knew the subject intimately and close up. It makes compelling reading. The entire Introduction (in fifteen chapters, of which the criminal justice essay is only one), has been translated into English—the only part of Dallet's opus for which that has so far been done—by the Human Relations Area Files, New Haven, Connecticut. See Charles Dallet, *Traditional Korea*, Behavioral Science Translations, Human Relations Area Files (New Haven, 1954), 68–69. "Traditional Korea" is HRAF's title, not Dallet's.

52. Dallet, 158; *HCK*, 500.

53. *HCK*, 478, n. 72.

54. Pokchŏm was a female slave (*sabi*) who was owned by "Kwŏn *saengwŏn*"

—apparently Amburosio (Ambrose) Kwŏn Ch'ŏlsin—but who worked in a number of other homes with Christian family members. She describes in her testimony her duties working for Kang in preparing for and cleaning up after a *ch'ŏmnye*. *SC*, 370–371.

55. *SC*, 96–97.

56. Dallet, 157–158; *HCK*, 500.

57. Dallet, 158–159; *HCK*, 501. Note that Kang speaks for the other women as their leader.

58. *SC*, 97–98.

59. Unfortunately, the earliest surviving version of that book, which is believed to have been supplemented and revised from Chŏng's original text, is a woodblock print edition of 1864. See Chŏng Yakchong, *Chugyo yoji*, ed. Ha Sŏngnae (Seoul: Sŏng Hwang Sŏktu Nuga Sŏwŏn, 1986).

60. Listed in the Korean Catholic encyclopedia. See n. 3.

61. In 2000, the Archdiocese of Suwŏn, in Kyŏnggi province, announced a general inquiry into the lives of seventeen early Catholics of the period we have considered here. The inquiry would be the first step in a long process that could lead to beatification and ultimately to sainthood. The list includes Kang Wansuk and, among those who have been mentioned in this chapter, these others (in alphabetical order): Saba Chi Hwang, Mathia Ch'oe In'gil, Parŭbara (Barbara) Chŏng Sunmae, Yakobo Chu Munmo (= Jacobo Zhou Wenmo), P'illippo Hong P'ilchu, Agada (Agatha) Yun Chŏmhye, and Paoro Yun Yuil. In addition to Kollumba Kang, Agada Yun, and Parŭbara Chŏng, there are two other women on the list: Parŭbara Sim Agi and Nusia Yun Unhye (cousin of Paoro Yun and sister of Agada Yun). In 1984, ninety-three saints were canonized, but these were all from the persecutions of 1839, 1846, or 1866. Of those, forty-seven were women, a bare majority. (In addition, ten French missionary priests were also canonized at that time, for a total of 103 Korean or Korea-related saints to date.)

62. *SC*, 108–109.

63. Dallet, 164–166; *HCK*, 510–512.

64. See Don Baker, "Unexpected fruit: Catholicism and the rise of civil society in Korea," in *Christianity in Korea*, ed. Young-Key Kim Renaud and R. Richard Grinker, Sigur Center Asia Papers, no. 12 (Washington, D.C.: George Washington University, 2001).

65. Obviously by that time the role of female entertainers, or *kisaeng*, had been long established in Korean society, and one might say that many of them were autonomous, public, female professionals. Shamans, Buddhist nuns, wet nurses, and some medical practitioners might also be included in such a group. These were all activities for which social niches had long existed. However, such women were marginalized and vulnerable to constant governmental harassment and regulation, and in that sense they were not the modern type of professional woman that I am speaking of here, even though in Kang Wansuk's case the government that executed her was not yet ready to make any such distinction. That very fact serves to highlight the precociousness of her emergence.

Glossary of Names, Terms, and Book Titles

NAMES OF PERSONS

An Ŭngnyŏl 安應烈
Chi Hwang 池璜
Cho Yesan 趙禮山
Chŏng Sunmae 鄭順每
Chŏng Yag'yong 丁若鏞
Chŏng'im 丁任
Chŏngjo (King) 正祖
Ch'oe Ch'anghyŏn 崔昌顯
Ch'oe In'gil 崔仁吉
Ch'oe P'ilche 崔必悌
Ch'oe Sŏg'u 崔奭祐
Chu Munmo 周文謨
Hong Chiyŏng 洪芝榮
Hong Ingman 洪翼萬
Hong Mun'gap 洪文甲
Hong P'ilchu 洪弼周
Hong Sunhŭi 洪順喜
Hwang Sayŏng 黃嗣永
Hwang Sŏktu 黃錫斗
Hyomyŏng 孝明
Kang Kyŏngbok 姜景福
Kang Wansuk 姜完淑
Kangmo 姜母
Kangnyŏ 姜女
Kangp'a 姜婆
Kim I'u 金履禹
Kim Nyŏm'i 金廉伊
Kim Pŏm'u 金範禹
Kim Wŏrim 金月任
Kong (Brother) 孔哥
Kwŏn Ch'ŏlsin 權哲身
Mun Yŏng'in 文榮仁
Nyŏn'i 連伊
O Sŏkch'ung 吳錫忠
Pokchŏm 福占
Sado (Prince) 思悼世子
Sanggye (Prince) 常溪君
Sim Agi 沈阿只

Sin Maria 申마리아
Sŏ Kyŏng'ŭi 徐景儀
Somyŏng 小明
Song Maria 宋마리아
Sun'i 順伊
Tasan 茶山
Tŏg'i 德伊
Tŏg'im 德任
Ŭnŏn (Prince) 恩彥君
Yamaguchi Masayuki 山口正之
Yi Chonch'ang 李存昌
Yi Hapkyu 李鴿逵
Yi In 李祵
Yi Kigyŏng 李基慶
Yi *Saengwŏn* 李生員
Yi Tam 李瑊
Yi Yuhŭi 李𥡴
Yŏngjo (King) 英祖
Yu Chungsŏng 柳重誠
Yun Chich'ung 尹持忠
Yun Chŏmhye 尹占惠
Yun Unhye 尹雲惠
Yun Yuil 尹有一
Zhou Wenmo 周文謨

KOREAN CHRISTIAN NAMES

Agada (Agatha) 아가다
Aleksanderŭ (Alexander) 알렉산데르
Ambŭrosio (Ambrose) 암브로시오
Antonio (Anthony) 안토니오
Kollumba (Columba) 골룸바
Maria (Mary) 마리아
Mat'ia (Mathias) 마티아
Nuga (Luke) 루가
Nugalda (Luthgarde) 루갈다
Nusia (Lucy) 루시아
Paoro (Paul) 바오로
Parŭbara (Barbara) 바르바라
Pedŭro (Peter) 베드로

Pibianna (Vivian) 비비안나
P'illippo (Phillip) 필립보
Saba (Sabas) 사바
Tasŭra (Theresa?) 다스라
Yuanna (Joanne?) 유안나

PLACES AND LOCALITIES
(EXCLUDING TOWNS, CITIES,
AND PROVINCES)

An'guktong 安國洞
Ch'angdong 倉洞
Chŏndong 磚洞
Naep'o 內浦
Sŏsomun 西小門
Taesadong 大侍洞

GENERAL TERMS

ch'ŏmnye 瞻禮
chŏnghak 正學
ch'onghoejang 總會長
chŏnjang 田庄（田莊）
ch'ŏnyŏ 處女
ch'uhaeng nangjŏk 醜行狼籍
chung'in 中人
churi chil 주리질
churoe chil 주릐질
hanmun 漢文
hoejang 會長
Hyŏngjo 刑曹
ilmyŏng 一名
Kabin 甲寅
kisaeng 妓生
kyoju 教主
Kyŏngsin 庚辛
kyŏranch'o 結案招
myŏngdo hoejang 明道會長
Myŏngdohoe 明道會
Myŏnghoe 明會
Nam'in 南人

oe sangjŏn 外上典
pansŏ 班庶
pu 付
puin 夫人
purok 附録
p'odoch'ŏng 捕盜廳
p'yegung 廢宮
sabi 私婢
sabon 寫本
sabu 士夫
sadaebu 士大夫
sahak 邪學
sahwan 仕宦
sajok 士族
se 歲
sin 神
sinbu 神夫
Sinhae 辛亥
Sin'yu 辛酉
sŏ 庶
sosa 召史
sŏlpŏp ch'ŏmnye 設法瞻禮
Sŏng (saint, St.) 聖
sŏyang'in 西洋人
Ŭigŭmbu 義禁府
Ŭlmyo 乙卯
ŭisin 矣身
yangban 兩班
yŏhoejang 女會長
yosŏ 妖書

BOOK TITLES

Chugyo yoji 主教要旨
Han'guk ch'ŏnju kyohoesa 韓國天主教會
　史
Hwang Sayŏng paeksŏ 黃嗣永帛書
Kō Shiei hakusho no kenkyū 黃嗣永帛書
　の研究
Paeksŏ 帛書
Pyŏgwi p'yŏn 闢衛編
Sahak ching'ŭi 邪學懲義

CHAPTER 4

Chinese Protestant Literature and Early Korean Protestantism

Sung-Deuk Oak

Since the 1870s when Chinese Protestant literature began making inroads into Korea and especially since the 1880s when missionaries from the United States began arriving in the peninsula, Protestantism made rapid progress in Korea. By the end of the twentieth century, as Donald Baker and Timothy S. Lee discuss in this volume, every fifth South Korean was a Protestant. Many a factor—ranging from the sociopolitical to the religious—has been proffered to explain this rapid growth. This is all good and proper: no relevant factor should be neglected if we are fully to appreciate the complexity and richness of the phenomenon. Nevertheless, one important factor has largely escaped the consideration of most students of the phenomenon: the contribution of Chinese Protestant literature—both in original Chinese and in vernacular Korean translations.

It is the thesis of this chapter that Chinese Protestant literature prepared the ground for the rapid growth of Protestantism in Korea by explaining Protestantism to Koreans in terms congenial to them, with untranslated Chinese tracts and books appealing mostly to the educated classes and vernacularly translated literature appealing mainly to less-educated commoner classes. As a subthesis, the chapter also argues that the contents of these texts do not support the stereotypical view that early Protestant missionaries' attitude toward East Asian religious cultures was unfailingly and unremittingly imperialistic, bent on a total supplantation of traditional religions.[1] Granted, the texts reveal that almost all of the missionaries held paternalistic attitudes toward East Asian religions—and some of them were indeed unremittingly imperialistic; yet they also reveal that many missionaries made bona fide efforts—within the scope of their ultimate commitment, to be sure—to look favorably on local religions.[2]

To this end, the chapter will provide a brief overview of the Chinese tracts and books that were distributed in Korea both in their original language and in Korean vernacular. Six representative texts will then be examined with some thoroughness to ferret out their key messages. Aside from the translated gospel texts, these tracts and books were the most important evangelistic tools of the early Korean Protestant church and reveal a great deal about the church's theological orientation. This is especially the case with the Chinese-language texts. A few studies have already been made examining the vernacular texts, usually underscoring the texts' imperialistic messages.[3] Scarce, however, are studies that focus on Chinese-language Protestant texts, which tended to be less antagonistic toward native religions. Before discussing these matters in detail, however, it behooves us to examine where these texts came from, what they were generally like, and how they made their ways into Korea.

Chinese Protestant Literature in the China–Korea Nexus

Geographical proximity and cultural similarities between the two nations enabled China to transmit to Korea Buddhism, Confucianism, and Daoism around the fourth century, and Roman Catholicism in the late eighteenth century. In the transmission of all these religions to Korea, Chinese literature about the respective religions played a key role. In this regard, Protestantism was no exception.

It is well known that the production of Chinese Christian literature began in earnest in the seventeenth century, with the arrival of Matteo Ricci and other Jesuit missionaries in Beijing. For Protestants, similar efforts began two centuries later. In 1811, in Canton, the British missionary Robert Morrison printed the first Chinese Protestant tract, *Shendao lunshu jiushi zongshou zhenben* (A True and Summary Statement of the Divine Doctrine on the Redemption of the World). By 1875, about eight hundred Chinese Protestant tracts, excepting scriptures, commentaries, and hymnals, were published.[4] By 1890, the number reached more than a thousand. Until 1842, such pioneer missionaries to China as Morrison, W. Milne, W. H. Medhurst, and Karl F. A. Gützlaff published their tracts in Canton, Malacca, Batavia, Macao, and Singapore. Among these first-generation works, Milne's *Zhang Yuan liangyou xianglun* (Dialogues between the Two Friends Chang and Yuan, 1819) and Medhurst's *Sanzi jing* (Three-Character Classic, 1823) and *Jingming saomu zhi lun* (Feast of Tombs, 1826) were still used in the 1880s. Because it was illegal to disseminate Christianity in China, missionaries usually smuggled Protestant literature into Chinese ports on opium boats or armed merchants' ships. In a similar manner Gützlaff visited and distributed Chinese tracts on the west coast of Korea in 1832.

With the Treaty of Nanking in 1842, a cohort of Western Protestant missionaries began producing in large numbers higher-quality Protestant books and tracts through the presses established on the Chinese mainland. William Burns's *Tianlu licheng* (Pilgrim's Progress, 1853) and William A. P. Martin's *Tiandao suyuan* (Evidences of Christianity, 1854) were representative works of the early second-generation missionaries.[5] Works of D. B. McCartee, W. Martin, A. Williamson, F. Genähr, Ernst Faber, and especially Griffith John ranked as best-sellers in the last decades of the nineteenth century. It is worth noting that it was Williamson who supported Robert J. Thomas, a Welsh missionary, who voyaged to Korea in 1865 and 1866 as a colporteur on the *General Sherman*, a heavily armed American merchant ship, seeking to distribute Chinese-language tracts in P'yŏngyang, a voyage that ultimately ended in disaster with Thomas and the rest of the crew losing their lives.

A great deal of the Protestant literature that eventually made its way into Korea was first printed outside the country and was read by Koreans living in places such as Mukden, Manchuria, and Yokohama, Japan. For example, Martin's *Tiandao suyuan* was read by Korean converts of the Scottish missionary John Ross in Manchuria in 1879–1882 and then, in 1882–1884, by Korean students and converts in Japan, including well-known figures such as Yi Su-jŏng, Son Pung-gu, and Kim Ok-kyun.[6] Later texts by Martin and other authors were smuggled into Korea, initially through the "Peking road," and then through the open ports.

A diplomatic treaty between Korea and the United States in 1882 "opened" Korea to more active missionary efforts on the land. Subsequently, between 1885 and 1894, a large number of Chinese Protestant books and tracts were imported into Korea, even though—strictly speaking—importation was prohibited by law. After the failure of the Kapsin (1884) coup, which was led by a pro-Japanese faction in Korean politics, Chinese influence predominated in Korea for about a decade, until the start of the Sino-Japanese War in 1894. In this decade, under the protection of Yuan Shikai, Chinese "director-general resident in Korea of diplomatic and commercial relations," commercial traffic between Korea and China increased, with Chinese merchants assuming the upper hand. In this situation, it was not difficult to import Chinese Protestant texts into Korea.

Missionaries in Korea only translated and circulated the Chinese texts they deemed to be of highest quality or best-sellers, texts that had stood the test of Chinese readers for two generations.[7] These texts were well adapted to the Chinese milieu. They were also congenial to Korean readers. This was not surprising given the common Confucian worldview that the Chinese and the Koreans shared. The texts were especially congenial to Korea's educated classes, whose traditional education was based on Chinese (Confucian) classics and who could read original Chinese Christian literature without much difficulty. The fact that the missionary H. G. Underwood distributed three thousand Chinese Protestant tracts in a few days at a *kwagŏ*, the governmental examination, held in Seoul in May 1894, points up how the Confucian educational system, coupled with the modern printing press, unwittingly aided the spread of the gospel in Korea.[8] By 1900, as shown in table 1, more than forty untranslated Chinese Christian books and tracts had been distributed among educated Koreans.

The majority of early Korean Protestant converts were of lower classes, a result largely due to the missionary strategy generally known as the Nevius method that Korea missionaries applied to their work. This method was developed by the China missionary John L. Nevius and targeted "the commoner classes" rather than the educated, upper classes, generally known as *yangban* in Korean. The commoner classes in Korea at the time, however, did not necessarily mean underclasses. Though the category included underclasses, it also included the newly rising, middle (*chungin*) class, a great many of whom were self-reliant merchants. By 1895, a large number of middle-class Koreans as well as some *yangban* entered the church in Seoul, P'yŏngyang, and Ŭiju. In the north, the middle classes became the backbone of the church, supplying its key leaders. In Seoul, as well, a great many of the early believers came from the middle and *yangban* classes. Some government officials and palace eunuchs also joined the church. Around 1904, at the start of the Russo-Japanese War, a year before Japan established a protectorate over Korea, a substantial number of *yangban*, mostly reform-minded political figures, gravitated toward the church. In the conversion of all these educated Koreans, Chinese-language Protestant tracts played an instrumental role. Worthy of note here is that from 1903 to 1904, more than dozen political leaders—including Syngman Rhee, who would later become the first president of South Korea—were converted in a Seoul prison after reading Chinese-language Protestant books and tracts.[9]

Whereas the Chinese-language editions were for educated *yangban*, vernacularly translated Protestant literature was mostly for commoners who lacked classical education. Fifty or more Chinese tracts were translated into Korean and published in Korea from 1881 to 1896, as shown in table 2. Most were translated and printed in Seoul.[10] To publish these texts, Korea missionaries organized in 1889 the Korean Religious Tract Society and the Trilingual Press, which was housed in a Methodist mission. During a one-year period—from June 1893 to July 1894—the Trilingual Press printed 6,000 copies of the gospels; 36,700 copies of leaflets; 44,800 copies of tracts (1,355,300 pages); and 1,385 English books, pamphlets, and miscellaneous items—to a total of 1,801,440 pages.[11] More copies were printed following the Sino-Japanese War (1894–1895). Korean colporteurs distributed most of these books and tracts, roaming all over the land.

TABLE 1. Chinese Books and Tracts Used in Korea without Translation, 1880–1900 (incomplete/chronological)

Christian teachings (theology, natural theology, apologetics, and comparative religions)

清明掃墓之論	William Medhurst, *On the Custom of Repairing the Graves* (Batavia, 1826).
耶穌教要訣	D. Bethune McCartee, *Fundamental Truth of Christianity* (Ningpo, 1849).
救靈魂說	————, *Discourse on the Salvation of the Soul* (Ningpo, 1852).
天道溯原	William A. P. Martin, *Evidences of Christianity* (Ningpo, 1854).
釋教正謬	Joseph Edkins, *Correction of Buddhist Errors* (Shanghai, 1857).
天路指南	John L. Nevius, *Guide to Heaven* (Ningpo, 1857).
喩道傳	William A. P. Martin, *Religious Allegories* (Ningpo, 1858).
社先辨謬	John L. Nevius, *Errors of Ancestral Worship* (Ningpo, 1859).
救世要論	William A. P. Martin, *Important Discourse on Salvation* (Ningpo, 1860).
天路指明	Griffith John, *Clear Indication of the Heavenly Way* (Hankou, 1862).
宣道指歸	John L. Nevius, *Manual for Evangelists* (Shanghai, 1862).
西士來意略論	D. Bethune McCartee, *Western Scholars' Reasons for Coming to China* (Zhengzhou, 1863).
正道啓蒙	William Burns, *Peep of Day* (Beijing, 1864).
訓子問答	Griffith John, *Child's Catechism* (Shanghai, 1864).
眞教權衡	William Muirhead, *Balance of the True Religion* (Shanghai, 1864).
天牖二光	John L. Nevius, *The Two Lights* (Shanghai, 1864).
神道總論	————, *Compendium of Theology* (Shanghai, 1864).
格物入門	William A. P. Martin, *Elements of Natural Philosophy and Chemistry* (Beijing, 1868).
眞教論衡	William Muirhead, *Balance of the True Religion* (Shanghai, 1868).
格物探原	Alexander Williamson, *Natural Theology* (Shanghai, 1876).
基督實錄	————, *Life of Christ Jesus the Light and Life of the World* (Shanghai, 1879).
聖徒堅忍	Mrs. Helen S. Nevius, *Christian Perseverance* (Ningpo, ca. 1880).
兩教辨正	John L. Nevius, *The Two Religions Set Right: Romism and Protestantism* (Shanghai, 1890).
兩教合辨	F. H. James, *A Comparison of the Two Religions: Protestantism and Romism* (N.p., n.d.).
聖會史記	Hunter Corbett, *Church History* (N.p., n.d.).

Civilization (history, international law, politics, and science)

大英國志	William Muirhead, *History of England* (Shanghai, 1856).
地球說略	Richard Q. Way, *Compendium of Geography* (Ningpo, 1856).
萬國公法	William A. P. Martin, *International Law* [H. Wheaton's] (Beijing, 1864).
公法會通	————, *International Law* [J. C. Bluntschli's] (Beijing, 1880).
天文學	Nathan Sites, *Elementary Principles of Astronomy* (Shanghai, ca. 1880).
自西徂東	Ernst Faber, *Civilization: East and West* (Hong Kong, 1884, 1902).
萬國通鑑	Devello Z. Sheffield, *Universal History* (Shanghai, 1892).

Presbyterianism (published by the Presbyterian Synodical Committee of the China Mission, Shanghai, ca. 1877)

信道揭要	*Confession of Faith*
禮拜模範	*Form of Worship*
教會政治	*Form of Church Government*
耶蘇教要理問答	*Shorter Catechism*
耶蘇教要理大問答	*Larger Catechism*
教會勸懲條例	*Book of Discipline*
婚喪公禮	*Marriage and Burial Forms*

Methodism

受洗禮之約	Robert S. Maclay, *The Baptismal Covenant* (Fuzhou, 1857).
美以美教會禮文	————, *Ritual of the Methodist Episcopal Church* (Fuzhou, 1865).
天道總論	James W. Lambuth, *Compendium of Theology* [Binney's] (Shanghai, 1879).
神之原道	————, *Elements of Divinity* [T. N. Ralston's] (Shanghai, 1879).

TABLE 2. Chinese Tracts Translated and Published in Korean, 1885–1896 (incomplete)

Year	Author	Title in Chinese	Title in Korean	Title in English	Translator
1881	J. Ross	[聖經問答]	예슈셩교문답	Bible Catechism	Yi Ŭng-ch'an, J. Ross
	J. MacIntyre	[新約要領]	예슈셩교요령	Summary of the New Testament	Yi Ŭng-ch'an, J. MacIntyre
1885	J. Legge, R. Maclay	浪子悔改	랑耭회耭	Prodigal Son	Yi Su-jŏng
	R. S. Maclay	美以美教會問答	미이미교회문답	Methodist Catechism	Yi Su-jŏng
1889	R. S. Maclay	美以美教會問答	미이미교회문답	Methodist Catechism	F. Ohlinger
	?	聖教撮要	셩교촬요	Summary of the Holy Teaching	H. G. Appenzeller
	Griffith John (?)	濟世論	제셰론	Salvation of the World	H. G. Underwood
	Griffith John (?)	贖罪之道	속죄지도	Redemption	H. G. Underwood
1890	G. John	聖教撮理	셩교촬리	Salient Doctrine of Christianity	H. G. Underwood
	F. Ohlinger	癩病論	라병론	Sin Like Leprosy	F. Ohlinger
	R. S. Maclay	信德統論	신덕통론	General Discourse on Faith	F. Ohlinger
1891	R. S. Maclay	美以美教會綱禮	미이미교회강례	Article of Religion	W. B. Scranton
	Mrs. J. L. Holmes	訓兒眞言	훈耭진언	Peep of Day	Mrs. M. F. Scranton
	A. Judson	天路指歸	텬로지귀	Guide to Heaven	W. M. Baird
	G. John	勸衆悔改	권즁회	Exhortation to Repentance	H. G. Underwood
	G. John	上帝眞理	샹뎨진리	True Doctrine of God	H. G. Underwood
	W. H. Medhurst	三字經	삼耭경	Three-Character Classic	Ohlinger/Moffett
1892	W. Milne	張袁兩友相論	장원량우샹론	Two Friends	S. A. Moffett
	Mrs. S. M. Sites	聖經圖說	셩경도셜	Bible Picture Book	Miss L. C. Rothweiler
	?	救世要言	구셰요언	Essentials of the World's Salvation	W. B. McGill
1893	G. John	德惠入門	덕혜입문	Gate of Virtue and Wisdom	H. G. Underwood
	G. John	重生之道	즁耭지도	Regeneration	H. G. Underwood
	G. John	信者所得之眞福	신耭소득지진복	True Way of Seeking Happiness	H. G. Underwood
	W. C. Milne	眞道入門問答	진도입문문답	Entrance to Truth Doctrine	F. Ohlinger
	F. Ohlinger	依經問答	의경문답	Nast's Larger Catechism	F. Ohlinger
	?	四福音合書	耭복음합셔	Harmony of the Gospels	W. B. Scranton
	Helen Nevius	耶蘇教問答	예슈교문답	Christian Catechism	H. G. Underwood
1894	G. John	引家歸道	인가귀도	Leading the Family in the Right Way	F. Ohlinger
	G. John	福音大旨	복음대지	Great Themes of the Gospels	H. G. Underwood
	?	地球略論	지구략론	Geography	Mrs. M. F. Scranton
	Ernest Faber	舊約工夫	구약공부	Study of the Old Testament	G. H. Jones
	W. A. P. Martin	三要錄	삼요록	Three Principles	H. G. Underwood
	J. K. MacKenzie	救世眞詮	구셰진쥬	True Plan of Salvation	S. A. Moffett
	?	天主耶蘇兩教不同問答	텬쥬예슈량교부동문답	Romism and Protestantism	S. F. Moore
1895	W. Burns	天路歷程	텬로력뎡	Pilgrim's Progress	J. S. Gale

(continued)

(Table 2 continued)

Year	Author	Title in Chinese	Title in Korean	Title in English	Translator
	D. B. McCartee	眞理易知	진리이지	*Easy Introduction to Christian Doctrine*	H. G. Underwood
	G. John (?)	大主之命	대주지명	*Order of the Lord*	H. G. Underwood
	?	靈魂問答	령혼문답	*Catechism on the Soul*	H. G. Underwood
	G. John	救世眞主	구셰진쥬	*True Savior of the World*	W. M. Baird
	?	救世論	구셰론	*Discourse on Salvation*	S. A. Moffett
	C. W. Foster	福音要史	복음요輧	*Story of the Gospel*	Mr. & Mrs. D. L. Gifford
	F. Genähr	廟祝問答	묘츅문답	*Dialogue with a Temple-Keeper*	H. G. Appenzeller
	R. S. Maclay	洗禮問答	세례문답	*Baptismal Catechism*	W. B. Scranton
	?	主日禮拜經	쥬일례輧경	*Wesleyan Sunday Worship*	W. B. Scranton
	W. Muirhead	來就耶蘇	輧취예슈	*Come to Jesus*	W. C. Swallen
	F. Ohlinger	丁德傳記	틴들뎐긔	*The Life of William Tyndale*	F. Ohlinger
	J. L. Nevius	爲原入敎人規條	위원입교인규됴	*Manual for Catechism*	S. A. Moffett
	?	撒世論	경셰론	*Warning to the World*	W. L. Swallen
1896	?	敎會史記	교회輧긔	*Church History*	W. L. Swallen
	?	新約問答	신약문답	*The New Testament Catechism*	W. B. Scranton
	?	舊約問答	구약문답	*The Old Testament Catechism*	W. B. Scranton
	?	復活主日禮拜	부활쥬일례輧	*Easter Sunday Worship*	H. G. Underwood

Key Themes in Chinese Protestant Literature

Chinese Protestant literature played a pivotal role in shaping the theology and missiology of the early Korean Protestant church, especially since a great deal of it became required reading at Methodist and Presbyterian seminaries and mission schools, whose combined numbers constituted the vast majority of mission schools in Korea.[12] The literature also affords an insight into the missionaries' view of East Asian religious culture. An examination of six influential texts from this literature will therefore give us an insight into what the literature espoused and what kind of theology early Korean Protestant converts were expected to believe in. The first four to be discussed below had been translated into Korean and distributed mainly among commoners, whom the missionaries generally believed to have been under the "superstitious" spell of shamanism and Buddhism. The last two—Martin's *Tiantao suyuan* and Faber's *Zixi cudong*—had not been translated into Korean and were distributed mainly among *yangban*.

WILLIAM MILNE'S *ZHANG YUAN LIANGYOU XIANGLUN*

William Milne (1775–1822), a Scottish Congregationalist, was sent to South China by the London Missionary Society in 1813. He had worked for ten years in various fields. He published *Zhang Yuan liangyou xianglun* (Dialogues between the Two Friends Chang and Yuan) in Malacca in 1819 (twenty leaves). In 1851 and 1857, his son, W. C. Milne, published revised and more accurately translated editions of the book. By 1906 at least seventeen editions and two million or so copies of the pamphlet circulated. For a century, it was a best-selling tract in China. Historian Daniel Bays attributes its popularity to its Chinese setting, its dialogical format, and its use of *wenli* semiclassical style.[13] The missionary Samuel A. Moffett translated it into Korean in 1892; by 1905 at least four editions of it had been published.

In a clear manner, *Two Friends* presents Christian doctrines that were representative of early nineteenth-century mainstream Protestantism. By contrasting various points on the spirituality of Christians with that of non-Christians, by contrasting Jesus Christ with Chinese sages, and by contrasting the mundane earthly existence with the blessedness of eternality, Milne expounds basic Protestant doctrines for his East Asian audience. The tract uses standard Chinese religious terms, especially Buddhist terms such as *zui* (sin), *shanren* (good person), *eren* (wicked person), *huigai* (repentance), *xin* (faith), *tiantang* (heaven), *diyu* (hell), *jinsheng* (this world), *laisheng* (the world to come), *yongsheng* (eternal life), *yongfu* (eternal blessing), and *yongfa* (eternal punishment). While castigating polytheism as idolatrous and criticizing Confucian ethics as imperfect, the tract lauds Confucianism's central principles of filial piety (*xiaodao*) and loyalty (*zhong*) and applies them to God—in short, insisting that worshiping God is the most authentic way of practicing filial piety (*zhen xiaodao*).

FERDINAND GENÄHR'S *MIAOZHU WENDA*

Ferdinand Genähr, of the Rhenish Missionary Society, arrived in Hong Kong in 1847. Having been placed under the direction of Gützlaff in connection with the Chinese Union, Genähr settled at Taiping in the Guangdong province. In 1848 he founded a station near Hong Kong and established a school there. In 1853 he married a Miss Lechler; in August 1864, he and his two sons died of cholera. The author's close contacts with common people enabled him to observe Chinese popular religions at close quarters. But his observations led him to form unfavorable views of the local religious culture, leading him to condemn Buddhism, Daoism, and spirit worship, as well as geomancy and ancestor worship.

Miaozhu wenda (Conversation with a Temple Keeper, 1856) was a frontal attack on native Chinese religions. It used "the popular dialogue format to explain Christian doctrine in the context of denouncing the follies of idolatry."[14] Exuding the typical iconoclastic attitude of nineteenth-century evangelicalism, the text denounces all forms of non-Protestant worship— including the worship of Buddhist icons, Daoist pictures, Confucian ances-tral tablets, and Shamanistic spirits—as idolatry. It condemns such worship as ignorant, superstitious, and perfidious, often invoking enlightened reason as a warrant.[15] Although the tract does not mention Roman Catholicism, its tenor assumes Catholicism to be another form of false religion. In the epi-logue of the Korean edition of the book, the missionary H. G. Appenzeller differentiated Protestantism from Roman Catholicism in part by Catholics' wearing of a crucifix and by their adoring portraits of Jesus.[16] From con-demning Chinese religious practices, *Conversation* went on to attack Con-fucian sociopolitical systems as a whole. Extended to Korea, the texts' sen-timents aspired ultimately to reform Korea's sociopolitical structures in addition to its religious and ethical culture.

GRIFFITH JOHN'S *DEHUI RUMEN*

John (1831–1912), the "boy preacher of Wales," became "the Apostle of Central China." He arrived in Shanghai in 1855 and founded the Han-kow mission in 1861. He traveled extensively to open new fields in central China. John had a passion for evangelism via direct preaching, building col-leges and seminaries, and erecting hospitals, especially for lepers. He was optimistic about evangelizing China, believing that "in due season we shall reap, if we faint not." He persistently stressed the power of the Holy Spirit in missionary work. He founded the Hankow Tract Society in 1876 and enlarged it into the Central China Religious Tract Society in 1884.[17] It was chiefly through his literary efforts that John became famous in China. He was a prolific writer, a master of written Chinese, authoring more than thirty best-selling books and tracts. He could write books dealing with his-tory, science, and philosophy, but he preferred to concentrate his talents on producing only those that had direct bearing on evangelism.

John published *Dehui rumen* (The Primer of Virtue and Wisdom, 1879) mainly for the educated classes. This book contains all his previously pub-lished tracts as well as several newly written for the book. It is thus the de-finitive edition of his theological output. And as soon as the volume was published, it became an instant classic in its genre. Nelson Bitton said, "The Chinese delight in it, not only for the good teaching it contains, but also on account of its easy, polished Chinese style. It possesses what the Chinese call 'flavor,' and without that 'flavor' no book may hope to be-come popular and obtain length of days."[18] In 1879, ten thousand copies of the volume were distributed at a state examination. Since then tens of thousands of copies have been distributed in various provinces and to mis-sionaries of various backgrounds.

The book consists of eighteen chapters. The first five chapters deal with the origin and source of heaven and earth and with natural theology. Chapters 6, 7, and 8 are on God—his nature, his names, and the Trinity. Chapters 9 and 10 are on Jesus Christ and his redemption of sin. Chapter 11 is on the Holy Spirit and regeneration. The remaining chapters deal with salvation by faith, resurrection, key biblical themes, Christian life, eternal blessings, and repentance.[19]

In the preface, John states that the True Way, which permeates the universe, does not discriminate between East and West. He emphasizes Christianity (by which he mainly means Protestantism) as a universal religion for the salvation of all souls, having its origin not in the West but in God. He stresses benefits that Christianity had brought to China: hospitals, relief work among the poor and opium addicts, modern education and civilization. He warns of the danger of the *zhongti xiyong* (Chinese substance and Western function) philosophy as putting the cart before the horse. The relationship of Christianity to Western technology, he argues, is like root and branch, such that the former is indispensable for the latter.

Since educated Chinese were drawn to natural theology and rational discussions on the origin of the world, John, in the first five chapters of the book, adopts moves used by Martin's *Evidences of Christianity*, discussed below. Thus to explain the Creator's deft design and management, chapter 1 invokes a variety of analogies: the literary work, the watch, the house, and the human soul. Chapter 2 argues that the relationship between heaven-cum-earth (which is *qi*) and God (who is Spirit) is like that between house and carpenter or between human body (which is *qi*) and soul (which is spirit). John denounces the Confucian theory of *wuji taiji* (the Great Ultimate) and *li* (principle). These cannot be equated with God, he argues, for they express neither sense nor spiritual wisdom. As a king governs a state with laws, God governs the world according to his nature, will, and law, which is his *li*. He concludes that *dao* (Way) or *wuji taiji* is not God, but mere empty chaos.

Chapter 3 criticizes the theory of *yinyang wuxing* (two forces and five agents). Here he resorts to the Western chemical theory of elements and compounds. John explains the theory of atoms and molecules by comparing it to the method of making Chinese characters by combining brush strokes, driving home the point about the existence of the Maker of the elements. The topic of chapter 4 is the glory of God exhibited in the universe. John uses modern astronomy to prove the divine creation and providence. He explains the Earth, the solar system, the phenomena of the eclipses of the sun and the moon, the comets, and the moving stars and fixed stars. Chapter 5 discusses the order of all things and their appropriate functions in the cosmos, with the cosmos compared to a sophisticated machine. John stresses the hierarchical relationships that purportedly exist among animals, human beings, and God. He argues that God differs from man-made gods such as the Buddha and Jade Emperor, declaring that the Buddha is an empty name, his teaching deceitful even when compared to Confucian ethics. As there is only one emperor in the empire, John argues, there is only one God in the world. He denounces the polytheistic assumption that God needs the help of other gods, such as of fire, water, wind, and rain, or the help of ancestors.

Chapter 6 follows W. Martin's argument on the names of God, accepting Shangdi, Tianzhu, Zhenshen, and Tianfu for God's name. Chapter 7 discusses the spiritual nature of God and the Trinity more clearly and figuratively than most other tracts. John compares the Trinity to a compound composed of elements, to the seven colors of the light, to heat and fire, and to a person's body and soul. Chapter 9 deals with the life and teachings of Jesus. Here John finds a point of reference in Chinese history. John states that Jesus was born in Judea, an Eastern country, in the first year of Emperor Ping of the Han dynasty. In Chapter 10, he pointedly makes note of the fact that in ancient times, sacrificial ceremonies were performed on behalf of people by Chinese sage-emperors. Jesus himself, he notes, offered a sort of sacrifice; unlike the emperors, however, Jesus offered himself as a sacrifice, on the cross—moreover, not just for one kingdom or empire but for the entire world.

Chapter 11 explains how one might be transformed through the power of the Holy Spirit, who enables a person to recover his or her original conscience and to become a new being. Only after defining regeneration does John introduce the doctrine of original sin. John uses a version of the watch analogy here: if a part of a watch is broken, it does not work properly, even if the other parts are in good repair. Likewise, since originally good human nature has been corrupted by original sin, it is prone to wickedness, even though it has five constant virtues. Therefore, human beings do not or cannot do what they think is good. John argues that the Confucian way of *gewu zhizhi* (the investigation of things and the extension of knowledge), which applies only to knowledge, cannot transform the human heart; only the power of the Holy Spirit can do so.

Chapter 12 emphasizes that human work cannot obtain salvation; faith alone can accept it through divine grace. Chapter 13 explains the resurrection by analogy with the butterfly. The final judgment is necessary, he also argues, in that historical justice is not sufficient. Chapter 14 summarizes the main themes of the Old and New Testaments. It emphasizes that the Bible is the revelation of God, not mere words of human beings. Chapter 15 is a polemic against anti-Christian tracts such as *Pixie shilu* (Essays on Exposing Heretical Teachings), which accuses Christians of being immoral. After summarizing the laws and ethical teachings of the Bible from the Ten Commandments to St. Paul's epistles, John concludes, "If the Chinese people from the emperor to the populace believe in Christianity, the whole nation will become one house without deception and dishonesty and all will enjoy peaceful blessings."

In Chapter 16, John lists what Christians should and should not do. Christians ought to study the Bible, pray to God, and attend worship services regularly. They should not engage in ancestor worship; worship of the dead body; worship of ancestral tablets; burning paper money; seeking auspicious days; using charms; fortune-telling; physiognomy; or geomancy. John discusses each topic in detail. In particular, he answers several questions regarding ancestor worship. He defines sacrificial rites as the rites for the reverence of God and divides them into two: one for the redemption of sin and the other for thanksgiving. John insists that although both have been offered to God by the emperors of ancient China, later generations forgot their original meanings and offered them to heaven and earth, idols, or ancestors. Inasmuch as Christ's redemptive sacrifice fulfilled the divine law, all other sacrificial rites are unnecessary and useless. What God wants now, he argues, is nothing more or less than the repenting mind and sincere heart.

A sacrifice to ancestors is useless, he argues, for ancestors cannot eat. Such is not an appropriate memorial; the more appropriate memorial would be to live sincerely, to keep alive good memories of ancestors, and to take good care of their tombs. John also insists that though one should follow ancestors' good teachings, doing so does not entail building shrines or worshiping the tablets, for the tablets are false and useless, worshiping them, idolatrous. Against the variety of fortune-telling that existed in China, John emphasizes the sovereignty and lordship of God, who governs all aspects of human life; and he urges his Chinese readers to use common sense rather than the dubious art of geomancy in choosing sites for a house or a grave site.

Chapter 17 expounds blessings of Christians in this life and in the life to come. He argues that Christianity not only reveals the truth through the Bible but also offers the comfort of and hope for the kingdom of God. He allows that Confucian humanism and its teachings on the five human relationships are good, but, he adds, they do not empower humans to actually practice them. Therefore, he asserts, Confucianism, is merely a hollow religion that has no power to save people. Christianity, on the other hand, provides a hope for a millennial paradise on Earth, a state wherein justice and peace will reign. Christianity, furthermore, promises blessings beyond death, about which Confucianism remains silent.

In the final chapter, John answers some common objections missionaries encountered while evangelizing in East China—such as why Easterners should accept Christianity when it did not originate in the East, why it should be necessary for one to believe in Jesus in addition to God, or why people shouldn't remain loyal only to their native gods. John answers that though missionaries came from the West, Christianity itself came from God, that the Great Way is not limited to a particular country, that its principles operate throughout the world. If a religion, domestic or foreign, is right and profitable to individuals and the world, it is acceptable to all, even to the Chinese. He adds that the relationship of Christianity and Confucianism is like that of the sun and the moon. Although Confucianism is good, its light is insufficient to show people the way of God; Christianity does not destroy but fulfills Confucianism.

GRIFFITH JOHN'S *YINJIA GUIDAO*

Despite the popularity of *Dehui rumen*, John was not satisfied with its didactic style. So he wrote a new tract, *Yinjia guidao* (Leading the Family in the Right Way, 1881), in the form of a novel and in the hope of letting the story express the Christian ideal. The book is the story of an ideal Chinese Christian and his family, a story based on facts John had observed in China. The book's setting and characters are all Chinese. John endows authority and leadership to Mr. Li, the head of the family. He becomes the first Christian of his family and then leads his wife and children, elder brother and his wife, and his parents to the Christian faith by dint of faith and patient teaching.

Even as it exudes literary charm, *Leading the Family in the Right Way* deals with doctrinal, religious, and social themes. It covers essential doctrines: God and the Trinity, creation and original human nature, Jesus and the Holy Spirit, and sin and salvation through the atonement of Jesus Christ. It treats ancestor worship, town gods, and Sabbath keeping. It also treats social themes such as child slavery and education for girls, almsgiving and polygamy, footbinding and work ethics, equal rights that should exist between men and women, and marriage between Christians and non-Christians.

The book espouses that Christian faith is not a matter of mastering a few theological propositions but of living out the faith in integrity and benevolence, prayer and justice, and truth-loving spirit. Mr. Li is the ideal pilgrim: he practices filial piety, loves his wife and children, and exercises brotherly love. His goodly behavior leads his neighbors to Christianity. A transformed life with a new heart in Christ—this was John's message to his Chinese readers. Yet most of Mr. Li's virtues were essentially Confucian: he is an ideal "Confucian" Christian. He practices the five human relationships (lord-subject, father-son, husband-wife, senior-junior, and friend-friend) and five cardinal virtues (humanity, righteousness, propriety, wisdom, and faithfulness) with sincere Christian faith. While neglecting larger issues of national welfare and world peace, John's narrative was an effective way to appeal to the practical bent in the Chinese mind and a solid defense against objections of nonbelievers.

WILLIAM A. P. MARTIN'S *TIANDAO SUYUAN*

William Martin (1827–1916) worked in China for sixty-six years in Ningpo (1850–1860) and then in Beijing until 1916.[20] His evening lectures to educated Chinese at the Ningpo Presbyterian Church became the basis for *Evidences of Christianity*. It was the most popular and best evangelistic book in China. Before 1912, it went through thirty or forty editions in Chinese, in addition to numerous editions in Japanese.[21] The book shared a great deal with other apologetic tracts in that it sought to provide "evidences" for Christianity.

Evidences of Christianity was published in circumstances similar to Ricci's *Tianzhu shiyi* (The True Meaning of the Lord of Heaven, 1593–1596).[22] Both books were published at critical periods of Chinese history: Ricci's book at the end of the Ming dynasty (when it was threatened by aggressive Manchu forces) and Martin's between the Taiping Rebellion (1850) and the onrush of Western imperialism in China at the end of the decade. As was the case with Ricci's book at the end of the tumultuous sixteenth century, Martin's caught the attention of the reform-minded educated class who sought new ways to envision their society, especially the Confucians who eschewed doctrinaire Confucianism in favor of more evidential learning of the Chinese classics. It is no wonder that many Confucian literati looked favorably upon Martin's emphasis on facts and tangible evidence.[23] Martin's book was similar to Ricci's also in that it was, like Ricci's, an intellectual defense of the Christian faith in philosophical and theological terms. Both believed that Confucian morality was compatible with Christian ethics and faith. They presented Christianity as a faith that could be adopted by Confucian scholars and translated "God" in words for deity that Chinese were already familiar with. And as was the case with some Confucian scholars influenced by Ricci at the end of the sixteenth century, at the beginning of the twentieth century, some educated Chinese accepted Martin's argument that Christianity was the fulfillment of Confucianism. Moreover, just as Ricci's accommodationist policy would later be criticized by Franciscans and other hard-liners in the eighteenth century, Martin's accommodationists views came in for criticism from Fundamentalist missionaries from the United States in the 1920s.

Martin regards superior achievements of the West as an aid in propagating Christianity. He identifies Christian faith with Western civilization and uses the latter as proof of the veracity of the former. Martin lifts up Enlightenment ideals and presents Christianity as a reasonable religion. In doing this, he draws from works of the British rationalist William Paley, who resorted to natural theology to prove a biblical worldview. Just as the Newtonian worldview holds the universe to be a harmonious system that operates according to the natural laws decreed by God, Martin asserts that there are comparable laws for morality and history.

Martin's concept of "divine providence" illustrates the confluence of biblical and Enlightenment influences in the formation of his evangelical worldview. Human history, in this view, is an ordered process, under the governance of God and the lordship of Christ, moving toward the fulfillment of the purposes and design of the divine will. In the nineteenth century, Anglo-Saxon missionaries believed that they had been uniquely commissioned by God to bring the gospel to the world. As one such missionary, Martin was convinced that he was called by God to disseminate a unique amalgam of Christian civilization—Christianity and Anglo-Saxon civilization—to China.[24]

Notwithstanding the apparent ethnocentrism, Martin takes pains in his book to appeal to Chinese modes of thought and Chinese points of reference. He utilizes Chinese terminology, illustrations, and concepts to gain points of contact. He expounds Christianity in a dialogical mode, in the classical Chinese style favored by educated Chinese. He believes that God had already been at work in China's philosophical, ethical, and religious system—in contrast to the majority of the missionaries, who assumed that they had brought a new God to China. Although he condemns idolatry and ancestor worship and is critical of the theory of *yinyang wuxing*, Martin does not denounce other Chinese beliefs and customs—such as geomancy, use of opium, and polygamy. Mission is not a question of either Christ or Confucius, but of both, an inclusive view evident in the following passage from chapter 5 of *Evidences of Christianity*:

> The Christian teachings came from God. As God created men in his own image, God and men are related to each other. As God created men, they should know the origin of their bodies. As serving God is their important duty, it is clear that the relationship between God and men ought to be the primary relationship. As the God-men relationship stands primary, the five relationships come secondary and thus in due order. This is like the foundation of a house, on which all the pillars and rafters should be built and then the house becomes safe and strong. The five relationships are like precious pearls, which have no flaw. The primary relationship is like a golden string on which the pearls are threaded not to be lost.[25]

A golden string of pearls—this is Martin's idea of harmony between Christian faith and Confucian teachings. Christianity brings Confucianism to perfection; Christianity complements the latter at critical points. What is important is the order of priority: the heavenly relationship—worshiping God, the Heavenly Father and Creator—takes precedence over the five human relationships. In the last chapter of the book Martin answers common objections and doubts about Christianity. To the most important question—"If I follow this way, must I turn my back on Confucius?"— Martin answers:

> Don't you know that Confucianism speaks of human relationships and Christianity also speaks of them, yet adds God to the five relationships as well. After the relationship between God and men is in harmony, the five relationships will naturally get their due order.... Confucianism affirms filial piety and brotherly love; Christianity lets men revere the Heavenly Father, respect their parents, make friends with others in brotherly love and with the same love search for the origin of filial piety and brotherly love. If God and men love, filial piety and brotherly love will reach out to the world. Confucianism and Christianity are differentiated in terms of breadth and narrowness, but not in terms of heterodoxy and orthodoxy. Then how can you talk about apostasy [if one turns to Christianity]?[26]

Martin lived in his Presbyterian faith and common-sense philosophy that enabled him to see God as the cause of historical, ethical, social, and religious effects in Chinese society. He believed that China's deep-seated religious needs were imperfectly met by Chinese religions and that such needs could be satisfied only if the Chinese put themselves in right relationship with the Christian God.

ERNST FABER'S ZIXI CUDONG

Ernst Faber (1839–1899), of the Evangelical Missionary Society of Basel, arrived in China in 1865. Among his numerous books, *Zixi cudong* (Civilization: West and East, 1884) was the most famous.[27] His basic attitude toward Confucianism was that it should be "an ally to Christianity."[28] The aim of the book was to awaken the Chinese by comparing Christian civilization to Chinese civilization and to introduce essentials of the former into the latter for the reformation of China, which he believed was in peril.

Faber's main idea is a "grafting theory"—cutting away the dead and decayed branches of Chinese civilization and grafting the good branches of Christian civilization to the old Chinese tree. He argues that reinvigorating the root of Chinese culture by grafting the Christian religion onto it is more important than resorting to short-lived and ultimately futile efforts of grafting Western technology and secular learning onto Chinese culture, which he likened to grafting a fresh stem onto a dying branch. He therefore criticizes the position of Chinese intellectuals who advocate *zhongti xiyong*. In another analogy, Faber propounds that Christianity is like the sun or rain, which has the power to grow the tree of China. Therefore, accepting Western technology without accepting Christian religion, Faber insists, is like Yang Zhu's heterodox materialism and hedonistic egoism or like Mozi's utilitarianism. Confucianism teaches humans to follow Heaven's mandate, while Christianity teaches people to follow God's will. These two religions therefore must have something important in common and should make efforts to accommodate each other.

The book consists of five parts, their titles coming from the traditional Confucian *wuchang* (five cardinal virtues). Part 1 deals with the social welfare system for the poor, the sick, the aged, the orphaned, the insane, the stranger, and the imprisoned. It also deals with the ending of wars, diplomatic efforts for peace with other nations, and humane treatment of animals. Part 2 discusses, among other things, the importance of honest administration for national wealth, of protecting good and honest people, of street improvements and a regulated tariff policy, of eschewing extravagance and gambling, and of prohibiting the slave trade and female infanticide. The prosperity of people, this part of the book argues, is the source of national power.

Part 3 discusses ceremonies and rites, which, Faber insists, should be based on one's maintaining sincerity in auspicious circumstances, moderation in unfortunate situations, rightness in court, reverence for guests, and authority in the military. In the section titled "The Errors of the False Rites," he criticizes ancestor worship. He advocates the type of filial piety that serves living parents with a whole heart, buries the dead with proper ceremony, and holds ancestors in cherished memory. On the other hand, he criticizes rites of the dead aimed at seeking fortunes, building a shrine and worshiping ancestral tablets, engaging in animal sacrifice, and holding extravagant memorials beyond a family's means. Faber also severely criticizes feng shui. Comparing what he regards as the vanity and falsehood of some Chinese rites with the practicality and truth of Western Christian rituals, he suggests that the former should be reformed and supplemented in light of the latter.

Part 4 deals with education and modern Western technology: classics and history, literature and newspapers, agriculture and manufacturing, handcrafts and mining, commerce and munitions, medicine and physics. Part 5 introduces works of missionary societies in China. It begins by explaining the main supports of the Christian Church: faith in Jesus Christ, hope for God's eternal blessing, and love of others as oneself. It emphasizes the oneness of the Church in the Holy Spirit. Even though there are numerous denominations and mission societies and various works, he argues, the Church's one purpose is to redeem the Chinese people from sin and to glorify God. The remaining chapters then validate aspects of Christian missions such as Bible and tract societies, temperance and Sabbath-observance society, and young Christian men's and women's societies.

In the last chapter, "How Can Western Civilization Be Practiced in China?" Faber concludes that the Chinese government should reform the old laws by appointing to important offices people who are awakened and well versed in Western civilization. The contemporary weakness of China, he claims, resulted from the worship of idols and false spirits and from neglecting the divine commandments. A stronger nation, he argues, should heal a weak and sick nation. But if a weaker country does not accept a doctor's prescription, then powerful countries will come and exact fees on it; then without being healed, the weak country will only become poorer. Thus a weak China should seek to become strong by appropriating Western civilization; Chinese should believe in the possibility of reformation and make a strenuous effort to achieve it. To this end, the Chinese should revere and seek aid from God. Good-natured Westerners would then cooperate to reform China.

Conclusion

Why was Protestantism readily accepted in Korea at the dawn of the twentieth century? One reason was that the messages of Chinese tracts like those discussed above were well suited to late-nineteenth-century Korea, whose religious culture, on the one hand, was still under the Neo-Confucian sway and whose many people, on the other hand, were searching for something new in the face of a collapsing traditional social order. While vernacularly translated literature tended to be more critical of native religions and customs, Chinese-language tracts and books assumed more accommodating attitudes toward them. They claimed that Christianity—more precisely, Protestantism—would not destroy traditional religious heritages but fulfill their spiritual longings. Many Koreans could readily accept such indigenized messages. Moreover, these tracts and books were relatively inexpensive and plentifully available. If I may use horticultural imagery, these missionaries did not bring a pot of Christian flowers already grown in North America and plunk it down in the garden of Korean religions, nor did they sprinkle New England gospel seeds directly on Korean soil; rather, they selected only the most promising seeds that had already been nursed in the seedbeds of China and sowed them in the fertile soil of the Korean mind.

NOTES

1. See David Chung, *Syncretism* (Albany: State University of New York Press, 2001); James H. Grayson, *Early Buddhism and Christianity in Korea: A Study in the Emplantation of Religion* (Leiden: E. J. Brill, 1985); and Sung-Deuk Oak, "The Indigenization of Christianity in Korea: North American Missionaries' Attitudes toward Korean Religions" (Th.D. diss., Boston University, 2002).

2. For a more conventional view on this issue, see Harvie M. Conn, "Studies in the Theology of the Korean Presbyterian Church: A Historical Outline (I)," *Westminster Theological Journal* 29 (Nov. 1966): 24–58; Park Yong-gyu, "Korea Presbyterian and Biblical Authority" (Ph.D. diss., Trinity Evangelical Divinity School, 1991); and Kim Kyoung-Jae, *Christianity and the Encounter of Asian Religions* (Zoetermeer, Netherlands: Uitgeverji Boekencentrum, 1995). Spencer Palmer, who had paid attention to the indigenization of Christianity in Korea, insisted that "the Christian movement in Korea was invariably conservative; it was concerned with personal conviction, not social program." He claimed that missionaries in Korea belonged to the Hudson Taylor type who accepted biblical literalism and fundamentalism, yet they held "favorable attitudes toward the native people and their traditional way of life" (Spencer J. Palmer, *Korea and Christianity: The Problem of Identification with Tradition* [Seoul: Hollym Corporation, 1967], 33). I think these two claims are contradictory. How could such a fundamentalist missionary readily accept native traditional religious heritage? Actually a Hudson Taylor–type missionary would have strongly attacked native customs, such as ancestor worship and polygamy.

3. See Yi Manyŏl, *Han'guk kidokkyo munhwa undong sa* [A History of the Cultural Movement of Korean Christianity] (Seoul: Taehan kidokkyo ch'ulp'ansa, 1987), 302–344; and idem, "Hanmal Kidokkyo sajo ŭi yangmyŏnsŏng sigo [A Review of the Dual Trend of Christian Thought in Late Chosŏn]," *Han'guk Kidokkyo wa minjok ŭisik* (Seoul: Chisiksanŏpsa, 1991), 221–229.

4. Alexander Wylie, *Memorials of Protestant Missionaries to the Chinese* (Shanghai: American Presbyterian Mission Press, 1867); S. L. Baldwin, "Christian Literature—What Has Been Done and What Is Needed," *Record of General Conference of Protestant Missionaries in China* (Shanghai: Presbyterian Mission Press, 1877), 206.

5. William Burns's *Tianlu licheng* (a Chinese version of Bunyan's *Pilgrim's Progress*) was used by Hong Xiuquan in the Taiping Uprising. Its Beijing edition (1863) was translated partly by John Ross of Manchuria and his Korean converts into Korean about 1882. James S. Gale translated it into Korean with the help of his wife (Mrs. Heron), and Yi Ch'ang-jik at Wŏnsan and published its first volume in 1895.

6. "Power of the Word in Corea," *Quarterly Report of the National Bible Society of Scotland* (Oct. 1880): 633–634; H. Loomis, "Rijutei, the Corean Convert," *Missionary Herald* (December 1883): 481–483. See Harry A. Rhodes, "Presbyterian Theological Seminary," *Korea Mission Field* 6 (June 1910): 149–151.

7. In May 1892, Mr. Kenmure, an agent of the British and Foreign Bible Society, investigated the most popular Christian tracts and books (exclusive of commentaries, hymnals, and prayer books) among missionaries in China. The following

was its final result of 169 votes: Martin's *Tiandao suyuan*, 32; Milne's *Zhang Yuan liangyou xianglun*, 31; Burns's *Tianlu licheng*, 24; G. John's *Dehui rumen*, 18; G. John's *Yinjia jiadao*, 16; Burns's *Zhengdao qimeng*, 12; Genähr's *Zhenjiao quanheng*, 11; Faber's *Zixi cudong*, 11; Williamson's *Gemu tanyuan* 8; Martin's *Yudao zhuan*, 6 (Alexander Kenmure, "The Ten Best Christian Books in Chinese," *Chinese Recorder* [July 1893]: 340). Kenmure was transferred to Seoul in 1895.

8. "A few weeks ago a great *quaga* was on. Hundreds of countrymen were here. Mr. Underwood suddenly conceived the idea and published three leaflets and two of these small tracts in two days (Mr. Hulbert worked the print all night) and nearly 3,000 tracts were immediately disposed of. He himself distributed nearly 1,000 leaflets" (Lillias H. Underwood to Frank F. Ellinwood, May 28, 1894, *Letters and Reports of the Board of the Foreign Mission, the PCUSA, the Korea Mission*, [Philadelphia: Presbyterian Historical Society, 1894] [hereafter *LP*]). This was the last governmental examination in Seoul. Board of Foreign Missions, PCUSA, *Missions Correspondence and Reports*. Microfilm series, Korea (Philadelphia: Department of History, PCUSA, 1957), reel 178.

9. After Syngman Rhee was arrested in January 1899, about thirty political leaders were imprisoned. About fifteen were converted to Christianity after reading Chinese Christian books borrowed from the prison library, opened in January 1903. For twenty months, 229 persons borrowed about 2,020 books. They also read books on Western history and civilization (Yi Nŭng-hwa, *Chosŏn Kidokkyo kŭp oegyosa* [Seoul: Chosŏn Kidokkyo Ch'angmunsa, 1928], 203-204; Yi Kwang-rin, "Kuhanmal okchung esŏŭi Kidokkyo sinang," *Han'guk kaehwa sa ŭi che munje* [Seoul: Ilchogak, 1986], 218–222). When released in 1904, they attended Gale's Yŏndong church and joined the YMCA. Their conversion stimulated other educated people to join the church. In December 1905, Yŏndong church had more than six hundred members, three-quarters of them from the nobility (C. A. Clark to A. J. Brown, Dec. 8, 1905, *LP*).

10. The following earlier tracts were published in Manchuria or Japan: Ross's *Yesu sŏnggyo mundap* and MacIntyre's *Yesu sŏnggyo yoryŏng* in Mukden in 1881; Maclay's *Rangja hoegae* and *Miimi kyohoe mundap* in Yokohama in 1885; Underwood's *Chyesyeron, Sokchoe chido*, and *Sŏnggyo ch'waryo* in Yokohama in 1889.

11. *Annual Report of the Board of Foreign Missions of the Methodist Episcopal Church for 1894*, 249. The tracts occupied 75 percent of all printed pages. From June 1897 to July 1898, the same press printed 5,157,195 pages of evangelistic literature (George C. Cobb, "Report VII. Trilingual Press," *Journal of the Fourteenth Annual Meeting of the Korea Mission of the MEC for 1898*, 41). See Yi Manyŏl, *Han'guk Kidokkyo munhwa undong sa*, 309–318. Some Korean tracts were printed in Yokohama, Japan, and at Underwood's private printing press.

12. See Oak Sung-Deuk, "Ch'ogi Han'guk Changnogyo sŏngyo chŏngch'aek, 1884–1903 [The Nevius-Ross Method of the Korean Presbyterian Church]," *Han'guk kidokkyo wa yŏksa* 9 (September 1998): 176–183; and idem, "Ch'ogi Han'guk kamnigyo sŏngyo sinhak, 1884–1893" [Franklin Ohlinger and Methodist Evangelical Mission Theology in Korea]," *Han'guk kidokkyo wa yŏksa* 11 (October 1999): 22–29.

13. Daniel Bays, "Christian Tracts: The Two Friends," in *Christianity in China*, ed. Suzanne W. Barnett and John K. Fairbanks (Cambridge, Mass.: Harvard University Press), 19–34.

14. Wylie, *Memorials of Protestant Missionaries to the Chinese*, 161–163; Ralph Covell, *Confucius, the Buddha and Christ* (Maryknoll, N.Y.: Orbis, 1986), 95.

15. The Protestant missions attacked the visible religious symbols and idols with the linear symbols of the printed pages. But they also used visual media of communication, such as modern machines and inventions; chapels, hospitals, and schools; pictures of Jesus and the cross; and magic lantern pictures. For "radical intellectualist anti-idolatry" in the early nineteenth century, see Kenneth Cracknell, *Justice, Courtesy and Love* (London: Epworth Press, 1995), 14–20.

16. H. G. Appenzeller translated the tract into Korean in 1893. He published the second edition, which had thirty-five leaves, at the Paejae School Press in 1895. The third one was published in 1899.

17. Ralph W. Thomson, *Griffith John: The Story of Fifty Years in China* (London: Religious Tract Society, 1906), 331–332. In 1884 the Central China Religious Tract Society reported a list of fifty new publications; of these, John wrote thirty-one.

18. Nelson Bitton, *Griffith John: The Apostle of Central China* (London: Sunday School Union, 1912), 126.

19. At least the following nine chapters were compiled from the previous tracts: 6, "Shangdi zhenli" [The Truth concerning God]; 9, "Jiushi zhenzhu" [The True Savior of the World]; 10, "Shuzui zhi dao" [On the Atonement]; 11, "Zhongsheng zhi dao" [On Regeneration]; 12, "*Xinzhe dejiu*" [Salvation through Faith]; 13, "Fusheng zhi dao" [On the Resurrection]; 14, "Shengjing dazhi" [Great Themes of the Gospel]; 15, "Xinzhe suode zhi zhenfu" [True Way of Seeking Happiness]; and 18, "*Quanzhong hougai*" [On Repentance].

20. For Martin's life and work in China see Ralph R. Covell, "The Life and Thought of W. A. P. Martin: Agent and Interpreter of Sino-American Contact in the Nineteenth and Early Twentieth Century" (Ph.D. diss., University of Denver, 1974); and idem, *W. A. P. Martin, Pioneer of Progress in China* (Washington, D.C.: Christian University Press, 1978), 10–19.

21. In 1907 a poll conducted by the Christian Literature Society voted it "the best single book" in Chinese (Arthur J. Brown, "The Death of the Rev. W. A. P. Martin," *Minutes of the Board of the Foreign Missions of the PCUSA for 1916* [Philadelphia: PCUSA, 1916], 321). In 1885 H. G. Underwood began to translate the book into Korean. A full Korean edition was not published.

22. In the appendixes of section 2, Martin introduced the text of the memorial on Roman Catholicism submitted by Xu Guangqi (baptized by Matteo Ricci) to the emperor in 1616 (Ming dynasty) and "the Nestorian Monument" (set up in 781), because the Chinese people thought highly of the traditions. Xu defended Christianity and called on the emperor to grant it the same status as Buddhism, Daoism, and Islam. Martin argued that the Nestorian Monument proved that Christianity was propagated in China not only by Westerners, but also by Asians in the Tang dynasty.

23. Tora Yoshida, *Chugoku Kirisutokyō dendō bunsho no kenkyū* [A Study on the Missionaries' Works Written in Chinese by American Protestant Clergies in China] (Tokyo: Kyuko Shoin, 1993), 103–104.

24. For the relationship between nineteenth-century evangelicalism and the Enlightenment, see Brian Stanley, *The Bible and the Flag* (Leicester, England: Apollos, 1990), 61–78; and idem, ed., *Christian Missions and the Enlightenment* (Grand Rapids, Mich.: Eerdmans, 2001).

25. W. A. P. Martin, *Jiandao suyuan* [Evidences of Christianity] (Shanghai: Chinese Tract Society, 1903), 29b.

26. Ibid., 36b.

27. First edition, *Zixi cudong: Civilization, Western and Chinese* (Hong Kong: Religious Tract Society, 1884); fourth edition, *Zixi cudong: Civilization, the Fruit of Christianity* (Shanghai: Society for the Diffusion of Christian and General Knowledge among the Chinese, 1902). For his understanding of Confucianism, see his paper "Confucianism" read at the Parliament of Religions, Chicago, 1893. A full text is in the *Chinese Recorder* 33 (April 1902): 159–175. His conclusion was that once China was an advanced civilization, yet now "the Western people are in advance of you. Therefore learn from them what they have good and correct their evil by what you have better; this is my meaning of the great principle of Reciprocity!"

28. Ernst Faber, "A Critique of the Chinese Notions and Practice of Filial Piety," *Chinese Recorder* 9 (March–April 1878): 94.

PART THREE

Christianity, Nationalism, and Japanese Colonialism

CHAPTER 5

Church and State Relations in the Japanese Colonial Period

Wi Jo Kang

Religious scholars have engaged in heated debates regarding alleged collusion versus firm resistance on the part of Christian churches during the era of Japanese colonial rule in Korea. The discussion below contends that church-state relations during the Japanese colonial period cannot be characterized monolithically or consistently as cooperative or contentious, but, instead, as evolving and changing in response to the unfolding of historical events over a number of years.

In the early years of Japanese annexation, many foreign missionaries and Korean church leaders applauded Japanese rule and sought cooperative, cordial relations with Japanese government officials. As the Japanese state enacted increasingly harsh and violent policies toward Korean churches and the Korean populace in general, many church leaders protested and criticized Japanese rule. However, the severity of suppression by the Japanese government eventually silenced these protests and forced acquiescence to state practices, ranging from participation in Shintō ceremonies to persecution of church leaders.

In 1910, when Japan annexed Korea, Christian missions and churches were already strongly established. Although the Roman Catholics were severely persecuted, the church had experienced more than a hundred years of fruitful history working in Korea and claimed forty-six expatriate missionaries, fifteen native priests, forty-one Korean seminarians, sixty-nine churches, and 73,517 members.[1] Protestant churches, after three decades of work among the Koreans, were also strong, especially as seen in the rapidly increasing influences of the Presbyterians and the Methodists, with Presbyterians numbering 12,202 and Methodists 3,621.[2]

Immediately following annexation, the initial church and state relationship seemed surprisingly friendly. One missionary praised the Japanese rule in these kind words: "Prior to the annexation, the administrative system was chaotic. By stern enforcement, the Japanese have introduced quiet and order, have commenced to exploit the natural resources of the country, set up a judiciary, developed the beginning of an educational system, improved communication and cultivated hygiene."[3] Such acceptance of Japanese rule by the missionaries was further reflected in a letter from the Reverend Arthur J. Brown, secretary of the Board of Foreign Missions of the Presbyterian Church in the United State of America, to a Japanese government official, Hanihara Masanao: "Japanese administration is far better than Korea would otherwise have had and far better than Korea had under its own rule."[4]

Acceptance of the Japanese administration was not merely a friendly gesture on the part of the missionaries; it was also the official policy of the Presbyterian mission, the largest mission in Korea. Mission board secretary Arthur Brown further wrote:

> What is the attitude of the missionaries toward the Japanese? There are four possible attitudes: First, opposition; second, aloofness; third, cooperation; fourth, loyal recognition.... [T]he fourth, loyal recognition, is I believe, the sound position. It is in accord with the example of Christ, who loyally submitted himself and advised His apostles to submit themselves to a far worse government than the Japanese and it is in line with the teaching of Paul in Romans xiii.[5]

The missionaries advised Korean Christians not to be involved in opposition to the Japanese, and Korean Christians also officially adopted the position of "loyal recognition" toward the Japanese colonial state. Consequently, any Korean Christians who were involved in political activities against the Japanese were "kept from responsible positions in the Church."[6]

Despite these policies in support of Japanese rule, the Japanese government did not trust the Christian churches. Sermons preached by missionaries or Korean pastors who were deemed suspicious were thus reported to the authorities. Suspicion of Korean Christians was especially strong in the winter of 1909–1910, during the revival movement referred to as the "campaign for a million souls." This great evangelistic effort by Protestant churches in Korea aimed to bring one million Koreans into the Christian faith. Many revival meetings were held and fiery sermons were preached. These meetings, too, were carefully watched by Japanese government officials.

Inevitably such suspicion brought oppression and hostility toward the churches. The culmination of this was the fabrication of the so-called Conspiracy Case. In October 1911, the Japanese colonial government began to arrest Korean Christian leaders from the cities where Christian populations were significant in number. A missionary stationed in Sŏnch'ŏn reported,

"Time after time arrests have been made, sometimes one or two and sometimes several at a time, until now there are fifty or more from our neighborhood. The parents and relatives of these men do not know why they were taken. The men themselves do not know why."[7] Finally, the colonial government issued a statement accusing these Korean Christians of plotting to assassinate Governor-General Terauchi as he passed through Sŏnch'ŏn in late December 1910. The government explained the conspiracy case in the following words: "In the course of the prosecution of a robber arrested in Sensen [Sŏnch'ŏn in Korean pronunciation], North Heian Province, in August, 1911, the fact that a gang of conspirators under the guidance of a certain ring-leader had been trying to assassinate Count Terauchi, Governor-General of Chōsen, was discovered."[8]

Arrests of Christians in Sŏnch'ŏn, where the attempted assassination was to have taken place, were so numerous that the Hugh O'Neill Jr. Industrial Academy, the largest Presbyterian mission school in the area, had to close. Those accused were imprisoned without a public hearing until June 28, 1912, when finally 123 of them were indicted and brought to trial before the District Court of Seoul. All of the accused complained about being tortured at the police station. One of the accused declared, "I was told by one of the officials that one man had been killed as a result of torture and I was threatened that if I did not stick to the statements I had made, I should meet the same fate."[9]

A veteran missionary who was in Korea during the trial later wrote in demonstration of the falsity of such confessions:

> I was able to secure a copy of the so-called confession before the police of the elder in whom I was especially interested. To my surprise and consternation I found that he had apparently not only confessed to the police that he had conspired with others to kill the governor-general when he came to Pyongyang, but that several missionaries including myself had attended one of their meetings and had urged the Koreans to be brave and kill the governor-general without fail. However, the record showed that the elder in his subsequent examination before the procurator had indignantly denied having had any part in or even knowledge of the alleged conspiracy.[10]

After three months, on September 28, 1912, the trial came to an end, and 105 men were sentenced even though there was no evidence of any crimes. Indeed, the evidence presented in the case was highly suspect from the start. On the dates that the prosecution charged Yun Ch'iho, a U.S-educated Christian leader, had met the other plotters in Seoul, he was in Kaesŏng City. Also, the confessions stated that toward the end of December 1910, the conspirators traveled to Sŏnch'ŏn to kill Governor-General

Terauchi. The investigation showed, however, that during the last six days of December the number of passengers arriving in Sŏnch'ŏn by two different railways did not exceed seventy people.

Finally, in a curious twist, the court did not try any missionaries. If they had been involved in the meetings, handing out revolvers and urging "the Koreans to be brave and kill the governor-general without fail," then they should have been charged as well. However, as missionaries were not called to account, neither were they allowed "to be called as witnesses for the defense."[11] Thus, the entire case and related trials were based almost completely on coerced or fabricated testimonies.

Nonetheless, numerous Korean Christians were convicted of "attempting to assassinate the governor-general." They appealed to the Seoul Appeals Court, which met fifty-one times between November 26, 1912, and February 25, 1913. The court reduced the ten-year sentences to six years of penal servitude. Some of the accused were acquitted. However, the accused refused to accept the decision of the appeals court and went to the Higher Court of the Governor-General. That court chose to reconsider only the cases of those sentenced to penal servitude; the retrial began on July 1, 1913, in Taegu Appeals Court. It ended three days later, and the decision was announced on July 15. The court upheld the previous court's decision with minor changes in terms of sentences. Again the defendants brought the case before the higher court, but on October 9, 1913, the court ruled against any further hearing and upheld the judgment of the Taegu court.

There is little historical question that those prosecuting the Conspiracy Case concocted evidence and that Japanese government officials were unable to prove any conspiracy on the part of Christians in Korea. This case demonstrates that despite the churches' efforts to cooperate with the Japanese government, church-state relations were strained from the early colonial period—and they grew increasingly so.

Missionary leaders were alarmed by the conspiracy case and interpreted it as evidence of Japan's political aim to suppress the Christian churches in Korea. Mission board secretary Arthur Brown strongly protested against the case and against the Japanese government:

We cannot be indifferent to the effect of the present policy of the Japanese police upon a mission work which now represents approximately 330 foreign missionaries, 962 schools, a medical college, a nurses' training school, thirteen hospitals, eighteen dispensaries, an orphanage, a school for the blind, a leper asylum, a printing press, 500 churches, a Christian community of 250,000, property worth approximately a million dollars and an annual expenditure of over $250,000. This extensive work is being injuriously affected by the reign of terror which now prevails among the Koreans.[12]

The Japanese government was surprised and disturbed to hear such harsh reactions. On February 13, 1915, the colonial government released all of the accused before the completion of their prison sentences. However, the Japanese government continued oppressive policies toward the Christian churches in various ways. In the area of medical work on the part of the missionaries, for example, the government was fully aware of the shortage of doctors and the great assistance rendered by medical missionaries. The need for doctors was so great that the government permitted some Japanese to practice medicine in Korea without official licenses and proper qualifications. Despite the obvious needs, the government persisted in restricting the medical practice of Christian missionaries by making it unusually difficult for them to obtain licenses. On November 15, 1913, the government issued General Ordinance number 100, which required all who desired to practice medicine to apply for permission from the governor-general. The ordinance listed the following as qualifications.

1. Those qualified according to the law in force in Japan
2. Those graduated from medical schools recognized by the governor-general
3. Those who have passed a medical examination prescribed by the governor-general
4. Those Japanese subjects graduated from medical schools of good standing in foreign countries
5. Those foreigners who have obtained a license in their respective countries, in which qualified Japanese subjects are permitted to practice medicine[13]

Without considering the difficulties of obtaining licenses under the requirements laid down in items one through four, item five alone limited foreign medical practice in Korea to those of British nationality. Only Great Britain permitted Japanese who had received medical training and certification in Japan to practice medicine in Britain. The ordinance was modified in July 1914 to allow more foreign doctors to obtain general licenses, but restrictions against the Christian missionaries were not altogether eliminated.

In the area of Christian education there was also significant government pressure. General Ordinance number 24, as contained in the Revision of Regulations for Private Schools issued in March 1915, excluded the Bible from all school curricula and required all teachers to learn the Japanese language within the next five years and teach only in that "national language."

On August 16 of the same year, in order to supervise the propagation of Christianity, General Ordinance number 83 stated that official permission had to be secured before one could open a new church or employ any paid workers in a church. Such permission was exceedingly difficult to obtain. Some churches were never able to secure permission to build and eventually had to disperse as a result. Regulations such as these tightened the control on all Christian activities.

For Korean Christians, it was unquestionably clear that the Japanese stance toward the Christian churches was oppressive and that the religious liberty guaranteed by the constitution of Japan was not being honored in Korea. Eventually, Korean Christians responded to such oppressive alien state policies with open protest and by aligning themselves with other religious groups opposed to Japanese rule. The first public demonstration of this solidarity was the nationwide March First Independence Movement of 1919, a direct reaction by the Korean public against the Japanese colonial state.

Korean Christians were active participants in this independence movement. Sixteen of the thirty-three signers of the declaration were Christian leaders, among them the Reverend Kil Sŏn-ju, one of the first ordained Korean Presbyterian ministers. Many Christian churches became gathering places for demonstrators and to hear the declaration of independence read.

The government placed primary blame for the protests on the Christians and retaliated against them. Police even more closely supervised Christian worship services, and many churches were ordered to close. Practically every Christian pastor in Seoul was arrested and jailed. Soldiers stopped people in the street in order to discover and punish more Christians.

The number of Christians arrested became so great that many Christian schools had to be closed. In some localities the police arrested all church officers. By the end of June 1919, the following numbers had been arrested: Presbyterians, 1,461; Methodists, 465; Roman Catholics, 57; others, 207.[14]

Less than four months later, the number of Presbyterians in jail had increased to 3,804, among them 134 pastors and elders. In the course of this persecution, forty-one Presbyterian leaders were shot and six others were beaten to death. Twelve Presbyterian churches were destroyed, and the homes of many missionaries were searched by the police, resulting in more property damage. Some of the missionaries were physically attacked by soldiers and severely beaten. Under these conditions, the work of the church was disastrously affected. One missionary reported:

> With the launching of the Independence Movement in March, 1919, the work suddenly stopped. Everything was changed. Schools had to be closed, Bible classes could not be held, Bible Institutes could not finish, trips to the country had to be cancelled, visiting in homes by missionaries was found to be inadvisable, many of our churches found their pastors, elders, helpers and other church officers carried off to prison; missionaries lost their secretaries,

language teachers, or literary assistants; every way we tried to turn regular work seemed impossible.[15]

Of all the repressive measures taken against Christians, surely the most tragic and brutal was the massacre in the village of Cheamni, near the Suwŏn City. Horace H. Underwood, the noted Presbyterian missionary, reported the bloody incident at Cheamni in detail. On April 16, 1919, he and some friends left Seoul to visit Suwŏn. Nearing the town, they saw a large cloud of smoke. While visiting a nearby home, Underwood talked with a local farmer:

UNDERWOOD: "What is that smoke?"
FARMER: "That is a village that has burned."
UNDERWOOD: "When was it burned?"
FARMER: "Yesterday."
UNDERWOOD: "How was it burned?"
FARMER (glancing around fearfully): "By the soldiers."
UNDERWOOD: "Why? Did the people riot or shout for independence?"
FARMER: "No, but that is a Christian village."[16]

Proceeding then to Cheamni, the group learned that on the previous day, Japanese soldiers had arrived in the village and ordered all male Christians into the church. When they had gathered, about thirty in all, the soldiers fired on them with rifles and killed the survivors with swords and bayonets. Afterward, the soldiers set fire to the church and left.

Such violently oppressive measures were quickly criticized and deplored by church leaders in Korea and abroad. The Reverend Herbert Welch, bishop of the Methodist Episcopal Church in Korea, visited Tokyo on his way to the United States and met with Prime Minister Hara Takashi on May 15, 1919. The prime minister in his diary described the meeting:

I asked him to express his frank opinion on the Korean incidents. Then he said he is going to the United States to raise funds of two million dollars for the work of the church in Korea. But he feels quite uncertain about the future of the church in Korea in consideration of the severeness of the military rule, lawless actions of the gendarmeries and police, the oppression of Christians in various places and discriminating treatment of Koreans by the Japanese and discrimination in education.[17]

The prime minister's diary also recounts that on the next day, May 16, a committee of Christian missionaries from Korea visited Tokyo to report on the tense nature of the relations between church and state.

The atrocities perpetrated against Korean Christians by Japanese soldiers and police were reported as well in the United States and in Europe, despite efforts by the Japanese authorities to conceal the facts through their control of the communication systems. Upon learning of this persecution in Korea, the Commission of Relations with the Orient of the Federal Council of Churches of Christ in America sent a cable on June 26, 1919, to Prime Minister Hara deploring Japanese actions and demanding administrative reform. The cable read: "Agitation regarding Chōsen abuses increasingly serious, endangering good will. Cannot withhold facts. Urgently important you publish ... that abuses have ceased and reasonable administrative reforms proceeding."[18]

On July 10, the commission received a cablegram from the prime minister stating, "I desire to assure you that the report of abuses committed by agents of the Japanese Government in Korea have been engaging my most serious attention. I am fully prepared to look squarely at actual facts. As I have declared on various occasions, the regime of administration inaugurated in Korea at the time of the annexation, nearly ten years ago, calls on us for substantial modification to meet the altered conditions of things."[19]

The desire for "substantial modification" seemed to have been sincere on the part of Prime Minister Hara. Already in early April he had seriously discussed with his cabinet the possibilities of recalling Governor-General Hasegawa, providing equal opportunity for both Japanese and Koreans in education, abolishing the gendarmerie system, and generally treating Koreans without prejudice.

In Hara's mind, it was clear that reform was needed if the Japanese administration was to continue, and he frequently brought up the Korean question in Tokyo cabinet meetings. On June 27, 1919, the cabinet discussed replacing Hasegawa Yoshimichi with Admiral Saitō Makoto as governor-general of Chōsen. In his diary, the prime minister wrote: "I visited Admiral Saitō Makoto and consulted about his willingness to assume the position of Governor-General and he consented. In the evening I invited Mizuno Rentaro and asked him to become the Administrative Superintendent (the next highest post) in Chōsen and I received his consent."[20] On August 4, 1919, the cabinet finally agreed to replace the governor-general and introduce political reforms. The Japanese emperor officially appointed Admiral Saitō as the new governor-general on August 12.

A week after Saitō's appointment to the Korean position, on August 19, 1919, the Imperial Rescript concerning the Reorganization of the Government-General of Chōsen was made public. Among other things it stated, "We are persuaded that the state of development at which the general situation has now arrived calls for certain reforms in the administrative organization of the Government-General of Korea and we issue our imperial command that such reforms be put into operation."[21]

In addition to this statement, another promising sign of reform was Admiral Saitō's meeting with missionary leaders soon after his arrival in Seoul. He asked them to frankly express their opinions on the Japanese rule and make suggestions. In response, the Federal Council of Protestant Evangelical Mission in Korea prepared a statement and submitted it in September 1919. After expressing gratitude for the planned reforms, the document went on to say:

> It was a keen disappointment to us, who had lived in Korea under the former government, to find that what we had expected from the Japanese administration after annexation, was not forthcoming, but that military rule to which the country was subjected, restricted the religious liberty and educational freedom which had been enjoyed, introduced unjust discrimination against the Koreans and eventually imposed upon the people such subjection and such harsh measures of oppression, as to call forth from them the protest of the independence agitation of this year. The unarmed demonstrations at that time were met with such brutality . . . and we were forced for the sake of humanity to give expression to our protests.[22]

The missionaries also said, "We urge that religious liberty, which is already guaranteed by the constitution of the Empire of Japan . . . be made effective" and then made the following important requests:

1. That fewer restrictions be placed upon the church and upon missionaries
2. That discrimination against Christians and against Christianity by officials not be allowed
3. That missionaries be allowed to include the teaching of the Bible and religious exercises in the curricula of church schools
4. That restrictions on the use of the Korean language be removed
5. That we be accorded more liberty in the management of our schools and freedom from unnecessary official interference
6. That teachers and pupils be allowed liberty of conscience
7. That the details of the management of our hospitals be left to the staff without interference from officials
8. That the censorship of Christian books be abolished[23]

Subsequent meetings between government officials and missionaries were frequent.

The new administration made some significant changes in regard to Christian education. The former administration had fixed a definite curriculum for all grades of Christian private schools that precluded additional courses on the Bible or religion. However, in March 1920, new regulations for private schools were issued. The only required subjects were on morals and the Japanese language. Religion was again allowed to be taught in Christian schools. Further modifications of the law in 1922 and 1923 permitted the Korean language to be taught and spoken in the Christian schools.

Policies governing Christian work in general were also changed. Before reform, specific permission from the governor-general was a prerequisite for the opening of a new church or other religious institution. If this was violated, a severe fine was levied. In April 1920, new regulations came out abolishing the fines and requiring only that new church openings be reported to the government. The Japanese government, however, reserved the right to close buildings if the institutions were found to have been used as "places for concocting plots injurious to the public peace and order."[24]

With these reforms in place, church workers and government officials began to maintain close, friendly contacts, and Japanese officials often praised the Christian church's contribution to the betterment of Korean life. The following statement by Mr. Mizuno at the Tenth Annual Conference of the Federal Council of Protestant Evangelical Missions in Korea on September 21, 1921, expressed this new attitude:

> I have made several trips into the country and the more familiar I become
> with the conditions in the peninsula, the more do I realize how painstakingly
> you labor for the uplift of the people. . . . It can be said without any
> appearance of flattery that Chōsen owes much of her advancement in
> civilization to your labors. . . . So we hold Christianity in high regard to give
> it every possible facility for its propagation.[25]

Christian churches in Korea welcomed the change in administration and appreciated the new relationship they enjoyed with the government. The churches' membership, which had declined in 1919, had begun to increase under the new administration. In 1918, Christians numbered 319,129; in 1919, 296,487; in 1920, 323,575; in 1921, 355,114; and in 1922, 372,920.[26]

Despite all these good signs, it would be overstating the case to conclude that Christians under the Saitō administration enjoyed full religious liberty with no restrictions placed on their Christian work. The Japanese maintained a distrust of Korean churches, and spying on Christian activities continued. One missionary wrote, "They [the policemen] often insist on attending the services of the churches and schools and in regulating what is said and done. They frequent the halls of the schools and arrest the students on all sorts of suspicion. They censor all publications and often object to articles in the weekly church's paper."[27]

In addition to the surveillance and interventions by Japanese government officials in church life, the greatest problem that Christians faced during this period arose from the worldwide economic depression and Japanese economic policies that created conditions of hardship for Korean Christians.

Japanese land and agricultural policies adversely affected large segments of the Korean population. Some 80 percent of Koreans depended on the land for their livelihood, but farmers who had tilled their land for generations lost their property overnight as a result of seizure or competition from the Japanese. A missionary recounted, "There are now immense Japanese holdings that once belonged to Koreans and hundreds of Japanese small farmers are taking the land and the place of a like or greater number of Koreans; for the man from Japan can farm more than a Korean can and always manage to get hold of the land."[28] Korean Christian farmers were especially vulnerable to this change of ownership. Japanese landowners who were antagonistic to Christians would often take away the land rights from their Christian tenants and give them to other Japanese or to non-Christian Korean farmers.

Admiral Saitō Makoto's second term ended in 1931, and General Ugaki Kazunari became Korea's new governor-general. The Ugaki administration seemed to maintain the policies of the Saito administration and so the "rule of culture" did not yet disappear. The prevailing attitudes even resulted in awards being presented in recognition of the positive contributions made by missionaries in Korea. Dr. O. R. Avison, a medical missionary and educator, received the fourth degree of the Order of the Sacred Treasure from the emperor of Japan, and early in 1937 the Imperial Educational Association presented Dr. Samuel Moffett with a gold medal.

In Tokyo, however, the militarists were expanding their influence and engaging in terrorist activities to suppress liberal democratic elements in Japanese politics. They attacked Western ideas of democracy and demanded chauvinistic devotion to the emperor from the people. With the establishment of Manchukuo in 1932, Korea gained new significance. The devotion of the Korean people to the empire became, from the Japanese viewpoint, more important than ever before. As a means of making Koreans more loyal subjects, the Japanese administration began urging all Koreans, including Christians, to participate in Shintō ceremonies, for which an increasing number of shrines were built throughout the country.[29]

To Christians, the Shintō religion became a serious issue after 1935, when the government ordered all educational institutions, including private Christian schools, to pay obeisance by attending the shrine ceremonies. In previous years when the government had asked Christian schools to participate, Christians had been able to excuse themselves by participating in some other forms of constructive activities.

On November 14, 1935, the governor of South Pyongan Province called a conference of educators. Before the meeting he wanted all of them to visit Shintō shrines. Dr. George McCune, president of Union Christian College in Pyongyang, and Velma L. Snook, principal of Sungui Girls' High School, refused to do so. The governor ordered them to leave the meeting and gave them sixty days to reconsider their action. He threatened to revoke their educational permits if they did not capitulate. The missionaries held their ground and the government did indeed revoke their educational permits.

Police guarded Dr. McCune's house and followed him wherever he went. On January 20, 1936, McCune was relieved of his college presidency and Snook was relieved of her position as principal. Yet despite these measures to weaken the churches' power and activities, Japanese officials claimed that, in trying to bring Koreans to the Shintō ceremonies, they were not imposing religious rites but instead encouraging patriotic acts that had nothing to do with religion: "The veneration of her illustrious dead in places specially dedicated to their memory has been a national custom of Japan for ages past and the state ceremonies for this purpose are treated by the Government as distinct from those of a purely religious nature."[30]

On January 29, 1936, seven Christian leaders, including Yun Ch'iho and Ryang Ju Sam (Yang Chusam), general superintendent of the Korea Methodist Church, visited the Department of Education of the Japanese colonial government to address this issue of forced participation in Shintō ceremonies. Mr. Watanabe, the head of the department, emphasized that attendance at the ceremonies was a civil, not a religious, act and that participation was simply a payment of the highest respect to one's ancestors.

Korean Christians who had abandoned their own ancient practice of ancestor worship as idolatry were not convinced that paying such respect to Japanese ancestral sprits was not worship. In spite of the efforts to persuade them, most Korean Christians rejected the government's definition and refused to participate in the ceremonies. Many believed that bowing to the shrines violated God's commandment against idolatry, and the overwhelming majority of expatriate missionaries also understood the shrine ceremonies as religious acts.

Roman Catholics especially took Shintō rites to be highly religious in nature. A Japanese bishop told his people in 1931, "The Shintō Shrines, so the high authorities of the government tell us, do not maintain a religion, but as a matter of fact the ceremonies that are performed therein have a full religious character. Thus the sacred right of religious freedom, given to the people in Article 28 of the Constitution, is forgotten and violated by the ministry of education."[31] The Roman Catholic position that participation in the shrine ceremonies was idolatrous was recanted in 1936 following specific instructions from Rome. The Reverend Edward Adams, a veteran Presbyterian missionary in Korea, recounts the shift in the position of Korean Catholics toward participation in Shintō ceremonies. Adams describes a meeting of educators called by the Japanese government in which Dr. McCune was challenged for his opposition toward participation in Shintō ceremonies. A Roman Catholic missionary seated next to McCune whispered to him in an ominous tone, "The blood of the martyrs is seed of the church."[32]

On May 25, 1936, the Sacred Congregation of the Propagation of the Faith instructed Catholics in the Japanese empire, including Korea at that time, to accept the government order. Item one of this order said:

> The ordinaries in the territories of the Japanese Empire shall teach their faithful that the ceremonies, conducted by the government at Jinja are civil affairs. According to the repeated, explicit declaration of the authorities and the common consensus of the educated, shrine ceremonies are mere expressions of patriotic love, that is filial reverence toward the royal family and the benefactors of their own nation; and that, consequently, these ceremonies have only civil value and that Catholics are permitted to participate in them and behave like the rest of the citizens.[33]

The instructions resolved the shrine issue as far as the Roman Catholics were concerned. However, for Protestants, especially Presbyterians, the problem remained serious to the point that one mission report stated, "At present, possibly no problem of missionary policy is more difficult than that occasioned by the requirement of the Japanese government of attendance at the national Shintō shrines."[34]

Protestants continued to reject the government's insistence on the non-religious nature of shrine ceremonies. A typical explanation for their opposition can be seen in a statement by the mission of the Presbyterian Church of Victoria (Australia):

> We wish to express the high respect and loyalty which we hold toward his Imperial Majesty, the Emperor of Japan; this we do in gratitude for the blessings of good government . . . but since we worship one God, alone, Creator and Ruler of the universe, revealed as the Father of Mankind, and because to comply with an order to make obeisance at shrines which are dedicated to other spirits and at which acts of worship are commonly performed, would constitute for us a disobedience to His expressed commands, we therefore are unable ourselves to make such obeisance or to instruct our schools to do so.[35]

The opposition of Presbyterian groups was so strong that the Executive Committee of the Board of Foreign Missions of the Presbyterian Church in the United States of America soon felt compelled to recommend closing Korean mission schools rather than support their participation in the shrine ceremonies: "Recognizing the increasing difficulties of maintaining our Mission schools and also of preserving in them the full purposes and ideals with which they were founded, we recommend that the Mission approve the policy of retiring from the field of secular education."[36]

Some schools in Taegu and Seoul had difficulty closing at first because of Korean clergy and missionary efforts to keep them open, but P'yŏngyang schools did not enroll any new students in 1937; finally, in March 1938, all schools were closed, including the Union Christian College.

In August 1936, General Minami Jiro, commanding officer of the Kwanto Army, became the new governor-general of Korea. With militarists in control in Tokyo, General Minami was able to place Korea under a firm military dictatorship as well. Meanwhile, government pressure on the Christian churches to participate in the Shintō ceremonies increased. Under the new regime, it became increasingly difficult to resist. In 1937, the Methodists decided to comply with the government's request, agreeing with the government's claim that shrine attendance was a patriotic rather than a religious rite. In February 1938, the Japanese government called a conference of Christians in Korea, intended to shape their thinking on the world situation at the time and to demand Christian support in the war efforts of the empire. The Presbyterians, at their General Assembly meeting of September 1938, in P'yŏngyang, finally agreed to obey the government order regarding shrine ceremonies.

It should be noted that strong government pressure and scare tactics affected the surrender of the Presbyterians. Before the meeting of four hundred delegates, each delegate was taken to a police station and told by the police to approve shrine participation. Then, when the session began, high-ranking police officials sat right in front facing the delegates. No debates or negative votes were allowed, and anyone who tried to leave was brought back by police escorts. With little other choice, the assembly resolved that participation in Shintō ceremonies was not a religious act and therefore did not conflict with the teachings of Christianity.

The official approval of shrine attendance by the largest and most powerful Christian denomination in Korea proved an effective means of suppressing any further Christian resistance. The vexing shrine issue was solved, as far as the government was concerned, but the war policies of the government were to bring about far more oppressive policies against Korean Christians.

In May 1939, the government called a meeting of Christian leaders in order to form an organic union of all Christian denominations under the

Nihon Kirisuto Kyodan (the United Church of Christ in Japan); such a union would allow for more effective governance of Korean church bodies. The gathering of more than seventeen hundred leaders, representing forty-seven Christian organizations, instituted an organization called the Chōsen Kirisuto-Kyo Rengokai (Federation of Korean Christian Churches).[37]

Japanese pressure on Korean Christians to conform to Japanese war policies continued relentlessly. Government interference in church affairs increased, and any activities of which the government disapproved became excuses to imprison church leaders or expel missionaries. The Day of Prayer Incident in September 1941 was a typical example. Christian women throughout the world observed the World Day of Prayer during the last week of February. In preparation for the day, the Reverend Herbert Blair, chairman of the Federal Council of Churches, asked Alice Butts of P'yŏngyang to make a short outline of the Day of Prayer program available to the churches. When the police examined the program, they discovered a prayer "for the Peace of the World" and charged that such a prayer was a sign of disloyalty to the war effort. Miss Butts was imprisoned for one month, and many Christian leaders were brought to police stations for interrogation.

At this point, the Christian churches in Korea were completely controlled by the Japanese state. A paper prepared by missionaries on November 22, 1949, four years after the end of Japanese rule in Korea, documented that during this period no church meeting could be held without police permission or without the presence of police representatives at every session. Restrictions imposed upon foreign missionaries were tight, including a restriction against their holding any administrative positions in the church.

As Japan progressed toward war, the missionaries were compelled to withdraw from Korea. In October 1940, the U.S. consul-general, Gaylord Marsh, called representatives of the missions and informed them of the U.S. State Department's order to evacuate all Americans. Marsh urged an early evacuation and arranged to bring the SS *Mariposa* to the Inchŏn port on November 16. On that day, 219 American citizens, practically all missionaries, were evacuated. Of the further withdrawal of missionaries up to March 31, 1941, the *Japan Christian Year Book* gave these figures: "Of the 108 reported in 1939 by the Methodist mission, only 3 remain and they will leave in April. Out of 66 Southern Presbyterians, 5 remain. Of 14 Anglicans, 3 are here, all plan to leave this spring. The Northern Presbyterians, with 118 members in 1939, have 14 now."[38]

With the main body of missionaries out of Korea, it seemed that the church simply became one more organization working for the Japanese cause. A statement adapted by the Executive of the Presbyterian Church at the General Assembly meeting in November 1940, proclaimed:

By following the guidance of the Government and adjusting to the national policy based on group organization, we will get rid of the wrong idea of depending on Europe and America and do our best to readjust and purify Japanese Christianity. At the same time the church members, as loyal subjects of the Emperor, offering public service without selfishness, should go forward bravely to join in establishing the New Order in Asia.[39]

This same outline added, "Like other people, the church members should attend the shrine worship."

On December 6, 1940, the Standing Committee of the Korean Presbyterian General Assembly called a meeting to form the Total National Force Union. The meeting was attended by some 220 delegates, persons from each presbytery, as well as by Vice-Governor-General Ohno and other officials of the colonial government. The assembly passed a resolution that "Chōsen Presbyterians are resolved to give up the principle of reliance on Europe and America and reform our church as purely Japanese Christianity."[40] The Methodists in Korea made a similar statement:

It is both urgent and proper that we Christians should bring to reality the true spirit of our national polity and the underlying principle of Naisen Ittai (Japan Proper and Korea form one body), perform adequately our duties as a people behind the gun and conform to the new order, therefore we, the General Board of the Korean Methodist Church, hereby take the lead in deciding upon and putting into effect the following:

I.   Right Guidance of Thought
II. Educational Reform
III. Social Education
IV. Support of the Army
V.   Unified Control of Organizations[41]

After Japan attacked Pearl Harbor, the Japanese imperial forces entered into direct confrontation with the United States. As the war progressed, the Japanese government attempted to force confessions of anti-Japanese activities in Christian churches. The remaining missionaries in Korea, including sixty-seven Roman Catholics, were imprisoned. During the war, many churches were without pastors, and Christians were forced to work on Sundays. Institutions such as the Christian Literature Society and the British and Foreign Bible Society were closed.

On July 29, 1945, less than a month before the end of the war, all Protestant churches under Japanese control were ordered to abolish their denominational distinctions and combine into the Nihon Kirisuto-kyo

Chōsen Kyodan (Korean-Japanese Christian Church). During an organizational meeting for this purpose, a Shintō priest even led the Christian pastors to the Han River for a purification ceremony. Following this forced union, about three thousand Christian leaders were arrested and fifty of them suffered martyrdom. It was also reported that the Japanese army was planning to massacre a great many more Korean Christians in the middle of August 1945 because of the fear that these Christians might aid the Allied forces. Dr. Helen Kim wrote:

> Some weeks after the atom bombs were dropped on Hiroshima and Nagasaki, we were told that over ten thousand leaders in Korean society who had been kept on the blacklist of the Japanese police were to have been arrested. In case of eventual Japanese defeat, the authorities thought these Koreans would become leaders and would retaliate against them. They had planned to massacre this group about the fifteenth of August, which proved to be the very day of the Japanese surrender.[42]

On that fateful day of August 15, 1945, rather than a wholesale massacre of the leadership of the Korean churches, the turbulent relations between the Korean churches and the Japanese state ended with the liberation of Korea from Japanese colonial rule.

NOTES

1. Yu Hong-yŏl, *Han'guk Ch'ŏnju kyohoesa* [History of the Roman Catholic Church in Korea] (Seoul: Catholic Publishers, 1963), 998.

2. Min Kyung Bae, *Han'guk Kidok kyohoesa* [History of the Christian Church in Korea] (Seoul: Christian Literature Society of Korea, 1972), 299–300.

3. The Commission on Relations with the Orient of the Federal Council of the Churches of Christ in America, *The Korean Situation: Authentic Accounts of Recent Events by Eye Witnesses* (New York: The Commission on Relations with the Orient of the Federal Council of the Churches of Christ in America, 1919), 8.

4. Letter from Arthur J. Brown to Masanao Hanihara, dated Feb. 16, 1912, in the Presbyterian Library, New York.

5. Ibid.

6. A "memorandum" of missionaries Samuel A. Moffet, Norman C. Whittemore, O. R. Avison, George S. McCune, and C. E. Sharp to His Excellency Count Terauchi, Governor-General of Chōsen, and received by Mr. Komatsu, Director of Chōsen, Jan. 8, 1912, in the Presbyterian Library, New York.

7. Letter of Alfred M. Sharrocks, M.D., to the Hon. M. Komatsu, Director of the Bureau of Foreign Affairs of the Governor-General of Chōsen, dated Dec. 16, 1911, in the Presbyterian Library, New York.

8. *Annual Report on Reforms and Progress in Chōsen, 1912–1913* (Keijō:

Government General of Chōsen, 1914), 56. Hereafter referred to as *Annual Report* (various years).

9. Special correspondence of the Japan Chronicle: *The Korean Conspiracy Trial: Full Report of the Proceedings* (Kobe, Japan: The Office of the Japan Chronicle, 1912), 4–5. This is the most comprehensive report of the proceedings of the conspiracy trial.

10. William Newton Blair, *Gold in Korea* (Topeka, Kan.: H. M. Ives & Sons, 1957), 175.

11. Letter of Missionary Samuel A. Moffett, reporting the Conspiracy Case to the Presbyterian Board of Foreign Missions, dated Aug. 26, 1912, in the Presbyterian Library, New York.

12. Arthur Judson Brown, *Korean Conspiracy Case* (Northfield, Mass.: Northfield Press, 1912), 22–23.

13. *Annual Report, 1912–1913*, 200, and *Annual Report, 1913–1914*, 127.

14. *Kodae Minjok Munhwa Yŏnguso, Minjok, Kukkasa* [History of the Korean People and the Nation] (Seoul: Koryo Daehak Minjok Munhwa Yŏn'guso, 1914), 657.

15. Board of Foreign Missions, Presbyterian Church in the U.S.A., *Chōsen Mission, Annual Report* (Philadelphia: Presbyterian Foreign Mission Board, 1920), 193.

16. For the report of Underwood, see "First Account of Massacres and Burning of Villages," *Korean Situation*, 68–72.

17. Keiichiro Hara, ed., *Hara Takashi Nikki* [Diary of Takashi Hara], 9 vols. (Tokyo: Kangen-sha, 1950), 8:261.

18. Quoted in *Korean Situation*, 3–4.

19. Quoted ibid., 3.

20. *Hara Nikki*, 8:260.

21. *Annual Report, 1918–1921*, 204.

22. *Korean Situation*, 9–10.

23. Ibid., 10–12.

24. Government-General of Chōsen, *Outline of Administrative Reforms in Chōsen* (Seoul: Seoul Press, 1920), 19.

25. *Address of Dr. Rentaro Mizuno* (N.p., 1921), Korean file, Missionary Research Library, Union Theological Seminary, New York.

26. These figures are based on *Chōsen Sōtoku-fu Tokei Nenpo, 1924* [*Annual Statistical Report of Chōsen Government-General, 1924*] (Keijō: Chōsen Sōtoku-fu, 1924), 7:86–87.

27. Harry A. Rhodes, *History of the Korean Mission Presbyterian Church, 1884–1934* (Seoul: Chōsen Mission Presbyterian Church U.S.A., 1934), 503.

28. L. T. Newland, "Is the Church Meeting Korea's Economic Problems?" *The Korean Mission Field* 25, no. 4 (April 1929): 69.

29. The following figures show the growth of shrines within the ten years from 1923 to 1933. These figures are based on *Chōsen Sōtoku-fu Tokei Yoran, 1925* [Statistical Index of Government-General of Chōsen] (Keijō: Chōsen Sōtoku-fu, 1925), 195, and *Tokei Nenpo, 1934*, 294.

Year	Number of *jinja*	Number of *jinshi*
1923	40	77
1924	41	103
1925	42	108
1926	43	107
1927	43	129
1928	47	152
1929	49	177
1930	49	182
1931	51	186
1932	51	199
1933	51	215

30. *Annual Report, 1933–1934*, 86.

31. D. C. Holtom, *Modern Japan and Shintō Nationalism* (New York: Paragon Book Reprint, 1963), 98.

32. Adams told me this story in a meeting in New York in 1964.

33. Sacra Congregatio de Propaganda Fide, "Instructio," *Acta Apostolicae Sedis* (Romae: Typis Polyglottis Vaticanis, 1936), annua 28, series 2, 3, 408–419.

34. Board of Foreign Missions, Presbyterian Church in the U.S.A., *Chōsen Mission, Annual Report, 1937*, 27.

35. This statement was adopted in the mission meeting in February 1936, at Chinju. See "The Situation in Korea," *The Mission Chronicle* 33, no. 3 (March 1939): 15.

36. *Minutes and Reports of the Chōsen Mission of the Presbyterian Church in the U.S.A., 1936* (Philadelphia: Presbyterian Foreign Mission Board, 1936), 37.

37. *Shisei Sanjunen-shi* [History of Thirty Years' Administration] (Keijō: Chōsen Sōtoku-fu, 1940), 856. This account is based on an official Japanese government source. However, it is questionable whether a large number of Christian leaders actually attended the meeting to form such a federation. Korean and English Christian sources are silent on this matter.

38. Darley Downs, ed., *The Japan Christian Year Book, 1941* (Tokyo: Christian Literature Society, 1941), 89. The yearbook of 1941 is the last yearbook published before the end of the World War II.

39. "Church and Mission in Korea: Report of a Visit to Korea by Bishop James C. Barker and Dr. R. E. Diffendorger to the Board of Missions and Church Extension of the Methodist Church" (mimeo., 1941), 16, Methodist Archives, New York.

40. Ibid., 18.

41. Ibid., 14–15.

42. J. Manning Potts, ed., *Grace Sufficient: The Story of Helen Kim by Herself* (Nashville, Tenn.: Upper Room, 1964), 105.

CHAPTER 6

Cradle of the Covenant
Ahn Changho and the Christian Roots of the Korean Constitution

Jacqueline Pak

The Korean quest for independence from Japanese colonial oppression between 1910 and 1945 occurred simultaneously
with a momentous Christian movement spreading throughout East Asia, a
movement that was unprecedented in the twentieth century.[1] The independence movement coalesced around Christian enlightenment reforms
and sought to create a new type of democracy, especially as Christianity
was not necessarily presumed by the late Chosŏn monarchy to be a menac-
ing tool of Western imperialism. Enabled by a historically serendipitous
partnership between Korean nationalism and Christianity against the threats
of foreign colonialism and loss of sovereignty, the rise of democracy and
Christianity profoundly transformed the political and spiritual landscape of
modern Korea.

Along with the emergence of republican constitutionalism during the
twilight years of the Chosŏn dynasty, the period also saw the rapid dissem-
ination of the vernacular-language Bible, also a rare phenomenon in East
Asia. Inculcating the values of equality, justice, and courage unto death as
well as proselytizing a new vision of society, the Christian church became
a site of political praxis, or do-it-yourself democracy, for Koreans. The
church offered a public forum for speech and discourse, and instructed its
congregation to live by both the rules of the promised covenant that governed individual and collective behavior and the procedures and mechanisms of self-government. Inspired by Christian learning-by-doing lessons,
this new sort of democracy became a compelling means and end for the
Korean nationalist struggle. For early Christian Koreans, the church was
far more than a consecrated temple or holy altar of worship; the church
instead became a sacred domain of Christ's body of togetherness in spirit
and flesh that empowered and nourished Korean nationalist activism. As a

sanctuary of spiritual refuge and protection immune from colonial repression, the church served as the public sphere of political action and protest, where the Korean independence struggle was launched and where early republican stirrings were translated into a new constitutional self-government.

An inquiry into the nationalist and Christian history of colonial Korea would explore how and why the Korean "nationalist-Christian (or Christian-nationalist) movement" evolved as an ambitious and expansive transnational project, strategy, and enterprise. As the Korean nationalist movement converged with the enlightenment and democracy movement, it was morally and spiritually undergirded by both domestic and foreign support and by the growth of Christianity on the peninsula. Given the formative and transformative interconnectedness between the Korean nationalist and Christian movements, it is inevitable that the intellectual inquiry and theoretical methodologies of the history of Korean nationalism and Korean Christianity are shared, or even analogized and parallelized. Indeed, the border-crossing and interdisciplinary problematiques and issues, as much as the hotly debated controversies, continue to cohabit and overlap within the historical and ethical narratives of Korean nationalism and Christianity.

The tumultuous drama of modern Korean history encompasses tension, irony, and ambiguities underlying the historical perspectives concerning Korean nationalism, Christianity, and democracy. The painful legacy of colonialism, the Korean War, political division, and successive military dictatorships is mirrored in the twists and turns of interpretations of the Korean colonial period, including the nationalist struggle and the role and fate of the Christian leadership and movement. In fact, historical facts remain hidden or distorted by colonial and post-colonial dictatorial repression, including government censorship against freedom of speech and political assembly, with both divided and diasporic Korea. In the overarching Cold War environment following the Korean War, the historical reality of the independence quest also became a victim of ideological and political division and conflict, which often led to misjudgments and misrepresentations as much as blind lacunae and silenced voices in both Korea and the West.

Increasingly, the Orientalism of the West has been charged with fundamental flaws from which the histories and identities of the former colonized countries of the East have been represented with racialist bias and perception. The case of colonial Korea, including the history of Korean nationalism and nationalist resistance, also suffered for generations from distortions fomented in Japan and the West. The fact of the matter was that Japan was, more often than not, unapologetic and unyielding, but possessed an exceptional economic and intellectual influence in the West. With the special postwar security arrangement with the American superpower, Japan continued to sacrifice historical truths and justice, as the United States primarily sought to contain communism in Asia and the world during the Cold War era.[2] From the standpoint of what post-colonial Korean historians consider an unfortunate colonial historical perspective (*singminsagwan*) on the part of Japan and the West during and after that era, the sheer scale and audacity of the Korean independence movement were frequently denied, distorted, and dismissed. Such often led to a gross underestimation, including abuse and contempt, of the evidential facts as well as of the inner logic and coherence of the Korean nationalist leadership and movement.

Arguably the foremost leader of the Korean independence movement and a Christian pioneer, modernizer, and reformer, Ahn Changho (An Ch'angho; 1878–1938) largely defined and configured the nature and direction of the nationalist-Christian movement to achieve sovereign freedom and democracy. Even so, Ahn Changho long remained an elusive, if not mysterious and misunderstood, figure in modern Korean history. He was an enduring enigma, and the leading intellectuals, writers, and scholars of Korea and the West could not figure him out. In a sense, his genius as an "undercover" revolutionary—i.e., his adoption of a moderate reformist stance to camouflage and yet advance his ultimate revolutionary agenda of waging an independence war to reclaim his country—who eluded the Japanese police for decades also eluded them. Well known and yet unknown, Ahn Changho was a man of principled moral dignity and a labyrinthine strategic mind. With preeminent political, strategic, organizational, and moral-spiritual influence, Ahn Changho led an international revolutionary network of exile and underground activists who evaded Japanese suppression from the 1900s to the 1930s and engaged in military operations and planning in Manchuria, Russia, China, and the United States. Committed to the patriotic cause of freedom for his people and his country, Ahn did not fully reveal his revolutionary aims or intentions even to those who were close to him. With multilayered and multidimensional strategic vision and planning, he eschewed neither violent tactics nor progressive socialist ideologies to champion his lifelong goal of independence. To reveal Ahn Changho's true identity as a Christian nationalist personality, therefore, is to discover a vital clue to unlocking the puzzling mystery surrounding both the Korean independence movement and the evolution of the Christian leadership.

Among Ahn Changho's documents, the most astonishing, if not providential, discovery is a series of his own constitutional drafts of the nationalist revolutionary organizations. Although previously unknown as the draftee of the earliest republican constitutions, Ahn Changho was an avid constitutionalist who trusted in God's historical guidance and participation in the search for justice and freedom. As the embryonic basis of the Constitution of the Korean Provisional Government, Ahn's original constitutions are the "founding documents" of the Republic of Korea. The elaborately constructed constitutions, with a keen sense of moral and aesthetic balance, serve as a window into his designing mind. Demonstrating a combination of creative intuition and conscious structuring, the constitutions reveal Ahn's aspiration to arrive at a unity of effect and a balanced order as revolutionary testimonials to achieve sovereign democracy. For Ahn, the constitutions were more than the political instruments of subversive anticolonial self-government; instead, he aspired for them to serve an epic moral and spiritual purpose as a heroic code of honor and dignity for his compatriots in their quest to build a new republic.

As a labor of hope, faith, and love, Ahn's constitutions for the revolutionary organizations demonstrate his creativity and imagination as well as the evolving and complex character of his constitutional philosophy and institutional experiments. Ahn Changho unfailingly wrote constitutions for his associations—including the Kongnip hyŏphoe (United Korean Association, 1905) in the United States; the Sinminhoe (New People Society, 1907) in Korea; the Taehan kungminhoe (Korean National Association, 1912) in Manchuria, Russia, and the United States; and the Hŭngsadan (Young Korean Academy, 1913) in the United States and subsequently in China and Korea—as well as for the Provisional Government of the Republic of Korea (1919), the National Representatives Congress (1923), and the Korean Independence Party (1929) in China, among others. A textual and philological analysis of Ahn's drafts reveals his pragmatic judgment as well as his farsighted intellectual-institutional ideals animated by the Christian model of constitutional self-government as a sacred covenant. The constitutions become patriotic testimonies to his future-oriented Christian conception of democracy and revolution and authenticate his theory and practice of self-government and institution-building as well as an ethics of civic rights and responsibilities. As the emblematic nucleus of his lifetime travail, the revolutionary oeuvre of Christian nationalist Ahn Changho indeed inaugurated the "democratic revolution," or constitutional birth, of modern Korea.[3]

If the dramatic success of Christianity in Korea is a historical fait accompli, the intimate relationship between Christianity and democracy in early modern Korea has not yet been adequately examined. In earlier scholarship, the Christian impetus, contribution, and inspiration during the formative phase of Korean democracy were not understood as necessarily premised upon the indigenous merger of the Korean independence movement and Protestant Christian enlightenment reforms. Also, in judging the Christian influence on early Korean nationalism and democracy, earlier scholarship has not accorded the historical significance of such missionary proselytizing techniques as the Nevius Method, which promoted self-government and other self-building measures, the credit it deserves. The Nevius Method was often merely seen as a successful mode of initial proselytization, but the broader implications of its democratic promise and aptitude, as well as its rich rapport and affinity with budding Korean democracy, had not been previously examined. The impact of the Presbyterian church and its relationship to the Korean nationalist struggle and the progress of a constitutional democracy have also not been sufficiently appraised, beyond the life stories and charity of early missionary and nationalist leaders.

With the new discoveries and insights gleaned from the documents and archival materials in the Ahn Changho Collection, I will here explore, first, the background to and debates concerning the "Ahn Changho Controversy" as it relates to the historical interpretations of Christianity, nationalism, and democracy; second, the revolutionary life of Ahn Changho as a Christian nationalist leader and pioneering constitutional democrat; and third, the historical circumstances that led to the creation of the founding document of the new Korean republic and the relationship between constitutional nationalism and Christian democracy, including the sources of Christian inspiration and the loci of influences, i.e., the Presbyterian church government and constitution. Here, the life events and social milieu of Ahn Changho as a Christian will be illumined to observe how Christianity inspired his nationalist career and leadership, including his moral-spiritual vision and his political aspirations. It will also investigate how Ahn's revolutionary ideals and career fused with Christianity and how his revolutionism was transfigured by his faith in the Christian church as a self-governing, constitutional democracy.

The Ahn Changho Controversy

Since Korea's liberation from Japanese colonialism in 1945, Ahn Changho has been a critical subject of literary and scholarly attention among colonial and post-colonial Korean intellectuals in Korea and the West. Caught at the nexus of modern Korean history and historiography, Ahn Changho was misinterpreted or misjudged as a "gradualist-pacifist" by Yi Kwangsu, Chu Yohan, Chong-sik Lee, and Arthur Gardner from 1945 to the 1970s;[4] as a "cultural nationalist" by Michael Robinson in the 1980s;[5] and as a "self-reconstruction nationalist" by Kenneth Wells in the 1990s, among others.[6] As biographers, Yi Kwangsu and Chu Yohan presented Ahn as a "gradualist-pacifist" and set the tone for subsequent interpretations of Ahn's life and thought. If their works were marked by inconsistencies and paradoxes, Yi and Chu's collaborations further clouded and complicated our understanding of Ahn and the Korean liberation struggle.

With the advent of civil democracy in Korea and the growth of global consciousness amid the end of the Cold War and the fall of communism, the "grand narrative" and epic of the Korean independence struggle began to be more systematically mined in the 1990s with newly discovered sources of leading revolutionaries, many of whom were Protestant Christians. In the past decade, one of the most spirited controversies in the international arena of Korean Studies has been the Ahn Changho Controversy, which engaged debates on the historiographical interpretation and reinterpretation of Ahn Changho. Given Ahn Changho's role and significance as the chief architect and strategist of the Korean independence movement, this was a controversy not only about Ahn Changho as a man and leader, including his patriotic vision, philosophy, and methodology, but also about getting at the truth of the shape and course of the Korean anticolonial struggle as a whole. At the heart of the controversy were the empirical and theoretical bases of historiography of the Korean nationalist leadership and movement and the possible paradigm-altering implications of new documentary findings that challenged us to rethink and reappraise the political and ideological dialectics of modern Korean history.

The Ahn Changho Controversy emerged, in part, from dramatic discoveries from the Dosan Ahn Changho Collection, which comprises his private papers, including diaries, speeches, letters, documents, books, photographs, and artifacts. (Dosan, meaning "Island-Mountain," is Ahn Changho's pen name.) Perhaps the most significant and extensive collection of the papers of the Korean nationalists, the Ahn Changho Collection of documents, sheds new light on the behind-the-scenes workings of the independence struggle as well as on the substance and scope of Ahn's revolutionary leadership as a diasporic transnational quest to attain national liberation.

For example, a new breakthrough in the interpretation of the Korean nationalist movement was a discovery that the Christian nationalist leadership of Ahn Changho merged successfully the "patriotic enlightenment" and "righteous army" movements (or what was often construed as the divisive "right" and "left" or the "cultural-educational" and "military-political" elements) in the course of anticolonial activism from the early twentieth century onward. The conventional wisdom, which is still widespread, upholds a rather crude and simplistic right/left divide within the independence movement, myopically viewing the epic nationalist phenomenon from the narrow and partial lens of the post–Korean War binary division. In this sense, the historiographical debates concerning the controversy brought to light a possible new interpretation of the much more fluid and dynamic nature of the underlying ideological and political patterns within the Korean independence movement as a whole. The nationalist quest also initiated the process of the Korean global diaspora. Despite its peaks and valleys, the diasporic liberation struggle sustained its momentum and lasted for decades with its share of martyrs, heroes, and heroines, as well as villains, collaborators, and opportunists.

Against Christian nationalist activism, the main critique and challenge came from the Communist movement of the 1920s. The Communists, however, being decades younger than the mainstream Christian nationalists as a politicized group, were far less cohesive and organized. They therefore increasingly adopted propaganda and underground organizations as their main political tools to redirect the leadership, discourse, and momentum of the liberation movement. In this more competitive discursive atmosphere, some Korean nationalist revolutionaries came to espouse the idealistic and anti-imperialistic dimensions of international communism. During this time and decades thereafter, Ahn persevered with much of his efforts toward political reconciliation of nationalists, Communists, and followers of other ideologies. The Christian nationalists continued to dominate the political terrain of the Korean anticolonial movement over the divided Communists, whose particular vulnerability and existential irony as nationalists derived from the fact of their being under the foreign control of the Comintern.[7] Contrary to the received wisdom, Ahn and other Christian nationalists were not always in divisive conflict or competition with the early Korean Communists in terms of revolutionary methods, strategies, and ideologies. Ahn sought to creatively embrace the revolutionary and democratic impulses and dynamics inherent in the independence struggle and eventually came to unify nationalists, Communists, and anarchists under his own indigenous, syncretic leadership umbrella. Among his diverse revolutionary colleagues and supporters were also Christians, Buddhists, and Confucians, as well as Taejonggyo followers who worshiped the mythical progenitor of Korea, Tan'gun.

Despite a visionary moral-spiritual leadership and formidable international organization with military and political objectives, the mainstream nationalist-Christian independence movement continued to face great obstacles and oppression both at home and abroad. With the arrest of Ahn Changho in 1932 and his death in 1938 from prison torture, the Korean nationalist movement could not triumph over the war-driven Japanese colonial regime, or the so-called East Asian holocaust. The inhumane cruelties of Japan spread far beyond colonial Korea, to include the Nanjing massacre in China, comfort women, and medical experiments on colonial subjects.[8] Prior to the liberation of Korea in 1945, Japan joined with Hitler's Germany and Fascist Italy in waging war against the Allied forces. It was also after 1938 that the younger disciples of Ahn Changho, including such famous and tragic literary figures as Yi Kwangsu, Chu Yohan, and others, subsequently came to be brutalized and compromised under the duress of the Japanese colonial police.[9]

In the post-Kwangju era of the 1980s, the leftist critique of Christian nationalists reemerged as an appropriated historiographical discourse with an ideological and political impetus. Following the Kwangju massacre in 1980, the political conscience of the time demanded that marginalized intellectuals take a more militant and activist (i.e., violent) stance against the brutal military dictatorship. This stance led to a subversive adoption by dissident intellectuals of a parallelizing colonial-nationalist discourse of oppression versus freedom. In this milieu of radicalized politics and discourse against illegitimate dictatorship, violence was frequently employed as the key criterion in writings ranging from the amateur-underground to semi-professional to academic historiography, with a pedantic and propagandistic tone marked by aggressive revisionism. At times, such an outpouring of self-styled vigilante revisionism was embraced to seek liberation from the old shackles of strident government-sanctioned historiography or narrow nationalist hagiography. Such a revisionist discourse, however, aimed to achieve a political correctness of ideological purity, or self-righteous "historical rectification," in search of new "historical correctness." And it often inadvertently led to intellectual and ideological excesses that, unintentionally and unfortunately, reduced or victimized historical past, truth, and identity in its political zeal for utility and action and substitute means of self-flagellation.[10] The new findings of the Ahn Changho Controversy critically interrogated such revisionist writings to address the politico-ideological excesses and internal contradictions of such historical correctness or the ideological rightness of the violence-scarred decade of the 1980s. Emblematically, the "violent" desire for democracy, but not necessarily the violent means or logic, in the end would topple the authoritarian government in that tumultuous decade, as Korea entered another phase of the "democratic revolution." The seeds of Korean democracy and democratic revolution were, of course, sown decades ago in the independence struggle.

In this vein, the Ahn Changho Controversy propelled the historical debates to new heights to move beyond the formulaic ideologico-political binaries, or dichotomies of historical forces, as the older dualisms maintained by the conventional conceptions of the Korean War, the division of the peninsula, and the Cold War continue to be reassessed. Still, broader debates crucially remain to challenge the historical problematiques of received wisdom concerning the nationalist-Christian movement versus the Communist movement of the colonial period, because a facile and widespread assumption of an a priori binary division of the nationalist movement prior to the division of an a posteriori Korean War must be reimagined, including the idées fixes of right versus left, Christianity versus communism, gradualism versus radicalism, pacifism versus militarism, and patriotism versus collaborationism, among others.

One of the highlights of the Ahn Changho Controversy included piquant debates on "cultural nationalism" as an analytical category. Cultural nationalism applied to the Korean colonial context came to mean passive collaborationist attitudes and lack of politico-military will on the part of the Korean nationalist response, especially with regard to Christian nationalist leaders. The conceptual weakness of cultural nationalism was that it depicted Korean nationalism (including the Christian nationalism of Ahn Changho) through the prism of writing by Christian patriot-turned-collaborator Yi Kwangsu and obfuscated or confused patriots with collaborators and vice versa. In this connection, the controversy touched upon the highly complex and potentially explosive issues of patriotism versus collaboration. The controversy ultimately problematized the previously ideologized binaries and essentialisms of Communist-left-patriot-militarist-righteous army versus Christian-right-collaborationist-cultural nationalist-patriotic enlightenment. As by-products of historical circumstances and interpretations, such ideological bifurcation reflected the intellectual limits and conceptual constraints of the reductive post hoc matrix of the bipolar Cold War alignments.[11]

Was Ahn Changho, then, a "gradualist-pacifist," "cultural nationalist," or "revolutionary-democrat"? It is beyond the scope of this chapter to delve into substantive details of documentary evidence or theoretical points of controversy. For instance, it can be mentioned only briefly that the most contentious debate concerns Ahn's "revolutionary militarism," and the new findings of the research point to a rich array of sources that testifies to decades of Ahn's prima facie commitment and the transnational scope of his military and paramilitary engagements, activities, and strategic leadership. Most likely, the debates and discourses of the Ahn Changho controversy concerning the interpretations of the Korean nationalist and Christian leadership and movement will resonate for years to come. The Ahn Changho Controversy can be summarized as follows: (1) the conventional analysis of Christian nationalism as "gradualist pacifist" versus a new perspective of it as "revolutionary militarist"; (2) the old view of Christian nationalism as consisting of the tripartite division of "diplomatism, militarism, and gradualism" versus a new view of it as a unique alignment of "revolutionism and democratism" or a rare indigenous synthesis of "revolutionary democratism"; (3) the post-Kwangju revisionist critique of mainstream Christian nationalism as "cultural nationalism" or passive collaborationism versus its neorevisionism as revolutionary-democratic nationalism or patriotic political nationalism; (4) the problems and issues of patriotism versus collaborationism among Christian nationalist leaders, personalities, ideologies, and strategies during the colonial period and the complicated legacy thereafter, including the Christian collaborationist apologetics of "self-reconstruction nationalism"; and (5) the origins of Korean democracy, including the surviving documents, authorship, and circumstances surrounding the drafting of the first Korean republican constitution.[12]

A Christian Leader

Perhaps the political, military, philosophical, and spiritual persona of Ahn Changho as a Christian nationalist leader can be delineated only through a painstaking process of research into his voluminous documents and sources. In fact, the myriad pieces of the puzzle of Korea's transnational revolutionary enterprise can be linked and layered like an epic tapestry from the turn of the century to the liberation. As records of the endeavors of his heart and soul, the documents bring to light the decades of his leadership and involvement in evolving military strategy and the formation of the Korean Independence Army. They also demonstrate the nationalist commitment to political transformation and the sometimes cultural-educational camouflage revolutionary leaders adopted to survive harsh repression in Korea and abroad. In his private papers, Ahn Changho emerges as an arch-patriot, a pioneering constitutional democrat, modernizer, institution-builder, and military strategist. Blessed with prodigious intellectual, oratorical, and political gifts and resolute will, Ahn was a profoundly spiritual man who provided the requisite ethico-spiritual and organizational leadership for the Korean nationalist movement.

The most talented visionary and expansive institution-builder of his time, Ahn was largely responsible for the global and revolutionary character of the Korean nationalist movement as a radical exile struggle. He was also an eloquent orator, a systematizer of nationalist ideology and methodology, a political leader who initially conceived and established the Korean Provisional Government, and an underground and exile revolutionary, as well as a grass-roots organizer, reformist educator, writer, publisher of leading journals, and composer of patriotic lyrics and songs, among other things.[13]

A LIFE: ENCOUNTERS
The life of Ahn Changho, a pioneering Korean democrat, can be viewed as a series of critical moments of encounter, or points of contact, with Christianity, especially the Presbyterian church. It was through such

encounters that his Christian faith grew, nourishing his enlightenment vision and his democratic praxis. Ten such encounters with Christianity were particularly compelling.

1. Ahn Changho was born in 1878 in P'yŏngyang. American Presbyterian missionary Samuel Moffett arrived in P'yŏngyang in 1893, before the Sino-Japanese War (1894–1895). While young Ahn did not meet Moffett during this time, the American missionary's newly founded Presbyterian church in P'yŏngyang undoubtedly awakened Ahn's interest in the world beyond his village, particularly after he witnessed the Sino-Japanese War that tore apart his city. Ahn later came to know Moffett.

2. The Underwood School was founded by Horace G. Underwood, an American Presbyterian missionary, in 1886. Ahn Changho became a student and later teacher at the Underwood School. He was baptized as a Presbyterian Christian.[14]

3. The Nevius Method (i.e., self-support, self-government, and self-propagation) was introduced to Korea in 1890. Ahn Changho learned and participated in the implementation of the Nevius Method by attending a Korean Presbyterian church. The experience profoundly changed the way he viewed individual and collective destinies and endeavors, as well as private and public spheres, imbuing them all with a sense of common purpose and community. Ahn was initially exposed to the idea of democracy and politics by the unique practice of the Nevius Method in the formative phase of Korean Protestant Christianity.[15]

4. The Independence Club was founded by Seo Jaepil (Sŏ Chaep'il or Philip Jaisohn), a Korean Presbyterian leader, in 1896. Ahn Changho became a young activist and a branch leader of the Independence Club in P'yŏngyang.[16]

5. In 1902, Ahn Changho went to the United States in the hopes of becoming a minister and educator. He studied theology, attending evening classes in California. He also established a Korean immigrant church in San Francisco. Even so, he later chose an activist path to aid and organize his compatriots.

6. Ahn returned to P'yŏngyang during the Great Revival of 1907. He went to Seoul, where he created the New People's Association, Sinminhoe, a secret revolutionary organization, with his Christian colleagues.

7. In the Case of the 105, the Japanese targeted the patriotic Christian Sinminhoe members after Japan annexed Korea in 1910. Immense patriotic courage was shown by Korean Christians, particularly the Presbyterians from the northwestern provinces, whom the Japanese considered the most influential and ardent nationalists.[17]

8. The March First Movement of 1919 was a nationwide uprising

against Japanese colonial rule. This event was initiated and planned largely by Ch'ŏndogyo (Religion of the Heavenly Way) and Christian leaders, especially Presbyterian leaders such as Yi Sŭnghun, who had abandoned his life as a wealthy merchant to become an enlightenment educator, inspired by the patriotic example of Ahn Changho.

9. In Shanghai, Ahn Changho unified the Provisional Government of the Republic of Korea and drafted the Constitution of the Republic of Korea in 1919. He was inspired by the constitutional self-government of the Presbyterian church.

10. In 1928 he founded the Korean Independence Party. Later he originated the Theory of Three Equalities (of economy, politics, and education). In 1932 he was arrested in China and extradited to Korea, where he was imprisoned.

11. Ahn Changho passed away at the age of fifty-nine in the spring of 1938 in Seoul from illnesses sustained from prolonged torture by the Japanese police. He had been released from prison on the previous Christmas Eve but remained under house arrest. He persisted with his independence struggles underground and stated at one time to the Japanese police interrogator, "I ate for independence, I slept for independence. This will not cease until I die."[18]

A WAY: THE NEVIUS METHOD

Introduced nearly a decade before the Tonghak Uprising of 1894 and the Independence Club of 1896, the Nevius principles of self-help, self-propagation, and self-government had profound and lasting effects on the formation and growth of Korean democracy. By assimilating and incorporating the Nevius Method, early Christian, especially Presbyterian, churches became the primordial loci of self-governing praxis in late Chosŏn Korea.

The foreign missionaries endeavored to establish native churches that would naturally express the religious experience of Korean Christians. This policy was based upon the Nevius Method, named after Dr. John Nevius of the China mission field, who originally elaborated it in a series of articles appearing in the 1883 issues of the *Chinese Recorder*. The method was neither popular nor successful in China but gained practically universal acceptance among the Korean missionaries after Dr. Nevius visited Seoul in 1890.[19] The Nevius Method may be summarized as follows:

1. Personal evangelism and wide itineration by the missionaries
2. The Bible central in every part of the work
3. Self-propagation
4. Self-government: every group under its chosen unpaid leaders;

circuit under their own paid helpers, who will later yield to
pastors; circuit meetings training the people for later district,
provincial, and national leadership

5. Self-support
6. Systematic Bible study for every believer under his group leader
   and circuit helper and for every leader and helper in the Bible
   classes
7. Strict discipline enforced by Bible penalties
8. Cooperation and union with other bodies, or at least territorial
   division
9. Noninterference in lawsuits or any such matters
10. General helpfulness where possible in the economic life problems
    of the people[20]

For Ahn Changho, the Christian church became the formative source
of inspiration to imbibe and absorb democratic ideals and procedures.
Through his participation in church activities of self-propagation and self-
support, Ahn Changho came to be exposed to wholly different organizing
principles of community within the evangelical Korean church. He came to
grasp the working dynamics of voluntary self-initiative and self-government
among Korean Christians. He also came to understand the organizational
essence and nature of self-government by participating in the governing
procedures and mechanisms within the public debates and discourses of
the Korean Christian church.

In previous scholarship, the democracy-building practice inherent in
the Nevius Method has not been much recognized for its formative significance and contribution to the democratic development in modern Korean
history. Through an examination of Ahn's early life, however, it becomes
apparent that the Nevius Method was of critical importance to Ahn Changho's emergence as a pioneering constitutional democrat. The Nevius
Method quintessentially embodied the self-defining path of Ahn, as he
came to translate and reconstitute the theory and praxis of Presbyterian
self-government into the Korean independence movement as a constitutional democracy movement. In fact, Ahn's life narrative as a nascent Christian and democrat begins with his coming of age as a baptized Presbyterian
educated at the Underwood School, being tutored English by Horace
Underwood and learning self-help and self-government as part of the curriculum.[21] Departing from the prevailing social norm and hierarchy of late
Chosŏn Korea, Ahn Changho was initiated into the Presbyterian church's
practice of self-government. And he would never forget the experience,
which led to his spiritual and political awakening as a republican revolutionary with patriotic ambitions.

A MEETING: UNDERWOOD SCHOOL

Ahn arrived in Seoul in 1895; his meager funds did not last him long. He stayed at an inn near the South Gate and toured the city. When he began to ponder his next step, he ran into a foreigner who invited him to study at his school with an offer of food and residence in Chŏngdong. The foreigner was the Reverend F. S. Miller, who was the principal of Kuse Haktang (Save the World School), a school operated by the American Presbyterian Mission in Korea. Though eager to receive "new learning" (*sin hangmun*), Ahn was at first hesitant: "How can a Korean who wishes to follow the *dao* of Confucius and Mencius study at a barbarian school?" Eventually, he enrolled at this school, informally known as the Underwood School (Wŏndu'u hakkyo) after its energetic founder, Horace G. Underwood (1851–1916).[22]

An American Presbyterian missionary, Underwood arrived in Seoul in April 1885, when the edict of 1866 that proscribed the propagation of Christianity was still in effect, and the Chosŏn government had not yet formally allowed any missionary to come into the country. Dr. Horace Allen (1858–1932), the first American Christian to arrive in Korea, was a Protestant physician-missionary who had arrived at Chemulpo on September 20, 1884. From Delaware, Ohio, Allen had earned his medical degree at Miami Medical College in Ohio and had gone to Beijing soon after graduation in 1883. Allen heard of the need for Western medical care from personnel in the various legations in Korea and received permission from the Presbyterian board to go to Korea. Thus, Allen entered Korea *not* as a missionary but as a physician to the U.S. legation. During this time of great political upheaval and turmoil, Allen fortuitously gained a critical opportunity to advance the Protestant cause in Korea as a doctor after successfully treating Min Yong'ik, a nephew of King Kojong, wounded in the Kapsin coup of 1884. The palace's favor strengthened Allen's position to gain a firmer foothold in Korea; he was given permission to open a clinic.[23]

Underwood, an English immigrant to America, received master's degrees in 1884 from the Dutch Reformed Theological Seminary and New York University. He went to Korea as a "young, idealistic, reform-minded and educated liberal" filled with the ideas of the various reform movements sweeping both the United States and England at the time.[24] He was not allowed to either preach or baptize, however, and could only informally engage in missionary work behind closed doors for his first five years. After Allen's hospital met with the Korean government's approval and proved successful, Underwood sought to establish an orphanage-school. He believed that Koreans would allow schools that charged no tuition and gave students food and clothing. In 1887, Underwood's orphanage and school came into being, it soon became full, and he had to turn down applications for admission. Underwood hoped to initiate a school for boys at which he could openly proselytize Christianity. By attaching a school to the orphanage, he entertained future hopes for a Christian college and a theological seminary. This was the beginning of what eventually became Yonsei University.

Developing a special bond with the missionaries, Ahn Changho began to learn English from Underwood and attended normal and superior classes while serving as a teaching assistant. The Underwood School was "something halfway between an old-fashioned and modern school" with about seventy students on two acres of land in Chŏngdong.[25] Instruction was in the Korean and Chinese translations of the Bible, Christian tracts, and science books in Chinese that replaced the canon of Confucian classics. With two or three primers, a classic on good manners, and a treatise on letter writing, the native Korean script was emphasized over literary Chinese composition in a curriculum that also included arithmetic, philosophy, music, geography, scripture, and catechism. The Nevius Method of self-help and self-support was vigorously emphasized, with the students required to pay all or a part of their school expenses through industrial or teaching work.[26]

As a missionary, Underwood was also known for his boldness in taking chances to convert and baptize Koreans, activities that at times caused great consternation among American diplomats and other missionaries. Close association with Underwood, nicknamed the "Great Fireball" (*pul tŏngŏri*) as an indefatigable and committed man of faith, left a strong impression on Ahn Changho.[27] Ahn was observed urging students to behave collectively in a more edifying manner, "full of P'yŏngyang zeal," at the Underwood School.[28]

AN EVENT: THE CONVERSION

At the Underwood School, Ahn Changho befriended Song Sunmyŏng, who was a few years older. Ahn was converted as a Presbyterian Christian by Song, one of the early Korean Christians proselytized by Underwood. Though skeptical and resistant at first to the idea of a new religion, Ahn became persuaded by the sincerity and truth of Song's words as a message of faith, love, and hope. Initially, Song discussed the commonality of Confucianism and Christianity by suggesting that Christianity was also the Way (*dao*) and the moral teachings of Heaven (*tian*). It was also, he explained, a universal religion without national or ethnic boundaries and a spiritual life of salvation, redemption, and eternity. Affirming that Christianity involves a covenant of love between man and God, Song spoke of human humility toward the almighty God and authentic inner freedom that can only be achieved by believing in Jesus Christ. As Song challenged and engaged

Ahn intellectually and spiritually, Ahn not only began to reflect deeply on the possible superiority of Christianity over Confucianism but also started to read the Bible.

After almost ten days of evening debates with Song, Ahn Changho embarked on a new spiritual journey toward Christianity. Becoming Christian, Ahn Changho related that "the idea of love in Christianity is akin to the philosophy of *ren* in Confucianism. Through the prayers derived from human humility, it is true that inner peace can be found within the embrace of the almighty God. This may be the nature of God's salvation, lacking in Confucianism."[29]

By accepting the Christian idea of God's immanence and divine transcendence, Ahn spiritually came to "meet that which is greater than himself, greater than his heart, and yet within his heart."[30] Song later became a senior elder at the Saemunan kyohoe, the first Korean Presbyterian church, founded by Underwood.

AN IDEAL: THE PROPHET

The inculcation of the ideal and praxis of constitutional democracy in transitional Korea entailed the transvaluation of values, rather than a mere transfer, importation, or appropriation of a foreign body or system of universal knowledge.[31] The process of transvaluation of values often created turmoil for Koreans, who charted an unknown path toward constitutional democracy from absolutist monarchy while facing impending threats from foreign nations. If moral and spiritual aspirations shaped the desire for a more egalitarian democracy from a class-based autocracy, Confucian values also insisted on building moral character and strength through self-cultivation in order to become responsible civic subjects—in accordance with the transforming potential of self.[32]

But what were to be reassessed and reimagined in terms of Confucian sociopolitical ideology and statecraft ideals that emphasized the precepts of humanity, social order, righteous government, and sound kingship? Did Confucian-Mencian humanism and reformism offer enough about equality, freedom, the rule of law, or administrative and institutional know-how?[33] What about virtues and duties as subjects vis-à-vis fundamental human rights as citizens?

For Ahn Changho, caught as he was in the sociopolitical tumult of late Chosŏn Korea, the event of Christian conversion signified a dramatic crossroads engaging the past and the future of his inner self. Becoming a Christian, Ahn Changho no longer desired only to emulate the sages of the golden past but to participate in God's prophetic plan for the future to build a new community of Koreans. Toward this end, not only was Ahn critical of the Neo-Confucian ethos and practices of the Chosŏn dynasty, he was no longer content with the idea of becoming a noble man (*junzi*) or sage (*shengren*) through self-cultivation and moral sincerity.[34] Ahn Changho yearned to be in faithful communion with a God who showers love on humankind and directly intervenes in history through the prophets, who has a "personal relation, engages in dialogue, and even 'wrestles'" with God, being responsible for "God's people specially called to fulfill the Covenant."[35] As "surely the Lord does nothing without revealing his plan to his servants, the prophets" (Amos 3:7), for God revealed himself to Moses as the God of Israel and the Fathers; the God of Abraham, Isaac, and Jacob (Matthew 15:31, Mark 12:26); and the God and Father of Jesus Christ (Romans 15:6, Corinthians 1:3).

In the Old Testament, God's divine design for man through the relationship of the prophets and the holy people of Israel is attested. For instance, God's experiential plan and purpose for the future salvation can be read from the given name of Abraham, the "father of many nations" (Genesis 17:4–10), with the implied meaning of "future" and divinely elected and covenantal Israel. In the New Testament, the miraculous birth, life, death, and resurrection of the ultimate prophet, Jesus Christ, are historically testified by his disciples, who had a personal revelation of God.

Jesus Christ is not only the consummate figure foreshadowed and promised by the earlier prophets as the Son of God but also the embodiment of love and sacrifice for human redemption and future salvation. In God's love, the love of brotherhood and charity toward others is also conceived in terms of grace and life that includes the Confucian notion of *ren*— of love as virtue and life. Thus, from the Neo-Confucian God of process and becoming to the direct I-Thou communion with and in Jesus Christ through his human affinity and form of flesh and blood, Ahn Changho came to embrace the Christian covenant of love (Nehemiah 9:32) between man and God and, above all, the God of love (1 John 4:16).[36]

Most central to the raison d'etre of the prophet is his intimate I-Thou association with God and engagement in God's purposive blueprint for the future. Thus, for the prophets who speak of the covenant between God and his people, an overriding concern is often "God's love for his people, his solicitude for them, his jealous demands, his anger, [and] his forgiveness of them."[37] As an aspiring reformer and patriotic spokesman, Ahn Changho could easily identify with the prophets, motivated by "the need to move people to action" with terrible urgency and intense and personal involvement with God and the fate of his people. Concerned with the moral state of the people, the prophet identifies with "the very life of a whole people" for he is existentially engaged in "what his words foreshadow." Accepting Jesus Christ as the prophet-ideal, Ahn Changho trusted in the future redemption and salvation of his people. His passionate sermons at a Korean church spoke of the "covenant of love and respect of individual freedom and rights."[38]

The Founding Documents

Following the creation of the Friendship Society in California, Ahn Changho founded the United Korean Association in 1905. Applying the principles of the American Federalist Constitution, Ahn wrote a pioneering democratic constitution for the association that prescribed a system of separation of powers and political checks and balances. He devised a two-tiered bicameral system of headquarters and local branches, a dual system of executive and legislative bodies of self-government that functioned as separate but equal powers. In the local branches, each of which had an executive and legislative system of its own, autonomy was stressed. A product of Ahn Changho's own inimitable interpretation and application of the Presbyterian church's self-government and constitution, the constitution was the earliest crystallization of Ahn's concept of constitutional democracy and practice of the rule of law.[39]

Returning to Korea in 1907, Ahn Changho founded a secret revolutionary organization, the New People's Association, with a self-governing constitution that reflected the transnational linkage of the republican revolutionary project of Korean-Americans and Koreans with a well-developed plan for the war of independence. Possibly influenced by the earlier Korean-American Sinminhoe of Hawai'i, established in 1903, the organization underscores Ahn's diasporic vision and revolutionary network of organizations. (The earlier view of the Sinminhoe was that it was mainly a homeland-initiated and homeland-centered organization.)[40]

In the years before the Japanese annexation of Korea in 1910, Ahn aspired to open regional branches of the Korean National Association as a constitutional self-governing organization in Russia, Manchuria, and China, and he continued his grassroots efforts to lead and strengthen the organization as a transnational enterprise in America. Following Ahn Changho's peripatetic organizational groundwork, the organization was solidified when he became chairman of the central assembly in 1912; it eventually had more than a hundred branches in Asia and the Americas.[41] Here, Ahn Changho laid the political foundation for diasporic Koreans and began to conceive the international framework for a government in exile. The Korean National Association already possessed the body and network of supranational structure and began to function as the central organ of the "provisional government." Thus it is not surprising that Ahn Changho would later head the Korean Provisional Government in Shanghai.

In 1913, Ahn Changho established a revolutionary leadership-training society, the Young Korean Academy, in California. From the draft of the Constitution of the Young Korean Academy (forty-five notebook pages written in pencil from 1913), one can observe his passionate commitment toward the democratic process of self-government, such as elections, the separation of powers, and the transfer of office by limited terms. With such a constitutional framework, Ahn Changho attempted to ensure the viability and longevity of the academy, which he hoped would be the role model of democracy for Koreans. Ahn Changho's emphatic insistence on democracy for Koreans derived from his belief that the very act of self-governing constituted an essential part of subversive anticolonial revolution. Such a constitution with a sophisticated grasp of democratic mechanisms prefigured that Ahn Changho would author the first Constitution of the Provisional Government of the Republic of Korea.

THE MASTER PLAN OF INDEPENDENCE AND DEMOCRACY

Among his papers, Ahn Changho's handwritten Master Plan for Independence and Democracy (my nomenclature) is an arresting document that addresses the most contentious element of the Ahn Changho Controversy, that is, his "revolutionary militarism." Most likely prepared before the outbreak of World War I in 1914, it is assumed that Ahn wrote the Master Plan as he conceived the Young Korean Academy and the leadership of the Korean National Association in America. It is, however, also possible that Ahn wrote it several years before then, as some of his revolutionary ideas reflect the independence scheme of the New People's Association created in 1907.

In the Master Plan, Ahn charted the entire course of the independence movement with comprehensive knowledge and systematic planning. A private and concrete articulation of a program of action for the nationalist movement, the outline manifests the totality of Ahn's revolutionary strategy. It is also a detailed diagrammatic chart that describes the necessary virtues, personnel, skills, means, and resources to achieve his ultimate aims—independence and democracy. Most of all, it reveals his future-oriented Christian faith and vision of sovereign democracy.

Underlying the Master Plan, in which Ahn envisioned a well-integrated stage-by-stage development, are his "philosophy of strength" by which to build the "moral, intellectual, and economic strength" of Koreans and his revolutionary conviction that national liberation could be achieved only by military means. The plan consists of five major stages and thirteen substages that progressively evolve toward his final goal, an all-out independence war to restore national sovereignty. The Master Plan is as much a mobilization road map for the independence war as a prophetic blueprint to create a new democratic nation. In fact, a striking feature of the Master

Plan is how Ahn entwined his dual aims of seemingly paradoxical democracy building and war preparation within a single, overarching structure.[42]

Prepared when Ahn Changho was thirty-six years old, the Master Plan can be also read as a synopsis of the philosophical currents of his time and place. For example, we can notice the formative influence of the Confucian classics in his insistence on building moral character and strength as fundamental requisites. Here, Social Darwinism was a transvaluated philosophy evolving from Confucian-Mencianism to Christian enlightenment to Faustian-Promethean democracy for Ahn Changho. His understanding of Social Darwinism was translated into dialectical self-strengthening and military revolutionism. Ultimately, however, his futuristic orientation and democratic vision of equality and freedom derived from his lifelong Christian faith.

Later called "Korea's Moses," Ahn Changho was motivated by an all-consuming desire to realize the aim of independent democracy for Koreans.[43] His Christian faith merged with his conception of sovereign democracy and independence revolution. Within his vision of Korea's special historic-spiritual identity and her role in world history, democratic nation building was necessarily to be a hard-won outcome of revolution, or an independence war. Indeed, the Christian Ahn Changho not only actively planned for an independence war throughout his nationalist life but also supported and engaged the Korean Independence Army in the Ch'ŏngsanni War after he established the Provisional Government.[44]

A NEW REPUBLIC: DRAFTING THE PROVISIONAL GOVERNMENT

Before the nationwide uprising of March 1, 1919, Ahn Changho had formulated a plan to create the Provisional Government and had signed the early, radical version of the declaration of independence with other overseas Korean revolutionaries. After the uprising, the Korean revolutionaries in Shanghai invited Ahn Changho, widely acknowledged as the most skilled conciliator and gifted institution-builder to meet with them. Following the meeting, Ahn was sent to Shanghai as a representative of the Korean National Association. From a young firebrand independence fighter, he had also become a seasoned revolutionary who, by his early forties, thought with his head as much as his heart.

In Shanghai, Ahn Changho purchased a house as the seat of government and his residence with funds provided by the Kungminhoe and Hungsadan.[45] Since three provisional governments had arisen—in Vladivostok, Seoul, and Shanghai—Ahn Changho consolidated the Provisional Government in Shanghai in August 1919, carefully balancing the Seoul and Vladivostok cabinet appointments (table 1). As acting premier, Ahn Changho considered the Seoul government to be the legitimate heir of the March First Movement. He followed the Seoul government as closely as possible, against those who insisted that the roster of Seoul government was merely an underground resistance group.

Aiming toward grand solidarity, Ahn appointed Syngman Rhee to be president, for he could potentially be the most critical agent in altering the direction of U.S. policy toward colonial Korea. Also, he appointed Yi Tonghwi, the most influential revolutionary leader in the Far East, as the premier of the Korean Provisional Government.

Though an unfair slight, Ahn Changho accepted for himself the insignificant title of chief of the Bureau of Labor (Nodongguk ch'ongp'an) assigned by the Seoul government. He accepted such a post for himself in the interests of the larger task of unification of the Korean Provisional Government. As a sincere Christian, Ahn entirely subsumed his personal ambition and reputation to a goal larger than himself; this act of charitable humility and earnest stewardship stunned the nationalist community, both at home and abroad.[46]

Upon unifying the Korean Provisional Government, Ahn Changho drafted the first Constitution of the Republic of Korea, which espoused a presidential system with three branches of government. Cognizant of his historic challenge to lay the cornerstone of a future independent democracy, he prepared a comprehensive constitution of eight chapters and fifty-eight articles as the Provisional Constitution of the Republic of Korea. After considerable debate, the constitution passed the Provisional Assembly on September 11, 1919. In the prefatory chapter, it reads:

I.   The Republic of Korea is composed of the people of Korea.

II.   The sovereignty of Korea rests entirely with the people of Korea.

III. The land of Korea is the peninsula of the old Chosŏn dynasty.

IV.   The people of Korea are all equal.

TABLE 1. The Unified Provisional Government in Shanghai

	Vladivostok	Seoul	Shanghai (Unified)
Head	Son Pyŏnghŭi Pak Yŏnghyo	Syngman Rhee	Syngman Rhee
Premier	Syngman Rhee	Yi Tonghwi	Yi Tonghwi
Minister of interior	Ahn Changho	Yi Tongnyŏng	Yi Tongnyŏng
Minister of diplomacy		Pak Yongman	Pak Yongman
Minister of finance	Yun Hyŏnjin	Yi Siyŏng	Ch'oe Chaehyŏng
Minister of military	Yi Tonghwi	No Paengnin	No Paengnin
Minister of education		Kim Kyusik	Kim Kyusik
Minister of justice		Sin Kyusik	Sin Kyusik
Minister of transportation		Mun Ch'angbŏm	Mun Ch'angbŏm
Minister of labor	Nam Hyŏng'u	Ahn Changho	Ahn Changho

V. Korea's legislative right belongs to the Assembly (Ŭijŏngwŏn), executive right belongs to the Executive (Kungmuwŏn), and judicial right belongs to the Judiciary (Pŏpwŏn).

VI. Within the limits of the Constitution, the governing of Korea is delegated to the Provisional President.

VII. Korea will courteously respect the monarch of the *ancien regime*.[47]

The constitution proclaimed the sovereign right and equality of Koreans and stipulated a presidential system based on the separation of powers. Emphasizing the Provisional Government as the legitimate government in exile, the declaration of the Provisional Constitution buttressed the overseas movement as the highest body of organized resistance to Japanese rule, with its legitimacy ultimately deriving from the Korean people's anticolonial democratic revolution of March 1, 1919.

A CHRISTIAN CONSTITUTION: GENESIS AND PRAXIS

Both a theoretician and practitioner of Korean democracy, Ahn Changho wrote constitutions that reveal Christian influence as his faith was translated into patriotic activism and a subversive self-governing agenda. He also incorporated the lessons of the Christian church into his own unique nationalist praxis and synthesis of constitutional democracy. In his continuous endeavor to draft a constitution and create a transnational framework for the Provisional Government, Ahn Changho particularly adopted the local self-governing constitutions and the ecumenical church government of the Presbyterian faith.

The relationship between Ahn Changho's democratic ideals and Presbyterian politics can be seen in the extant library of his books. Ahn Changho's volumes can be broadly divided into the following categories: (1) religion, especially Christianity; (2) military and sciences, including tactics, chemistry, and mathematics; (3) society, including history, government, law, and social sciences and social issues; Americana, and Koreana; (4) humanities, including art, classical studies and languages, and English language and literature; (5) biography, education, and self-help; (6) references, such as almanacs, atlases, encyclopedias, and dictionaries, and (7) various types of periodicals.[48] In his library, Ahn possessed numerous books on Christianity and Christian church government: *Systematic Theology*; *A Dictionary of the Bible*; *Church Politics*; *Gospels and the Acts of Apostles*; *The Constitution of Presbyterian Church*; *History of Christian Church*; *Building the Bible Class*; *For the Work of Ministry*; *God, Home, and Native Land*; *What the Bible Teaches*; *A Syllabus of Systematic Theology*; *Outline of Systematic Theology*; *Greek Testament*; *Paul's Joy in Christ*; *How to Know the Bible*; *Outline of Theology*; *Thayer's Greek-English Lexicon of the New Testament*; *A Study of the*

Book of Revelation; and *Faith and Life.*[49] Evidently, Ahn studied these Christian books over the years when he wrote an array of constitutions and established myriad revolutionary organizations.

As the acting premier in charge of instituting the fundamental structure and constitution of the Provisional Government in Shanghai, Ahn Changho apparently closely consulted *Church Politics* (1905) in Chinese and *The Constitution of the Presbyterian Church in the United States of America* (1920) in English,[50] among other books in his library. By November 1919, Ahn had completed the Provisional Constitution in ninety-five articles. The document elaborated the role of the various ministries of the Provisional Government and included a detailed delineation of the military's role, leadership, assembly, and affairs. Meanwhile, in the following year Ahn continued to refine his constitutional philosophy, method, and strategy with his "revolutionary-democratic" (or anticolonial military) agenda and transnational aims to mold the Provisional Government in colonial diaspora.

Ahn Changho paid great attention to the Constitution of the Presbyterian Church in the United States of America, especially part 5, "The Form of Government," which includes the chapters "Preliminary Principles," "Of the Church," "Officers of the Church," "Bishops or Pastors," "Ruling Elders," "Deacons," "Ordinances in a Particular Church," "Church Government and Judicatories," "Church Session," "The Presbytery," "The Synod," "The General Assembly," "Electing and Ordaining Ruling Elders and Deacons," and "Resigning a Pastoral Charge," among others.[51] Here, Ahn saw that the presbyterial assembly of the elders "as the representatives of the people" behaved and operated as a legislative assembly, and the minister served as the executive head of the church government. The minister and elders were chosen by the people of the church "in the mode most approved and in use in that congregation," and the pastor and the assembly of elders deliberated and voted on important church decisions and issues.[52] Regarding the terms of appointments and terms of the minister, the assembly of elders as the presbytery of the church congregations had the constitutional right to discharge the minister.[53] As for the "judicatories," the assemblies "ought not to possess any civil jurisdiction, nor to inflict any civil penalties. Their power is wholly moral or spiritual, and that only ministerial and declarative ... but the highest punishment to which their authority extends, is to exclude the contumacious and impenitent from the congregation of believers." Ahn Changho's own penned notes on the first page of "The Form of Government," a volume in his library are revealing:

1. Ruling by elder[s] and minister
2. Minister[,] equal power
3. System of apply[ing] the courts[54]

The "ruling by elder[s] and minister" demonstrates his awareness of the cooperative yet competitive style of governing between the legislative and executive by sharing "equal power" between the elders and the minister, in addition to the system of judicial courts. He also wrote "elder" before "minister," suggesting his understanding of the importance of a legislative decision-making body rather than the prerogative of the executive leader or the supremacy of the executive as a branch of government.

On the same page are more of Ahn's handwritten notes:

1. Episcopal
2. Congregation[al]
3. Presbyterian[55]

Referring to the denominational distinctions, he observed the variances in the method of organization between the Episcopalian, Congregational, and Presbyterian churches. Episcopalian church government, for example, possessed a hierarchical, pyramidal structure with an appointed bishop at the top, while the Congregational church tended to have far less authoritarian and more individualistic, if too atomized, structures. The Presbyterian church, as a form of self-government, often designated territorial jurisdictions for effective self-management.

From this work, Presbyterian Ahn Changho also grasped the distinction between the constituent parts and the processes of the "congregation, presbytery, and synod" of the Presbyterian church organization as a worldwide General Assembly, which acted as the higher forum of elected presbyterial and synodical assemblies.[56] While respectful of the special autonomous conditions of each local congregation, the Presbyterian Church had an ecumenical organization that managed the global affairs of the church through the "church session," as described in part 5, chapter 9, which Ahn Changho carefully studied, underlining the categories of responsible personnel and operation.[57]

Ahn Changho's reliance on the Presbyterian constitution during the formative period of the Korean Provisional Government reveals not only his spiritual commitment but also his understanding of sociopolitical organization and governance as fundamentally based on the Christian, and particularly Presbyterian, ideals of democracy. For Ahn, the worldwide proselytizing strategy of the management and operation of the Presbyterian Church was analogous to his own full-scale transnational struggle for national freedom. Although a hierarchical network existed, an intrinsically enlightened democratic system of local autonomy and the separation of powers underscored the constitutional governing of the national and global organization of the Presbyterian Church. Ahn Changho too envisioned the Korean nationalist revolution in a global manner, with a multilayered magnitude and systematic complexity, or evangelical ecumenism.

CORPUS CHRISTI: AN INSPIRATION

In creating the first presidential constitution of the Republic of Korea, which became the comprehensive framework and working cabinet of the Provisional Government in Shanghai, Ahn Changho was deeply influenced by the American Presbyterian constitutional structure and government, but more precisely, by the Presbyterian self-governing mode of administration. Essentially, Ahn's source of Christian and revolutionary inspiration was the United States, which had fought a revolutionary war against tyrannical Britain and established a new sovereign democracy. America was the emulatory historical model of independence not only for Ahn Changho, but also for his close friend Ahn Chunggŭn and other Korean revolutionaries of his time.[58] Ahn Changho's constitutions also embraced distinctly American constitutional accoutrements, such as the system of the separation of powers, checks and balances, and even bicameral federalism, which were influenced by Montesquieu's *Spirit of Laws* with Jeffersonian constitutional imprint.[59]

Concerning the historical development between Puritanism, or Presbyterianism, and American democracy, theologians such as Reinhold Niebuhr, notably in his *Moral Man and Immoral Society* (1932), H. Richard Niebuhr in his *Kingdom of God in America* (1936), and Perry Miller have assessed, but, more importantly reassessed, the manner by which the Puritan ethic and heritage have forged the American way of democratic life with secular and religious implications.[60] What was the relationship between the progressive reformist impetus of the early beginnings of Presbyterianism and its underlying philosophy of government? In fact, Puritanic Presbyterianism contributed much to the unique manner in which the institutions as well as the ideal and praxis of democracy evolved in America.

In terms of the origins of American Presbyterianism and its relationship to democracy, what were John Calvin's (1509–1564) notion of government and law, for instance? In *Institution de la Religion Chretienne*, Calvin's treatise on law and government, which first appeared in 1536, it seems that he clearly preferred a combination of aristocracy and democracy, although he "repudiated absolute monarchy" and resisted tyranny.[61] Was that not also Plato's (367–427 BCE) preference? The ancient Greek philosopher and writer of *The Republic* believed that a democracy could potentially become a mob-acracy. Calvin's conception of the so-called aristocracy in Geneva, however, is still a far cry from what Chosŏn Korea or any other part of traditional East Asia would have considered aristocracy. His understanding of aristocracy was classical in the sense of Plato and Aristotle inasmuch as his language refers to the Platonic terms of aristocracy as the "government by the best," the rule of "truly good and just men." For Aristotle, aristocracy is "the distribution of honors according to virtue *(arete)*, with virtue as the defining factor of aristocracy, as wealth is of oligarchy and freedom of democracy."[62] Calvin's Geneva was conceived as rule by a council of the "best men" in the classical Platonic and Aristotelian sense, not of men from a few selected families based on birth. In fact, the council that governed Geneva at the time of Calvin was not hereditary; members were elected by popular vote.[63]

As a student trained in law and the son of a lawyer, Calvin conceived of law and government as tied to acceptance of the covenantal kingdom of God based on divine sovereignty and divine law, or the unity of will and word of God as the creator and redeemer. What of the law and the covenant? The covenant springs from a covenant of God's grace, and the law is God's gift. Thus the covenant is the cradle of law wherein the love of paterfamilias God is to be translated into the love of neighbor.[64] Indeed, some writers have noted Calvin's faith in the divine basis of government as "theocracy, bibliocracy, or christocracy," describing his ideal of a political society as well as the disciplined community of Geneva.[65] Perhaps, it can be said that Jean Jacques Rousseau's *Social Contract* was influenced by this earlier Christian notion of the covenantal relationship between the Christian God and his people.

The Christian Ahn Changho extended the covenantal relationship between God and man to the constitutional relationship between brothers and sisters whose fundamental God-given rights and responsibilities allowed them to be the people of a nation of freedom, justice, and democracy. Ahn's pragmatism and emphasis on learning-by-doing is reminiscent of the modern American philosophers of pragmatism and democracy William James and John Dewey. There are powerful corresponding democratic impulses in both Ahn's and Dewey's appreciation of immediate applicability and trial-and-error practice as the best civic education.[66] There also appear to be parallels between Woodrow Wilson, a Presbyterian president of the United States and visionary of the League of Nations who was also a son of a Scottish Presbyterian minister, and Ahn Changho. Wilson, a man with a complex legacy, is best known to Koreans as the American president who, at the end of World War I, declared the Fourteen Points (principles for peace and self-determination), which influenced the March First Movement. Apparently, Wilson "forever wrote constitutions for college debating societies, and he crowned this activity by writing one for the government of the world."[67] Young Ahn Changho too devotedly wrote constitutions for the secret revolutionary societies he created in Korea and abroad, and he crowned this activity by writing the founding constitution for the Provisional Government of the Republic of Korea.

For Ahn Changho, life was a courageous quest for democracy and sovereign freedom from Japanese colonial rule. Though Ahn's holistic pursuit of independence and democracy often blurred the distinction of self and country for him, Ahn labored to reclaim and repossess the self, or individual dignity of life, for himself and his compatriots. Thus Ahn's strivings toward individual and national freedom were ultimately based on an understanding of his historic-spiritual self/nation. Yet Ahn Changho expanded his own destined sense of self to further affirm individual self-dignity for all Koreans toward recovering independence and building democracy. The essence of independence as well as democracy for Ahn Changho, too, came to be defined as the courageous and free self. Whether Ahn's heroism or courage was a being itself or was derived from a sense of self-preservation, affirmation, or cultivation or from a transcendent faith in and relationship with God, he undoubtedly possessed a dynamic sense of self and courage toward the cause of national freedom as a man and leader.

Nicknamed "Mr. Unification" (T'ong'il Ahn Changho) for his unceasing efforts to reconcile and unify his compatriots in order to sustain the nationalist movement to liberate Korea, Ahn Changho especially championed his democratic ideal of "sacred unity" for the Young Korean Academy. This notion was an outgrowth of his spiritual conception of democracy as a collectivity of strength and solidarity with esprit de corps. Here, his vision of Christian democratic polity may be understood in relation to the spiritual message of the Apostle Paul. Paul portrayed the church as a sacred body politic or "unity in the body of Christ" with necessary differences in the roles of the people according to the "apportioned grace" or "gifts," yet affirmed the oneness of the Lord as the sacred corporal locus of the spiritual unity of the people as "one body and one Spirit—just as you were called to one hope when you were called—one Lord, one faith, one baptism; one God and Father of all, who is over all and through all and in all" (Ephesians 4:4–5). Paul sought to prepare God's people for works of service to build the unified body of Christ as "mature, attaining to the whole measure of the fullness of Christ" (Ephesians 4:13). With a prophetic gaze, Ahn Changho too envisaged a sacred unity of compatriots as a collective body of togetherness in spirit and flesh for the blessed future of his homeland.

NOTES

The McCune-Reischauer transliteration of the subject of this chapter is Tosan An Ch'angho; since, however, he wrote his name as Dosan Ahn Changho, I will use that form here. The McCune-Reischauer transliteration for the name of his mentor is Sŏ Chaep'il, but he preferred Seo Jaepil or the Anglicized Philip Jaisohn.

1. For an overview of early Christian history in Asia, see Samuel Hugh Moffett, *A History of Christianity in Asia: Beginnings to 1500* (Maryknoll, N.Y.: Orbis, 1998), and *History of Christianity in Asia: 1500–1900* (Maryknoll, N.Y.: Orbis, 2004). For a survey of Korean Christian history, see Han'guk Kidokkyosa yŏn'guhoe, *Han'guk Kidokkyo ŭi yŏksa* [A History of Korean Christianity], vols. 1–2 (Seoul: Kidokkyo Munhwasa, 1989–1990).

2. Jacqueline Pak, "Pioneers, Controversies and Paradigm Shifts: So Chaep'il, An Ch'angho, and Syngman Rhee" (Paper delivered at the 2003 Annual Meeting of the Association of Asian Studies, New York, March 29, 2003), explored the idea of paradigm shifts in modern Korean history and Korean Studies, including new discourses on nationalism, Orientalism, regional studies, and ethnic studies. The new research findings, which called for a paradigm shift in the decade-long Ahn Changho Controversy, are included in Jacqueline Pak, *The Founding Father: Ahn Changho and the Origins of Korean Democracy* (forthcoming). That monograph is based on my thesis "An Ch'angho and the Nationalist Origins of Korean Democracy" (Ph.D. diss., University of London, 2000). See also Edward W. Said, *Orientalism: Western Conceptions of the Orient* (1978; repr., London: Penguin, 1995), and idem, *Culture and Imperialism* (London: Vintage, 1993).

3. For a brief introduction to the subject, see Jacqueline Pak, "An Ch'angho and the Origins of Korean Democracy" (paper delivered at the "Origins of Korean Democracy" conference, Woodrow Wilson Center for International Scholars, Washington, D.C., 2001). Also, Jacqueline Pak, Review of *Tosan Ahn Ch'ang-ho: A Profile of a Prophetic Patriot*, by Kim Hyung-chan (1996), *Korean Studies*, July 2001.

4. Yi Kwangsu, *Tosan An Ch'angho* (Seoul: Hungsadan, 1947); Chu Yohan, *An Tosan chŏnsŏ* [Complete Works of An Tosan] (Seoul: Samjungdang, 1963); Chang Iuk and Chu Yohan, *Naŭi sarang Hanbandoya* [My Love, the Korean Peninsula] (Seoul: Hungsadan, 1987); and An Byŏnguk, *Tosan sasang* [The Philosophy of Tosan] (Seoul: Samyuk, 1991), among others. The "tripartite division" of "diplomatism, militarism, and gradualism" first appeared in Chong-sik Lee, *Politics of Korean Nationalism* (Berkeley and Los Angeles: University of California Press, 1965). Adopting this approach, Arthur Gardner wrote "The Korean Nationalist Movement and An Ch'angho, Advocate of Gradualism" (Ph.D. diss., University of Hawai'i, 1979). For a critique of the "tripartite division" paradigm, see Jacqueline Pak, "The An Ch'angho Controversy—Gradualist-Pacifism, Cultural Nationalism, or Revolutionary-Democracy," *International Journal of Korean Studies* 6, no. 1 (Spring/Summer 2002): 109–135.

5. Michael Robinson, *Cultural Nationalism in Colonial Korea, 1920–1925* (Seattle: University of Washington Press, 1988). Other "revisionist" books with similar ideological problems include Kang Tongjin, *Ilche Han'guk ch'imnyak chŏngch'aeksa* [History of the Strategy of Japanese Colonial Aggression toward Korea] (Seoul: Han'gilsa, 1980); Sŏ Chungsŏk, *Hanmal Ilche ch'imnyakha ŭi chabon chuŭi kŭndaehwaron ŭi sŏnggyŏk—Tosan An Ch'angho ŭi sasang ŭl chungsim ŭro* [The Character of Capitalistic Modernization Theory under Japanese Colonial Aggression at the End of the Chosŏn—Focusing on Tosan An Ch'angho's Philosophy], *Han'guk kŭnhyŏndae ŭi minjok munje yŏn'gu* (Seoul: Chisik Sanŏpsa, 1989); Pak Ch'ansung,

Han'guk kŭndae chŏngch'i sasangsa yŏn'gu: Minjok chuŭi upa ŭi sillyŏk yangsŏng undong-non [A Study of the History of Modern Korean Political Philosophy: Theory of the Rightist Nationalist Ability-Cultivationist Movement] (Seoul: Yŏksa Pipy'ŏngsa, 1992); and Kang Man'gil, *Han'guk kŭndaesa* [Modern Korean History] (Seoul: Ch'angjakkwa Pip'yŏngsa, 1984), 230–242. This was reprinted as *Koch'yŏssŭn Han'guk kŭndaesa* [Revised Modern Korean History] in 1994. In the past decade, these works were widely problematized and interrogated. Some of the works were also actively debated in the Ahn Changho Controversy, in terms of the pertinent issues involving Korean nationalism and the nationalist movement.

6. Kenneth Wells, *New God, New Nation: Protestants and Self-Reconstruction Nationalism in Korea, 1896–1937* (Honolulu: University of Hawai'i Press, 1990). Koen de Ceuster also examined the life and milieu of prominent Christian leader-turned-collaborator Yun Ch'iho in "From Modernization to Collaboration, the Dilemma of Korean Cultural Nationalism" (Ph.D. diss., Katholieke Universiteit Leuven, 1993), based on Yun's English diary and other sources. De Ceuster later revised his "cultural nationalism" framework concerning Yun Ch'iho.

7. Jacqueline Pak, "Reform or Revolution?: Reassessment of Late-Nineteenth-Century Korea" (paper delivered at the "Conference on Nineteenth-Century Korea," University of British Columbia, Vancouver, Canada, June 16, 2001). This paper re-investigated the nature and dynamics of the "patriotic enlightenment" and "righteous army" movements in the late Chosŏn period and interrogated the oft-cited conventional bifurcated view of modern Korean history.

8. Iris Chang, *The Rape of Nanking: The Forgotten Holocaust of World War II* (New York: Penguin, 1997), and Herbert P. Bix, *Hirohito and the Making of Modern Japan* (New York: Perennial, 2001). See also, among many other such works, George L. Hicks, *The Comfort Women: Japan's Brutal Regime of Enforced Prostitution in the Second World War* (New York: W. W. Norton, 1997), and Sheldon H. Harris, *Factories of Death: Japanese Biological Warfare, 1932–1945, and the American Cover-Up* (London: Routledge, 2001).

9. For discussions on the collaboration of Yi Kwangsu and Chu Yohan, read the circumstances of the Hungsadan trial, *Hungsadan undong ch'ilsimnyŏnsa* [The Seventy-Year History of the Hungsadan Movement] (Seoul: Hungsadan, 1983), and Kim Yunsik, *Yi Kwangsu wa kŭŭi sidae* [Yi Kwangsu and His Time] (Seoul: Han'gilsa, 1986).

10. I have critiqued the problematics of the overly ideologized and politicized historiography of the 1980s and early 1990s in Jacqueline Pak, "History or Ideology?: Problematique of *New History* as the post-Kwangju Historiography" (paper delivered at the Identity through History Workshop at Leiden University, August 29–September 1, 1996).

11. The critique of the earlier, conventional, "bifurcated historiography" of twentieth-century Korea based on the current peninsular division is further discussed in Pak, "The An Ch'angho Controversy."

12. Ibid.

13. Since Ahn Changho's eldest daughter, Susan Cuddy, donated the papers in the 1980s, the Tosan An Ch'angho Collection of papers is stored at the Indepen-

dence Hall of Korea, Ch'ŏnan, Korea. The Independence Hall is a museum dedicated to the Korean independence movement.

14. About the Underwoods in Korea and the Underwood School, see Lillias H. Underwood, *Fifteen Years among the Topknots* (Boston: American Tract Society, 1904), and Horace G. Underwood, *The Call of Korea* (New York: Fleming H. Revell, 1908).

15. Lak-Geoon George Paik, *The History of the Protestant Mission in Korea, 1832–1910* (1929; repr., Seoul: Yonsei University Press, 1971), explores the earnest Korean participation in the self-government and democracy-building practices of the early Christian churches.

16. The first biography of Dr. Seo Jaepil was written by his assistant Channing Liem: *Philip Jaisohn: The First Korean-American—A Forgotten Hero* (Philadelphia: Philip Jaisohn Memorial Foundation, 1984).

17. Yun Kyŏngno, *105in sagŏn kwa Sinminhoe yŏn'gu* [Study of the 105 Incident and the New People's Society] (Seoul: Ilchinsa, 1991).

18. For further reference on the life, thought, and legacy of Ahn Changho, as well as the circumstances of his arrest, imprisonment, and death, see my works based on his papers, as well as those of Sŏ Chaep'il and An Chunggun. The documents and letters of other leading Korean revolutionaries of his time, such as Yi Tonghwi, Syngman Rhee, and Kim Kyusik, are also included.

19. Charles Allen Clark, *The Korean Church and the Nevius Method* (New York: Fleming H. Revell, n.d.).

20. Ibid. Also, interviews with Professor Sam Moffett Jr. in Princeton, New Jersey, 2001–2004. For the missionary work of Samuel Moffett Sr. in Korea, see the Moffett Collection, Princeton Theological Seminary, Princeton, New Jersey.

21. See the Moffett Collection.

22. Interviews with the family members of Ahn Changho, including daughter Susan Cuddy in Northridge, California, and niece An Sŏnggyŏl in Seoul, Korea. Also, Lillias H. Underwood, *Underwood of Korea* (1918; repr., Seoul: Yonsei University Press, 1983), 44–45, and Won-Mo Kim, ed. and trans., *Horace Newton Allen's Diary* (Seoul: Dankook University Press, 1991), 510.

23. Everett N. Hunt Jr., *Protestant Pioneers in Korea* (Maryknoll, N.Y.: Orbis, 1980), 9. Also, Fred Harvey Harrington, *God, Mammon, and the Japanese: Dr. Horace N. Allen and Korean-American Relations, 1884–1905* (Madison: University of Wisconsin Press, 1980).

24. Key S. Ryang, "Horace Grant Underwood (1851–1916) in Korea: The First American Protestant Missionary and Educator," *Journal of Modern Korean Studies* 3 (1987): 76–77.

25. Paik, *History*, 130. Chu Yohan, *An Tosan chŏnso*, 23–25.

26. Underwood, *Fifteen Years among the Topknots*, 10–12.

27. Ibid. Ryang, "Horace Grant Underwood," 78–79 and 86. Also, In Soo Kim, *Protestants and the Formation of Modern Korean Nationalism, 1885–1920: A Study of the Contributions of Horace G. Underwood and Sun Chu Kil* (New York: Peter Lang, 1996).

28. The Reverend Miller's Memorandum at the Underwood School in the Tosan An Ch'angho Collection describes Ahn as a youth and student.

29. Kim Yongje, *Tosan An Ch'angho* (Seoul: Chŏngmunsa, 1964), 43–37, in the Susan Cuddy Collection. According to Susan Cuddy, eldest daughter of Ahn Changho, Kim Yongje was a Protestant Christian from P'yŏngyang who met Ahn Changho.

30. Julia Ching, *Confucianism and Christianity: A Comparative Study* (Tokyo: Kodansha International, 1977), 168.

31. Benjamin Schwartz, *In Search of Wealth and Power: Yen Fu and the West* (Cambridge, Mass.: Harvard University Press, 1967).

32. Tu Wei-ming, *Confucian Thought: Selfhood as Creative Transformation* (Albany: State University of New York Press, 1985).

33. Benjamin Schwartz, *The World of Thought in Ancient China* (Cambridge, Mass.: Harvard University Press, 1985). The Four Books of the Confucian classics are the *Great Learning, Doctrine of the Mean, Confucian Analects,* and *Works of Mencius.*

34. Ibid.

35. William Theodore de Bary, *The Trouble with Confucianism* (Cambridge, Mass.: Harvard University Press, 1991), 12. Max Weber discusses his conception of a prophet and "ideal types" in *The Sociology of Religion* (Boston: Beacon Press, 1963).

36. Ching, *Confucianism and Christianity,* 113 and 139. See also Gregory Blue, "Traditional China in Western Social Thought: An Historical Inquiry with Special Reference to Contribution from Montesquieu to Max Weber" (Ph.D. diss., Cambridge University, 1988).

37. De Bary, *Trouble,* 17–18. See also Martin Buber, *I and Thou,* trans. Walter Kaufmann (New York: Charles Scribner's Sons, 1970).

38. Chu Yohan, *An Tosan chŏnso,* 26.

39. About the Kongnip hyŏphoe, Yun Pyŏngsŏk, *Kukoe hanin sahoe wa minjok undong* [Exile Korean Communities and the Nationalist Movement] (Seoul: Ilchogak, 1997).

40. The Korean-American component of the Sinminhoe is further reinforced in Wayne Patterson, *The Ilse: First-Generation Korean Immigrants in Hawaii, 1903–1973* (Honolulu: University of Hawai'i Press, 2000), 49–52.

41. Ahn Changho's grassroots organizational endeavors in building the Kungminhoe in Manchuria, China, and Russia are described in Ban Byong Yool, "Korean Nationalist Activities in the Russian Far East and North Chientao, 1905–1921" (Ph.D. diss., University of Hawai'i, 1996). The biography by Jacqueline Pak, *The Founding Father: Ahn Changho and the Origins of Korean Democracy,* includes a critique of the characterization of Ahn Changho's nationalist activities abroad as being merely "cultural-educational," as made by Ban and others.

42. The unique paradigm of the Master Plan for Independence and Democracy was initially presented by Jacqueline Pak, "An Ch'angho as a Nationalist Leader: A Revisionist Perspective" (paper delivered at the Association of Korean Studies in Europe Conference, Prague, Czech Republic, April 23, 1995).

43. A Korean historian, Shin Ilcheol, was the first to call Ahn Changho "Korea's Moses." See also Jacqueline Pak, "Korea's Moses: Ahn Changho and the

Colonial Diaspora" (paper delivered at the Colloquium on Korean Christianity, UCLA, Center for Korean Studies, Los Angeles, November 9, 2000).

44. As the most contentious element of the Ahn Changho controversy, Ahn's "revolutionary militarism" has been a source of much debate in Korean Studies. For Ahn's crucial military and strategic role in the Provisional Government and the Chŏngsanni War, see Pak, *Founding Father*.

45. The Constitution of the Hungsadan, the Tosan An Ch'angho Collection. There are a number of drafts of the Hungsadan constitution in the collection. Newly discovered Hungsadan documents indicate the purchase of bonds issued by the Provisional Government and reveal that the Hungsadan assumed perhaps the greatest financial burden in supporting the Korean Provisional Government from its inception.

46. About the Korean Provisional Government, Yi Hyŏnhŭi, *Taehan min'guk imsi chŏngbusa* [History of the Korean Provisional Government] (Seoul: Chipmundang, 1983), among others.

47. *Sanghae Ilgi* [Shanghai Diaries], the Tosan An Ch'angho Collection; Kukhoe Tosŏgwan, *Tosan An Ch'angho charyo chip: Chosŏn ch'ongdokpu kyŏngmuguk sojang pimil munsŏ* [Sources on Tosan An Ch'angho: Secret Documents from Governor-General's Police Bureau] (Seoul, 1997), 172; and Kim Yŏngsu, "*Taehan minguk imsi hŏnjang*" [The Constitution of the Provisional Government of the Republic of Korea] in *Taehan min'guk imsi chŏngbu hŏnpomnon* [Theory of the Korean Provisional Constitution] (Seoul: Samyŏngsa, 1980), 85–86.

48. Ahn Changho's library and the book list he prepared are part of the Tosan An Ch'angho Collection. Since Ahn was last in the United States in 1926, only books published before this date were considered.

49. *Sojang charyo mongnok* [The List of Source Holdings] (Ch'ŏnan, Korea: The Independence Hall of Korea, 1993).

50. Presbyterian Board of Publication, *The Constitution of the Presbyterian Church in the United States of America* (Philadelphia, 1920).

51. Ibid., 405–438. Also, Thomas G. Sanders, *Protestant Concepts of Church and State* (New York: Holt, Rinehart and Winston, 1964), and Elwyn A. Smith, *Church-State Relations in Ecumenical Perspective* (Pittsburgh, Pa.: Duquesne University Press, 1966).

52. Ibid., 357, 360, and 372.

53. Ibid.

54. Ibid., 351.

55. Ibid.

56. Ibid., 360.

57. Ibid., 361–370.

58. A new interpretation of the life and philosophy of An Chunggun, who was a close friend and colleague of Ahn Changho, is included in Jacqueline Pak, *The Founding Father: Ahn Changho and the Origins of Korean Democracy* (forthcoming), with a new perspective on the circumstances of the assassination of Ito Hirobumi.

59. David N. Mayer, *The Constitutional Thought of Thomas Jefferson* (Charlottesville: University Press of Virginia, 1994).

60. About an influential American Puritan theologian-philosopher, see Sang Hyun Lee, *The Philosophical Theology of Jonathan Edwards* (Princeton, N.J.: Princeton University Press, 1988).

61. George L. Hunt, ed., *Calvinism and the Political Order: Essays Prepared for the Woodrow Wilson Lectureship of the National Presbyterian Center, Washington, D.C.* (Philadelphia: Westminster Press, 1965), and Stephen Strehle, *Calvinism, Federalism, and Scholasticism: A Study of the Reformed Doctrine of Covenant* (Bern: Peter Lang, 1988).

62. Hunt, *Calvinism*, 37. Also, Bradley J. Longfield, *The Presbyterian Controversy: Fundamentalists, Modernists, and Moderates* (New York: Oxford University Press, 1991).

63. Ibid.

64. I. John Hesselink, *Calvin's Concept of the Law* (Allison Park, Pa.: Pickwick Publications, 1992).

65. Hunt, *Calvinism*, 35.

66. Robert B. Westbrook, *John Dewey and American Democracy* (Ithaca, N.Y.: Cornell University Press, 1991). Also, James Earnest Fisher, *Democracy and Mission Education in Korea* (Seoul: Yonsei University Press, 1970), demonstrates John Dewey's influence on the ideas and practice of democracy building in early Korean education.

67. Hunt, *Calvinism*, 167. About the life and politics of Woodrow Wilson, see John Milton Cooper, *The Warrior and the Priest* (Cambridge: Harvard University Press, 1985), and Kendrick A. Clements, *Woodrow Wilson: World Statesman* (Chicago: Ivan R. Dee, 1999).

CHAPTER 7

Preaching the Apocalypse in Colonial Korea

The Protestant Millennialism of Kil Sŏn-ju

Chong Bum Kim

Protestant Christianity has often been guilty of cultural imperialism. Guided by the idea of the "white man's burden" to "civilize" the world, Victorian-era missionaries regarded with contempt the cultures and religions of non-Western peoples and imposed upon them not only a new faith, but also a new way of life. Korea was no exception. When the first Protestant missionaries arrived in the late nineteenth and early twentieth centuries, they condemned ancestor veneration as "idol worship" and instructed converts to burn traditional ritual objects. They also carried out a whole range of social reforms, from temperance to hygiene. The missionaries saw themselves as liberating the benighted masses from false religion and a stagnant, backward society. To become Protestant was to throw off the shackles of tradition and enter the modern age. Mission schools and hospitals were the two most powerful symbols of this transformation.

Yet while cultural imperialism was undoubtedly part of early missionary ideology in Korea, the actual situation was more complex. To begin with, not all missionaries held a dismissive attitude toward tradition. In fact, some missionary scholars, such as James S. Gale (1863–1937), Homer B. Hulbert (1863–1949), and Mark N. Trollope (1862–1930), became pioneers in the study of Korean history, literature, and religion. More important, the Korean converts themselves were not merely victims who passively allowed the erasure of their culture. To be sure, there were instances of wholesale Westernization; a privileged few even went to study in the United States. However, these represented the elite. For the majority of Korean Protestants, the break between the old and the new was not so clear and decisive. In spite of the general intolerance and exclusivism that characterized the brand of Protestantism that entered Korea, traditional beliefs and customs continued in the lives of the converts. This was especially true in the villages, where missionaries were few and native leaders took charge of the spiritual guidance.[1] Indeed, at the popular level, the old religions not only survived their encounter with the new religion; they had a powerful influence on the kind of Protestantism that would emerge in Korea.

One example of the persistence and vitality of traditional religions is found in the thought and ministry of Kil Sŏn-ju (1869–1935). Considered by some to be the "father of Korean Christianity," Kil played a central role in the growth and expansion of Protestantism in its early stages.[2] Perhaps more than anyone else, he helped shape the form and character of Protestantism in Korea. The revivalist tradition, of which he was one of the pioneers, has become a permanent feature of Korean church life.[3] Together with his friend, Elder Pak Ch'i-rok, Kil began the tradition of *saebyŏk kido* or "day-break prayer meetings," the daily gathering of the faithful in the early hours of the morning.[4] Today the practice is one of the hallmarks of Korean Protestant devotion. Kil was also instrumental in establishing the dominance of fundamentalist theology, vigorously defending such doctrines as biblical inerrancy against the inroads of liberal scholarship. In many other areas as well, including church organization and social programs, he left a profound mark on Korean Protestantism.[5]

As part of the first generation of native-born church leaders, Kil inherited from the missionaries the task of making the new, alien beliefs and practices of Christianity accessible to the Koreans. Kil's approach to the problem was to employ resources within traditional culture. His sermons and theological works are thus filled with references that range from Korean history to Chinese literature and philosophy. Especially striking is his strong Confucian orientation.[6] Kil even turned his energies to music, advocating the use of traditional instruments and tunes in the worship service. In a way, this process of indigenization was inevitable. When Kil converted to Christianity he was steeped in the traditional culture and religions of Korea.[7] Thus, he carried over into his new faith many of the old habits, inclinations, and ways of thinking.

Kil's appropriation of tradition was, moreover, far from being limited to a sprinkling of cosmetic touches to give Protestantism a Korean look; it extended to the very content of his faith. One Christian doctrine, in particular, had a powerful hold on Kil: the Second Coming, the belief that Jesus would come again in the near future to establish his kingdom. Toward the end of Kil's life, this millennialist conviction became almost an obsession, as he became a kind of doomsday prophet preaching the imminent end of the world and divine judgment. Belief in the Second Coming was a major part of missionary teaching, and Kil's understanding of it was rooted in his study of the Bible. Yet at the same time, his vision of the end reflected the continuing influence of traditional religions. Kil added his own emphases and interpretation to Protestant millennialism and salvation theology, even making room for Confucius and the Buddha.

The Second Coming preached by Kil found a receptive audience. Millennialism was a major feature of folk religion and instilled the idea of a future messianic deliverer in the popular consciousness. Belief in the prophecies of the *Chŏnggam nok* (Record of Chŏng Kam), which predicted the fall of the Chosŏn dynasty (1392–1910) and the establishment of subsequent dynasties, was widespread in late Chosŏn, especially during periods of social and political turbulence. Also prominent was faith in the coming of Mirŭk or Maitreya, the Buddha of the Future, who would descend from heaven and rule over a new age. Christianity, with its own message of a messiah to come, came to represent another way in which collective hope for a better life found expression. Some converts even drew direct connections between the older millennialist traditions and Christianity, seeing the latter as the ultimate fulfillment of the former.

Thus, for Kil and his fellow converts, a lively interaction took place between the old religions and Christianity, as the Korean Protestants engaged in a selective appropriation of tradition. For example, they heeded the instructions of the missionaries and abandoned ancestor veneration, but they retained Confucian ethics. They gave up the practice of going to *mudang* (shamans) for fortune-telling, but they continued to see the *Chŏnggam nok* as a book of genuine prophecy. In a way, the older traditions even provided a certain validation for Christianity. Jesus the moral teacher was reminiscent of Confucius the revered sage, and Jesus the messiah resembled Chŏng To-ryŏng, the promised deliverer of the *Chŏnggam nok*. Thus, Christianity was not entirely new and alien to the Koreans; it provided significant areas of continuity and compatibility with the older traditions.

This chapter is a study of Protestant millennialism and its relationship to the traditional cultural and religious context, focusing on its main proponent during the Japanese colonial period (1910–1945), Kil Sŏn-ju. For Kil and his fellow Korean Protestants, various aspects of their backgrounds in other religious traditions helped them make sense of the Christian doctrine of the Second Coming. At the same time, the doctrine itself was transformed in the process. The vision of the ultimate end, the consummation of history, took on a Korean ethos.

Crisis of Church and Nation

Kil's Protestant millennialism took shape in the social and political context of the colonial period. The March First Movement of 1919, a series of demonstrations against Japanese rule, failed to bring about its goal of national independence. As one of the leaders of the movement, Kil was arrested and jailed for two and a half years. While in prison, Kil became drawn to the last book of the Bible, the Apocalypse of John or the Book of Revelation, which describes the end of the world and the Second Coming. He reputedly memorized the entire book.[8] In addition to Revelation, Kil also studied other prophetic books of the Bible. Following his release from prison in 1921 he preached a sermon titled "The Dawning of Peace." In it, he concluded that there was no peace in the world for the weak; the only thing the weak could do was to pray for God to stretch out his hands from above and extend his rule.[9]

Thereafter, Kil divorced himself from any further political involvement. Political action was futile; the only hope lay in preparing for the coming apocalypse and the establishment of a new, divine order. Kil turned his gaze away from the Korean nation to the Kingdom of God. From 1921 until his death in 1935, he preached the end of the world and the Second Coming of Christ everywhere he went.[10] In 1929, Kil was jailed again, this time for twenty days in the town of Andong, after the Japanese police arrested him for being a "disturber of the minds of the people" with his millennialist message.[11]

In the last five years of his life, Kil's millennialism took on a feverish pitch. Following a 1931 conflict between Chinese and Korean farmers in an area of Manchuria called Manbosan, a group of Korean youths looted and killed some Chinese residents of P'yŏngyang. Kil was shocked by the incident, but he was also surprised to find support for the massacre among fellow Protestants. He condemned P'yŏngyang, once the "Jerusalem of Korea," as having become the "lair of the Devil" and prophesied the city's destruction. Kil and many of his followers subsequently began to flee P'yŏngyang.[12]

Kil's sense of impending doom was heightened by a series of personal conflicts. He contended with the increasing number of socialists in Protestant congregations in northwestern Korea in the 1920s and 1930s, even within his own congregation.[13] In 1927 a group of socialists disrupted a service in Wŏnsan and attempted to harm Kil.[14] Then, in 1933, a long struggle with younger, more theologically liberal members of his congregation forced him to leave the Changdaehyŏn Church, where he had been pastoring since 1907, and to found another church with a group of followers.[15] Such developments must have led Kil to sense that his religious community was undergoing subversion from within.

On the broader political scene, 1931 marked the end of the so-called cultural policy (K. *munhwa chŏngch'i*; J. *bunka seiji*) of the government-general, which had allowed relative freedom for Korean social and cultural life following the March First Movement of 1919. In contrast, the 1930s represented a period of forced assimilation and participation in the expanding Japanese colonial empire.[16] The pressure proved so unbearable, especially during the wartime mobilization of the late 1930s and early 1940s, that many nationalists, including some signatories of the Declaration of Independence, gave in and collaborated with the Japanese. Kil, however, passed from the scene just as this period of colonial oppression was beginning and was thus spared its most brutal moments.[17]

On November 20, 1935, while Kil was leading a revival, he fainted from a stroke. When he regained consciousness, he was unable to speak, but he asked for a piece of paper and wrote a line in classical Chinese—his last words before he died: "Why is it that I cannot speak? When will I be able to speak? What use is it to have a mouth? Do not enter P'yŏngyang."[18]

Kil's response to the crisis in the church and the nation was to find hope in the future, when God would directly intervene and end history itself. The faithful, not only in Korea but also throughout the world, would find redemption as the old world of pain and suffering came to an end and a new world of joy and peace began.[19]

The End of the World

Kil presented his vision of the end in a work titled *Malsehak* (Eschatology, or study of the end times).[20] Based on his studies of the prophetic books of the Bible, *Malsehak* provides a detailed description of the signs that herald the end of the old and the subsequent events that will usher in the new era.

In pointing to the signs of the end, Kil begins with examples of moral disorder: the rise in the power of women, the contempt of the young toward their elders, parents and children killing each other, and the arrogance of the base (*ch'ŏn*) toward the noble (*kwi*).[21] The examples reveal Kil's conservative social attitude and Confucian moral orientation, subscribing to a normative social order in which women are subordinate to men and there are clearly defined roles between elder and younger, and noble and base.

The list of signs continues with examples from the human and natural worlds. In addition to such natural disasters as earthquakes and famines, Kil also cites technological innovations. For example, he believes that the invention of the telephone is a fulfillment of the biblical prophecy found in the Gospel of Matthew that "what you whispered, proclaim upon the housetops."[22]

Furthermore, Kil explains that even non-Christian religions point to the Second Coming of Christ. He cites three examples. First, Kil brings up a prophecy made by an Indian Buddhist in 1902 that a world savior would come in 1966 and establish a new empire. Then, Kil mentions an Egyptian Muslim prophet in Cairo who predicted that the religion of Islam would end and that a new, eternal heavenly kingdom would be established in 1972. The third example comes from an Indian mystic who prophesied in 1922 that a world savior would come within twenty years and, in fact, might already have come.[23] Kil's conclusion is that the unknown world savior of which all three prophets speak is none other than Jesus. He points out that as all three religions oppose Christianity, the Buddhist should have prophesied about the coming of the Buddha; the Muslim, the Prophet; and the Hindu, one of the deities. Nevertheless, the fact that they do not do so but rather leave the identity anonymous is a sign that God is using other religions to give evidence of the Second Coming of Jesus.[24]

Thus, Kil saw signs of the end everywhere, from moral and political crises to natural disasters and religious prophecies. Evildoers had penetrated and corrupted his beloved community—Jerusalem was doomed. The time was ripe for the fulfillment of prophecy. A new divine order was dawning.

Eden Restored

Kil's vision of the end of the world is based on the Book of Revelation.[25] The faithful—those who are resurrected from the dead and those on earth—are caught up in the air and participate in the heavenly banquet prepared for Jesus the bridegroom and his bride, the Church. However, the lazy believers who have not adequately prepared must remain on earth and endure seven years of tribulation. During the first three and a half years, two witnesses resembling Moses and Elijah will preach to them, but during the last three and a half years, the tribulation will become more severe. The two witnesses will be martyred but will be resurrected and taken to heaven. Angels in the air will then proclaim the Gospel. The believers who have kept the faith will witness the coming of Jesus on earth and the establishment of the millennial kingdom, in which people will continue to live in physical bodies as before but in a state of bliss; they will also continue to marry. At the end of the millennium, devils that had been locked up will be released, and the residents of the millennial kingdom will face trials and tribulations. At that point, the Last Judgment will take place. Sinners resurrected from the dead, and those unable to resist the devils, will be judged and sent to hell, along with the devils.

Following the Last Judgment, three eternal worlds will be established: a heavenly paradise, the "new Jerusalem"; an earthly paradise, the "new heaven and new earth"; and hell.[26] The first and third worlds, that is, heaven and hell, are familiar aspects of Christian theology, but the second, an earthly paradise, seems distinctive to Kil.[27] He calls it *pyŏnhwa mugung segye* (transformed eternal world) and identifies it as the restored Garden of Eden.[28]

A postapocalyptic, restored Eden was not part of the millennialist vision of the Western missionaries; it was Kil's personal interpretation of the biblical expression "new heaven and new earth."[29] He takes a highly symbolic and cryptic text and gives literal meaning to the phrase "new earth." Poetic language about a restored Eden occurs in the prophetic books of Ezekiel and Isaiah.[30] However, literal belief in the restoration of Eden is usually not associated with Christian millennialism.

The idea of an earthly paradise was, however, familiar to the religious imagination of Kil's audience. The shamanistic landscape was one of sacred mountains and rivers where gods, fairies, and immortals resided.[31] Pure Land Buddhism promised the Western Paradise (Skt. Sukhāvatī), a place of bliss for the faithful before they enter nirvana. Practitioners believed the Western Paradise to be an actual location on earth.[32] Furthermore, Daoist lore spoke of the Peach Blossom Land, a hidden paradise where the people lived simple, happy lives free from the turmoil and suffering of the world.[33] Korean folk religion was thus full of Edens, and Kil, in his sermons and theological works, employed the traditional term *nagwŏn* (paradise) to refer to Christian heaven. For Koreans at the end of the nineteenth century and the beginning of the twentieth, not yet versed in the European iconography of angels and cherubs flying in the clouds, *nagwŏn* would have conjured up images of the Western Paradise or the Peach Blossom Land rather than St. Peter at the pearly gates.[34]

In general, Korean folk religion seemed to have had a more positive view of the natural world than that which prevailed in the West. The forest, for instance, was not the abode of evil spirits and frightening creatures such as witches, goblins, and dragons, as the Western literary imagination often presented it. On the contrary, in Korean folklore, it was a place of hidden paradises and sacred sites. Kil's idea of a restored Eden seems to reflect this positive view of the natural world in traditional thinking. In the *Malsehak*, he argues against the view of those Christians who believe that in the end the present world will be consumed by fire. The Garden of Eden, the earthly paradise where Adam and Eve lived in harmony with God and nature, was originally conceived without sin, and only in the aftermath of Adam's disobedience and the Fall did sin and corruption enter Creation. In the end, far from destroying the world, God will restore it to the state of original paradise.[35]

This restored earthly paradise is, however, of a lower order than the heavenly paradise. The inhabitants of the heavenly paradise—the new Jerusalem—are the Christians who participated in the heavenly banquet and were caught up in the air with Jesus in the Second Coming; they now reside in the new Jerusalem, with their bodies transformed. The residents of the earthly paradise—the restored Garden of Eden—are those who did not join Jesus at first but who endured and overcame all the trials and tribulations.[36] The former can freely travel back and forth between the two realms experiencing the joys and pleasures of both, but the latter must await the time when they too will be allowed to enter the realm of ultimate paradise.[37]

Kil's scheme of an ultimate and penultimate paradise appears in another work—his 1916 *Mansa sŏngch'wi* (Fulfillment of All Things). A revision of an earlier work published in 1904 as *Haet'aron* (Treatise on laziness), *Mansa sŏngch'wi* can be seen as a Korean version of John Bunyan's *Pilgrim's Progress*, which played a key role in Kil's conversion experience.[38] *Mansa sŏngch'wi* is an allegory of the Christian journey from Sowŏnsŏng (City of Wishes), the present world, to Yŏngsaengguk (Kingdom of Eternal Life). It depicts the many stray roads that tempt the traveler, such as those that lead to drinking, womanizing, opium, and vanity. The greatest obstacle is a creature called *Haet'a* (Laziness), which blocks the road and swallows those who try to pass.[39]

Before one reaches Yŏngsaengguk, there is a penultimate destination, Sŏngchw'iguk (Kingdom of Fulfillment), a place where all desires and expectations have been fulfilled. Kil describes this idealized place in Confucian terms. The king and his ministers are sagely, and the kingdom is overflowing with the benevolence of sages (K. *sŏnghyŏn*; C. *shengxian*) and gentlemen (K. *kunja*; C. *junzi*) and the courage of heroes (K. *yŏng'ung yŏlsa*). It is a kingdom of great peace (K. *t'aep'yŏngguk*; C. *taipingguo*).[40] *Sŏngch'wiguk* is Kil's vision of utopia, an earthly paradise.

The residents of this kingdom are diverse. Kil begins the list with the Han dynasty philosopher Dong Zhongshu (179–104 BCE) and goes on to mention several other figures from Chinese history and literature, including Confucius, the mythical kings Yao and Shun, and the Tang poet Li Bai (710–761 CE). Kil praises them for the diligence with which they overcame personal obstacles and made great contributions to culture and history. Then, he discusses the Buddha's attainment of enlightenment, Paul's experience of becoming an apostle, and Jesus' diligence in prayer, preaching, and doing good for the people.[41] All are residents of Sŏngch'wiguk by virtue of the fact that they have kept to the correct path on their journey and have overcome Haet'a by wearing the Kyŏngsŏng kabot (Armor of Awakening).[42] What is striking about the roster of residents is that Jesus shares company with Confucius and the Buddha, as well as literary, historical, and mythical figures from China's past.

Kil does not, however, leave Jesus permanently in this position. Jesus goes on to the ultimate destination, Yŏngsaengguk, where the Eternal God the Father reigns—a kingdom built of precious metals and jewels—and the only way to enter this kingdom is by believing in Jesus and following him.[43]

Kil creates a two-tiered conception of paradise in both *Mansa sŏngch'wi* and *Malsehak*. His motive for the division seems to be, in part, to make room in the Christian theology of salvation for the "noble pagans," in much the same way that many medieval Christian thinkers could not bear the thought of sending their beloved classical authors to hell. Because he continues to view the cultural and religious heroes of his past in a positive light, it is difficult to imagine Kil condemning them to a life of eternal torment. In other words, the penultimate paradise is Kil's resolution of the problem of what happens to the good people who died without hearing the Gospel. Unlike some Christians who took a narrow view and saw them as beyond salvation, Kil makes space for them. They cannot yet reach the ultimate destination because they did not believe in Jesus in their lifetimes, but at the same time because of their accomplishments and contributions, they do not deserve hell. Therefore, they will reside for a while in an earthly paradise until God will ultimately receive them into heaven.

Popular Millennialism in Korea

Kil Sŏn-ju's millennialist vision reflected his continuing attachment to the figures and ideas from his religious past. Noble pagans entered the Garden of Eden and stood at the gates of the new Jerusalem itself. Kil's fellow Protestant converts made yet more connections with traditional religion. Popular millennialism in late Chosŏn embraced prophesies in the *Chŏnggam nok* that, based on geomancy and other omens, foretold the collapse of the Chosŏn dynasty and the establishment of future, successive dynasties. The first copy of the document is supposed to have been found in 1785.[44] Its ideas, however, may have circulated as early as the late sixteenth century.[45] The main part consists of a dialogue that takes place in the Diamond Mountains between Chŏng Kam, a reputed ancestor of the Chŏng clans who makes the predictions, and Yi Tam, an ancestor of the Yi clans who records the conversation. According to Chŏng, the Chosŏn dynasty based in Hanyang (Seoul) will fall, and a Chŏng dynasty will be set up on Mount Kyeryong in South Ch'ungch'ŏng province. Other dynasties, including the Cho, Pŏm, and Wang, each with different capitals, will then succeed the Chŏng.[46] The *Chŏnggam nok* also includes the supposed prophecies of the Silla monk Tosŏn (827–898), the Koryŏ-Chosŏn monk Muhak Chach'o (1327–1405), and the Chosŏn-period seers T'ojong (Yi Chiham, 1517–1578) and Kyŏgam.[47] The people of late Chosŏn read and circulated this book of prognostications as they awaited the coming of their deliverer, Chŏng To-ryŏng.

The Chosŏn government periodically gathered and burned copies of the book because of its subversive message. The government, in fact, did have cause for concern, as *Chŏnggam nok* belief played a major role in rebellion. Throughout late Chosŏn, numerous disturbances found their inspiration in the book.[48] Two major rebellions influenced by the *Chŏnggam nok* were the Hong Kyŏng-nae Rebellion of 1812 and the Tonghak Rebellion of 1894. The root causes of the Hong Kyŏng-nae Rebellion, which swept the northern province of P'yŏng'an, included regional discrimination and bad harvests. Nevertheless, prophetic belief based on the *Chŏnggam nok* also gave inspiration to the rebels and the people who rallied behind them.[49] The Tonghak Rebellion was a peasant uprising that arose as a result of the devastating effects from the social and economic turbulence within the country; antiforeign sentiments against Japan and the Western powers further provoked the rebellion. It took its name, however, from Tonghak (Eastern Learning), a new syncretic religion founded in 1860 that combined aspects of Confucianism and shamanism, as well as Christianity.[50] Like the Hong Kyŏng-nae Rebellion, the Tonghak Rebellion, too, found a source of inspiration and legitimacy in the *Chŏnggam nok*.[51] The book thus had a powerful hold on the popular religious imagination and could even challenge the authority of the state.

Another source of disturbances during the late Chosŏn was faith in Mirŭk (Maitreya) who would descend to establish a utopian order free from the suffering and evil of this world.[52] Like belief in the prophecies in the *Chŏnggam nok*, faith in Mirŭk was strongest in times of crisis. The late seventeenth and early eighteenth centuries were plagued by nationwide famine and epidemics, leading to widespread social unrest.[53] In 1688, a Buddhist monk named Yŏhwan predicted the fall of the Chosŏn dynasty and the establishment of the era of Mirŭk. Claiming that Mirŭk had promised him the country, Yŏhwan gathered a group of followers around him in anticipation of taking over the government, but their movement was quickly discovered and suppressed by the government. The aftereffects of the rebellion were felt in two provinces.[54] During the same period, there were other, smaller millennialist disturbances.[55] Then, in 1758, another major incident involving Mirŭk occurred, when a female shaman named Yŏngmu claimed to be the incarnation of Mirŭk and demanded that her followers abandon all other religious practices and worship her exclusively. The movement spread throughout three provinces before the government arrested and executed her.[56]

It is interesting to note that these millennialist movements, though centered on Mirŭk, also drew on various other beliefs.[57] For example, although Yŏngmu claimed to be the incarnation of the Buddha, she was a shamaness. Yŏhwan was a Buddhist monk, but his movement involved shamanism, Daoism, geomancy, and the *Chŏnggam nok*. Folk religion is, by nature, fluid and syncretic.

In the modern period, Mirŭk has given birth to several new messianic religions. The most prominent one is Chŭngsan-gyo, founded by Kang Il-sun (1871–1909), a former Tonghak who prophesied that an epidemic would destroy all of humankind unless he and his followers prevented its spread by performing magical practices using mantras, charms, and amulets. Kang told his followers that he would return to earth someday as Mirŭk. During the colonial period, Chŭngsan-gyo sects proliferated, numbering eighty by 1945.[58]

The arrival of Protestantism represented the addition of another layer to the tradition of messianic millennialism in Korean religious culture. Some Protestant converts, in fact, saw a direct relationship between the *Chŏnggam nok* and Christianity. When Kim Sang-nim, a Confucian scholar, came upon the *sipchagajido* (the way of the cross) of the Bible, he believed it to be the true meaning of the *sipsŭngjiji* (the ten auspicious places) prophesied in the *Chŏnggam nok* and converted to Christianity.[59] The two terms share the Chinese character for *sip*, meaning "ten"; the translation of *sipchaga*, the term for "cross," is literally "the wooden structure in the shape of the (Chinese) character for 'ten.'" Kim believed that Christianity was what he had been waiting for all along. Another Christian, Yi Sŭng-ryun, drew further links by looking at the form and meaning of other Chinese characters in the *Chŏnggam nok*, including Chŏng To-ryŏng's name, in light of Christianity.[60] Thus, for Yi, Kim, and others steeped in the tradition of the *Chŏnggam nok*, Christianity was true because it fulfilled the prophecies in the book.[61] The *Chŏnggam nok* was the basis, the source of validation, on which they accepted the new faith.

The identification of Jesus with Chŏng To-ryŏng seems to have been widespread among the early Protestant converts. Easurk Emsen Charr, who was one of the earliest Korean immigrants to the United States, recalls in his autobiography the time his family first heard of Christianity. An uncle who had converted came home to share the faith. After listening to him, another uncle immediately thought that Jesus was Chŏng To-ryŏng.[62] Charr himself makes a direct historical comparison: "Indeed, the people were looking for and longing for Prince Jung-Do-Ryung (Chŏng To-ryŏng), as did the Israelites of old for the Messiah, to come to claim the kingship of the land and enthrone himself in his new capital to be built at the base of the Gay-Riong (Kyeryong) Mountain in Choong-Chung (Ch'ungch'ŏng) province in the south."[63] Charr compares the Koreans to the Jews in their messianic expectations, but his analogy is significant in another respect as well. Like the Jews of first-century Palestine, whose millennialist hopes for a political revolution against the Roman Empire were transformed by Jesus and his followers into a spiritual revolution, the Koreans, too, accepted Jesus as the Prince of Peace.[64] Unlike the millennialist rebellions of late Chosŏn, Protestant millennialism during the colonial period never translated into a mass movement against the Japanese.[65] Because a new world was dawning through divine intervention, human effort was pointless.

The preaching of Kil and other revivalists to wait patiently for the Second Coming did not encourage political action. Indeed, after March First, Kil became one of the foremost opponents of Protestant involvement in nationalist politics, believing that the Church should occupy itself with strictly spiritual matters.[66] He called on his flock to look to the heavens for their salvation, proclaiming that Christ would soon descend on the clouds to gather the faithful unto him.[67]

Waiting for the Apocalypse

The vision of the Second Coming of Christ thus resonated with a rich millennialist tradition in Korean popular religion. For many, the millennialist expectation that had pervaded popular piety in late Chosŏn found new expression in Christianity; Jesus replaced Chŏng To-ryŏng and Mirŭk as the future deliverer. In the hands of Kil and other great revivalists, such as Kim Ik-tu (1874–1950) and Yi Sŏng-bong (1909–1965), who placed the belief in the Second Coming at the center of their faith, the tradition of popular millennialism continued into the colonial period, albeit now in Christian dress. The loss of nation and the tumultuous changes that followed gave even greater urgency and power to the collective hope for future deliverance.

Today, Korean Protestants are still waiting. Millennialist expectation remains strong. The majority of Korean Protestants believe in the imminent return of Christ and speak of Hyugŏ (Rapture), in which they will be caught up in the air with Jesus when he comes again. In a much publicized incident, one preacher, Yi Chang-nim, predicted October 28, 1992, as the precise date for the event, causing his followers to sell their possessions and abandon their families. Millennialist groups such as the Seventh-Day Adventists and Jehovah's Witnesses have large, significant followings in Korea. The emphasis on the Second Coming in Korean Protestantism has also produced new messianic religions derived from Christianity. Pak Tae-sŏn, a former Presbyterian elder, founded the Chŏndogwan (Hall of Evangelism), proclaiming himself the "olive tree" prophesied in *Revelation*.[68] Perhaps the best-known Korean religious leader in the world, Sun Myung Moon, the head of the Unification Church, claims to be the second Jesus who will complete the unfinished work of the first Jesus. Furthermore, on Mount Kyeryong, the site where Chŏng To-ryŏng is prophesied to appear, numerous new religions have emerged that combine Christianity and belief in the *Chŏnggam nok*. Many are based on the conviction that Korea will be the center of the new divine world order.

Interestingly, a similar attitude prevails among mainstream Protestant denominations as well.[69] Korean Protestants feel that Christianity has declined in the West, both numerically and doctrinally, and that Korea is now the last bastion of the true faith.[70] Korea sends missionaries not only to Africa, South America, and other parts of Asia, but also to Europe and the United States. In little over a century, Korea has grown from a mission field to a major center of Protestantism, and in the process has developed a distinctive Christian tradition. Protestantism entered Korea at the end of the 1800s with the social and cultural trappings of Anglo-American civilization. Today, it is a Korean religion.

NOTES

1. The growth of Protestantism during the colonial period was largely a rural phenomenon, the typical church being the village church. See Myoung-Woo Cho, "Regional Peasant Social and Religious Structures and Differential Rates of Social Change in Rural Colonial Korea" (Ph.D. diss., University of Washington, 1997), 246–247.

2. Kil Chin-gyŏng, *Yŏnggye Kil Sŏn-ju* (Seoul: Chongno Sŏjŏk Chusik Hoesa, 1980), 129.

3. "Revivalism" is a mass movement in Protestantism aimed at the personal experience of salvation. It is characterized by intensive preaching and prayer, and often involves a high level of emotion. Kil began the first Korean-led "revival meeting" in 1906 at his church, the Central Presbyterian Church (also called Changdaehyŏn Church). Later, the Great Revival of 1907 took place, beginning with Changdaehyŏn and other churches in P'yŏngyang but rapidly spreading to the rest of the country. Kil was called to lead many of the revival meetings in different areas. He was Korea's first great revivalist; he made the entire peninsula as well as parts of Manchuria his parish and spread the new faith through countless conversions. "Kil Sŏn-ju," *Kidokkyo taebaekkwa sajŏn* [Christian encyclopedia], ed. Pak Kŭn-yong et al. (Seoul: Kidok Kyomunsa, 1980–1985), 152–153. For a historical analysis of revivalism in Korea, see Timothy S. Lee, "Born-Again in Korea: The Rise and Character of Revivalism in (South) Korea, 1885–1988" (Ph.D. diss., University of Chicago, 1996).

4. Charles F. Bernheisel, "Kil Sunju," *The Korea Mission Field: A Monthly Journal of Christian Progress* 32 (February 1936): 30.

5. Kil's historical significance goes beyond his religious activities. Honored as a national hero, he participated in the March First Movement of 1919 as a *minjok taep'yo* (representative of the people), one of the thirty-three signers of the Korean Declaration of Independence. Kil was also an educator, one of the first Koreans to found a modern private school, and a reformer, who was engaged in a variety of movements, from rural development to women's issues.

6. One of his sermons portrays Jesus as the ultimate filial son, who, even as he hung on the cross dying, expressed love for his mother by leaving her in the care of

a close disciple. Kil Sŏn-ju, *Kil Sŏn-ju Moksa sŏlgyo* [Sermons of Pastor Kil Sŏn-ju] (Seoul: Hyemunsa, 1977), 1:130.

7. Kil received a Confucian education in his youth. In his teens, he entered the temple of Kwansŏnggyo, a cult devoted to the worship of Kwan U (C. Kuan Yu, one of the heroes of *The Romance of the Three Kingdoms*) and practiced severe asceticism, often staying awake for several days and nights. Before his conversion to Christianity, Kil was a Taoist master, famous for his physical and even supernatural skills. He also engaged in shamanistic practices involving communication with spirits. See Kil Chin-gyŏng, *Yŏnggye Kil Sŏn-ju*, 15 and 30. See also Bernheisel, "Kil Sunju," 29. For a description of the Kwan U cult, see Boudewijn Walraven, "Shamans and Popular Religion around 1900," in *Religions in Traditional Korea*, ed. Henrik H. Sorensen (Copenhagen: Seminar for Buddhist Studies, 1995), 124–128.

8. Bernheisel, "Kil Sunju," 29.

9. Yi Tŏk-chu, *Ch'ogi Han'guk Kidokkyosa yŏn'gu* [Study of early Korean Christian history] (Seoul: Han'guk Kidokkyo Yŏksa Yŏn'guso, 1995), 512.

10. Kil Chin-gyŏng, *Yŏnggye Kil Sŏn-ju*, 308. His son and biographer, Kil Chin-gyŏng, calculates that during the fourteen years of his father's ministry, 90 percent of morning Bible studies held during the revivals was devoted to the topic of the end of the world. See ibid., 329.

11. Bernheisel, "Kil Sunju," 30.

12. Kil Chin-gyŏng, *Yŏnggye Kil Sŏn-ju*, 311–313.

13. Ibid., 302.

14. Ibid., 306–307. The leader of the socialist gang was the husband of a female church worker.

15. Ibid., 301–305.

16. Carter J. Eckert et al., eds., *Korea Old and New: A History* (Seoul: Ilchogak, 1990), 306.

17. In 1935 the Japanese colonial government issued an order requiring all students and government employees to attend Shintō shrine ceremonies. Many Protestants resisted, considering the act idolatrous. The Japanese cracked down by closing schools and churches, expelling foreign missionaries, and arresting Korean clergy. The persecution also produced several martyrs. Although a small minority resisted to the end, most Christians were eventually forced into compliance. After the liberation of Korea from colonial rule in 1945, the Shintō shrine controversy caused deep divisions in the Protestant churches over who resisted and who did not.

18. Yi Tŏk-chu, *Ch'ogi Han'guk Kidokkyosa yŏn'gu*, 513. Kil Chin-gyŏng, who was present when his father passed away, gives a different account, in which Kil Sŏn-ju drew on the floor with his finger, but no one could decipher the writing. See Kil Chin-gyŏng, *Yŏnggye Kil Sŏn-ju*, 320.

19. Kil Chin-gyŏng credits his father as having foreseen World War II and the liberation of Korea. See Kil Chin-gyŏng, *Yŏnggye Kil Sŏn-ju*, 282.

20. The work was published posthumously in 1968 because of colonial-period censorship. See ibid., 254.

21. Kil Sŏn-ju, *Yŏnggye Kil Sŏn-ju Moksa yugo sŏnjip* [Selection of Pastor Kil

Sŏn-ju's posthumous works, vol. 1] (Seoul: Taehan Kidokkyo Sŏhoe, 1968), 39–41.

22. Ibid., 41–42 (the verse is Matthew 10:27).

23. Ibid., 72–73. For a summary of the millennialism found in Buddhism, Islam, and Hinduism, see entries for "millenarianism," "eschatology," and "messianism" in *Encyclopedia of Religion*, ed. Mircea Eliade et al. (New York: Macmillan, 1987).

24. Kil Sŏn-ju, *Yŏnggye Kil Sŏn-ju Moksa yugo sŏnjip*, 72.

25. Kil follows closely the narrative in the last chapters of Revelation (19–22). Kil Sŏn-ju, *Yŏnggye Kil Sŏn-ju Moksa yugo sŏnjip*, 89–135. Kil and most other Korean Protestants at the time were premillennialists, who believed that Christ would come before the thousand-year kingdom. Postmillennialists, on the other hand, believed that Christ would come at the end of the thousand years.

26. Ibid., 138.

27. Yi, *Ch'ogi Han'guk Kidokkyosa yŏn'gu*, 515.

28. Kil Sŏn-ju, *Yŏnggye Kil Sŏn-ju moksa yugo sŏnjip*, 135–140.

29. "Then I saw a new heaven and a new earth; for the first heaven and the first earth had passed away, and the sea was no more. And I saw the holy city, new Jerusalem, coming down out of heaven from God, prepared as a bride adorned for her husband" (Revelation 21.1–2). *The New Oxford Annotated Bible with the Apocrypha, Revised Standard Version*, ed. Herbert G. May and Bruce M. Metzger (New York: Oxford University Press, 1977), 1511–1512. The expression "new heaven and new earth" also appears in the book of Isaiah (65.17, 66.22) in the vision of a restored Jerusalem.

30. Ezekiel 36.35, 47.12. Isaiah 51.3.

31. Duk-Whang Kim, *A History of Religions in Korea* (Seoul: Daeji Moonhwasa, 1988), 56–59.

32. Stephan Schuhmacher et al., eds., *The Encyclopedia of Eastern Philosophy and Religion: Buddhism, Hinduism, Taoism, Zen* (Boston: Shambhala, 1994), 340–341.

33. The famous Chinese poet Tao Yuanming (Tao Qian, 365–427) tells the story in a prose poem. A fisherman accidentally discovers in the midst of a peach blossom forest a group of people who had escaped war and conflict several generations before and had established an ideal agrarian community. The people urge the fisherman to stay, but he leaves in order to share his discovery with the outside world. But when he goes back, he finds that he cannot rediscover the hidden community.

34. Even in Western Christian conceptions of heaven, there is great diversity, ranging from heavenly visions of singing angels to theological abstractions about the eternal. In the absence of specific details of what the afterlife will be like in the Bible or church doctrines, the idea of heaven seems largely left to the popular imagination. The tendency in recent times has been to see heaven as an extension of all the good things that one experiences in this world. See Colleen McDannell and Bernhard Lang, *Heaven: A History* (New Haven, Conn.: Yale University Press, 1988), 307–308.

35. Kil Sŏn-ju, *Kil Sŏn-ju Moksa yugo sŏnjip*, 135–138. Kil explains that the fires will be only partial, allowing the faithful to escape harm. Moreover, the fires will serve to purify Creation as it is restored to the original state of paradise.

36. Ibid., 139.

37. Ibid., 139–140.

38. Yi, *Ch'ogi Han'guk Kidokkyosa yŏn'gu*, 514.

39. Kil Sŏn-ju, *Mansa sŏngch'wi* [Fulfillment of all things] (P'yŏngyang: Kwangmyŏng Sŏgwan, 1921), 28–30.

40. Ibid., 46–47. It is interesting to note that *yŏng'ung* is a traditional term for heroes, but *yŏlsa* is a modern term, usually referring to patriots or even revolutionaries.

41. Ibid., 48–49.

42. Ibid., 30.

43. Ibid., 50–51.

44. James Huntley Grayson, *Korea: A Religious History* (New York: Oxford University Press, 1989), 242–243.

45. Keith Pratt and Richard Rutt, *Korea: A Historical and Cultural Dictionary* (Surrey: Curzon Press, 1999), 57.

46. Ibid. See also Grayson, *Korea*, 242–243.

47. Grayson, *Korea*, 242–243.

48. See Sun Joo Kim, "Marginalized Elite, Regional Discrimination, and the Tradition of Prophetic Belief in the Hong Kyŏngnae Rebellion" (Ph.D. diss., University of Washington, 2000), 184–190.

49. Ibid., 190–203.

50. Benjamin B. Weems, *Reform, Rebellion, and the Heavenly Way* (Tucson: The University of Arizona Press, 1964), 8.

51. Ibid., 8–9.

52. For studies of Maitreya in East Asian history, see Alan Sponberg and Helen Hardacre, eds., *Maitreya, the Future Buddha* (Cambridge: Cambridge University Press, 1988). Works on Maitreya in Korea include Kim Sam-yong, *Han'guk Mirŭk sinang yŏn'gu* [Study on Mirŭk belief in Korea] (Seoul: Tonghwa Ch'ulp'ansa, 1983), and Han'guk Pulgyo Munhwa Yŏn'guwŏn, ed., *Han'guk Mirŭk sasang yŏn'gu* [Study of Mirŭk thought in Korea] (Seoul: Tongguk Taehakkyo Ch'ulp'anbu, 1987).

53. See Chŏng Sŏk-chong, "Chosŏn hugi Sukchong nyŏn'gan ŭi Mirŭk sinang kwa sahoe undong" [Mirŭk belief and social movements during the reign of Sukchong in late Chosŏn], in *Han U-gŭn Paksa chŏngnyŏn kinyŏm sahak nonch'ong* [Historical studies in honor of Dr. Han U-gŭn's retirement], ed. Han U-gŭn Paksa Chŏngnyŏn Kinyŏm Sahak Nonch'ong Kanhaeng Chunbi Wiwŏnhoe (Seoul: Chisik Sanŏpsa, 1981), 417–422.

54. The incident is recorded in the official annals of the Chosŏn dynasty, the *Sillok* [Veritable records]. For a translation of the passage dealing with Yŏhwan and his followers, see Yŏngho Ch'oe, Peter H. Lee, and Wm. Theodore de Bary, eds., *Sources of Korean Tradition, vol. 2: From the Sixteenth Century to the Twentieth Century* (New York: Columbia University Press, 2000), 174–176. The disturbance is ana-

lyzed in Chŏng Sŏk-chong, "Chosŏn hugi Sukchong nyŏn'gan ŭi Mirŭk sinang kwa sahoe undong," 409–446.

55. Ko Sŏng-hun, "Sukchong pyŏllan ŭi iltan" [An aspect of disturbances during the reign of Sukchong], in *Sohŏn Nam To-yŏng Paksa kohŭi kinyŏm yŏksahak nonch'ong* [Historical studies in honor of Dr. Nam To-yŏng's seventieth birthday], ed. Sohŏn Nam To-yŏng Paksa Kohŭi Kinyŏm Yŏksahak Nonch'ong Kanhaeng Wiwŏnhoe (Seoul: Minjok Munhwasa, 1993), 405–425.

56. The disturbance caused by the female shaman is recounted in the writings of the Confucian historian An Chŏng-bok (1712–1791; pen name Sunam). Set in the context of a polemical piece against Roman Catholicism, An compares Yŏngmu's claim to be Mirŭk to the Christian doctrine of the incarnation, finding the latter just as dangerous in deluding people and causing unrest. See his "Ch'ŏnhak mundap" [Questions and answers on heavenly learning], in *Sunam chŏnjip* [Complete works of Sunam], ed. Yi U-sŏng (Seoul: Yŏgang Ch'ulp'ansa, 1984), 1:379–380. A translation of the passage dealing with Yŏngmu is found in Ch'oe, Lee, and de Bary, eds., *Sources of Korean Tradition*, 176–177.

57. One incident, in 1718, involved a man claiming to be Confucius. See Ko, "Sukchong pyŏllan ŭi iltan," 414–415.

58. Lewis Lancaster, "Maitreya in Korea," in *Maitreya, the Future Buddha*, ed. Alan Sponberg and Helen Hardacre (Cambridge: Cambridge University Press, 1988), 147. For a study of new religions during the colonial period, see Murayama Chijun, *Chōsen no ruiji shūkyō* [Pseudo-religions of Korea] (Keijō: Chōsen Sōtokufu, 1935). On new religions in general, see H. Byron Earhart, "The New Religions of Korea: A Preliminary Interpretation," *Transactions of the Korea Branch of the Royal Asiatic Society* 49 (1974): 7–25, and Spencer J. Palmer, "The New Religions of Korea," *Transactions of the Korea Branch of the Royal Asiatic Society* 43 (1967).

59. Yi Tŏk-chu and Cho Yi-je, *Kanghwa Kidokkyo 100-nyŏnsa* [The one-hundred-year history of Christianity on Kanghwa] (Seoul: Kanghwa Moguhoe, 1994), 106.

60. Yi Tŏk-chu, *Han'guk t'och'ak kyohoe hyŏngsŏngsa yŏn'gu* [Study of the growth of an indigenous Korean church] (Seoul: Han'guk Kidokkyo Yŏksa Yŏn'guso, 2000), 365–366.

61. After the failure of the Tonghak Rebellion, many former rebels converted to Protestantism. The nationalist leader Kim Ku (1876–1949) is probably the most famous example.

62. Easurk Emsen Charr, *The Golden Mountain: The Autobiography of a Korean Immigrant, 1895–1960*, edited and with an introduction by Wayne Patterson (Urbana: University of Illinois Press, 1996), 46. Charr's uncle had been a Tonghak before his conversion to Christianity.

63. Ibid., 42.

64. Ibid., 45–57.

65. Some believed that Kil was in a position to mobilize Protestants for armed conflict. In 1907, Korean Protestants debated whether to join the ŭibyŏng (righteous armies), who had risen up in arms following the abdication of Emperor Kojong. Kil took the lead in opposing the move. The missionaries credited him as having

successfully prevented the whole region around P'yŏngyang, the center of Korean Protestantism but also "famous for the sturdy fighters," from insurrection; he "delivered Korea from tremendous bloodshed." L. George Paik, *The History of Protestant Missions in Korea, 1832–1910*, Series of Reprints of Western Books on Korea, no. 6 (Seoul: Yonsei University Press, 1980), 416.

66. See Min Kyoung-Bae (Min Kyŏng-bae), "The Korean Churches and the Organisation of the Nationalist Movements," *Yonsei Journal of Theology* 3 (1998): 115–130.

67. *The Book of Revelation*, the text on which Christian millennialism is based, is itself no manual for political revolution. The original audience was first-century Christians suffering persecution and martyrdom under imperial Rome. Writing in the form of a letter to the community, the author encourages them to patiently bear the hardships and remain faithful. Divine action will bring justice and reward.

68. In the final days, two "witnesses," symbolized by two olive trees and two lamps, will appear and display prophetic and other supernatural powers. Revelation 11:3–13.

69. Even in Kil's time, Korean Protestants seem to have had the sense of a special place for Korea in a new Christendom, as evidenced by the fact that they appropriated the name "Jerusalem" for the city of P'yŏngyang.

70. There appears to be a historical pattern for this kind of zealous adherence to orthodoxy. Korean Neo-Confucians believed that they were the last upholders of Cheng-Chu orthodoxy after the fall of the Ming dynasty. A more recent example is North Korea, the last Marxist-Stalinist state.

CHAPTER 8

Mothers, Daughters, Biblewomen, and Sisters
An Account of "Women's Work" in the Korea Mission Field

Donald N. Clark

In 1984, the publication of Jane Hunter's study of women missionaries in China opened a new window of scholarly inquiry about the work and interactions of Western and Chinese Christian women, particularly single women, in the promotion of Christian institutions and opportunities for "native" women.[1] Especially notable is the field of women's education. Less familiar is the work of evangelistic missionaries and their local counterparts. The contributions and achievements of the "agents and actors" in these areas are not in doubt. However, the practitioners remain objects for study rather than people to identify with, and missionaries—and again this seems especially true for unmarried women missionaries—remain an odd lot reminiscent of something outdated or even outlandish.

In Jane Hunter's book *The Gospel of Gentility*, the formidable and talented women missionaries are reorganized into a mildly feminist category of people with indomitable personalities but peculiar private lives. One type, for example, is the female graduate of the Midwestern denominational college who chooses a career in China over the drudgery of life as a farmer's wife; who finds fulfillment in work but no eligible men in China; and who poses prickly social problems for Chinese men and married missionaries, male and female, who end up treating her as if she were gender neutral. This caricature can be the starting point for painting single women missionaries as restless reformers or even social revolutionaries. It does not, however, paint the picture fully or in enough colors. One needs to move beyond the caricature to discover more about what these remarkable women actually did.

Women missionaries and their local counterparts were an important part of the missionary effort in Korea just as they were in China, and in many of the same ways. In their assignments they found roles and ways to make a difference that outshone many of the likely possibilities back home.

A hundred years ago, Western society also was far from according women equal rights, especially in the public sphere. In church they could not be ordained as ministers and thus always ranked behind male pastors in their roles as Sunday school teachers and in "softer" kinds of service. However, in the mission field, including Korea, the emphasis on "women's evangelism"—the contacting and teaching of Korean girls and women in homes, schools, and churches throughout the country—offered a special opportunity to function as fully franchised professional. Women were of inestimable importance to the success of the overall Korea mission effort.

The need for women missionaries in Korea was clear from the fact that males, and especially foreign males, were barred from contact with respectable Korean women. Horace Allen, the first Protestant missionary doctor, found that he was discouraged from treating female patients. When he founded his clinic in 1885, he had to borrow palace women, *kisaeng* entertainers actually, to be "nurses" to assist in the treatment of women. Lillias Horton, M.D., the first woman doctor in Korea, was recruited to work with women explicitly because of this cultural taboo.[2]

Northern Presbyterians Cyril and Susan Ross were a typical Korea missionary couple in the early 1900s. Like many Americans of his generation, Cyril Ross was an immigrant, born and educated in Scotland before his family moved to Canada and then to the United States. He earned degrees at Park College and eventually at Princeton Theological Seminary, two schools that emphasized missionary training and had alumni in Korea. Susan Shank Ross was an Illinois native who earned her medical degree at Northwestern in 1896. In 1897 she volunteered for service with the Presbyterian Board of Foreign Missions and was assigned to the newly opened field of Korea. Eleven days before she sailed she married Cyril Ross, who was by then a fellow missionary-designate.

In Korea, the Rosses were first stationed in Pusan, where their main business was language study. Cyril tried out Korean phrases with his teacher on short trips to nearby villages while Susan practiced her Korean in the station clinic, treating women patients.

It was not long before the Rosses had begun to learn the price for volunteering to serve in Korea. Their first child, Dewey, born in Pusan in 1897, died suddenly while the family was visiting Seoul the following year. As she awaited the birth of her second child in the summer of 1900, Susan looked back upon their loss and the empathy it had generated:

It has been a comfort in our sorrow to know that friends at home have been with us in prayer and sympathy. Our Korean friends seemed to come nearer to us, in that time, than ever before. It seems to me that the real soul is alike in us all, though scarcely anything else is. The day when we came back to our lonely home, the Koreans came in one after another, all day, to tell us of their sympathy and their prayers for us. Some who had loved the little baby wept when they spoke of him. As they came and went, I felt that all the differences of complexion and feature, of physical and mental habits, were but the merest incidental circumstances and the people themselves are exactly like us. I had felt this before when some of our people had themselves been in sorrow.[3]

The Rosses' second child, Lilian, was born in Pusan in November 1900. By then, Susan had become accustomed to making the hundred-mile journey to Taegu to work as the women's doctor in the Presbyterian hospital there, and in the spring of 1900 baby Lilian went with her. "It has been a nice opportunity to see the work in a new inland station," wrote Susan Ross.

Miss Nourse, with whom I have been staying, and Mrs. Adams receive Korean women who call and Mrs. Adams has a class which meets every Wednesday afternoon while Miss Nourse meets with and teaches women who come in, on Sunday morning especially. There are as yet no women who are even catechumens, but there are six in Mrs. Adams' class who are interested and say they believe.[4]

In 1902, the Rosses were sent to join the newly opened mission station at Sŏnch'ŏn near the Manchurian border. Cyril Ross started "itinerating" to nearby villages, visiting the homes of students in the Sŏnch'ŏn Presbyterian boys' school, seeking out parents for possible conversion to Christianity. As the students' families became Christians and started little home churches, they invited relatives and neighbors to join, increasing the Christian community in the Sŏnch'ŏn territory from 677 to 4,039 between 1902 and 1907. The boys' and girls' academies on the Sŏnch'ŏn mission compound became important regional institutions along with the Presbyterian clinic run by Drs. Alfred Sharrocks and Susan Ross, the men's and women's physicians.

When she was not seeing patients, Susan Ross ran a class in her living room for women who wanted to join the church, taught hygiene at the girls' academy, and paid visits of her own to women in homes throughout the city—dropping in unannounced to talk on the women's porches and invite them to church or to communicant classes. Like all other women missionaries, Susan Ross did not go calling alone. She was always accompanied by a Korean companion known as a "Biblewoman." Biblewomen were workers paid by the mission to act as assistants to missionary women doing evangelistic work. Some did double duty as the missionaries' language teachers, accompanying them whenever they went out on what amounted to language laboratory sessions in public. Some Biblewomen were students, or former students; others were deaconesses in the local church; and still others were simply Christian women who applied for positions as Biblewomen in an employment climate that otherwise offered them very little chance to earn an income. The foreign women depended on them and respected them both for their dedication as Christians and their strength as women.[5]

Biblewomen were major sources of cultural information for the missionaries and often spared them from embarrassing failures. Once, for example, Susan Ross wanted to do some calling on women in "unbelieving homes."

> The Biblewoman told me the women in such homes would be so embarrassed by [my] coming upon them in the dishabille to which they let themselves down in August heat that I could do them no good. So we waited for cooler weather. We had some good times calling until the weather grew cold and the women went into their houses and shut their doors. After that we could still call where we knew the people but it was not so easy to approach perfect strangers as it had been when we would find the women in their yards or sitting in their open doorways.[6]

Susan Ross and her Biblewomen conducted classes for village women in Sŏnch'ŏn, teaching them how to read and understand the Bible and encouraging them to develop leadership skills. The Biblewomen helped her attract local women to the mothers' clubs (ŏmŏni-hoe) that she started in order to provide maternal and child health. Dr. Ross's activities in this work reflected an interesting blend of Calvinism and modern science.

"So many children are fed whatever they want whenever they want it," she wrote, echoing a common Western criticism. "No system at all. Not only digestion suffers, but when such practices are carried to extreme, disobedience and lack of self-control are the result." She was not the first or last Westerner to comment disapprovingly on the freedom permitted Korean toddlers, but she was just as quick to acknowledge the futility of many Western remedies for what ailed the local population.

Once she returned from a trip to Seoul full of ideas, charts, posters, recipes for a milk substitute made of beans, and a substitute for orange juice made from cabbage.

> Some of the mothers know and put into practice already some of the modern ideas of child hygiene. Babies are very much better taken care of now than when we first came to town. Still the most willing mother has so little with which to do that it is small wonder if she sometimes grows tired of hearing foreigners who have all the milk, soap, clean clothes, orange juice, etc.... tell her how to do things. She would be glad to do so also if only she could.[7]

As younger missionaries arrived to staff the Sŏnch'ŏn clinic, Susan Ross devoted increasing amounts of time to teaching in the girls' academy and the Women's Bible Institute. The *institute* classes were short courses on the Bible aimed at non-Christians recruited by the Biblewomen, who promoted them as chances to attend school—a rare privilege for ordinary Korean village women. Some classes were more advanced and aimed at leadership training for churchwomen. Hundreds of women turned out for sessions of the Sŏnch'ŏn mission's Bible Institute. Some failed the courses and simply returned to try again. Susan Ross sympathized with women who were ill-prepared for school by life in rural Korea. As she once observed, "Minds that have not only been untrained but have been dulled by grief are slow in awakening."[8]

Dr. Ross also devoted much of her time to her children, Lilian and Albert, who grew up in a mission station that was full of foreign and Korean playmates. Sŏnch'ŏn was a fertile place, and the missionary mothers had much child care to occupy them, even with the help of Korean amahs, the female servants employed as babysitters.

The mothers took turns homeschooling the compound's children through the early grades, while the older children went to boarding school in P'yŏngyang. In 1918 the Rosses' neighbors included the George McCunes (four children), the Stacy Robertses (five), the Alfred Sharrockses (four), the Henry Lampes (eight), and the Norman Whittemores (one), for a total of twenty-four children under age eighteen. In that year, Lilian Ross graduated from Pyeng Yang Foreign School and was sent to her father's alma mater, Park College, in Parkville, Missouri.

Studies at Park and later Huron College, and graduate work at Biblical Seminary for Women in New York, prepared Lilian Ross to return to Korea as a missionary in her own right. No doubt there was an element of "going home" in her decision to apply to the Presbyterian Board for service in the country where she had grown up. As with other second-generationers who were returning to Korea in the 1920s, it was thought that her experience with the language and gladness to serve in the land of her birth were important indicators of effectiveness as a missionary, so she was welcomed home not only as a daughter of the mission but as a valuable mission asset.

As a teacher, Lilian was eager to get started gathering classes of women and children to learn the Bible through storytelling. In the United States she had studied teaching methods, including storytelling via simple visual media such as the flannel graph, a plain flannel-covered easel on which colored flannel cutouts of Bible story characters and all the other elements of scenery for storytelling could be stuck and moved around as the story continued. In Korea the Presbyterian Mission assigned her to general evangelism in the provincial town of Kanggye.

Kanggye was a regional center of eighteen thousand inhabitants, accessible via a railroad spur that ran from Sinanju on the west coast up through the mountains to the Yalu River. It was an ancient walled frontier town, an erstwhile fortress that had recently been transformed into a regional base of operations by the Japanese colonial regime. In the mid-1930s the Japanese upgraded the railroad connections in keeping with their plans to open more access points between Korea and Manchuria, for which reason there was a significant increase in the Japanese population.

The Presbyterian Mission compound commanded a view of the valley junction in which Kanggye was nestled, and from her bedroom window Lilian could look out on the woods nearby, the terraced fields in the valley beyond, and a distant range of mountains that were covered with snow in winter. The Kanggye mission compound had its own garden plots, and Lilian spent much time watching the weather and tending her household economy. Winters in Kanggye were so cold that it took hours to warm up the house in the morning; on some days Lilian simply stayed in bed reading until it was possible to function. Summers were milder, but the Korean rainy season made things soggy and sometimes dangerous.

"The river is flooded," she wrote one July day in 1937, "carrying away pigs and houses and covering fields. What the drought did not destroy the floods aim to ruin. The ceiling is leaking in our dining room; plaster is falling. There has been a lot of sickness this summer and not a few deaths among our church families."[9]

In most years, however, the Kanggye valley was rich with the fruits and vegetables that ripened in sequence through the spring and summer months. Lilian spent a lot of time tending the garden:

> Our grapes are huge but it is some time before they will ripen. Some sunny day I might check the disease started among them. I shall pick them over a

little tomorrow. Have already canned quite a little tomatoes. We pick and ripen [them] on the sunporch to reduce loss by decay. I want to put up plenty. Shall serve for dessert fruit this winter, for salad or vegetable, or for appetizers. If plums and grapes fail, strawberries and tomatoes will be my stock of fruit! Sometimes I'll be reckless and buy apples or pumalo [pomelo?]. (Never fear, stingy Scotchman that I be, I always live on the fat of the land.) Have had watermelon, peaches, apples—and not failed for meat either.[10]

Every two or three days, Lilian took sheets of onionskin letter paper and handwrote letters to her parents, addressing them in *hangul* script as *abu* or *ŏmma*, childhood forms of the words for father and mother. The letters, cathartic for her to write and a joy for the Rosses to receive and file, constitute a diary of Lilian's early career on the mission field.

Between the lines, as Lilian wrote of happiness when new missionaries were assigned to Kanggye and particularly when women were assigned to terms as "companion" missionaries in the single ladies' house on the compound, one detects suggestions of loneliness. However, her expressions seem never to have transgressed family propriety by mentioning a longing for romance or a fear of spinsterhood. Women missionaries were free to have relationships and marry, but in Lilian Ross's case one senses a renunciation, something like that of a Catholic nun. Her letters tell of small pleasures, such as working in her garden, receiving visits from old friends, and doing small deeds for others such as sewing a sleep outfit for a new baby in the neighborhood. They reveal her struggle to upgrade her childhood Korean as she worked with a tutor to learn the proper forms of address for use by a mature woman.

This was a matter of polish for second-generation missionaries who were quite confident in their ability to speak street Korean but needed a more dignified vocabulary to function effectively as teachers and command respect from Korean peers and students. Perhaps as important was the fact that passing the second-year-level exam in Korean would qualify her to vote on mission matters.

Lilian Ross easily found women who needed her attention. Kanggye too had a Bible Institute that offered classes for men and women during farming's slack season. Her women's Bible Institute alumnae formed her network of contacts in the surrounding villages and provided her with welcoming places to visit when she went out to conduct classes at village churches, welcomes that she reciprocated when they came calling in Kanggye. At home she also opened her living room to classes for the town's lone women, the castaways and runaways who worked in restaurants, bars, and coffee shops and often engaged in prostitution. These were women who

routinely endured degrading abuse, and on their rare days off Lilian Ross
tried to give them a warm environment in which they could talk and sing
and regain some dignity through study:

> Tomorrow I am hoping to have a group of cafe girls. The Jap. keeper is not
> sending his girls (only 3 of 12 are Korean) but the [Korean] keeper said he
> would. He is reported to have said, "And does the foreigner consider us as
> folks? Then invite us!" We shall see what happens. Then next I want to
> return to the *kisaeng* house where Ch'anghi was and where I have called
> several times, and see if I can have them come for a party. How else can one
> get on the inside? There is so much to be done and so little being tried for
> these neediest ones. I love to have more folks to love, with music, flowers,
> and books, but most of all our Savior to share with eager ones—His lambs
> and sheep for whom I too am responsible. Just how could I not be happy![11]

One of her forays into social work with young working women was
her class for "bus girls," the undereducated teenagers who operated the
doors and collected the fares on public autos and buses. Bus girls worked
cruel hours, often starting work in the freezing predawn hours and staying
on their vehicles with little time for rest or food until the last run in the
evening. They answered to several "bosses" at once: the drivers, their super-
visors, and the customers, and they suffered considerable psychological and
physical abuse. Lilian Ross considered them prime candidates for evangelism, and despite the hardships of their working days they were still endear-
ing as teenagers:

> Yesterday evening the bus girls came to play. Of the nine, three have had
> some church training. When I led in prayer one of the youngsters started
> giggling and that started one or two more. The others called them down.
> (One of the girls came today and said the one who started giggling said she
> was sorry and that she did badly and that she wanted to be a Christian after
> this.) While we ate I said each one of us should do a stunt. One girl had
> brought her hymnbook and so the stunts consisted of hymn singing. I told
> them the story of the boy who had to pay store price for the boat that he
> himself had made and lost and found on sale—and ended up "Ye are bought
> with a price." The girls asked one of their number to lead in prayer before
> they left. We had a good time getting acquainted and playing games. They
> seldom have time off to go to church working on Sunday. They are a
> responsive bunch well worth some effort and help.... The child who came
> back today said she was leaving the bus work, no future to it, unable to be a
> Christian. She hoped there would be some opening at our hospital, which
> there isn't.[12]

The hardships of working-class Korean women were revealed a little differently in another letter about a recent Bible Institute graduate.

> Her younger daughter (17 years) was sold to a *yorichip* (roadside restaurant) by her husband. She did not know any better than to go and did not even notify her mother for some months. Now she is kept here in town. She has been spending her spare time weeping at her mother's. The mother is distracted. The price of the girl has gone from ¥100, which the husband received, to ¥230. The police doctor [has] sent her to the hospital and already the price is ¥240. [I received] ¥60 from the US. recently. The mother thinks she can raise ¥60 by selling her sewing machine. I do not have the [funds] even to advance [the rest].[13]

In 1927, the same year that Lilian Ross began her work in Kanggye, the Southern Presbyterian Mission acquired a single missionary named Florence Root for similar work with women in Kwangju, far to the southwest, in the region known as Honam. From the arrival of the first seven missionaries in 1892, the Southern Presbyterians laid considerable emphasis on girls' education and women's evangelism, and by 1927 women comprised fully 60 percent of the Honam Protestant community. The mission employed many single women who were renowned for braving weather, distance, bad food, and illness to hold classes for country women in tiny *anpang*, the "inner rooms" of farmhouses that sequestered the women of the region and isolated them from education and mental exercise.

Elise Shepping, to cite one example, started a school for girls, founded the first Korean branch of the Women's Christian Temperance Union (WCTU), and created a chain of dozens of "auxiliaries," or "circles," for women to meet and practice reading the Bible, teaching each other without male interference. When Florence Root arrived in Honam, it was as a successor to an already formidable line of missionary women.

Born in 1893 in Oswego County, New York, "Miss Florence" attended Smith College, taught in public schools in upstate New York, and did office work as a secretary and a bookkeeper before she decided to volunteer for missionary work in Korea. After a period of language study she was assigned to the Speer School for Girls in Kwangju, where she taught English and Bible and soon became the principal.

One of Florence Root's first letters home included this assessment of what the Christian gospel could do for rural Koreans, particularly women:

> To the skeptics and others who feel that the missionaries are forcing an undesired and unneeded religion on non-Christian people I would like to say, "Come with me to these villages I have just visited, and let me show you

how the Christian stands head and shoulders above his non-Christian brothers in the community." One little village called White Stone, straggling along beside a clear mountain stream, in one of the most picturesque places I have seen, was almost entirely heathen. But there was a 17-year-old Christian girl who had attended our mission school for girls in Chunju [Chŏnju] for several years. Her clothes were clean, she herself was neat and clean and alert—a marked contrast to the passiveness and slovenliness of most of the women there. This contrast prevails in greater or less degree wherever one finds Christians and non-believers together.[14]

Kwangju, Korea, was a long way from Root's native New York, but she lost no time becoming thoroughly countrified in the Southern Presbyterian territory. Before the end of her first term in Korea she already looked on Seoul as mecca of civilization "with its wide streets, beautiful stores and hurrying automobiles and streetcars."

However, Korea was always playing tricks on foreigners. One day, sated with shopping and good food from Seoul, as she was waiting for her train in the city's new baroque railway station, a pair of middle-aged males opened their parcels and held up sets of brand-new long johns:

They were very much pleased with the appearance of these garments, and— apparently not content to wait until they got home—proceeded to disrobe, completely, e'en down to nature, don the new purchases, reclothe themselves and go on their way rejoicing to catch their train. All this in absolute unconcern and unconsciousness of their surroundings, and in the main waiting room of a railway station that would do credit to one of our American cities![15]

Like Lilian Ross and other single women missionaries in Korea, Florence Root shared a home with other unmarried women in what was referred to in most locations as the "ladies' house" but in Southern Presbyterian territory was called the "saxie house," using the colloquial term for "maiden" or "bride." Normally in Korea a "saxie" (*ssaeksi*) was someone young and marriageable, ready to become a faithful wife, a filial daughter-in-law, and a bearer of sons.

In the daily speech of missionaries, the term "saxies" attached to single women missionaries with a certain irony inasmuch as missionary saxies were likely to remain unmarried and were established in careers where they often had considerable autonomy. It derived from the colloquial speech of Koreans, particularly servants, who had no other word to fit the situation.[16] Indeed, the combined strangeness of being foreign, female, and single occasioned much comment, often within earshot. Florence Root enjoyed telling this anecdote:

> I overheard two women in the hospital talking about me the other day. One said to the other: "Look at that foreign woman—do you suppose she is a Big Baby?" The other one who knows me well replied, "Yes." "How many rice cakes has she eaten?" (being interpreted, how old is she?) "You must not ask that: American ladies don't like to answer that question."
>
> A Big Baby is a daughter who is in her middle teens or above who has not yet married. In the old days, it was not necessary to ask that question among Koreans at all, because no unmarried girl could wear her hair done up, but had to wear it in a braid down her back. But now that girls are going to school and on to higher schools the custom has changed so that even some of our high school girls who are older than the majority wear their hair up, and no questions asked.[17]

Florence Root kept her blondish hair in a long braid, which she coiled around her head in a fashion statement that helped define her as a special case. Passersby and students soon learned that her Korean was too good to allow them to make rude comments where she could overhear them. Like her contemporary Lilian Ross, as her command of the language progressed she was able to learn more about the condition and needs of Korean women in general.

It seemed urgently necessary not only to teach girls via an organized curriculum in the Speer School but also to offer adult education that would lift mothers and grandmothers out of illiteracy and, it was hoped, to knowledge of the Gospel. During winter breaks, the slack season for farming, she taught women's classes in the Bible Institute, the Koreawide effort by Presbyterians to provide ordinary country people with a two-week series of laypeople's classes in hangul literacy and Bible study. The institutes were fun, partly because they involved music, singing, and scripture memorization games and contests, and the job forced Florence to sharpen her musical skills.

Mentors and Students: The Ewha Scene

Florence Root was never prouder than when her Speer girls went on to college, often in Seoul at the Methodist Ewha Womans College (now Ewha Womans University). Ewha was a project of the women's division of the American Methodist Episcopal Church and the flagship institution of the entire pan-denominational effort in women's education. It began in

June 1886 with a single pupil, a child found lying against the city wall with her mother, who was suffering from typhus. The mother, once recovered, briefly pulled her out of the school for fear that she was going to be kidnaped and taken to America. Such was the fear of foreigners and indifference toward education for lower-class girls in Korea. The school's founder, Mary Scranton, then recruited a second student who happened to be an orphan. Within a year she had seven students. The Protestant effort in girls' education was under way. By 1935, in all of Korea there were twenty-three thousand girls in Protestant mission and church schools, and thousands of adult women had been taught to read in Sunday schools and Bible institutes.

Mary Fletcher Benton Scranton, a fifty-two-year-old widow from Belchertown, Massachusetts, arrived in Korea in 1885 with her son William, a pioneer Methodist missionary. Because Mary Scranton was not a formally appointed missionary herself, her school soon was taken over as a regular mission project by the Women's Board of the Methodist Church, which has retained an interest in it ever since.

The early faculty of Ewha were all women appointed directly by the Women's Board to teach in what was not yet a college but a middle and high school—advanced enough for turn-of-the-century Korea. It was in Chŏng-dong, on property still occupied by Ewha Girls' High School, until 1935, when the present campus in Sinch'on was dedicated. That dedication was a triumph of missionary planning and effort as well as the result of substantial gifts from leading Methodist laywomen in the United States. The land for the school was purchased for $30,000 by Mrs. Philip Gray of Detroit and her two daughters. Mrs. Henry Pfeiffer of New York, who wanted to be first with the gift for the land, had to settle for Pfeiffer Hall, the donation for which brought her accumulated gifts to the $50,000 mark, later supplemented by an additional $104,000.

Missionary educators did the daily work of building Ewha, and the bonds that were forged between foreign and Korean women and between foreign teachers and their Korean students are clearly visible in every aspect of the school's history. Jeannette Walter, a teacher at Ewha from 1911 to 1926, spent her middle years in the school's family of missionaries, workers, and students. Her life revolved around the Chŏng-dong campus and the faculty house with "Sunamie" the cook, "Ye Subang" the outside man, and "Pedro" the houseboy. Ewha had many dormitory students, and Walter was the dorm supervisor with duties that included room inspections and bed checks. Student health was her concern, and it was her job to nurse the girls when they had the flu and to organize medicine-taking sessions to fight parasites.

Jeannette Walter taught English. She never learned Korean well enough to get acquainted with her students on a level that would have opened up their home experiences or their attitudes toward the political turmoil then affecting the city's new student culture. Instead she expressed her feelings in maternal ways, finding much fulfillment in the girls' academic successes and their development as young Christians. The curious dissonance between her orientation and theirs is seen in her account of how Ewha girls tried to join the student demonstrations during the March First Independence Movement in 1919:

> At Ewha ... the big gate was bolted, but when the girls, en masse, ordered it to be opened, the gateman opened it. Miss Frey [the principal] stood there with arms outstretched and announced, "Well, girls, you will go over my dead body." Some went back to their rooms, but others were taken to prison from the streets. In a few days we dismissed school and sent the girls to their homes, where many became leaders in their own communities. Induk Pak and Julia Syn, two of our teachers, were in prison for long terms.
>
> Months afterward, Yu Kwansoon, a little 16-year-old girl, died in prison. We had her body brought back to the school, and the girls prepared cotton garments for her burial. Then, during the night hours, they decided that she was a real heroine and they hunted up silk materials and re-dressed her in silk. We were allowed to have a quiet service at the church with only her classmates present. They all wanted to walk to the cemetery, but there was no permit for that, and I thought I was going to have trouble. Then Helen [Kim] told them that she would go with me to the gravesite as their representative and homeroom teacher, so we went, and that incident ended quietly. But Yu Kwansoon has not been forgotten. Much later, when Korea was free, a movie was made about her life.... I was featured in the picture [played by a later missionary, Emma Wilson]. However, when I was in Korea in 1959, I was interviewed by a group from Kwansoon's school, and I assured them on tape that her body was not mutilated. I had dressed her for burial.[18]

Among Walter's junior colleagues at Ewha were two who forged a particularly significant relationship: Alice Appenzeller, the second-generation president of Ewha during the 1930s, and her Korean understudy, Helen Kim (Kim Hwallan). Kim was born in 1899, the daughter of a Chemulp'o businessman. Her mother was persuaded to become a Christian by a Methodist Biblewoman, following which her parents adopted the revolutionary idea of sending their daughters to school as well as their sons. Helen was one of the first students to go all the way through Ewha, beginning in 1907 and graduating from the college in 1918. In 1922 she entered Ohio

Wesleyan University, earned a B.A. in 1924, and then went on for an M.A. in philosophy at Boston University before returning to join the Ewha faculty in 1925.

Alice Appenzeller, meanwhile, had been accruing her own seniority. Born in 1885 and commonly referred to by the other missionaries as "the first white child born in Korea," Appenzeller returned to the United States with her mother when her father, Henry Gerhardt Appenzeller, died in a ferryboat mishap in 1902. Twenty years later, after her education at Wellesley College and Columbia University, she returned to Seoul to become principal of Ewha. Three years later, Helen Kim joined her there and began rising as Appenzeller's understudy. Kim's prominence as a leader of the Korean women's movement was established early on when she helped found the Korean YWCA.

However, she also acquired detractors who exploited the tension created by her obvious ambition to succeed Alice Appenzeller as president of Ewha. In 1933 a Korean acquaintance wrote, "I gather that the gradual estrangement between Miss Appenzeller and Miss Kim Helen has taken a definite shape and form. Miss A. indignantly said to a Korean friend that K. H. [Helen Kim] would be glad if [Appenzeller] dropped out and that [Appenzeller] after having worked so hard for Ewha College, wouldn't play a figurehead."[19]

To almost everyone in the foreign community, the Appenzeller-Kim pairing seemed ideal, the embodiment of what was intended in the missionary effort: well-developed institutions, a trained Korean leadership, and a missionary withdrawal. But when Kim's ambition surfaced in the mid-1930s, Alice Appenzeller was in her forties—much too young to retire or be kicked upstairs. Kim, on the other hand, was no younger than many of the missionaries when they arrived in the field to manage comparable enterprises—and she knew in her heart that she was much better prepared than they. She had plans for Ewha; she wanted to add a women's medical department.[20] She was thinking ahead about the terms of a possible merger with Chosen Christian College.[21] Appenzeller, a conservative like most missionaries, thought the Ewha enterprise overextended already; but Helen Kim thought "the Lord will provide."[22] Though the pressure from Kim may have helped keep Ewha moving, it was personally unpleasant for Alice Appenzeller.[23] In 1939, the Japanese settled the matter by forcing all missionary school administrators to resign, and Appenzeller was able to make the gracious gesture of nominating Helen Kim to be Ewha's new president. As she capitulated she quoted Shakespeare to Kim: "Some are born great, some achieve greatness, and some have greatness thrust upon them. You are in the third category. You will have to take the presidency whether you like it or not."[24]

Sister Agneta Chang and the Maryknolls

A bond of a similar kind within the Catholic church was the relationship that formed between foreign and Korean nuns, a bond enhanced through communal living and daily rituals, and by the Catholic missions' policy of integrating religious orders.

In P'yŏngyang at the Maryknoll convent, two of the fifteen sisters in 1930 were Korean, officially part of the Maryknoll Mission and vested with the responsibility for leading the Korean sisterhood. One of them was Chang Chŏng'ŏn, otherwise known as Sister Mary Agneta Chang, known to history as the sister of John M. Chang (Chang Myŏn), sometime ambassador, vice president, and prime minister of the Republic of Korea from 1960 to 1961. John, Mary, and their siblings—Louis, Cunegunda, and Martha—were the children of Leo and Lucia Chang, the descendants of two nineteenth-century Catholic martyrs.

Leo Chang made his living as a comprador for foreign trading firms in Inch'on and Seoul and sent his children to Catholic schools. In 1913, the year the family moved into a new house in Seoul's Hyehwa-dong neighborhood, Mary Chang took her first communion and started attending the nearby parish church of St. Benedict, the center of the German Benedictine Mission.

During the week she went to a school run by the French Sisters of St. Paul de Chartres, where she acquired her multilingual Western education. The crowning event of her model Catholic upbringing was her confirmation in Seoul's great Myŏng-dong Cathedral by the patriarch of the regenerated Korean church, Archbishop Gustave Charles-Marie Mutel.

Not long after her two brothers began studying in the United States at Manhattan College, Mary Chang and her sister Cunegunda began their religious careers at a convent in Seattle, studying religion and serving in a "home for Japanese children"[25] because they knew Japanese. In 1922, when Mary was seventeen, the sisters entered the Maryknoll novitiate at the motherhouse in New York. There the way of life involved poverty, manual labor, and a rigorous schedule of study and prayer. The Chang sisters, although Catholic, had been reared in a Confucian culture that taught them stoicism in such circumstances, and the American novices quickly learned to admire them for their discipline. Eventually they were received into the order, Mary with the name Sister Mary Agneta, and Cunegunda with the name Sister Mary Clara.

In 1925 Sister Mary Agneta—alone by that time because Cunegunda had left the order—was assigned to return to Korea as a Maryknoll missionary sister. Her first assignment was at the new Maryknoll station in Ŭiju, teaching religion in the mission school, visiting the sick, and helping the

American sisters learn Korean. As the only Korean among the Maryknoll sisters, it fell to Sister Mary Agneta to explain her country to the Americans. She was also the most likely candidate for the new work of training a community of Korean nuns to be attached to the Maryknoll prefecture. To prepare for this she went to Tokyo for further study between 1932 and 1935.

It was during breaks from her training in Tokyo and in the early years of training the Korean sisterhood that she learned to treasure being a Maryknoller. "Our school is closed . . . and I am now enjoying the happiness of being with the Sisters again," she wrote one Sunday in 1931. "Needless to say, how wonderful it seems to be in our own community after being away even for a short time. . . . Sister Richard is trying to make me fat!"[26]

Like all the Maryknoll sisters, Sister Mary Agneta was required to write a journal made of letters addressed to Mother Mary Joseph Rogers, the superior of the Maryknoll sisterhood in New York. Mary Agneta's letters glow with not-necessarily-contrived happiness. "I really love my work—I mean my life, Mother," she wrote in 1938 during a stint teaching novices in Yŏngyu near Ŭiju. "I am preparing some things for their classes. One of them is translating our vow book—Cotel's. In helping Sr. Sylvester and in preparing the classes and spiritual talks, I realize what a privilege it is, and I feel as though I am having my own novitiate again."[27]

One of Mary Agneta's closest friends was Sister Mary Gabriella Mulherin, with whom she shared many interests besides the work. They read the same books, shared opinions about trends in the church, and had a special sympathy for each other as women and sisters. Sister Gabriella thought Mary Agneta was like the proverbial bamboo plant, fragile seeming but able to withstand fierce gales. That assessment was to prove prophetic in the two wars that separated the Maryknollers from Korea and left Agneta in charge of the work—a duty for which she ultimately gave her life in 1950.

A Korean Mother-in-Law

Marriages between Koreans and foreigners were not unheard of, but they were rare. One instance—famous because the bride wrote a book with the matter-of-fact title *I Married a Korean*—was the union of the American-educated Methodist student David Kim and his Drew University classmate Agnes Davis. The wedding took place in Korea in 1934 after a number of American missionary women had attempted to dissuade the bride upon her arrival in Seoul. Agnes Davis was troubled by the attitudes that she encountered in the expatriate community, not only because they were so racist but because she needed to be accepted by the missionary women in Seoul who were her natural social set. There were the direst predictions of a life of slavery under a domineering mother-in-law, the type of mother-in-law the missionary wives said was typical. Once she went through with the marriage, however, Davis had a very different experience. She grew into a close relationship with David's mother, whom she called O-man-ee (ŏmŏni, "mother").

In *I Married a Korean*, Agnes Davis recollects learning from O-man-ee the work of a Korean wife: how to fire the *ondol* floor; how to grind grain; how to make *kimch'i*, *tubu* (tofu), *ttŏk*, and myriad side-dishes for the table; how to spin cotton and silk; how to design and make Korean clothes; and how to wash and starch them, and then iron them by pounding them with paddles. Seated across from O-man-ee she learned the intricate rhythms of the ironing paddles—rhythms that also taught her something deeper about the love and intimacy between women and their families. O-man-ee was not just slaving endlessly at housework; she was smart and tender and endlessly resourceful, someone not to be pitied, but admired.

The final chapter of Agnes Davis's book, which was published in 1953, was titled "Would I Do It Again?" On this she equivocated: there were ways she felt she had held her husband back because she was a foreigner. And there were stressful times during which Agnes' own American-bred unwillingness always to keep to second place threatened the marriage. But her respect for O-man-ee pulled her through. "O-man-ee had learned more perfectly than anyone I ever knew the secret of losing her life to find it," wrote Agnes. "Her energies were not wasted in anger or vain regrets or desire for what she could not have. The only time she was not up and doing more than her share of the load of work was when she was too sick to lift her head from her pillow."[28]

Miss Florence and the Shintō Shrines

The Japanese colonial government-general's pushing of the Shintō religion on Koreans in the 1930s is a well-known story, and associated with it are many episodes of missionary resistance and attempts to dissuade Korean Christians from bowing at Shintō shrines.

There was no more anguished area for the problem than the question of whether to continue operating Christian schools whose students had to engage in Shintō rituals as part of their normal school day. Several missions opted to close their schools altogether rather than see their Christian students engage in Shintō observances while under their educational authority. The missionaries' decision to close the schools, however, infuriated many Christian students and their parents, who saw it as an arbitrary action that robbed them of their chance at an education, since there was scant opportunity to enter Japanese and government schools that were already fully enrolled. Protests ensued, and there were even threats of violence. One notable example was in Kwangju, where the Southern Presbyterian Mission voted to close Florence Root's Speer School for Girls.

The announcement that the mission was closing the Speer School set off a student strike against the missionaries. Principal Florence Root was a hard-liner on the Shintō issue and early on in the controversy had absolutely forbidden her girls to obey the government's order to bow at the shrines. At the time, the local authorities in Kwangju had let her defiance slide. However, when the new school term began in September 1937, the Speer girls were ordered to the city's Shintō shrine for a back-to-school ceremony. Miss Florence told them not to go and literally stood in the schoolhouse door to block their egress. Police soon arrived bringing an order to close the school. Several Korean teachers were taken in for questioning. Then there followed a student demonstration in which one missionary was actually taken hostage for a short time. Florence Root herself was subjected to death threats, although she remained firm in her own conviction that the Japanese were entirely in the wrong. She argued that it was the Japanese who had made Christian schooling impossible and that it was their order that had shut down the school. "It nearly broke my heart," she wrote, "as the children of our Speer School stood this morning in front of the building to receive instructions from the educational office about going to another school, to tell them good-bye, knowing that they would never be my children again."[29]

Because it involved hostage taking and threats to American life and property, the fracas in Kwangju was of interest to the newly arrived American consul-general in Seoul, a sternly secular official named Gaylord Marsh, who had little patience with missionaries and their exotic principles. Marsh thought Miss Florence was the cause of the trouble. On the school issue he wrote that missionaries like her were "disposed to assume the role of martyrs, and are afflicted with an extraordinary conditions of 'nerves.'" He noted that not all the missions took the same stand against Shintō worship and that the Japanese were actually going out of their way to reward the Methodists (for example) for cooperating.[30] He drew his own conclusions:

> There seems to be no doubt that there is a Korean nationalistic element connected with certain mission stations that is eager to use . . . the Christian churches and schools to further their nationalist aspirations and to oppose the Japanese. . . . Some of the missionaries are perhaps lending themselves to that purpose, a few willingly by reason of a prejudgment formed long years ago and others by fear of violence from their adherents of nationalistic sentiments.[31]

The Women's Day of Prayer Incident, 1941

As Japanese rule got tighter in Korea, there were more and more instances of outright conflict between missionaries and the government. The late 1930s brought political conditions that made it so difficult for Westerners and Koreans to remain in contact with each other that it seemed in 1940 that mission work was effectively at an end. By mid-1940, Koreans who associated with foreigners were subjected to such reprisals that breaking contact seemed to be the kindest thing to do. After U.S. ambassador Joseph Grew flashed his "green light message" to Washington and ceased objecting to U.S. pressure against Japanese aggression in China, the State Department decided to evacuate American civilians from the Japanese empire. Ships were sent to bring "nonessential" civilians home, and by the end of November the missionary community in Korea had been decimated.

Among the hardy individuals who elected to stay behind and face further trouble with the authorities were a number of missionary women. These soon ran afoul of the government during the 1941 observance of the International Women's Day of Prayer.

Christian women around the world had long since organized an international day of prayer to coincide with International Women's Day. By coincidence, the date for the observance fell on February 28, 1941, the eve of the anniversary of the 1919 independence uprising against Japan in Korea and a day on which the colonial police were especially jittery. In P'yŏng-yang, Presbyterian missionary Alice Butts was the member of the organizing committee in charge of devising the program for services. Mindful of the government's prohibition against unapproved printed matter, Miss Butts took the international organizers' suggested program and adapted it carefully to the Korean situation. When she thought it was sufficiently innocuous, she ordered fifteen thousand copies printed up and distributed across northern Korea without first showing it to the local police. When she was finished, it included the following:[32]

ORDER OF WORSHIP

Opening Hymn: "All Hail the Power of Jesus' Name"

Scriptures: Daniel 4:3. "His Kingdom is an everlasting kingdom, and his dominion is from generation to generation."

Psalm 22:27–28. "For the Kingdom is the Lord's and He is governor among the nations."

Revelation 11:15. "Then the seventh angel blew his trumpet, and there were loud voices in heaven, saying, 'The kingdom of the world has become the kingdom of our Lord and of his Christ, and he shall reign forever and ever.'"

Confession: "We must confess that for the interests of our own country we afflict other countries . . . making war against other nations for our own gain. . . ."

Sermon, prayers, etc.

Closing Hymn: "Must Jesus Bear the Cross Alone?"

Closing Scripture: Revelation 21:1–4. "And God himself shall be with them; He will wipe away every tear from their eyes, and death shall be no more, neither shall there be mourning nor crying nor pain any more, for the former things have passed away."

The women's prayer services took place on February 28 and the independence movement anniversary passed without incident on March 1; but on March 2 the police came to arrest Alice Butts on charges of circulating seditious literature. Nineteen of her alleged accomplices on the planning committee were arrested over the next several weeks.

The Japanese press in Korea used the opportunity to attack missionary "subversion" once again, accusing the detainees of an "anti-war plot" and of "craftily arousing anti-war and anti-state ideas" among the Koreans. The printed program had been "exceedingly seditious," grumbled the *Maeil sinbo*, the government's Korean-language paper. "The people in general should take care not to commit un-national crimes unwittingly, and at the same time they should strengthen the consciousness of their being Imperial subjects and whole-heartedly render service for the state behind the gun."[33]

American officials were appalled by the missionaries' poor sense. In New York, Methodist Board secretary George Sutherland said, "Phrases of this kind in printed documents circulated in any country in wartime would be questionable."[34] And in Seoul, Consul-General Gaylord Marsh was predictably livid. On March 4, 1941, he fired off a cablegram to Ambassador Joseph Grew in Tokyo:

> I suggest the Presbyterian Mission, New York City, be urged to withdraw all unessential, militant, and indiscreet missionaries from this field. . . . We cannot afford to have to defend individual indiscretion nor support self-appointed candidates for international martyrdom.[35]

Most of those arrested in the World Day of Prayer case were held for only a few days, although they were often brought back later for interrogation. In Kanggye, the police had a practice of summoning Lilian Ross for questioning in the middle of the night. The interrogation was never abusive and in fact took on a ritual quality. The sessions were not much more than conversations, and an hour or two later, when they were over, she would be given a choice between spending the rest of the night in jail and going home to her own bed.

She always chose to go home, and on the way she would pass the town's roving night watchman. "Oh, it's you!" he would say. "Are they through questioning you for the night?"

"Yes," Lilian would answer.

"Good," he would say. "Have a good sleep."[36]

The Years of Living Dangerously

In July 1941, the Presbyterian Mission and the colonial government worked out a compromise whereby the missionaries in the case would confess, apologize for breaking the law, and leave Korea forthwith.[37] Some returned to the United States via Shanghai; others, including Lilian Ross, volunteered for reassignment in the Philippines. By the end of November the remaining Protestant missionary community in the country numbered twenty-four men, women, and children.

When the War of the Pacific broke out in December 1941, all Americans and most other Westerners were interned, either in their own homes or in detention centers. In north Korea, the Maryknoll sisters kept in touch between buildings and across distances thanks to their Korean counterparts, servants, and houseboys who willingly risked everything to carry messages between the convents and tend to the captives' daily needs. Sister Agneta Chang traded her Maryknoll habit for a Korean nun's dress to make it easier to travel between points on the regular trains. On December 23, 1941, the P'yŏngyang and Chinnamp'o sisters were moved north to the Ŭiju convent. After that there were seven in all. They took turns with cooking and housework but were not allowed to do any work outside. Sister Agneta Chang, suffering from a progressive spinal deterioration that was already causing her much pain, brightened the American sisters' confinement with her energy and news of life on the outside. One day a Japanese detective let it slip that negotiations about a prisoner exchange were under way. Immediately the sisters started planning for Sister Agneta to take charge of their work and the Maryknoll property if they should suddenly be ordered to travel. Sister Agneta chose the Korean nuns to take over the assignments teaching in the mission school, working in the hospital, and training the novitiate.[38]

Epilogue

From these stories it is possible to extract many meanings. The story of the Maryknoll sisters is an example of the devolution of leadership to Koreans, not only through the leadership of Sister Agneta, who was technically a missionary, but also through the Korean nuns and the church women in their groups and sodalities across north Korea. Similarly, the withdrawal of Protestant missions meant a forced devolution in all institutions and on all levels, something that the Appenzeller/Kim case demonstrates was not always easy and certainly not painless.

One might logically start by concluding that the Second World War spared many missionaries and their Korean counterparts the most difficult experiences by setting the Korean church, women's institutions included, on its own foundations and requiring it to survive. It seems ironic that postwar conditions reversed this condition and put missionaries back in a position to help reconstruct the church, only to go through the process of devolution anyway, in the 1960s through 1980s.

And what about the people in the stories? Lilian Ross, ever willing to work, opted to be reassigned to the Philippines in 1941 and was soon captured by the invading Japanese and interned, to be released in 1945. She returned to Korea in 1948 and remained there doing evangelistic work with women and children in the Taegu area until retirement. She insisted on staying in Korea until her health required that she be transported to a Presbyterian retirement facility in California, where she died at the age of 93.

Florence Root was one of the 101 American internees in Korea who were collected and taken to Japan for repatriation in June 1942, first on a Japanese ship and then, from Africa, on the MV *Gripsholm*. She too returned to Korea and resumed her work. In 1950, when the North Koreans invaded the south, she refused to be moved from her place in Kwangju and ended up having to be hidden by Christians in caves and groves in the mountains near Kwangju at great personal risk to everyone involved. Remaining in Korea throughout the war, she shifted her emphasis to country evangelism and spent the rest of her career visiting village churches and holding classes for women. Eventually she retired; she died in North Carolina at the age of 101.

Alice Appenzeller suffered a stroke while giving a chapel talk at Ewha in the spring of 1950 at the age of sixty-four. She died within hours; her body is buried at the Seoul Foreigners' Cemetery at Yanghwajin. One usually finds flowers provided by faithful Ewha alumnae at her grave and that of Ewha's founder, Mary Scranton.

Appenzeller's protégé, Helen Kim, went on to a distinguished career as president of Ewha and became a symbol of women's education in Korea. During her lifetime Ewha grew from a small girls' school to the largest women's university in Asia—some would say, the world. She died in 1970 at the age of seventy-one.

Agnes Davis Kim spent the war years in America and returned to Korea to join her husband, David, on their farm in Susaek in 1961. After David's death, although she never learned Korean well, she taught English Bible classes in their home and spent her old age there, dying in 1986 at the age of eighty-five.

Sister Agneta Chang proved to be the linchpin of the Catholic community in P'yŏngyang through the years following liberation, being the only Maryknoller allowed to keep on working. She remained in directly in contact with Mother Mary Joseph Rogers in New York until it was no longer possible to send mail. Underground couriers then carried messages back and forth across the thirty-eighth parallel to Monsignor George Carroll and the Vatican's ambassador in Korea, the Vicar Apostolic Patrick Byrne, himself a Maryknoller. Her health, however, began to deteriorate badly, and her back bothered her so much that by 1950 she could hardly walk. She was put under house arrest when the Korean War broke out in the summer of 1950, as much because her brother was Syngman Rhee's ambassador to Washington as because she was a Christian. After the Inch'ŏn landing, however, as Republic of Korea and United Nations forces were approaching P'yŏngyang, she was formally arrested, loaded onto an oxcart, and taken away, presumably to join the distinguished roster of Korean Catholic martyrs.

NOTES

Elements of this chapter also appear in my book *Living Dangerously in Korea: The Western Experience, 1900–1950* (Norwalk, Conn.: EastBridge, 2003).

1. Jane Hunter, *The Gospel of Gentility* (New Haven, Conn.: Yale University Press, 1984).

2. One of Lillias Horton Underwood's first patients was Queen Min, who had been getting medical attention by means of a cord tied to her wrist and passed to a male doctor who was in another room and alternately by direct examination of her tongue, which "was protruded through a slit in a screen for the [male] physician's observation." Lillias Horton Underwood, *Fifteen Years among the Topknots* (New York: The American Tract Society, 1904), 25.

3. Quoted in correspondence between Eileen F. Moffett and Lilian Ross, November 4, 1990, in the papers of Lilian Ross, in the author's possession. Eventually the Rosses lost three of their five children. Son Willard, born in 1904, died of diphtheria in 1912, and son Lawrence, born in 1907, died of vaccination poisoning in 1908. Son Albert, born in Nagasaki in 1902, survived, as did Lilian (1900–1993).

4. Ibid.

5. *Eleventh Annual Report of the Korea Woman's Conference of the Methodist Episcopal Church* (Seoul: Methodist Publishing House, 1909), passim; Harriet Pollard, "The History of the Missionary Enterprise of the Presbyterian Church, USA, in

Korea, with Special Emphasis on the Personnel" (M.A. thesis, Northwestern University, 1927), 70–72; Louise B. Hayes, "The Korean Bible Woman and Her Work," *Korea Mission Field* 30, no. 7 (July 1935): 151–153 and other issues, passim, especially special issues devoted to women's work, such as 18, no. 11 (November 1922) and 19, no. 11 (November 1923).

6. "Personal Narrative of (Mrs. Cyril) Susan Ross, Year 1929–1930," in the papers of Lilian Ross.

7. Material in this paragraph is from the memorial minute for Mrs. Cyril Ross, M.D., adopted by the Presbyterian Board of Foreign Missions, June 22, 1954, in the papers of Lilian Ross.

8. "Personal Narrative of (Mrs. Cyril) Susan Ross, Year 1929–1930."

9. Lilian Ross, letter to her family, July 30, 1937, in the papers of Lilian Ross.

10. Lilian Ross, letter to Cyril Ross, August 17, 1941, in the papers of Lilian Ross.

11. Lilian Ross, letter to Susan Ross, January 12, 1938, in the papers of Lilian Ross.

12. Lilian Ross, letter to Susan Ross, January 12, 1938, in the papers of Lilian Ross.

13. Lilian Ross, letter to her family, July 30, 1937, in the papers of Lilian Ross.

14. Florence Root, "Dear Friends" letter, November 4, 1927, Presbyterian Church, USA, Department of History, Montreat, North Carolina.

15. Florence Root, "Dear Friends" letter, November 26, 1933, ibid.

16. The term "saxie" was used by both single and married male and female missionaries, especially in the Southern Presbyterian Mission. Other missions, however, failed to find less awkward terminology. The author recalls hearing a married male missionary refer to the single women present at a meeting of Northern Presbyterians in 1968 as "unclaimed blessings."

17. Florence Root, "Dear Friends" letter, May 16, 1931, Presbyterian Church, USA, Department of History, Montreat, North Carolina.

18. Jeannette Walter, *Aunt Jean* (Boulder, Colo.: Johnson, 1968), 142–143.

19. Yun Ch'iho, *Yun Ch'iho Ilgi* (Seoul: Kuksa P'yŏnch'an Wiwŏnhoe, 1976–1979) [hereafter referred to as *YCH*] 10:177. This is the diary that Yun started in Korean in 1882 and switched to English in 1889, continuing in English almost until his death in the 1940s.

20. *YCH*, 10:184.

21. L. George Paik (Paek Nakchun); interview with the author, Seoul, March 16, 1984.

22. *YCH*, 10:186.

23. For example see *YCH*, 10:208–209; 272; 310; 320–321; 340; 347; 349–352; 388; 391; and 11:67 and 131.

24. Helen Kim, *Grace Sufficient* (Nashville, Tenn.: Upper Room, 1964), 93.

25. This account of Sister Mary Agneta Chang follows Sister M. Gabriella Mulherin, M.M., "Flower of the Martyrs" (typescript biography in the Maryknoll Mission Archives, Maryknoll [Ossining], New York).

26. "Flower of the Martyrs," 15.

27. Ibid.

28. Agnes Davis Kim, *I Married a Korean* (New York: John Day, 1953), 228–229.

29. Many of the nine hundred students at the Speer School were able to enroll in government schools when they agreed to follow orders about Shintō worship. Of the teachers who were thrown out of work by the closure, four agreed to obey the government and were employed immediately to teach their former Speer pupils in government schools. Two teachers publicly refused to keep teaching under the circumstances, and a number of others retired. "We are sad at heart to think of those whose faith was not strong enough to keep them, but when we realize that the seven teachers who stayed at home will never get another permit to teach under the present regime, we can but honor them the more for their courage. Obedience to their Lord's commands meant real sacrifices on their part." Florence Root, "Dear Friends" letter from Kwangju, begun on September 7 and mailed on November 18, 1937 (PCUSA archives, Montreat, North Carolina).

30. National Archives and Records Service, record group 84: General Records of the Department of State, Correspondence Relating to the Internal Affairs of Korea. Dispatch from Marsh to Grew, February 10, 1939 (file number 360: Methodist Mission in Chosen).

31. Marsh to Secretary of State, April 20, 1937 (395.1163/50).

32. Program enclosed in Herbert E. Blair to J. L. Hooper, October 8, 1941, Presbyterian Historical Society, Philadelphia.

33. Enclosed with Marsh to Grew, April 1, 1941 (395.1121/22).

34. George Sutherland, memorandum for the file, August 8, 1941, Methodist Episcopal Church, Korea Mission archives at Drew University; microfilm in the possession of Professor Yi Manyŏl of Sungmyŏng Women's University, Seoul.

35. Marsh to Grew, March 4, 1941, quoted in Grew to Secretary of State, March 5, 1941 (390.1115A/400). In a follow-up report he described to Grew the injudicious language used by the missionaries in "the prayer circular with its several statements so well understood in Christendom and so open to misinterpretation by intention or lack of comprehension" and explained how the Japanese authorities must have resented "the activity of strong-minded missionary women who contrast so greatly with the present Japanese conception of a woman's lack of any place in affairs in general." Marsh to Grew, April 1, 1941. This was Marsh's carefully tempered report on the matter, less colorful than an earlier telegram to Grew in which he said, "This consulate general regards her [Miss Butts] as having been stupid and indiscreet." Marsh to Grew, quoted in Grew to Secretary of State, March 11, 1941 (390.115A/419).

36. Lilian Ross, interview, Duarte, California, May 26, 1987.

37. The text of the confession was as follows: "In connection with the International Women's Prayer Meeting I apologize for having acted in violation of the 'Chosen Pernicious Papers Temporary Control Ordinance.' I have now received generous treatment with special consideration and a kind admonition for the future, for which I am highly grateful. I therefore respectfully pledge myself not only to

desist henceforth from doing such improper things, but also to return to my country immediately."

38. Sister Mary Eugenia (Mary Agnes Gorman) Memorandum on Six Months' Internment, no date, and Sister Gabriella Mulherin to Mother Mary Joseph Rogers, August 28, 1942, H3.7a, box 1, file F-3, Personal Narratives of WWII. Heijō (P'yŏngyang), Korea, Maryknoll Mission Archives.

PART FOUR

Christianity and the Struggles for Democracy and Reunification

CHAPTER 9

Carrying the Torch in the Darkest Hours
The Sociopolitical Origins of Minjung Protestant Movements

Paul Yunsik Chang

During his tenure as South Korea's leader (1961–1979), President Park Chung-hee exercised his authority by developing laws and various state apparatuses aimed at controlling all dissident movements. For this end, the Korean military, the national police, and the Korean Central Intelligence Agency (KCIA) became useful coercive structures Park employed to maintain his rule. In addition to these structures of domination, Park also attempted to legitimize and justify his seizure of power as well as his plans to modernize South Korea. These legitimizing discourses revolved around two main themes. Park initially justified his seizure of power as an issue of "national security" and continually used the sentiment of "anticommunism" as a trump card to frame and imprison dissidents. During his reign, Park subsequently added to this a justification by "economic growth," which he held to be the most significant priority of his government.

The year 1972 marked a significant shift in how Park exercised his power over South Korean society. For various reasons detailed below, Park gave up the idea of maintaining a democratic polity and enacted the Yusin Constitution, which gave Park absolute control. The Yusin Constitution transformed Park's government into an authoritarian regime that afforded very little space for dissenting voices. Park continued to cite the threat to national security and the need for economic development as reasons why Yusin was necessary. Through these two pillars of Park's legitimizing discourse, authoritarian rule, economic policies detrimental to Korea's labor class, and harsh repression of dissident movements were justified.

Korean Christians responded to this political and economic situation in different ways.[1] During this time, when the need for rapid industrialization justified labor exploitation and when hysterical levels of McCarthyism restricted any criticism of the government, a minority of Protestant leaders became champions of democracy and human rights.[2] Evolving from a small but visible group of dissident ministers and churches into a thoroughly developed Christian social movement, these protesting Christians became a salient voice in the burgeoning democracy movement that eventually helped transform South Korea into a liberal democracy.

The protest of these dissident Christians constituted both the founding of social movement organizations and developing counterhegemonic discourses. Christians formed organizations to mobilize resources that were used in their strategic challenge to the Yusin regime. Through these organizations Christians attempted to educate and organize laborers, carry out various petition drives in the hopes of changing oppressive laws, and monitor the ways in which Park Chung-hee utilized groups like the KCIA to forcefully dominate Korean society. As the movement progressed, and with experiences of repression by the government, Christian organizations more thoroughly developed their networks to consolidate resources. Thus, what began as individual organizations fighting the regime on various fronts evolved into a networked group of Christian social movement organizations working together to challenge the Yusin regime.

In direct reaction to Park's legitimizing discourse, Christians initially began their discursive challenge by centering on political themes such as democracy. Quickly though, the discursive challenge incorporated the notion of human rights in reaction to the government's repressive measures. Thus "democracy" and "human rights" became the two main ideal symbols put forth by Christian protestors as a response to Park's Yusin regime. But what started with political and humanitarian symbols evolved into questions of identity and purpose for these dissenting Christians. Specifically, the identity of *minjung* (roughly translated as "the masses") came to inform the rhetoric of Christian protest. More generally, throughout the 1970s, what Nancy Abelmann has called the "*minjung* imaginary" became the source for a more thoroughly developed master narrative of protesting groups.[3] This master narrative became manifest in the discursive contest waged by Christians as well, and what began as a liberal Christian concern for the social welfare of the Korean people evolved into a fully developed systematic liberation theology. Thus Minjung Theology was born after years of protest by dissenting Christians and became a rhetorical weapon in the discursive struggle against authoritarianism.

The goals of this chapter are twofold. First, I attempt a descriptive task of Christian protest at both the organizational and discursive levels. Regarding the social movement organizations, the questions are, What were the formal social movement organizations that constituted the network of Christian groups? When and why did they appear? What were their main concerns and activities?

Christians also waged a discursive battle that challenged Park Chung-hee's rhetorical justification of the Yusin regime. To illustrate how a group of theologians made sense of their protest, I attempt to explicate the logic of Minjung Theology through the theological subcategories of soteriology, Christology, and biblical hermeneutics. Here the questions are, What constituted salvation for *minjung* theologians? How did they theologically construe Jesus? Moreover, how did the *minjung* imaginary influence their reading of the Bible?

The second goal of this chapter is to analyze movement transformation, and I attempt to explicate the origins of the *minjung* Protestant movement by situating it in its sociopolitical context. To achieve this second goal I attempt to answer the following questions: What were the factors that galvanized the formation and networking of Christian social movement organizations? How could, and why did, the *minjung* sentiment become the master symbol for a Korean liberation theology? Finally, how did state repression of Christian organizational and discursive protest facilitate changes in the structure of Christian organizations and Minjung Theology?

I use archival data to answer the above questions. The main source is the UCLA Archival Collection on Democracy and Unification in Korea. This archive was compiled by the Korea Church Coalition for Peace, Justice, and Reunification. Included in this prodigious collection are various types of primary documents including publications by the coalition, the Korean National Council of Churches (KNCC), various Christian social movement organizations, and formal declarations of protest by individuals and groups of Christian activists. This archive also includes official statements of the Korean government including proclamations of the National Assembly. A second archival source I use is the *1970-nyŏndae minjuhwa undong* (1970s Democracy Movement). This eight-volume collection was compiled by the Human Rights Committee of the KNCC and published in 1986. This set of primary sources includes mission statements of various Christian social movement organizations, official histories of these organizations, and most of the formal protest statements declared by Christian activists during the Yusin era. Finally, I draw upon the South Korean government's publication of Park Chung-hee's public speeches given throughout his tenure.

Historical Context: The Park Chung-hee Era

FROM COUP D'ETAT TO THE YUSIN CONSTITUTION (1961–1972)

In April 1960, the first Republic of South Korea under Syngman Rhee came to an end as pressure from university students, professors, and the broader urban mass became overwhelming. The subsequent government under Yun Posŏn and Chang Myŏn proved to be ephemeral, and on May 16, 1961, General Park Chung-hee, through a military coup d'etat, assumed political charge of South Korea. Immediately after the coup, Park Chung-hee temporarily dissolved the National Assembly and established the Supreme Council for National Reconstruction as the main governmental body. Martial law was enacted, and Park began the campaign to consolidate his power by arresting, threatening, and eliminating opposing figures. Park also strategically placed many of his military peers in positions of power. In 1961, Kim Chongp'il (Park's military junior and nephew by marriage) created the KCIA, and within three years this repressive organization developed a vast network of agents that monitored any opposition in Korean society.

Initially the military coup did not face the formidable challenge of those participating in the April revolution because of Park's promise to re-establish civilian rule as soon as some degree of stability was maintained. But the longer Park waited, the more the promise was held in question. It was this tension between promise and deed that led to the strategic decision to hold "democratic" elections in 1963. Park himself formally retired from the military in December 1962 and announced his intent to run for the presidency in the upcoming election. Through various manipulative methods, Park succeeded in winning the election and thus became the third president of South Korea. He organized the third republic into an executive branch, a judicial branch, and a two-party legislative branch.

Throughout the 1960s Park focused governmental efforts at industrializing and developing the economy of the country with a series of five-year plans. Orchestrated by the Economic Planning Board, the first five-year plan (1962–1966) began molding Korea's burgeoning economy into one concentrated in exports (mostly in textiles). This concerted effort by the government succeeded in raising the GNP by 7.8 percent during those five years. The second five-year plan (1967–1971) continued the trend of the first, and the GNP rose another 10.5 percent. Overall per capita real income rose from US$87 in 1962 to US$293 in 1972. As the export-driven economy created the demand for labor, unemployment dropped from 8.3 percent in 1963 to 4.5 percent by 1971.[4]

Park's economic policies then, proved highly successful, and "South Korea was unrivaled, even by Japan, in the speed with which it went from having almost no industrial technology to taking its place among the world's industrialized nations."[5] Park hoped that this growth would legitimate his regime as "he needed economic progress to defend his political base against those who regarded his seizure of power as illegitimate."[6] Park used economic success as his main platform to win reelection in 1967 for his second and supposedly last term as president.

Park, however, did not abdicate at the end of his second term but rather forced the National Assembly to amend the existing constitution to allow him to run for a third term. Again through coercive measures Park won the election, but by the end of 1972 frustrations with the existing political system led Park to enact the Yusin Constitution. The Yusin Constitution ended Korea's brief experiment with democracy and concentrated all political power in the executive branch. Although the National Assembly was allowed to meet again, under the Yusin Constitution the president had the power to directly appoint one-third of the Assembly. The Yusin Constitution also made it possible to propagate and enforce special emergency decrees that the president could use in an ad hoc way as situations arose. All of these political moves severed whatever democratic processes were upheld in the 1960s and in all practicality "transformed the presidency into a legal dictatorship."[7]

JUSTIFICATION BY ECONOMIC GROWTH AND NATIONAL SECURITY

Although Park did rely on coercive measures (e.g., arresting various dissenting National Assembly members) to enact and carry out the Yusin Constitution, he also tried to garner legitimacy by proffering various justifications. First, Park noted shifts in the international political sphere that compromised Korea's security. Referring to U.S. efforts at rapprochement with Communist China and progress in relations between the United States and the Soviet Union, Park declared, "Under these circumstances, we must guard ourselves against the possibility that the interests of the Third World or small countries might be sacrificed for the relaxation of tension between big powers."[8] Compounded with the legitimizing discourse of national security was the continual salience of economic prosperity as a primary goal and the need for authoritarian policies to ensure its possibility. For this end, Park declared on November 30, 1972, "The purpose of the [political] reforms we are now undertaking is to ... ensure our national prosperity by boosting and solidifying our national strength."[9] For Park, this goal of economic progress surpassed other political goals including the formation of a liberal democratic polity, and he always "emphasized that without 'economic equality,' political democracy is no more than an 'abstract, useless concept.'"[10] Even more poignantly put, Park declared that sometimes

Asian countries, including Korea, "have to resort to undemocratic and extraordinary measures in order to improve the living conditions of the masses.... One cannot deny that people are more frightened of poverty and hunger than totalitarianism."[11]

Christian Social Movement Organizations and Minjung Theology

CHRISTIAN SOCIAL MOVEMENT ORGANIZATIONS

Throughout the 1970s, Christians who found fault with Park Chunghee's Yusin regime organized themselves to better acquire resources. By 1979, the network of Christian social movement organizations (SMOs) constituted multiple types of organizations varied along several dimensions. First, the organizations were differentiated by the characteristics of their members. Different Christian SMOs specifically mobilized students, youths, clergy, urban poor, laborers, women, and prisoners of conscience. Second, SMOs varied depending on the focus of their main activities—unionization of labor, urban poverty relief, monitoring of human rights violations, women's rights, aiding political prisoners, and monitoring voting booths during elections. In addition to these task-oriented SMOs, there were SMOs that played the critical role of providing a centralizing structure through which many organizations were networked. These umbrella organizations provided various resources to individual groups including communication channels between SMOs and financial assistance for various organizations. The network of Christian SMOs that emerged in the 1970s was, and is still today, a highly organized community of Christian activists. Below I detail a sample of some of the more important SMOs in the struggle of Christians against the Yusin regime.[12] All together, and with others not mentioned, this collection of SMOs constitutes a well-developed Christian social movement working toward the goal of attaining democracy and human rights in South Korea.

On November 1, 1969, various Christian student groups came together to form the Korean Student Christian Federation (KSCF).[13] Despite the presence of such principal older individuals as Na Sanggi and Pak Hyŏnggyu, Christian student leaders primarily conducted the decision-making process. This umbrella organization became the central bureaucratic structure mobilizing specifically Christian university students and young adults during the Yusin era. Various activities of this organization included leading Bible studies and study groups for students, monitoring voting, organizing petition drives, and participating in street demonstrations. For example, on April 19, 1970, the KSCF took the lead role in organizing the 4-19 Memorial Event to commemorate the student revolution that brought down

Syngman Rhee's first republic exactly a decade earlier. This kind of activity contributed to keeping the overall historical memory of struggle and protest alive in the imagination of the larger democracy movement.

Another prominent youth organization was the Ecumenical Youth Council (EYC), created on January 29, 1976, by the KNCC. This organization focused on facilitating solidarity work between Christian youths from different denominational backgrounds. It was involved in ecumenical training, Good Samaritan training, organizing the annual Christian Youth Week, human rights monitoring, and protesting the draft. Both the ecumenical training and Good Samaritan training programs were educational programs for youths who after completion would participate in various relief efforts for the urban poor. The EYC's annual Youth Week was a time for Christian youths to come together in both worship and political solidarity. Its work relating to the human rights situation focused on the release of political prisoners, on whose behalf the EYC conducted petition drives and demonstrations. The EYC also demonstrated and petitioned against the government's illegal drafting of university students into the military.

The Protestant clergy also mobilized during the Yusin era and on March 20, 1975, formed the National Protestant Clergy Corps for the Realization of Justice (NPCCRJ). Principal individuals in the NPCCRJ included Kang Sinmyŏng, Kang Wŏnyong, and Kim Kwansŏk among the more than five hundred clergy members from eight different Protestant denominations. The corps' activities included holding prayer meetings, petitioning for the release of political prisoners, and attempting to reinstate professors and students who were forced to leave their universities. Because members of the NPCCRJ were church leaders, this organization had the added benefit of using its existing church networks for their cause. Church services sometimes became opportunities for dissent when these ministers worked their political concerns into their Sunday sermons.

Church Women United (CWU), founded in 1967, was another Christian organization that recruited members based on specific characteristics. Led by Yi Ujŏng, the CWU in Korea was especially inspired by the Church Women United chapter of the United States (a mainline liberal Christian organization). The CWU worked closely with the KNCC to free political prisoners and monitor human rights violations of the Yusin regime, as well as working for women's rights. For example, in a public declaration on December 3, 1973, CWU condemned the development of a prostitution circuit that catered mostly to Japanese foreign businessmen visiting Korea. Although prostitution was not an "official" activity of the government, CWU assumed government's knowledge and laissez-faire attitude as complicit support of this growing industry. Throughout the Yusin period,

CWU brought women together to strategize on how their particular gendered position could contribute to the larger movement for democracy and human rights.

Along with these member-specific SMOs were organizations differentiated according to their main topic of concern. The Seoul Metropolitan Community Organization (SMCO) was founded on September 1, 1971, to specifically address the needs of the urban poor, whose numbers had grown rapidly with the industrialization and urbanization of the first two economic five-year plans (1962–1971). Several years earlier, in 1968, Protestant leaders—including Pak Hyŏnggyu, Kwŏn Hogyŏng, Kim Tongwŏn, Yi Haehak, Yi Kyusang, Hŏ Pyŏngsŏp, and Mo Kapgyŏng—had become concerned with the growing level of urban poverty and had developed the Institute of Urban Studies at Yonsei University in Seoul to systematically study the conditions and welfare of the urban poor. A few years later, some of the same church leaders created the SMCO to not only research and study the conditions of the poor but also to help ameliorate these atrocious conditions.[14] Activities of the SMCO included counseling the residents of Seoul's slums in educational and spiritual matters and organizing them to demonstrate against government plans to force evacuation from the slum areas. In May 1976, SMCO changed its name to the Korean Metropolitan Community Organization (KMCO) to reflect the geographical spread of urban poverty and their commitment in these other areas.

The labor movement was also another area in which Christian SMOs played a significant part. The Urban Industrial Mission (UIM) was a loose network of church-based labor organizers that included foreign missionary George Ogle, who worked with the unions in the city of Inchŏn, and Methodist minister Cho Wha-soon, who worked with the Tongil Textile Company. Although each district UIM worked mostly with the laborers in its city, all city chapters had common motives and goals. These Christians were concerned with the exploitation of laborers in Park Chung-hee's mass-production-oriented economy. Activities of the UIM consisted of educating workers about labor laws, training them in the organization and administration of a labor union, providing Bible studies for them, and advising them on strategies for collective bargaining. It is estimated that the UIM aided in the formation of 20 percent of all labor unions founded in the 1970s.[15] The feeling of solidarity that UIM members had with the laborers is manifest in their informal policy of working in the companies of the same laborers they were trying to help organize. On February 8, 1975, the loose network of city-specific UIMs became more centralized under the auspices of the Korean Christian Action Organization (KCAO).[16] Renamed the KCAO–Urban Rural Mission, these Christians broadened their activities to include the mobilization of farmers in the rural areas of South Korea. This new ecumenical SMO consisted of Catholics as well as Protestants.

Along with women's rights, the urban poor, and labor relations, Christians were also concerned with the social education of the general public. The Christian Academy (CA), founded in 1956, was one of the few Christian SMOs that predated the Yusin era and was part of the larger literati movement to rebuild Korea from the rubble of war by educating the public. Much of its earlier work revolved around discussions about the church's role in society, but by the 1970s, when it was led by Kang Wŏnyong, the Christian Academy held various study groups around more political issues. It formed independent-democratic groups, self-reformation groups, and *minjung* groups. While the first two groups brought together educated Christians to discuss and critique Park Chung-hee's domestic policies, the *minjung* groups attempted to draw the lesser-educated public into informed discussions about the rapid changes then taking place in Korean society. In addition, the Christian Academy maintained a formal relationship with the Ecumenical Church of Germany, from whom it received funds and general encouragement.

The issue of human rights violations was one of the most salient topics for Christian activists. The Human Rights Committee (HRC) of the Korean National Council of Churches was formed on April 11, 1974, to specifically address and monitor the human rights situation during the Yusin period. The HRC became the cornerstone organization in the network of Christian SMOs by establishing a centralized structure for inter-organizational work. Spearheaded by Kim Kwansŏk, its activities included organizing the annual Human Rights Week, publishing a human rights newsletter, speaking out against the brutal use of force to repress antigovernment demonstrations, petitioning for the release of political prisoners, and organizing public talks by released political prisoners. Together with Kong Tŏkkwi, the wife of former president Yun Posŏn, the HRC helped form the Association of Families of Prisoners of Conscience (AFPC, September 1974) and the Association of Prisoners for the Restoration of Democracy (APRD, March 1975). These organizations provided opportunities for prisoners and their families to share their experiences of oppression and garner support. The activities of the AFPC included monitoring the trials of those arrested for antigovernment protest, petitioning for the release of prisoners, raising funds by knitting and selling shawls, and organizing prayer meetings.

Starting from September 18, 1974, the HRC, and later the AFPC, organized the Thursday Prayer Meeting. Although not a formal organization, this group of concerned Christians gathered every Thursday to pray for those oppressed by the Yusin regime. The Thursday Prayer Meeting became an important opportunity for Christian activists to gather and pray, as well as to make public declarations against the Yusin government. On May 3, 1976, this group became the Friday Prayer Meeting, scheduled so that they could more closely monitor the trials of those arrested for the March First Declaration of Salvation for the Nation, which was held on Saturdays (see below).

Although the network of Christian social movement organizations involved many different types of groups focusing on multiple issues, all together they constituted a cohesive Christian front against the Yusin regime. Christian protest, however, was not limited to praxis at the organizational level but also included expressive protest. Throughout the 1970s Christians waged a discursive battle using political, humanitarian, and Christian symbols that both motivated and justified their actions. For a group of theologians, this discursive protest culminated in the formation of a Korean systematic liberation theology known as Minjung Theology.

MINJUNG THEOLOGY

Minjung Theology was developed by a group of theologians, biblical scholars, and ministers concerned with making the Christian message relevant for their particular historical and political situation. This impetus comes from the understanding that "the function and task of theology is to test, criticize and revise the language which the Church uses about God.... [Theology] must be regularly revised in order to maintain a continuity of meaning."[17] This revision started taking place in Korean liberal theological circles in October 1979, as concerned theologians began to systematize the articulation of their experience of struggle in the democracy–human rights movement. At the time of the first meeting of these *minjung* theologians, as they would later be called, most were forced out of their positions in universities, Christian seminaries, and social movement organizations. The scars accumulated from nearly a decade of struggle colored the formation of Minjung Theology.

The various meetings of these theologians over the next few years came to be known as the Commission on Theological Concerns of the Christian Conference of Asia. Although the theme of their first meeting was "The People of God and the Mission of the Church," their main concern was to struggle with, and incorporate, the concept of *minjung* into their theologies. It was the aim of this conference to create a "living theology"—one that "must speak to the actual questions men in Asia are asking in the midst of their dilemmas: their hopes, aspirations and achievements; their doubts, despair and suffering."[18]

Derived from two Chinese characters, *min* (people) and *chung* (masses), the notion of *minjung* identified all those in Korean society who were suffering oppression at the hands of Park's dictatorial regime. *Minjung* began as a term denoting the *populace* but was transformed into a *populist* theology as theologians started to use it as the master symbol in the construction of their version of liberation theology. Through this theological reformulation, the collective identified as the *minjung* gained a kind of ontological status pointing to their preferred status in the eyes of God. Like all systematic theologies, Minjung Theology manifests itself in various subcategories. Below I provide brief descriptions for only the three theological subcategories of soteriology, Christology, and biblical hermeneutics.

Soteriology and the Notion of *han*

In systematic theology, soteriology has to do with doctrines that comprise notions of salvation. According to the traditional view of more orthodox Christian theological circles, salvation consists of individuals' repenting of their sins, accepting the resurrection of Jesus, and acknowledging Jesus as the only begotten son of God. For the *minjung* theologians, salvation was not an individual process but a social one. This point of view stems from the notion of "social sin" that blamed the suffering of the *minjung* on social structures rather than on personal sin. The condition of the *minjung*, one from which they have to be saved, has to do with the suffering stemming from these social structures. This condition of suffering is what *minjung* theologians called *han*. According to *minjung* theologians, *han* is unique to the experience of the Korean *minjung*: "It is a repressed murmuring, unexpressed in words or actions. It does not change anything. It might arouse a sense of revenge at most. But usually it would be limited to submission or resignation to fate."[19] Suh Nam-dong, one of the important founders of Minjung Theology, notes the "helplessly defeated" theme in defining *han* but adds to it the possibility of salvation from suffering: "Han is an underlying feeling of Korean people. On the one hand, it is a dominant feeling of defeat, resignation, and nothingness. On the other, it is a feeling with a tenacity of will for life which comes to weaker beings."[20]

The *minjung* of Korea release their *han* through a process of "cutting out" or *tan*. Literally it denotes "cutting away," but theologically, *minjung* theologians understood *tan* as a process of transcendence and transformation. Transcendence from the condition of *han* can only come about as the *minjung* actively struggle for their own liberation. Through this process, the *minjung* are able to exorcise their *han* as the systems that generate societal injustices are transformed. Regarding this point, the Catholic *minjung* poet Kim Chiha reinterprets the resurrection of Christ as a symbol of how *han* can be ameliorated and salvation brought about:

This is the mystery of resurrection—this is revolution. That resurrection fashions people in God's image, opens their eyes to their own dignity and turns their frustration and self-hatred into eschatological hope. This kind of resurrection changes a selfish, individualistic, escapist anomie into a communal, united realistic commitment to the common good.... This is a revolutionary religion.[21]

One important point regarding the salvation theme in Minjung Theology has to do with the conscious absence of "sin" as a defining characteristic of Christian soteriology. From the beginning, *minjung* theologians have focused on *han* rather than sin as the core issue for salvation. *Minjung* theologians advocate the position that one must be saved not only from personal sin but also from the collective *han* stemming from societal injustices. Therefore, the salvation of the *minjung* is not tied to the acceptance of grace, which reconciles God and man in more orthodox theological views, but rather comes from a group process as the *minjung* struggle for their own social liberation.

CHRISTOLOGY

Christology in systematic theology has to do with beliefs about Jesus Christ. Broadly speaking, notions of Christ are categorized as either "high Christology" or "low Christology." Whereas high Christology focuses attention on Jesus as the divine son of God and equal to God, low Christology highlights his humanness and life on Earth. Understandings of Jesus by Minjung Theology go beyond the low Christology emphasized by liberal theologians. *Minjung* theologians constructed a radical new Christology, one that apotheosized the *minjung*.

In articulating their own Christology, *minjung* theologians have focused not on the "personal savior" motif found in more conservative theologies, but rather on the "Jesus-event" itself. Biblical scholar Ahn Byung-mu interprets Jesus' ministry in the gospels as the first *minjung* movement and Jesus' crucifixion as the symbolic sacrifice of the *minjung*. This interpretation argues that the story of Jesus in the Gospels is not a time-bound unique story but rather a common story that is enacted through the lives of all suffering people. One example of *minjung* Christology manifesting itself in readings of the Bible has to do with the interpretation of the parable of the good Samaritan (Luke 10:25–37). While traditional interpretations identify the good Samaritan as the Christian "neighbor" and the robbed man as the individual representative of humanity's suffering, *minjung* theologians identify Jesus as the suffering man. In this way, Jesus becomes one with the *minjung*.

This understanding of Christ emphasizes the historical person of Jesus and the suffering that Jesus had to go through as the suffering of all *minjung*. As Ahn notes, "This Jesus is not the Christ who is facing man from God's side, but the Christ who is facing God from man's side."[22] For Ahn, and other *minjung* theologians, Jesus becomes the Messiah not because he is in fact God, but because as a fellow *minjung*, he carries on his shoulders the social sins of an unjust world. Thus the purpose of the parable of the good Samaritan in the Gospel of Luke is not to reveal the generosity and compassion of a Christian neighbor, but rather to invite the Christian to identify with Jesus and the suffering *minjung* robbed and beaten on the road to Jericho.

MINJUNG BIBLICAL HERMENEUTICS

Since the post-Enlightenment emphasis on higher criticism of sacred texts (including the Bible), liberal biblical scholars have questioned the assertion that the Bible is the revealed word of God leading to automatically given interpretations. On the contrary, biblical scholars working out of the liberal tradition have tried to situate the Bible in its various historical contexts in an attempt to make obvious the connections between text and the "life-world" of the author. Drawing upon developments in hermeneutical theory and textual analysis, these biblical scholars argue that readings of texts are always influenced by preexisting interpretive frameworks (conscious or unconscious).[23] In this vein, *minjung* theologians purposefully and consciously developed their own biblical hermeneutic (a *minjung* biblical hermeneutic so to speak) that colored their reading of the Bible.

In his paper "An Old Testament Understanding of Minjung," Cyris Moon argues that the essence of the Old Testament is "the history of belief about the minjung's liberation movement (the Exodus event) and creation of humanity."[24] This creative connection between humans as God's most important creation and the Exodus story highlights a key aspect in Minjung Theology: the suffering of the *minjung* is not the original condition meant for God's people but rather a consequence of the Fall (here interpreted as not from Adam and Eve's sin but from social injustices). The Exodus story is an archetypical story for Moon and shows how God restores Israel's enslaved *minjung* to their original purpose.

In respect to New Testament accounts of the *minjung*, Ahn Byung-mu focuses his philological lens on the Greek word *ochlos*. Found thirty-six times in the Gospel of Mark to connote the crowds surrounding Jesus, Ahn argues that the word *ochlos* is intentionally used by the author of Mark as a referent to a social historical class. Working through a *minjung* hermeneutical lens, Ahn argues that the masses of people surrounding Jesus' ministry are a witness to his faithfulness to them. For Ahn, then, the *ochlos* "were the minjung of Galilee."[25] This interpretation of Jesus' ministry leads

Ahn to affirm a fundamental axiom in liberation theology—namely, that God prefers and stands alongside marginalized oppressed groups.

Origins of Christian Social Movement Organizations and Minjung Theology

FROM INDIVIDUAL GROUPS TO A NETWORK OF SOCIAL MOVEMENT ORGANIZATIONS

The Christian organizational network was indeed thoroughly developed by the end of the Yusin era, incorporating a variety of activities by many types of formal social movement organizations. However, the founding dates of the Christian SMOs indicate that most did not exist in the 1960s, but came into existence and became part of the network only in the 1970s. To understand this evolution of a few individual SMOs into multiple networked organizations, we need a detailed knowledge of the historical condition and experiences that facilitated this change. Only through understanding the Christian SMOs in relation to the oppressive state apparatuses of the Yusin regime can we gain insight into the factors that gave rise to these organizations. Whereas some arose as a reaction to the injustices originating in Park's economic policies and others as a reaction to the repressive measures of the regime, all the SMOs in the network were in some way related to the Yusin government.

As mentioned above, the Economic Planning Board set Korea on an economic path that required large numbers of unskilled manual workers. Urbanization accompanied the rapid industrialization of the 1960s as people in the rural areas flocked to the cities in hopes of finding a modern and more lucrative life. The first two five-year economic plans generated and fostered textile companies while at the same time encouraging the migration of potential laborers from farming-dominated communities. As in other industrializing nations, including the United States, the early years of industrialization were a witness to atrocious working situations, poor wages, and the general exploitation of laborers.[26] The self-immolation protest of garment worker Chŏn T'aeil, on November 13, 1970, "became part of South Korea's labor history and signified the beginning of a new working class activism."[27] As public knowledge about these working conditions spread, Protestant Christian leaders resolved to work in the labor movement. Contact between Christians and the laborers was inevitable as the rapid growth of the Korean churches during this time was symbiotically tied to the industrialization-urbanization process.[28]

UIM ministers and church leaders first indirectly learned of the situation from the laborers themselves who attended their churches. The ministers and leaders then obtained jobs as manual laborers in order to work alongside laborers and help them organize. Their direct experience with the working conditions solidified their conviction that something had to be done for the rights of workers. The UIM continued its educational, organizational, and strategizing work with laborers throughout the 1970s. Through these programs, the UIM not only contributed to the formation of unions in various companies but also galvanized "worker's conscious- ness" among laborers.[29] In particular their work with two labor unions cat- apulted the UIM into the forefront of the labor movement. The Reverend Cho Wha-soon of the UIM involved herself in the aforementioned Tongil Textile Company union. On February 21, 1978, when women workers (who constituted the majority of workers) were about to win the election for union leadership for the second consecutive time, Tongil management hired street thugs to disrupt the union election. The hired strongmen beat up the women and threw human excrement on them.

After this incident, Tongil management fired 124 union members for "causing damage to company property" and dismissed the union com- pletely.[30] Various Christian organizations protested what happened to the women workers of the Tongil Textile Company. On March 12, at Tap- dong Cathedral, UIM ministers joined fired workers, Human Rights Com- mittee members, Ecumenical Youth Council members, various Catholic SMOs, and journalists from the daily newspaper *Tonga Ilbo* in a fast to pro- test the harsh repression of the Tongil company union. In this way, the Tongil Textile Company labor struggle, led by the UIM, became a rallying point for diverse elements in the democracy–human rights movement.[31]

A second union dispute led by the UIM also facilitated solidarity work between Christian SMOs. On August 11, 1979, one thousand riot police- men gathered at the YH Company to suppress a sit-in strike by 250 women workers.[32] During the violent exchange, one woman was killed and many more seriously injured. Three days later, on August 14, the Human Rights Committee of the Korean National Council of Churches held a press con- ference in front of both Korean and international reporters decrying the police brutality against the YH Company workers. The next day, the Asso- ciation of Families of Prisoners of Conscience held a sit-in demonstration at Hanbit Church and demanded the freedom of those arrested. Both the Tongil Textile Company and YH Company incidents came about as UIM ministers helped organize workers against their employers who, with state backing, severely repressed these efforts at unionizing. The repression, in turn, strengthened the role of the UIM in the labor movement and solidi- fied the connections between various organizations.

The Ecumenical Youth Council is another SMO whose origin is in- tricately tied to state repression. After Pastor Pak Hyŏnggyu's protest on Easter Sunday at Namsan Mountain in 1973, the Yusin regime began a pattern of arresting Christian protestors under the National Security Law. This pattern became even more accentuated with Presidential Emergency Decree number 1 and number 2 (January 8, 1974), Emergency Decree number 4 (April 3, 1974), and Emergency Decree number 9 (May 13, 1975). These emergency decrees (EDs) restricted the already limited freedoms accorded by law by disallowing the collection of signatures for antigovernment petitions (EDs nos. 1 and 2), subduing protest activities in the university campuses (ED no. 4), and proclaiming illegal any criticism of the Yusin regime or the decrees themselves (ED no. 9). Emergency Decree number 4 and number 9 especially became useful tools for the government, which used them as justifications for the harsh repression of student protestors.

Following the promulgation of Emergency Decree number 4, the state began a campaign to arrest and incarcerate student protestors. This period of mass student arrests has come to be known as the *minch'ŏng* incident after the name of the most salient leftist student organization, the National Federation of Democratic Youth and Students (*minch'ŏng hangnyŏn*). However, Christian students, especially those affiliated with the Korea Student Christian Federation, were also arrested, and student activism was for the most part silenced. The Korean National Council of Churches, realizing that the university campus could no longer serve as a space for antigovernment protest, began to make efforts to fill the void left by arrested students. To this end, the Human Rights Committee formed the Ecumenical Youth Council to mobilize students and youths outside their university settings.[33] The purpose of forming the EYC was to draw upon the potential power of students and youths while moving their activities away from the campuses to avoid restrictions set by Emergency Decree number 4. Thus, the addition of the EYC to the larger network of Christian SMOs is best understood in light of the activities of the KSCF, the repression of the KSCF by the Yusin regime, and finally, the Christian movement's reaction to state repression.

The formation of the Human Rights Committee of the Korean National Council of Churches was itself a manifestation of the shift in protest rhetoric due to repression by the Yusin regime. Initially, the discursive challenge of Christian activists began with political ideals such as the recovery of democracy. The aforementioned Easter Sunday in 1973 marked the beginning of direct Christian protest against the government, as opposed to such activism as the UIM's work with laborers or the Christian Academy's work in educating the public. The arrest of Reverend Pak Hyŏnggyu under the National Security Law and the mass arrests of students under the Emergency Decrees, facilitated the change in Christian protest rhetoric from political ideals (democracy) to humanitarian concerns (human rights).

As stories of the appalling treatment of political prisoners leaked out to the public, Christians became concerned with changing not only the policies of the government but also the harsh treatment of dissidents. The arrests of Pak Hyŏnggyu and junior pastors prompted the KNCC to sponsor a week-long Church and Human Rights Week,[34] during which leaders in the Christian dissident movement came together to strategize about how to work more efficiently toward the amelioration of the government's human rights violations. This desire for a strategic front grew with the promulgation of Emergency Decree number 4 and the arrests that followed it. It was with these motives that the KNCC officially formed the Human Rights Committee on April 11, 1974. This organization quickly became the central SMO by linking together a variety of organizations and by forming various new ad hoc organizations, thereby furthering the growth of the network.

The Association of Families of Prisoners of Conscience was one of the ad hoc organizations that the HRC helped form (September 1974). Headed by Kong Tŏkkwi, the AFPC specifically concentrated its efforts on monitoring the arrest and incarceration tactics of the Yusin regime under Emergency Decrees 1, 2, 4, and 9. The government used Emergency Decree number 9 as the legal justification for conducting mass arrests following the March First Declaration of Salvation for the Nation. As more and more Christian dissidents were incarcerated, greater numbers of family members of political prisoners found themselves in need of a community that could sympathize with and support them in their distress. As the AFPC made concerted efforts to mobilize these people, its membership grew accordingly. Similarly, the Association of Prisoners for the Restoration of Democracy grew in proportion to the numbers of Christian dissidents arrested. While unable to act freely, political prisoners at the very least were able to come together to share their experiences of arrest, torture, trial, and incarceration. APRD members continued their work by publicly sharing experiences of prison after some were released.

The Yusin regime issued Emergency Decree number 9 on May 13, 1975, and used it to legally constrain any open criticism of the government, or of the decree itself. It was during this critical time in the movement, when the KCIA effectively monitored and suppressed activities of most Christian SMOs, that the Friday Prayer Meeting (formerly Thursday Prayer Meeting) became an important part of the Christian organizational network. Although these gatherings were not technically formal SMOs, they nevertheless provided a consistent space for Christian dissidents to gather and further their cause. Indeed, the Friday Prayer Meetings (FPMs) provided just about the only opportunity left for indirect criticism of the government following Emergency Decree number 9.[35]

As the name implies, the main activity of the Friday Prayer Meeting was group prayer. Dissident Christians gathered for a short liturgy, then spent the rest of the time praying for the general state of the nation, as well as for specific people arrested and specific court cases. It was because of this overtly spiritual agenda that the KCIA hesitated to infiltrate and repress the Friday Prayer Meetings.[36] We would, however, miss the subtleties of the Friday Prayer Meeting if we were to ignore its subversive activities. After Emergency Decree number 9 suppressed most of their other activities, the Human Rights Committee continued to distribute its Human Rights Newsletter through the networks at the Friday Prayer Meetings. Political prisoners also gave their testimonies regarding the prison experience at these prayer meetings. Overall, the Friday Prayer Meetings were able to sustain Christian dissident praxis when the Yusin regime made great efforts to repress Christian protest.

FROM POLITICAL AND HUMANITARIAN IDEALS TO A SYSTEMATIC LIBERATION THEOLOGY

Understanding the rise and networking of Christian organizations during the Yusin era is critical to the overall comprehension of *minjung* Protestantism at the organizational level. Along with this development of an organizational network, a handful of Christian theologians developed Minjung Theology. Like the network, however, Minjung Theology did not approach its full form until the end of the Yusin era. It is also crucial to understand the formation of Minjung Theology in relation to the rhetorical aspects of the Yusin regime.

Christian discursive protest of the Yusin regime began in 1973 on various fronts. In a pivotal event, Reverend Pak Hyŏnggyu and two younger ministers of his church gathered their congregation at Seoul's Namsan Mountain on April 22 for Easter Sunday services and, in response to the "passing" of the Yusin Constitution, disseminated leaflets that read "Politicians Repent," "The Resurrection of Democracy Is the Liberation of the People," and "Lord, Show Thy Mercy to the Ignorant King."[37] The government accused Pak and his supporters of trying to "overthrow the government" and promptly arrested them under the National Security Law.

In this seminal conflict between Christian protestors and the Yusin regime, a pattern emerged that was to become characteristic of the discursive battle for the remainder of the 1970s. For Pak Hyŏnggyu, protest was a direct expression of the Christian faith, and it was the duty of all Christians to help alleviate the suffering caused by the Yusin regime's political and economic policies. The government, on the other hand, refused to acknowledge these religious motives and identified these ministers as a threat to national security. By arresting them under the National Security Law (NSL), Park Chung-hee insinuated that the protest at Namsan was pro-

Communist, thereby framing it as a political and not religious act. It is significant that Park Chung-hee could not simply repress the protest without having some kind of justification. Since the Korean War, the label of communism had constituted a serious charge, and Park Chung-hee's reliance on the NSL was an attempt to strike a common chord within the larger Korean society, whose memory of the war was still vivid.

Pak Hyŏnggyu attempted to challenge the rhetorical justification put forth by the Yusin regime, which argued for the necessity of an authoritarian political system to ensure national security and economic prosperity for the sake of the nation (*minjok*). In his legitimizing discourse, Park Chung-hee claimed to speak for, and protect the will of, the Korean people. Pak Hyŏnggyu, on the other hand, was proffering a new signifier—democracy—to refer to the will of the people. In this event of protest, symbols came into a binary relationship with each other as Pak Hyŏnggyu defined democracy to be the true referent to the will of the Korean people as opposed to Park Chung-hee's symbolic gesture of national security and economic prosperity. Not surprisingly this contest between opposing binary symbols did have an evaluative component as both Pak Hyŏnggyu and Park Chung-hee assumed to know what was truly best for the Korean masses.

The arrest of Pak Hyŏnggyu under the National Security Law led a group of concerned Christian leaders to propagate the 1973 Theological Declaration of Korean Christians. This declaration was a forerunner to Minjung Theology in that it was the first attempt to publicize Christian protest theologically or specifically as a Christian duty. In reaction to the state's framing of Pak Hyŏnggyu as a threat to national security, the declaration first established theological motives for protest: "We are under God's command that we should be faithful to his Word in concrete historical situations."[38] The declaration then applied these concerns to the specific context of Park Chung-hee's Yusin system:

> The present dictatorship in Korea is destroying rule by Law and persuasion.... Our position is that no one is above the law except God.... If anyone poses himself above the law and betrays the divine mandate for justice, he is in rebellion against God. The present regime is destroying freedom of religion.[39]

As can be seen from this theological declaration, Christians were contesting Park Chung-hee's rhetoric of maintaining national security via authoritarianism with the argument that his government impinged on their religious rights. The declaration also challenged the second pillar in Park's legitimizing discourse, economic policy:

The present dictatorship is responsible for the economic system in Korea, in which the powerful dominate the poor. The people, poor urban workers and rural peasants, are victims of severe exploitation and social and economic injustice. So-called "economic development" in Korea turned out to be the conspiracy of a few rulers against the poor people, and a curse to our environment.[40]

Overall, this declaration had the effect of challenging both of Park's justifications for the Yusin Constitution. For both Park Chung-hee and these Christians, the ultimate referent was the will and benefit of the Korean masses. While Park insisted that the Yusin system protected the Korean nation, Christians argued that only the restoration of democracy and a change in economic policy would ensure the rights of the people. The cultural contest between Christians and the Yusin regime, then, re-volved around the antithetical symbols of democracy and workers' rights versus national security and economic prosperity.

The contest for the sole right to speak for the Korean masses continued between Christians and Park Chung-hee throughout the 1970s. The Chris-tians presented their alternative interpretation of the state in sermons and public declarations. In particular, the Declaration of Conscience by Bishop Chi Haksŏn (July 16, 1974) and the Declaration for the Salvation of the Nation by Catholic, Protestant, and oppositional political leaders (March 1, 1976) were important for their highly publicized nature. These pre-dominantly discursive protests gave Christians the opportunity to challenge Park's justification of Yusin while upholding the ideals of democracy and human rights. The state's repression of the dissenting voices was quick and harsh. Both Bishop Chi and the group of eleven signers of the March First Declaration received long prison sentences (ranging from three to eight years).[41] The National Security Law provided the warrant for arrest and conviction in each case. Along with this material and instrumental repres-sion, the state's discursive responses to this counterhegemonic challenge were threefold. In various speeches, Park Chung-hee continued to propa-gate the rhetoric of prosperity for the *minjok*. In court cases, the govern-ment's prosecutors used the threat-to-national-security discourse to identify and frame Christian protestors as pro-Communists. Finally, in a few rare occasions, the state directly responded to Christians' continual use of the term "democracy" by offering their own definition.[42]

Two aspects of Park Chung-hee's rhetorical battle were important in the shaping of Minjung Theology. The first has to do with the collec-tive term used to identify the true will of the Korean masses. Christians criticized Park's assumption that he had the will of the Korean people in mind. The symbolic aspect of this contentious point became manifest in the Christians' use of the term *minjung* in opposition to Park's favored term *minjok*. Park, through various speeches, constantly referred to the *minjok* to convince larger society that his policies were for the betterment of the Korean nation. For Christians however, the true voice of the Korean people was the "groaning of the minjung"[43] and not the gratitude of the *minjok* implied in the state's public interpretation of Korea's economic growth. For some Christians, such as Ahn Byung-mu, relying on *minjung* rather than *minjok* was a conscious effort to raise an alternative rallying symbol for the Korean collective over and opposed to the state's use of *minjok*.[44] Thus, the collective identity of *minjung* became a sacred symbol in a binary relationship with Park Chung-hee's vision of the *minjok*. While not necessarily profaning the nation, Christians understood *minjung* as a "sacred-ontological category" of the Korean people, while the advocate of *minjok*—Park Chung-hee—was literally framed as demonic. In this way, as other scholars have noted, *minjung* versus *minjok* became "antonymic partners" in the symbolic contest over who represented the true voice of the Korean masses.[45]

The second aspect of Park's discursive critique of protesting Christians has to do with the identity of the latter. By arresting Christian activists under the National Security Law, Park was framing Christian praxis as (1) political, and therefore not religious in nature, and (2) as pro-Communist. This accusation vexed Christians who not only saw themselves and their protest as fundamentally different from the atheistic political ideology of Marxist-informed communism, but who also had historical reason to detest this association.[46]

Two events in the discursive struggle of the 1970s gave the state the opportunity to make pro-Communist accusations and the Christians a chance to rebut. The activities of the Urban Industrial Mission, while part of the instrumental challenge that Christians waged against Park Chung-hee, led to developments in the symbolic contest as well. On November 30, 1977, the government sponsored the publication of Hong Chiyŏng's pamphlet *What Is the UIM Aiming At?* in which the state framed the UIM as a Communist organization that "shakes the base of society ... because they imply companies belong to workers not to employers."[47] The state then passed out these pamphlets to workers and used this identification with communism as a justification for the violent repression of UIM-sponsored labor strikes.[48] In response to the pamphlet, Christians made various public declarations refuting this framing of the UIM. On March 20, 1978, the Catholic Justice and Peace Committee issued a public statement decrying the association of the UIM with Communists. Two days later the Human Rights Committee followed suit. More important, the committee directly and more thoroughly addressed this issue during the

"Consultation on Ideology" conference they held on October 19, 1978.[49] During the two-day conference Christian activist leaders studied the ways in which the government historically used anti-Communist ideology to frame political dissidents. Again, on August 29, 1979, three denominations affiliated with the Korean National Council of Churches held a press conference to denounce the government's framing of the UIM as Communists.[50] In all the public declarations and the Human Rights Committee conference, Christians first rejected the identification of their praxis with communism and then proceeded to argue that their activities stemmed from their religious faiths.

A similar incident was the case of the Christian Academy in 1979. On May 28 of that year Professor Chŏng Changyŏl and six staff members of the Christian Academy were arrested by the government under the Anti-Communist Law for their work in educating farmers and workers. Definitional elements crucial to the discursive struggle for both the state and Christians arose during the trial. On August 6, the presiding judge asked defendant Yi Ujae to define "socialism" since this was the formal accusation by the prosecutors.[51] In his response, Yi and all the other defendants insisted that their work with the farmers was a manifestation of their belief system, claiming that this was what their faith called them to do. Thus, Park Chung-hee's efforts at labeling Christian protestors as Communists not only gave Christians opportunities to reflect on their motives, but also helped facilitate and solidify their sense of self and praxis as religious in nature.

Conclusion

In his prison notebooks, the neo-Marxist theorist Antonio Gramsci made a keen observation regarding the powers that dominate societies. He noted that the ruling classes hold power over subordinate groups in at least two distinct ways. This "dual perspective" of power bifurcates hierarchical relations as a function of either "domination" or "hegemony."[52] Gramsci articulated the notion of domination to describe the relationship between ruler and ruled in which the latter enters the unequal relationship without consent. The forced relationship is held together as long as the ruler retains enough power to coerce the ruled. The other side to this dual perspective is what he called hegemony; the maintaining of an unequal relationship partly depends on rulers' ability to persuade, lead, and draw consent from those they attempt to control.[53] Gramsci speculated that the most thorough and efficient form of exercising power is to combine both of these strategies so that both the body and mind of subordinate groups are convinced and accepting of the existing relationship. For aspiring rulers, to have material power without hegemony is to rely strictly on the employment of brute force to maintain control. Likewise, to have consent without material power is to be at the whims of subordinate groups' shifting loyalties.

Park Chung-hee instinctively understood Gramsci's dual perspective of power and acted accordingly. Throughout his tenure, Park formed and utilized coercive state apparatuses to maintain control of South Korean society. In particular the Korean Central Intelligence Agency represented the "sophisticated and systematic repression" of any element within South Korea's society that challenged his political power.[54] Alongside this material repression of dissident groups, Park also developed legitimizing discourses in hopes of justifying his position as South Korea's undisputed leader. To this end, Park constantly referred to an impending threat to the nation's security as well as the need to industrialize the country as reasons why the authoritarian policies of the Yusin system were necessary. Thus from 1961 to 1979, Park Chung-hee consolidated his power over South Korean society through both the iron hand of material might and the softer voice of a father figure who knows best.

As a direct complement to Gramsci's dual perspective of power, the protest of dissident Christians constituted both strategic-material protest and expressive-discursive protest. Social movement organizations such as the Korean Student Christian Federation and the Urban Industrial Mission were founded to consolidate resources in an effort to strategically challenge the political and economic policies of the Yusin regime. In fact, increasing levels of repression of Christian dissidents gave rise to certain types of organizations as Christians responded to Park Chung-hee's Emergency Decrees. That is to say, the origins of organizations such as the Human Rights Committee, the Association of the Families of Prisoners of Conscience, and the Association of Prisoners for the Restoration of Democracy are to be found in the repressive measures of the Yusin regime itself. All of these SMOs exist even today, in some form, contributing to the present strength of the community of Christian activists.

In addition to these forms of strategic protest, Korean theologians also waged a discursive battle that challenged the justifying rhetoric of the Yusin regime. The Christian democracy movement established at the beginning of the Yusin era soon became a human rights movement following the repression of Christian political demonstrations. The continuing protest of Christians for democracy and human rights led to the arrests of many Christians under the National Security Law and the Anti-Communist Law, which in turn facilitated the motivational reappraisal of protest for these Christians. This rearticulation of motive for protest consciously utilized symbols that were the binary antithesis to Park Chung-hee's own legitimizing rhetoric. This process eventually culminated, for a group of theologians, in the formation of Minjung Theology.

Despite their efforts, Christians were not in the end the direct agents responsible for the fall of Park's regime. Ironically, the catalyst came from within his own government. On October 26, 1979, Kim Chaegyu (director of the KCIA) shot and killed Park Chung-hee, ending his eighteen-year reign. Following the assassination, hopes for a true democratic polity were once again shattered as General Chun Doo-hwan forcibly assumed control of the government. In the political period under Chun, Christians maintained their active role as the voice for the *minjung* and continued to suffer persecution for their activism.

NOTES

1. In the most general sense, we can roughly define two main positions among the Korean Christian leadership. A majority of the Christian leadership seems to have accepted, and even supported, the political status quo while a minority became a conspicuous force in opposing Park's Yusin regime.

2. Although not discussed in this chapter, the contribution by the Korean Catholic clergy cannot be overstated. For an in-depth study of the Catholic church during this time, see Nyŏng Kim, "Politics of Religion in South Korea 1974–1989: Catholic Church's Opposition to Authoritarian State" (Ph.D. diss., University of Washington, 1993). Also, although the heart of the Christian *minjung* movement is the countless number of marginalized people living and struggling during the Yusin era, this chapter focuses attention on the organizational and discursive manifestations of the movement.

3. Nancy Abelmann, *Echoes of the Past, Epics of Dissent: A South Korea Social Movement* (Berkeley: University of California Press, 1996).

4. All figures are quoted in Chang Hun Oh, "A Study of the Dynamics of an Authoritarian Regime: The Case of the Yushin System under Park Chung Hee, 1972–1979" (Ph.D. diss., Ohio State University, 1991).

5. Ezra F. Vogel, *The Four Little Dragons: The Spread of Industrialization in East Asia* (Cambridge, Mass.: Harvard University Press, 1991), 59.

6. Ibid., 51.

7. Carter J. Eckert, Ki-baik Lee, Young Ick Lew, Michael Robinson, and Edward W. Wagner, *Korea Old and New: A History* (Seoul: Ilchokak, 1990), 365.

8. From a special declaration announced on October 17, 1972. Quoted in Chung Hee Park, *Major Speeches* (Seoul: Samhwa, 1973), 25, 26.

9. Quoted from a speech given at the ceremony of the Ninth Export Day on November 30, 1972. Ibid., 130.

10. John Kie-chiang Oh, *Korean Politics: The Quest for Democratization and Economic Development* (Ithaca, N.Y.: Cornell University Press, 1999), 52.

11. Quoted ibid., 53.

12. The SMOs in this sample were the most prevalent in the archival sources.

13. *1970-nyŏndae minjuhwa undong* (Seoul: Human Rights Committee of the Korean National Council of Churches, 1986), 1:92. The groups were the Korean Student Christian Movement, the Korean Student Christian Council, and the youth group of the Korean YMCA.

14. Ibid., 132–140.

15. Hagen Koo, ed., *State and Society in Contemporary Korea* (Ithaca, N.Y.: Cornell University Press, 1993), 141.

16. Ibid., 170.

17. Owen C. Thomas, *Introduction to Theology* (Harrisburg, Pa.: Morehouse, 1983), 2.

18. D. Preman Niles, Introduction to *Minjung Theology: People as the Subjects of History*, ed. Commission on Theological Concern of the Christian Conference of Asia (Singapore: Christian Council of Asia, 1981), 6.

19. Ibid., 25.

20. Nam-dong Suh, "Towards a Theology of Han." In *Minjung Theology*, 58.

21. Chi-ha Kim, "The Dream of Revolutionary Religion," in *Living Theology in Asia*, ed. John C. England (Maryknoll, N.Y.: Orbis, 1982), 21, 22.

22. Byung Mu Ahn, "Jesus and the People (Minjung)," in *Asian Faces of Jesus*, ed. R. S. Sugirtharajah (Maryknoll, N.Y.: Orbis, 1993), 169.

23. Hermeneutical theory has been an important field of study for biblical scholars since the former's inception. See, for example, Gayle L. Ormiston and Alan D. Schrift, *The Hermeneutic Tradition: From Ast to Ricoeur* (New York: SUNY Press, 1990).

24. Cyris H. S. Moon, "An Old Testament Understanding in the Narratives of the Exodus and Creation Events," in *Minjung Theology*, 120. See also Wonil Kim's chapter (10) in this volume.

25. Byung-mu Ahn, "Jesus and the Minjung in the Gospel of Mark," in *Minjung Theology*, 141.

26. It is true that sweeping generalizations of this sort will necessarily overlook the positive experiences of some segments of Korean society. But still, what is maybe more important than the "objective truth" of labor conditions, is the fact that UIM members understood their own experiences in Park Chung-hee's economic program as fundamentally exploitive in nature.

27. Eckert et al., *Korea Old and New*, 369.

28. For further discussion see, Byong-suh Kim, "Modernization and the Rise of Religiosity in Korea: The Case of the Protestant Church and Sectarian Groups," *Industrializing East Asia* (1989): 152–168.

29. Hagen Koo, *Korean Workers: The Culture and Politics of Class Formation* (Ithaca, N.Y.: Cornell University Press, 2001), 75.

30. George E. Ogle, *South Korea: Dissent within the Economic Miracle* (London: Zed Books, 1990), 86.

31. UCLA Archival Collection on Democracy and Unification in Korea, box 09-1, folder 09-1-05.

32. Ibid., folder 09-1-06.

33. *1970-nyŏndae minjuhwa undong*, 3:1294.

34. Ibid., 1:295.

35. Ibid., 3:1039.

36. Ibid.

37. Wi Jo Kang, *Christ and Caesar in Modern Korea: A History of Christianity and Politics* (New York: SUNY Press, 1997), 102.

38. UCLA Archive, box 08-1, folder 1973.

39. Ibid.

40. Ibid.

41. Ibid., box 09-1, folder 09-1-03.

42. The government at this time started to put forth the notion of a "Korean-style democracy." For example in a press conference (July 19, 1979), assemblyman T'ae Wansŏn said that the threat to collective existence of Korea "makes the meaning of freedom here different from that existing in the Western Democracies." Quoted in UCLA Archive, box 09-1, folder 09-1-06.

43. In the mission statement of the Korean Christian Action Organization, a Christian based social movement organization.

44. David Suh Kwang-sun, "Korean Theological Development in the 1970s." In *Minjung Theology*, 41.

45. See, for example, Gi-Wook Shin, "Nation, History, and Politics," in *Nationalism and the Construction of Korean Identity*, ed. Hyung Il Pai and Timothy R. Tangherlini (Berkeley: Institute of East Asian Studies, University of California, 1998).

46. Although outside the scope of this chapter, I briefly mention here the fact that in prewar Korea, many Christians in the northern regions were heavily persecuted by Korean Communist groups. See, for example, Charles Armstrong, *The North Korean Revolution, 1945–1950* (Ithaca, N.Y.: Cornell University Press, 2004).

47. UCLA Archive, box 09-1, folders 09-1-04, 09-1-06.

48. Koo, *Korean Workers*, 83.

49. UCLA Archive, box 09-1, folder 09-1-05.

50. Ibid., folder 09-1-06.

51. Ibid.

52. Quintin Hoare and Geoffrey Nowell Smith, eds., *Selections from the Prison Notebooks of Antonio Gramsci* (New York: International Publishers, 1999), 169–170.

53. It is helpful to note the ambiguous nature of this term in Gramsci's writings. As the editors note (ibid., xiv), "hegemony" has two usages, and although it is defined in opposition to "domination," highlighting the subjective or interpretative qualities to power relations, it is also used to denote relationships where groups have been dominated in both the material and cultural spheres, leading to the total hegemonic control over a society.

54. Eckert et al., *Korea Old and New*, 341.

CHAPTER 10

Minjung Theology's Biblical Hermeneutics

An Examination of Minjung Theology's Appropriation of the Exodus Account

Wonil Kim

Traditional Christian theology—at least that is its claim—has been a Bible-based theology. It is a theology built first and foremost on the Bible.

As has been the case with liberation theologians of the Americas, it is therefore not surprising that *minjung* theologians do their work by showing that the theology they are constructing is rooted in the Bible in some significant way, and therefore credible. While we can hardly label them biblicists, their reliance on the Bible as an indispensable primary source of their theology is unmistakable.

Again, as has been the case with Liberation Theology,[1] one of the founding Biblical narratives for Minjung Theology is the Exodus story. An Byŏng-mu, one of the first and the most influential *minjung* theologians, sums up well what Minjung Theology takes for granted in this regard: "From the perspective of Minjung Theology, the Exodus is after all the most important event, and this perspective corresponds to the Bible's own perception, which takes the Exodus as the root of everything that is in the Bible."[2] Similarly, we regularly encounter the same sentiment expressed by second-generation *minjung* theologians. Chae Hyŏng-muk and Cho Ha-mu, for instance, assert that "the Old Testament texts most preferred [by Minjung Theology] are the ones related to the Exodus event."[3] Likewise, Kim Chi-ch'ŏl maintains that "the Bible witnesses to the God who reveals the divine will and carries it out in the concrete historical realm. And the defining moment of God's involvement in history in the Old Testament is the Exodus event."[4]

As is evident in this last statement by Kim, the modus operandi for Minjung Theology's biblical hermeneutics is the notion that history, and not the conceptual world, is the chief medium of divine revelation. This hermeneutical approach has underpinned Minjung Theology's reading of the Bible from its inception. Sŏ Nam-dong, one of the founding *minjung* theologians, is already absolutely clear about this methodological footing. In his groundbreaking book *Minjung Sinhak ŭi T'amgu*,[5] the chapter that deals with Minjung Theology's biblical connection is titled ("Minjung Sinhak ŭi sŏngsŏjŏk chŏn'gŏ"), and not "Minjung Sinhak ŭi sŏngsŏjŏk Kŭn'gŏ"—that is, "Biblical Reference of *Minjung* Theology," not "Biblical Basis of Minjung Theology."[6] He explains this deliberate choice of the word "reference" over "basis" in a way that is diametrically and programmatically opposed to the conceptual discourse of the traditional theology:

> The reason for using the word "reference" over the more usual "basis" is as follows. The word "basis" implies philosophical [= conceptual] grounding. But here we choose "reference" because we do not mean to say conceptual discourse but historical thinking. And the reason we must engage in historical thinking rather than in philosophical conceptuality is because that is the way the Bible thinks. The Bible does not inquire philosophically [= conceptually]. It only presents historical evidence. Historical referencing is the logic and the language of the Bible.[7]

Echoing this view, Kim Ch'ang-nak insists that "the biblical text does not so much convey concepts and ideologies as it addresses historical reality and witnesses the event that stands behind the text"; he then argues that "the Exodus event unmistakably shows that the Hebrews were a social class that was liberated," and therefore it is "unnecessary even to elaborate [the Exodus] as a liberation event."[8]

This history- and event-oriented approach of Minjung Theology to the Bible has taken on another methodological route in the form of narrative theology. From early on, Sŏ Nam-dong secures a clear methodological position that takes narrative as the fundamental and authentic medium of communicating and transmitting historical event. He stipulates methodological terms for narrative that are equally anti-conceptual discourse as they are when he speaks of the category of history:

> According to the biblical traditions and precedents, the primary, chief medium of God's self-revelation is salvific act, namely, historical event.... [It is not] a revelation through a theologian's hermeneutics. Laws, doctrines, theology, or even the Bible, which was edited according to a specific theological perspective, are not the primary media of divine revelation....
> The primary mode of God's self-revelation is the salvific, historical event, and the authentic transmitting medium of such an event is "story." For this

reason, most of the Old and the New Testament materials consist of narrative. God's language is [a language of] narrative.... [Contrary to what the traditional theology would have us believe], the authentic medium of divine revelation is narrative, inductively bearing the real and concrete experiences and cases.... Narrative theology is [therefore] ... a countertheology (*Gegentheologie*).[9]

There is of course a wide and divergent spectrum of what *minjung* theologians mean by "narrative," "narrative theology," or "narrative methodology." But the primacy of narrative over conceptual discourse as a fundamental method of Minjung Theology in general, and of Minjung Theology's biblical hermeneutics in particular, emerges as a common axis.[10]

The most distinctive characteristic of history-, event-, and narrative-oriented biblical hermeneutics of Minjung Theology therefore is the methodological primacy of history, event, and narrative over conceptual analysis. We may call it an action-oriented, anti-conceptual-discourse streak. Kim Yong-bok's call for narrative as virtually the only self-defining category of *minjung* itself clearly echoes the fundamental import of this underlying methodological assumption: "*Minjung* cannot, must not, be defined objectively and conceptually. Only *Minjung* can define itself—but again, not in an abstract category. *Minjung* can define itself [only] by its story that it owns and constructs."[11] And according to Kim Ch'ang-nak, the "story" of "Minjung Theology story" is "not an object of study by Minjung Theology but Minjung Theology's method of narrating."[12] He distinguishes Minjung Theology even from Liberation Theology in this regard:

The traditional theology can be defined as "an academic endeavor that systematizes the Christian religion through critical examination," and Liberation Theology as "a critical self-examination of the praxis of liberation." There remains thus a common denominator between these two theologies that is academic. Minjung Theology, on the contrary, emphasizes witnessing the *minjung* event from faith perspective. Minjung Theology places its theological task in the confessional, rather than academic, realm.[13]

By "academic task" Kim apparently means a conceptual discourse, and by "confessional task," a narrative task.

When *minjung* theologians construct their narrative Minjung Theology, they are modeling their hermeneutics after biblical paradigm. They build their case on what they perceive to be the central hermeneutics found in the Bible, which does not inquire conceptually but only references historical reality, as we hear Sŏ Nam-dong say in his programmatic statement. For

Sŏ and subsequent *minjung* theologians, then, historical event and its narrative have an indisputable and irrevocable methodological primacy over a conceptual approach.

What is Korean about this biblical hermeneutics? Before answering this question, I would like to take a detour and look at a few aspects of Liberation Theology first. Long before Liberation Theology emerged, Ernest Wright's phrase had become a truism: "History is the chief medium of revelation."[14] This famous phrase, of course, reflects the long-established tradition of *Heilsgeschichte* out of which Wright speaks. As Albrektson, Childs, and a host of others have pointed out, "revelation in history" has long been stressed by this school of thought in contrast with an alternative view of how revelation takes place, namely, through the word, or through a static, propositional doctrine of eternal truth.[15] The classic Protestant view of the divine word in the Bible has given way to this other concept of revelation that emphasizes "the action of God in history, his revelation in events."

Gerhard von Rad, the main player in this school of thought, therefore does not hesitate to call the Old Testament "a history book."[16] And Bernhard Anderson finds the most distinctive feature of the Jewish people in their "sense of history," and maintains that "biblical faith, to the bewilderment of many philosophers, is fundamentally historical in character." Anderson then asserts that "if historical memory were destroyed, the Jewish community would soon dissolve." This historical memory, simply put, is the memory of what God has done for and in the community. The Old Testament, according to Anderson, is therefore "the narration of God's action."[17]

Among many of God's actions, the event of the Exodus of course stands out as by far the most important occurrence in Israel's history. And the chief task of biblical theology is not to study it in conceptual terms but to simply narrate it because that is what the Bible does. Thus notes Ernest Wright:

> At the center of Israel's faith was this Supreme act of divine love and grace. The very existence of the nation was due solely to this act; the beginning of Israel's history as a nation was traced to this miraculous happening. In confessions of faith it is the central affirmation.... Who is God? For Israel it was unnecessary to elaborate abstract terms and phrases.... It was only necessary to say that he is the "God who brought thee out of the land of Egypt, out of the house of bondage" (Ex. 20:2).[18]

Thus, by the time of the Medellin conference, and by the time Cone and Gutierrez first published their works, "history" as the main category of biblical theology had been well established.[19] And Liberation Theology's affinity to this legacy of the *Heilsgeschichte* school is more than obvious.[20] We note, for instance, James Cone's assertion that "in the Bible revelation is inseparable from history," and "history is the arena in which God's revelation takes place. . . . The God of the Bible is a God who makes his will and purpose known through his participation in human history." And directly relying on von Rad's notion that even "creation is a work of Yahweh in history," Gutierrez maintains that "biblical faith is, above all, faith in a God who reveals himself through historical events," and "the God of Exodus is the God of history."[21] Liberation Theology thus enters into dialogue with biblical theology already permeated with the vocabulary of "history" as the main theological lingo and predicates its theology on that nomenclature from the beginning.

It is immediately evident that the history- and event-oriented biblical hermeneutics of Minjung Theology has a Western counterpart in this long trajectory of *Heilsgeschichte* school. It is the trajectory that stretches at least from, if not before, J. C. K. von Hofmann of nineteenth-century Germany to Gerhard von Rad of twentieth-century Germany, and on to the same school of thought represented by Richard Niebuhr, Ernest Wright, Bernhard Anderson, and others in the United States, finally reaching the shores of Liberation Theology, and in my opinion, of narrative theology as well.

Minjung theologians' focus on the Exodus event as a foundational text and their focus on historical event as the locus of revelation clearly echo the main thrust of this trajectory, which, not coincidentally, has the same built-in streak of anti-conceptual discourse, as we shall see later.

In addition to history as the primary hermeneutical category, narrative also plays a significant role in Liberation Theology's biblical hermeneutics, sometimes elaborated in detailed methodological studies. J. S. Croatto's works are a case in point.[22] As would be expected, the "God of history" provides the "hermeneutic key" for Croatto. Like other liberationists, he takes "salvific happening" as the point of departure for theology and insists that theology born of praxis is the starting point for biblical theology itself.[23]

Croatto's objective, however, is a narrative epistemology. Salvific events are, of course, most important to Croatto. But he concentrates on the question of "*how* the kerygma of liberation is treated as a theme in the Bible." In other words, he wants to know how the Exodus account works as a narrative. To accomplish this goal, Croatto turns to the field of *signs*, that is, narrative semiotics. And in doing so, he fully subscribes to the tenets of the Gadamar-Ricoeurian axis of hermeneutics.[24]

Croatto's methodological articulation is of course part of another long Western trajectory of hermeneutical discourse traversing the spectrum that includes, in addition to Gadamar and Ricoeur, Wilhelm Dilthey of nineteenth-century Germany, Karl Barth and Gerhard von Rad of twentieth-century Germany, Richard Niehbur of twentieth-century America, and Alasdair MacIntyre and Stanley Hauerwas of present-day America, to name just a few. In that spectrum, James Barr of England also has argued that story is better-suited than history to discourse on the Bible.[25]

Almost two decades after Sŏ Nam-dong declared narrative as the most fundamental category of Minjung Theology hermeneutics, *minjung* theologians were admitting that for them there was yet neither a clearly defined methodology of biblical hermeneutics in general, nor of the narrative aspect of that methodology.[26] In this milieu some second-generation *minjung* theologians attempted to move toward a more precisely rendered methodology, and in doing so, they unabashedly and without reservation resorted to the discourse on narrative taking place in the West.

Kim Ch'ang-nak, for example, concludes with W. G. Stroup that narrative is the only resource for establishing the Christian community's identity; that the God of the Bible is revealed through historical events and their narratives; that the defining biblical events—the Exodus and the Cross—are thus most naturally and most effectively transmitted by the genre of story; and most important, that the language that Christian theology must adopt for its authentic task is the language of narrative. Chae Hyŏng-muk and Cho Ha-mu, in their "search of a methodology for biblical hermeneutics by *Minjung*," rely heavily on Croatto, whose methodology I have briefly described above.[27]

At this point we may ask what is then so Korean about Minjung Theology's biblical hermeneutics. The survey above seems to lend itself to an unequivocal answer: Korean *minjung* theologians directly and extensively rely on the Western theology as they construct their biblical hermeneutics in general, and their hermeneutics of the Exodus account in particular. Both Sŏ Nam-dong and Ahn Byung-mu in fact acknowledge their methodological and substantive dependence on the West.[28] To the criticism that he is too dependent on Western trends to claim his own [Korean] theology, Sŏ admits unabashedly that his theological journey reflects the footsteps of the general trajectory of theology in the West. At the end of that trajectory he encounters Liberation Theology and engages it because the Korean situation of *minjung* demands it. The result of course is his Minjung Theology.[29]

In response to his critics Sŏ insists that theology is never a solo performance. One does theology by participating in the global discourse, and that means one develops her or his theology within the flow of that discourse. This argument reminds us of a similar charge leveled against liberation theologians and the subsequent debate. Admonishing Liberation Theology for what they see as its overreliance on the North, some critics, such as William

P. Lowe, have demanded that it draw its theological material from Latin sources in total independence from the North. In defense against this criticism, Christine E. Gudorf argues that the northern theology would not have taken Liberation Theology seriously enough had it relied solely on Latin sources.[30] Sŏ would only concur in response to the similar criticism of his Minjung Theology. But Sŏ's response above shows that for him the issue is more than just a practical matter of securing a global audience. It is the matter also of the substantive formation of his theology. He does not seem daunted at all by the idea that his own theology should be shaped by the global dialogue, because "a theologian must have an open attitude toward truth [regardless of its source]. One's [originality] is not [more] important [than one's openness]."[31]

This defense of course does not mean that Sŏ has nothing to say about the indigenous material as a source of Minjung Theology. On the contrary, he makes a bold suggestion that there is a methodology of Minjung Theology that is "developed uniquely in Korea, and therefore is in a position to make a singular contribution to global theological discourse" and that that methodology comes from *mindam* (Korean folktale).[32] Observing that "there is a confluence of the *minjung* tradition in Christianity and the Korean *minjung* tradition," Sŏ argues that "a task for Korean Minjung Theology is to testify" to that confluence. Then, using poet Kim Chi-ha's folktale plot of *Chang-il-dam*, he develops what can be considered a germinal programmatic statement for his "pneumatological historical interpretation."[33] But for him, this obligation of "testifying to the confluence" is not the paramount task of Minjung Theology. He would have developed Minjung Theology with or without Korean indigenous material. He uses Korean indigenous material in the service of Minjung Theology, not vice versa.

Many of the later-generation *minjung* theologians take a similar position. While not rejecting the label bestowed upon Minjung Theology as a "Korean theology," they nonetheless ask what is "Korean" about Minjung Theology and conclude that the adjective "Korean" should mean not so much a theology "of" Korea as a theology "for" Korean *minjung*.[34] The unique identity of Minjung Theology therefore does not lie in its theological originality arising ontogenically out of Korean soil but in a theological thinking that has converged with the tradition of Korean *minjung* liberation.[35] Furthermore, unlike their first-generation predecessors, many second-generation *minjung* theologians openly and programmatically borrow from Marxist theories as they construct their version of Minjung Theology (Kang Wŏn-don, Pak Sŏng-jun, and Sŏ Chin-han, to name a few).[36] Kim Chi-ch'ŏl fittingly summarizes the thrust of this self-perception of Minjung Theology when he calls Minjung Theology a "situation theology":

> Minjung Theology is better understood as a situation theology [than as a
> Korean theology] because its "Koreanness" does not depend on its theological
> and hermeneutical originality so much as on its ability to deal sensitively with
> the *minjung* reality in the Korean situation. Therefore the label that suits
> Minjung Theology best is perhaps "the situation theology of Korean
> *minjung*."[37]

It appears, therefore, that most *minjung* theologians would say that Minjung Theology's appropriation of the Exodus narrative is Korean because, and to the extent that, Koreans are using the Exodus account in the Korean situation of *minjung*.

My critique of Minjung Theology's hermeneutics of the Exodus story is not that it plugs directly into the trajectory of Western discourse to adopt its methodological lingo and categories. My criticism applies primarily to the schools of thought of which Minjung Theology partakes, then secondarily to Minjung Theology to the extent that it does not exercise a critical acumen in an important aspect as it adopts the Western idiom.

We have noted that Minjung Theology, like its Western counterpart, evidences an unmistakable streak of anti-conceptual discourse. For both Minjung Theology's biblical hermeneutics of the Exodus and that of its Western counterpart, which influences it, the Exodus is not an object of conceptual description, much less an object of conceptual analysis. Rather, it is a historical referent couched in narrative. The Exodus is not for us to analyze conceptually but to narrate as a historical event, as a narrative referent.

This methodological approach finds its earliest explicit precedent in the nineteenth-century German theologian J. C. K. von Hofmann, who sees the scripture "not [as] a textbook teaching conceptual truths but rather a document of an historical process . . . [which] has originated within the history recorded therein."[38] This methodological turn marks the beginning of *Heilsgeschichte* school in which others follow suit: for all his difference from von Hofmann, von Rad continues with the same methodological motif. As James Crenshaw describes him, von Rad has a "deep-seated fear of a rational system" and always resorts to history, insisting that "the Old Testament believes that God always and forever 'glorified himself' in his acts, that is to say . . . the *doxa* of his activity [in history and not in conceptual world]."[39] Wright likewise contends that "for Israel it was unnecessary to elaborate abstract terms and phrases [in order to explicate the question of God]. . . . It was only necessary to say that he is the 'God who brought thee out of the land of Egypt, out of the house of bondage'"; and the liberationists on their part insist that "[conceptual] wisdom and rational knowledge . . . [take]

praxis [in history] as their point of departure," and that conceptual reflection at best follows historical praxis, not vice versa.[40]

This methodological line continues with narrative theologians such as MacIntyre, Hauerwas, Stroup, and others who insist that narrative, and not conceptual analysis, is the most, in fact the only, authentic language of theology and ethics. Hauerwas, for instance, rejects the standard account's assumption that language describes conceptual reality in and of itself. He then speaks of skill, the know-how of proper utility, as a main narrative concern. The question for him is not whether our moral notion conforms to an objective theoretical norm, but whether the narrative language describing the notion does the job skillfully, thus enhancing its utility and purpose in a given context. He believes that conceptual analysis is not necessary because narrative structure lends itself to rational discourse that would lead us to a "reasoned act," and argues that narrative structure does not become rational discourse of necessary logic. Hauerwas does not exaggerate, therefore, when he says the rules governing narrative structure "are not those of logic but stem from some more mysterious source."[41] Story does not derive its assessing, evaluative function from its logical implication, but from its "grammar of actions." We do not gain moral insight by extrapolating a theory or a moral from the story. The story with its structure *is* insight. Narrative *is* the rational form on which ethics should depend. The reason lies within the narrative structure.

As for Croatto, after a book-length discourse on the indispensable role of narrative semiotics to show how the Exodus event becomes the effective Exodus narrative, he declares, in language strongly reminiscent of von Hofmann, von Rad, Wright, Anderson, and Hauerwas, "The biblical God is not the God of the Sources (an object of study and of reason) but the God-of-history of which the Sources speak to us as a kerygmatic "memory" [i.e., narrative] that sheds light on the God in action.... The biblical message wells up from the [narrated] salvific happening—this is the hermeneutic key."[42] And as we have seen, Minjung Theology absorbs this entire trajectory of von Hofmann, von Rad, Wright, Anderson, Hauerwas, Gadamar, Ricoeur, and Croatto and reads the Exodus account from their methodological standpoint, placing history, event, and narrative over conceptual and logical analyses and arguments.

Despite all the well-known merits of history- and narrative-oriented hermeneutics, however, its methodology manifests a fundamental flaw in its reading of the Exodus account. And this flaw is built into its methodological assumption that is very much in the spirit of the Kierkegaardian axiom, Live forward and understand backward.

No matter how much we may wish to simply narrate the Exodus event and reenact it—not as a conceptual construal but only as a historical and narrative referent—we cannot ignore one of its most fundamental elements that is constitutive of narrative: its conceptual basis. It is a story to be sure, but a story with, not without, a concept. In fact, there is no such thing as a story, a narrative, without a concept. And in the case of the Exodus, we cannot help but ask what the concept of its story is. Is it liberation, the beginning of a conquest, or a strange hybrid of both?[43] What about "the Hittites, the Amorites, the Perizzites, the Hivites, and the Jebusites" of Exodus 3:8 into whose land Yahweh is about to lead the Israelites, as stated programmatically in the same sentence structure that announces the plan for liberation?

Rolf P. Knierim, who solidly counts himself among the liberationists, has noted this problem and gives it a systematic treatment by scrutinizing Exodus 3:7–8 in the context of the Pentateuch narrative. While acknowledging that Yahweh's programmatic statement in this text is part of a "story" that "refers [not to an abstract idea but] to a real impending event," he nonetheless strives to find the "concept" of the story. By moving beyond the hermeneutical categories of history and narrative he engages the story in its relation to its "concept." He asks, "Without a concept, the story would be without clarity. What is the theological concept of the story?" After a meticulous conceptual analysis of the text in its literary environment, he concludes that

> the theology of Exodus 3:7–8 is the theology of the land of Israel as
> Yahweh's own people. All other notions, including the notion of liberation
> from oppression, stand in the service of this theology.... [The] story of
> liberation is not self-evidently based on a concept or theology of
> liberation.... [I]t is [therefore] not automatically clear in a given case whether
> liberation aims at nothing but the removal of injustice, or whether it serves an
> alien purpose which itself involves oppression of others by the liberated, and
> which discredits the credibility of liberation itself.[44]

In other words, the entry into the land of conquest, and not the departure from Egypt, is the main concept of our text. Both the oppression in Egypt and the liberation from it serve this concept. When we read the narrative of the Exodus conceptually and analytically, we can only conclude that the conquest theology is already embedded in the language of liberation.

As far as I can surmise, *minjung* theologians in general have embraced the hermeneutical trajectories of the West without addressing this problem.[45] It appears that *minjung* theologians overlook this conceptual aspect of the Exodus narrative because they, too, are caught up in a flawed methodological premise characteristic of the Western trajectories they adopt. Historical event rarely, if ever, becomes a narrative without a conceptual basis on which it is cameoed. Our theological task, therefore, is not simply to narrate it but also to examine its concept, and do so not only within but outside its narrative structure. As Habermas rightly observes, history writing as narrative is "action-oriented knowledge." We should of course expect history writing to continue in a narrative form, as does Habermas. Without returning to medieval scholasticism or Protestant orthodoxy, however, we must argue, as does Habermas, that the theory and the argument regarding the moral validity of the narrative are found in discursive moment outside the narrative. Thus notes Habermas: "The flow of the narrative would [therefore] be interrupted by argumentations; for history writing does not comprise theoretical knowledge, it is a form of application of theoretical knowledge."[46]

Just on the form of critical ground alone, the language of the Bible in general is already more than a language of historical/narrative referencing. But even when the language it uses is the language of historical/narrative referencing, as is the case with the Exodus narrative, it is only deceptively so—at least by the generic definition of narrative as such because narrative hides the conceptual reality that regulates it, consciously or unconsciously.[47] If Minjung Theology simply does historical/narrative referencing without doing any conceptual grounding, believing that is what the Bible does, then it does so at its own peril because biblical/historical narrative itself, to which Minjung Theology references, never simply does historical/narrative referencing without doing conceptual grounding of its own. Sŏ Nam-dong is apparently aware of this when he comes short of accepting the Bible as the ultimate authority because of its redactional biases.[48]

Despite this awareness, however, his affiliation with the lingo of the history and narrative schools of the West seems to prevent him, and the subsequent *minjung* theologians, from seeing the concept of conquest that accompanies, and is served by, the concept of liberation in the Exodus account. I do not believe this is so much an oversight as a result of a methodological flaw that puts a premium on history, event, and narrative at the expense of necessary conceptual analysis of history, event, and narrative. The sad irony is that, as a result, Korean Minjung Theology's hermeneutics of the Exodus history, event, and narrative unwittingly sidesteps the history, event, and narrative of the impending plight of the other *minjung* on the other side of the Red Sea.

As was noted earlier, the question of "Koreanness" of Minjung Theology's biblical hermeneutics does not seem to have preoccupied *minjung* theologians themselves. They appear neither to think that its methodology has to be necessarily uniquely Korean nor to hide their extensive reliance on biblical hermeneutics of the West. The issue they seem to consider more pertinent is how well Minjung Theology is served by its own biblical hermeneutics without agonizing over how Korean such a hermeneutics is or should be.

I wonder if *minjung* theologians have been relatively unperturbed by their reliance on Western methodology because Minjung Theology at its core is not dealing with the problems of culture, race, and ethnicity so much as with the problems of class struggle, which are often related to but also fundamentally distinct from those of culture, race, and ethnicity.

Just as Korean Marxists do not give a second thought to the fact that Marx was German or Bolsheviks were Russian, *minjung* theologians do not consider it problematic that their methodology of biblical interpretation depends so heavily on that of the West.

Perhaps the more pertinent question then is not how Korean but how *minjung* Minjung Theology's appropriation of the Exodus account is. And the answer is, as I have tried to show, that Minjung Theology's hermeneutics of the Exodus is not as *minjung* as we would have hoped it to be because the text does not really lend itself to such a hermeneutics. *Minjung* biblical hermeneutics has misread the text just as the Western hermeneutics it imports has misread it.

The question here is not just one of theory and method. At issue is not only *minjung*'s liberation, but *minjung*'s "logos" of "theos" in its struggle for liberation. We are therefore ultimately faced with the question of whether or not we can trust this god of the exodus to liberate *minjung* as the universal God of universal justice. The conceptual analysis of the account raises a serious doubt that we can. The analysis shows that the god of the exodus is capable not only of liberating his own elected people, but also of turning them into a group of oppressors. No righteous *minjung*, a phrase I hope is tautological, will ever trust such a god. This is not to suggest that we jettison the story of the Exodus or the Bible. On the contrary, it is to suggest that we keep searching for the God of *minjung* in, through, and beyond the god of the exodus, and that we search for that God dialectically in, among many places, the Bible.

NOTES

I dedicate this paper to the "the Hittites, the Amorites, the Perizzites, the Hivites, and the Jebusites" of Exodus 3:8, especially to their women, children, and underclass, and to their descendants, real or symbolic, in Palestine as they face the twenty-first-century Common Era.

I also dedicate this paper to Sŏ Nam-dong, for whom I have nothing but utmost and profound respect and admiration, and whose untimely death two decades ago I shall forever deplore.

1. Arthur McGovern, "The Bible in Latin American Liberation Theology," *The Bible and Liberation: Political and Social Hermeneutics*, ed. Norman K. Gottwald (Maryknoll, N.Y.: Orbis, 1984), 462.

2. Kim Ch'ang-nak, Min Yŏng-jin, and An Pyŏng-mu, "Minjung sinhak ŭi sŏngsŏ haesŏk pangbŏp" [Methodology of Minjung Theology's Biblical Hermeneutics], *Simp'ojium* [Symposium] 57.

3. Ch'oe Hyŏng-muk and Cho Ha-mu, "Han'guk Kŭrisŭdogyo minjung kongdongch'e ŭi sŏngsŏ haesŏk" [Biblical Hermeneutics of Korean Christian *Minjung* Community], *Sinhak sasang* [Christian Thought], 63 (1988): 818.

4. Kim Chi-ch'ŏl, "Minjung sinhak ŭi sŏngsŏ ilggi e taehan bip'anjŏk koch'al" [A Critical Observation on Minjung Theology's Bible Reading], *Sinhak sasang* 69 (1990).

5. Sŏ Nam-dong, *Minjung sinhak ŭi t'amgu* [Investigations into *Minjung* Theology] (Seoul: Han'gilsa, 1983).

6. Ibid., 221–244.

7. Ibid., 231–232. Hi-sŏk Cyris Moon is therefore less than precise when he says that Sŏ "regards the Exodus event as the biblical *basis* for the people's movement for liberation" (my emphasis) (Hi-sŏk Cyrus Moon, "An Old Testament Understanding of *Minjung*," in *Minjung Theology: People as the Subjects of History*, ed. Commission on Theological Concerns of the Christian Conference of Asia [Maryknoll, N.Y.: Orbis, 1983], 124. Curiously, however, Sŏ himself uses the word "basis" in the title of a section in the chapter. Sŏ, *Minjung sinhak*, 231.

8. Kim Ch'ang-nak, Min Yŏng-jin, and An Pyŏng-mu, "Minjung sinhak," *Simp'ojium* 57:417 and 423.

9. Sŏ, *Minjung sinhak*, 304–305.

10. Thus, we have, among others, An Pyŏng-mu, who speaks of "*minjung sinhak iyagi*" [*minjung* theology story] in his book of the same title (Seoul: Han'guk Sinhak Yŏn'guso, 1987); and Kim Yong-bok, who proposes "*Minjung ŭi sahoe chŏn'gi wa sinhak*" [*Minjung*'s Social Biography and Theology], *Sinhak sasang* 54:1 (1979): 58–77. See also Kim Yong-bok, *Han'guk minjung ŭi sahoe chŏn'gi* [Social Biography of Korean *Minjung*] (Seoul: Han'gilsa, 1987); and Kim Ch'ang-nak, who looks at "Minjung Theology as a narrative theology"; see Kim Ch'ang-nak, "Iyaki sinhak ŭrosŏ ŭi minjung sinhak," *Sinhak sasang* 64:1 (1989): 5–24.

11. Kim Yong-bok, *Han'guk minjung*, 61.

12. Kim Ch'ang-nak, "Iyaki sinhak ŭrosŏ ŭi minjung sinhak," 6.

13. Ibid., 7.

14. G. Ernest Wright and Reginald H. Fuller, *The Book of the Acts of God* (New York: Double day, 1957), 13.

15. B. Albrektson, *History and the Gods* (Lund, Sweden: CWK Gleerup, 1967), 11–13; Brevard Childs, *Biblical Theology in Crisis* (Philadelphia: The Westminster Press, 1976), 39–40.

16. Gerhard von Rad, "Typological Interpretation of the Old Testament,"

trans. John Bright, in *Essays on Old Testament Hermeneutics*, ed. Claus Westermann; English Translation ed. James Leither Mays (Atlanta: John Knox Press, 1979), 25ff.

17. B. Anderson, *Understanding the Old Testament* (Englewood Cliffs, N.J.: Prentice Hall, 1966), 2 (in the 1986 edition he changed "sense of history" to "sense of tradition"). Subsequent quotations ibid., 13 (in the 1986 edition, he changed "destroyed" to "erased").

18. Wright, *The Book of the Acts of God*, 77.

19. The Second General Conference of the Latin American Bishops held in Medellin, Colombia, in 1968, considered not only the official beginning of liberation theology but also one of the most important events in the history of Latin American Christianity. See Enrique Dussel, *History and the Theology of Liberation* (Maryknoll, N.Y.: Orbis, 1976), 113; James Cone, *A Black Theology of Liberation* (Philadelphia: Lippincott, 1970); and Gustavo Gutierrez, *A Theology of Liberation* (Maryknoll, N.Y.: Orbis, 1973).

20. This affinity has been equally well recognized. See, for example, Cone, *Black Theology*, 92–106. See also J. Severino Croatto, *Exodus: A Hermeneutics of Freedom*, trans. Salvador Attanasio (Maryknoll, N.Y.: Orbis, 1981), v. For a defense of this affinity, see Christine E. Gudorf, "Liberation Theology's Use of Scripture: A Response to First World Critics," *Interpretation* 41, no. 1 (January 1987): 10.

21. Cone, *Black Theology*, 93; Gerhard von Rad, *Old Testament Theology*, vol. 1, trans. D. M. G. Stalker (New York: Harper & Row, 1965), 139; Gutierrez, *Theology of Liberation*, 154 and 157.

22. Croatto, *Exodus*, and especially his later work, *Biblical Hermeneutics: Toward a Theory of Reading as the Production of Meaning* (Maryknoll, N.Y.: Orbis, 1987).

23. Croatto, *Exodus*, v.

24. Ibid., 13–35.

25. James Barr, "Story and History in Biblical Theology," *Journal of Religion* 56 (1976): 1–17.

26. Ch'oe and Cho, "Han'guk Kŭrisŭdogyo," 811–812; Kim Ch'ang-nak, 6–7.

27. Kim Ch'ang-nak, 7; Ch'oe and Cho, "Han'guk Kŭrisŭdogyo," 828–838.

28. Sŏ, *minjung sinhak*, 202ff.; An, *minjung sinhak iyagi*, 21ff.

29. Sŏ, *minjung sinhak*.

30. William P. Lowe, Review of Sobrino's *Christology at the Crossroad*, *America*, Aug. 5, 1978, 67; Gudorf, "Liberation Theology's Use of Scripture," 10–11.

31. Sŏ, *minjung sinhak*, 202.

32. Ibid., 228.

33. Ibid., 45–82 and 301–312.

34. Song Ki-dŏk, "Minjung sinhak ŭi chŏngch'e" [The Identity of *Minjung* Theology], *Kidokkyo sasang* [Christian Thought], 33, no. 2 (1988): 139ff.

35. Pak Chae-sun, "Minjung sinhak, muŏsi kwaje in'ga" [*Minjung* Theology: What Is Its Task?], *Kidokkyo sasang* [Christian Thought], 34, no. 1 (1990): 37.

36. Kang Wŏn-don, "Sinhak hanŭn pangbŏp ŭi saeroun mosaek—undong

hanŭn chŏnch'erosŏ ŭi hyŏnsil e taehan sinhakchŏk insik kwa silch'ŏn" [A New Search for Theological Method: Theological Understanding and Praxis], in *Sinhak kwa silch'ŏn* [Theology and Praxis] (Seoul: Minjungsa, 1989), 131–153; Pak Sŏng-jun, "Han'guk Kidokkyo ŭi pyŏnhyŏk kwa Kidokkyo undong ŭi kwaje [Changing Korean Christianity and the Task of the Christian Movement], *Sinhak kwa silch'ŏn* [Theology and Praxis] (Seoul: Minjungsa, 1989), 154–189; Sŏ Chin-han, "80-nyŏndae Minjung sinhak ŭi kwahaksŏng kwa taejungsŏng" [The Scientific Nature and Grass-Roots Nature of *Minjung* Theology of the '80s], in *Chint'ong hanŭn Han'guk kyohoe* [The Korean Church in Travail] (Seoul: Han'guk Kidokkyo Sahoe Munje Yŏn'guwŏn [Center for Studies of Problems in Christianity and Society], 1990), 103–143.

37. Kim Chi-ch'ŏl, "Minjung sinhak," 442.

38. Von Hofmann, *Interpreting the Bible* (originally, *Biblische Hermeneutik* [Nördlingen: C. H. Beck, 1860]), trans. Christian Preus (Minneapolis: Augsburg Publishing House, 1959), as cited in John H. Hayes and Frederick Prussner, *Old Testament Theology: Its History and Development* (Atlanta: John Knox Press, 1985), 83. Some may argue that this methodological approach begins with Blaise Pascal, who says that the God of the Bible is not the God of the philosophers and the sages but "the God of Abraham, Isaac, and Jacob."

39. J. Crenshaw, *Gerhard von Rad* (Waco, Tex.: Word Books, 1978), 33. Gerhard von Rad, *Old Testament Theology*, trans. D. M. G. Stalker (New York: Harper & Row, 1965), 2:358; cf. 379.

40. Gutierrez, *Theology of Liberation*, 3–15.

41. Stanley Hauerwas, with Richard Bondi and David B. Burrell, *Truthfulness and Tragedy: Further Investigations in Christian Ethics* (Notre Dame, Ind.: University of Notre Dame Press, 1977), 15–39 and 28.

42. Croatto, *Biblical Hermeneutics*, v.

43. Croatto does not answer these questions because he does not raise them to begin with. Neither do the majority of critics. Strangely, many "faulty" aspects of the Exodus model preoccupy them, but not this. We encounter some exceptions, such as Klaus Nürnberger, who criticize liberation theology for its silence on this question. See Klaus Nürnberger, *Power and Beliefs in South Africa* (Pretoria: University of South Africa Press, 1988), 218ff. See also Naim Ateek, *Justice, and Only Justice: A Palestinian Theology of Justice* (Maryknoll, N.Y.: Orbis, 1998), especially his chapter "The Bible and Liberation: A Palestinian Perspective," 74–114.

44. In 1978 Knierim gave a lecture on this problem that was subsequently published as "Israel and the Nations in the Land of Palestine in the Old Testament," *Bulletin* 58, no. 4 (November 1978), 11–21 and is now in *The Task of Old Testament Theology: Methods and Cases* (Grand Rapids, Mich.: Eerdmanns, 1995), 309–321. For a fuller understanding of Knierim's treatment of this question we also need to see his arguments in *Task*, 130ff. Extended quotation is on 133. See also 309–321, esp. 318. Knierim distinguishes between the cause and the reason for the Exodus. On the most immediate level, the oppression is the cause for the liberation, but the reason for the liberation lies elsewhere: "The need for the Exodus." Read within the context of the entire Pentateuch narrative, it can even be argued that "the

need for Israel's exodus is in the first place the reason for their oppression." He substantiates this notion by observing that Yahweh considers no alternatives for solving the problem of the oppression. Not all the Pharaohs were oppressive. Taking care of this one Pharaoh, therefore, could have solved the problem. Nor does Yahweh introduce any of "the viable alternatives also [found] in the Old Testament." In other words, "The intention to lead Israel away from Egypt is at the outset the conceptual reason for the liberation of Israel for which the oppression is the actual cause." And finally and most important, Yahweh has his mind set on the Exodus because of the promised land. Knierim notes "how directly our text connects Israel's departure from Egypt with the goal of its subsequent immigration.... No alternatives are considered, not even Sinai." Knierim notes the two aspects that comprise the text's depiction of this goal, the land: permanent settlement (land with milk and honey) and the conquest (the six peoples occupying the land). To confirm the second of these, he refers to the text's place in the tradition-history of the conquest and to its deuteronomic-deuteronomistic language. Furthermore, this conquest theology is based on the theology of the land. And the ultimate rationale for the theology of the land comes from another theology on which it stands: the theology of election. (ibid., 131).

45. Sometimes they turn to the sociological model of Gottwald and others and refer to it as the evidence of God's revelation through the Exodus (Sŏ, *Minjung sinhak*, 236ff.). Sŏ Nam-dong thus tells us that "[the peasant revolt] is God's revelation.... With this the God who protects *minjung* emerges through the revelation of the Old Testament" (240). In saying this Sŏ mixes two incompatible methodologies. Gottwald himself is very clear about the methodological incompatibility between biblical theology and biblical sociology. See Norman K. Gottwald, *The Tribes of Yahweh: A Sociology of the Religion of Liberated Israel, 1250–1050 B.C.E.* (Maryknoll, N.Y.: Orbis, 1979), 665–709. After an extensive exposition of Croatto's methodology, Ch'oe and Cho seem to commit a similar error. They fully accept Croatto's methodological premise that "every textual interpretation has to begin with *the text* ... [and] must strive to be a reading of the received *text* ... hence the supreme importance of any reading as a *reading of a text*" (Croatto, *Biblical Hermeneutics*, 29–30 (emphasis in original); Ch'oe and Cho, "Han'guk Kŭrisŭdogyo," 834). Yet they make a methodological jump and fall back on Gottwald's revolt theory and his socio-religious model of "mono-Yahwism" to make a case for *minjung*'s privileged hermeneutical stance regarding the Bible (836ff.). For them, the liberation of *habiru* (= the *minjung* of the Old Testament) forms the central axis of the Old Testament, which coincides with the life conditions and experiences of Korean *minjung*. This correspondence gives the Korean *minjung* a privileged hermeneutical position that "provides the only hermeneutical key for the interpretation of the Bible by *minjung*" (838). Yet again, the biblical text does not render a simple picture of liberation. The Hebrews of the Exodus, *habiru* or not, do not simply constitute *minjung* as Ch'oe and Cho define it, and identify it with Korean *minjung*.

46. Jürgen Habermas, "History and Evolution," *Telos*, no. 39 (1979): 41.

47. Habermas offers a penetrating analysis of our act of narrating in a manner analogous to psychoanalysis. Narrative does not just serve a parochial purpose as

MacIntyre and Hauerwas suggest. Habermas agrees with U. Anacker and H. M. Baumgartner's claim that narrative is indeed conceivable only with a totality of history in view as a regulative principle:

> The interest in narrating . . . conceals the interest in totality in the sense of the whole of temporal reality, which though not realizable is nonetheless necessarily presupposed and for whose very sake narrative structures are intended. . . . The "subject" of history is precisely in this sense a regulative idea like history itself: both have the positional validity of a principle of organization for constructions, a principle stemming from the practical interest in construction, i.e., in knowledge and action. But history is, therefore, necessary as a regulative principle. (U. Anacker and H. M. Baumgartner, "*Geschichte*," in *Handbuch philosophischer Grundbegriffe* (Munich, 1973), 2:555ff., as cited in Habermas, "History and Evolution," 42)

48. Sŏ, *minjung sinhak*, 304–305.

CHAPTER 11

Korean Protestants and the Reunification Movement

Yi Mahn-yol
Translated by Timothy S. Lee

orean Protestants joined the movement for national reunification in earnest in the 1980s. The movement was spearheaded
by the progressive wing of the Protestant church, but conservatives also
participated in due course. In the face of hostile dictatorships, Protestants
persisted in their efforts and in the end helped to shape the South Korean
government's reunification policy and make it possible for nongovernmental agencies and individuals to take part in the movement.

Historically, Korean Protestants have taken active roles in national issues akin to the reunification movement. In their early history, for example,
they led efforts to reform the feudalistic practices of the late Chosŏn dynasty
and opposed foreign encroachments in Korea. During the Japanese occupation of Korea, Protestants wholeheartedly participated in movements to
restore national sovereignty and to establish an independent Korean state.
After liberation, as their church became entwined with the unsavory right-
wing politics of Syngman Rhee, the Protestants temporarily lapsed into social irresponsibility. But following the 1960s, during a period of continuous
military rule, they once again resumed a more responsible role, taking the
lead in furthering human rights and democratization in South Korea. Entering the 1980s, their advocacy for human rights and democratization was
suppressed by the military government, in the name of national security.
Given Korea's national division and the heavy military buildup along the
demilitarized zone, the government's claim seemed plausible to the South
Korean public, enough for the government to suppress the Protestants' democratization efforts without provoking widespread opposition. Consequently, Protestants shifted their activist strategies and made the movement
for national reunification their top priority, not only because they believed
reunification to be a worthy goal in of itself but also because they believed

that as long as the nation remain divided, a government could always suppress pro-democratization or human-rights movements in the name of national security. This chapter examines the national unification movement as pursued by Korean Protestants.

The Policy of Reunification by "Northern Expedition" and the Transformation of the Korean Protestant Church

OPPOSITION TO A TRUCE DURING THE KOREAN WAR AND THE EMERGENCE OF THE POLICY OF REUNIFICATION BY "NORTHERN EXPEDITION"

After Korea was freed from Japanese rule in 1945, U.S. troops arrived and established a military government in South Korea.[1] Thereafter the American government assisted in establishing Syngman Rhee's rightist regime in 1948. Since most Protestants were pro-American and anticommunist and Rhee was a Protestant, many Korean Protestants made their way into high positions in both the U.S. military government and Rhee's administration. They also outnumbered adherents of other religions by substantial margins in the Korean national assembly and political parties.[2]

Such close association with the rightist government predisposed the Protestants to support the government's policy vis-à-vis the North. Taking their cues from Rhee, even before the outbreak of all-out war in 1950, Protestants opposed the withdrawal of U.S. forces.[3] During the Korean War itself, Protestants suffered greatly at Communist hands. At least 408 clergy were verified as having been killed; 1,373 churches were totally burned, and 666 churches partially burned.[4] Because, in part, of such losses, Protestants advocated the total eradication of communism from the peninsula and opposed truce negotiations during the war. In conjunction with opposing a truce with the North, Protestants supported Rhee's efforts to unify the peninsula by an armed incursion into the North, the so-called policy of reunification by northern expedition.

On December 27, 1950, an interdenominational association of the Protestant churches sent a message to U.N. Secretary-General Trygve Lie, U.S. President Harry S Truman, and U.S. General Douglas MacArthur. They expressed their clear opposition to a Korean War truce. When their message went unheeded and truce negotiations became more earnest, Protestants held a rally in Pusan on July 12, 1951, where they declared their desire to "resolutely march forward to achieve a complete reunification of North and South Korea by driving Communist forces out beyond national borders."[5] On June 15, 1953, they sent a similar message to President Dwight D. Eisenhower and Christian churches throughout the world.

After a standoff truce was reached despite Protestant opposition, the

South Korean government espoused a two-level unification policy. On one level, it continued to promote the familiar northern expedition policy; on another level, it put forward the idea of reunification by holding a comprehensive North-South election under the auspices of the United Nations. The former proposal was mainly for internal consumption and for fueling anticommunist fervor, whereas the latter was mainly for the outside world, a ploy to garner the moral high ground. Of these two alternatives, Protestants favored the northern expedition persuasion.

THE PROTESTANT CHURCH'S ANTICOMMUNIST OUTLOOK ON REUNIFICATION IN THE 1960s

The Protestants' anticommunist stance persisted into the 1960s, and became more institutionalized. In 1966, an anticommunist alliance was formed among Korean Protestant churches. In October 1967, a Christian anticommunist conference attended by 150 conferees from ten countries took place in South Korea.

On April 19, 1960, a popular uprising erupted, leading to Syngman Rhee's ouster by month's end. This event prompted Protestants to rethink their commitment to the ideologies of the 1950s. This new assessment included a revision of their unswerving hostility toward northern communism and, more important, a search for ways to promote true democracy in Korea. In July 1960 the government of Yun Posŏn and Chang Myŏn was elected to succeed Rhee's government, but it lasted scarcely a year, as General Park Chung Hee took power in a military coup. His military government reinstated unrelenting anticommunism, setting up a barrier to any softening of the hostility toward the north and a search for democracy in Korea.

Park's subsequent military—and later civilian—government insisted that to bring about reunification, and to confront communism, South Korea first had to gain superior strength in all levels of society. It pushed social and economic modernization to the top of the national agenda. But in instituting its policy, the government also insisted on the priority of national security. In time, in the name of national security, the government trampled on human rights and civil liberties, suppressing critical voices and thwarting free learning and thought.

The government sought to justify its repressive policy by contending that the Communist threat compelled it "temporarily" to restrain criticism, human rights, and social justice. But the regime's true intention was to preserve its hold on power by suppressing any kind of dissent. Given this situation, the Protestants concluded that inasmuch as the government could plausibly wield the "security doctrine" as its trump card, little headway could occur in democratization efforts.

National division gave plausibility to the security doctrine, and unless the division was supplanted by reunification, no democratization movement stood a chance of success in the South. Accepting this reality, the Protestants now saw democratization and reunification as two sides of the same coin. They eschewed more generally touted notions, such as the two-system approach or the "democratization first, reunification later" stance.[6]

REUNIFICATION ISSUE'S INABILITY TO MOVE BEYOND GOVERNMENTAL POLICY LEVEL

From the beginning, talk of reunification was monopolized as the property of the governments of North and South Korea. Civilians found it almost impossible to shape the debate over the issues, let alone to become actively involved in resolving the problem. In the 1970s, Protestants began challenging this trend. An encouragement in this regard was found in the North-South Joint Declaration (on Peaceful Reunification) of July 4, 1972, presented by the governments of the two Koreas, ostensibly as a step toward reunification.

Early on, however, Protestant leaders saw through this political showmanship. They criticized the joint declaration as a "reunification discussion of expedience enmeshed with the interests of the governments" and cautioned vigilance lest the ploy lead to a permanent division of the nation.[7] In this vein, on July 18, 1973, the Korean National Council of Churches (KNCC) issued its Declaration on the July 4 Joint Declaration, in which it stated that the council could not endorse the spirit of the joint declaration. The KNCC expressed its fear that the South Korean government could use the declaration—and its purported agenda for dialogue with the North—as one more bit of rationale to inhibit democracy in South Korea.[8] In time, it became apparent that the joint declaration was indeed just a ploy of the two governments. Not long after the declaration was issued, the South in 1972 declared a Yusin (revitalization) regime, with a fanatical anticommunist agenda, and the North revised its socialist constitution, cementing its monolithic hold on the populace.

Cognizant of this development, a year after the joint declaration was issued Protestants attempted to hold the two parties accountable to the publicized intent of the declaration: from a safe overseas venue, they issued statements that the July 4 joint declaration must serve as an occasion to realize the desired reunification of all Korea.[9]

The Protestants did not allow the failure of the North-South dialogue to stymie their reunification endeavors. In early 1974, about three thousand members of the Christian Youth Association held a service to pray for reunification and staged a street demonstration in Seoul. In the context of the Yusin regime, this was an extremely bold action. On March 1, 1976, at Myŏngdong Cathedral, a group of ministers issued a Declaration for the Democratization and Salvation of the Nation. As a result, many ministers suffered arrest and imprisonment. Predictably, the government accused the KNCC and other kindred organizations of being procommunist. The KNCC strongly refuted the accusation, and to defend itself against similar accusations in the future, formed a Committee on the Church and Society, a Human Rights Committee, and a Council on Christian Faith and Ideological Problems.[10] An ordeal such as that suffered by the KNCC was what awaited all Christians engaged in the reunification movement during the Yusin regime.[11]

On October 17, 1978, when the Yusin regime was at its maddening height, 402 opposition leaders, led by Christians such as Ham Sŏkhwan, Mun Ikhwan, Yun Posŏn, and Yi Munyŏng, jointly published the October 17 Democratic People's Declaration. In it, the signatories voiced their resolve to oppose the dictatorship, struggle for democratization, and work toward the long-cherished national dream of reunification. As this declaration attests, in the Protestants' overt opposition to the government, the issue of reunification usually emerged as an adjunct to the more prominent issues of human rights and democratization—largely because the Protestant church in the 1970s, for the most part, adhered to the view that if it discussed reunification, it would risk being drawn into the dictatorial regime's prolonged stratagem.

In spite of this strategic consideration, some have criticized the church as "dubiously espousing the rightness of the cause of reunification, on the one hand, while not taking much action to promote it, on the other."[12] It was only in the 1980s that Protestants took on the reunification movement with as much vigor as they had the democratization movement.

Alliance with World Church and Tozanzo Conference

CIRCUMSTANCE OF NORTH AND SOUTH KOREA IN THE 1980s

Having successfully staged a coup d'etat on December 12, 1979, Chun Doo Hwan succeeded Park Chung Hee as South Korea's next strongman. In 1981 he proposed in a policy speech that the heads of the South and the North visit each other's sphere. In another policy speech the following year, he proposed a Plan for National Reconciliation and Reunification. The idea called for a Council of National Reconciliation and adoption of a Reconciliation Constitution and, on the basis of such a constitution, a national election was to be held to form a Reunified Democratic Republic. To implement this plan, he even proposed a provisional agreement on basic relations between the South and the North. But, in truth, this was nothing more than a show of ostentation by a government that lacked legitimacy.

In the North, on October 10, 1980, at the sixth conference of the Workers' Party, Kim Il Sung proposed a Koryŏ Democratic Confederate Republic as a plan for reunification. Briefly, this plan provided for North Korea and the United States to change the truce agreement into a permanent peace treaty and for the two Korean states to work toward forming one confederate state, putting aside the existing ideologies and systems. To implement this plan, he also proposed the establishment of a Supreme National Council Conference (decision body) and a Confederate Standing Committee (permanent organ), through which the North and the South could individually administer their respective governments. On April 9, 1985, the North also suggested a conference of South-North national assemblies.

Another noteworthy development was that the Red Cross in the North and in the South resumed their conferences in the 1980s. A September 18, 1984, contact between working-level representatives of these two bodies was the first such meeting since their sessions of the 1970s. It ended without much result; but as a consequence of that session, the two Red Cross agencies exchanged relief materials. In May 1985, a Red Cross conference was held in Seoul between the two countries, the first such in twelve years. Those talks resulted in the exchange of cultural troupes. Of greater significance, some Koreans from both sides visited surviving relatives in the other side for the first time since the war.

VISITS OF OVERSEAS KOREANS TO NORTH KOREA

Since the division of their land, Koreans in the peninsula were prohibited from meeting with each other, but such prohibition did not bar overseas Koreans from visiting North Korea. In 1979, Kim Sŏngnak visited North Korea and met Kim Il Sung. Kim was a Korean American Protestant, a former dean of Sungsil College in Pyŏngyang who originally hailed from North Korea. Kim's visit was catalytic, for thereafter more and more overseas Protestants not only visited the North but also met with North Koreans outside the Korean peninsula and discussed unification issues.

From November 3 to 6, 1981, a historic meeting occurred in Vienna, Austria, as overseas Koreans and North Korean Christian representatives, forty-five in total, discussed national reconciliation and reunification, in the presence of thirty outside observers.[13] This meeting came to be known as the "Dialogue on Korean Reunification between Christians of North Korea and Overseas."

Subsequently, from December 3 to 5, 1982, a second such meeting took place in Helsinki, Finland, amidst enormous interest and expectations on the part of Koreans inside and outside Korea.[14] Both meetings produced a joint declaration. These announcements tended to follow the North's request to avoid criticism of Kim Il Sung and his son, even as they criticized

"U.S. imperialism" and urged U.S. withdrawal from South Korea and democratization of South Korea. On December 17, 1984, a third conference was held, this time in Vienna.

Given the biased slant of the discussions, these meetings were scarcely made known inside South Korea. But they were extremely meaningful in that they "were the first of its kind to have taken place in the thirty-six-year-long history of division since 1945, in or outside of Korea" and in that they led to overseas meetings between Christians of North and South.[15]

ALLIANCE WITH WORLD CHURCH

As a result of the May 1980 Kwangju Democratic Movement, churches around the world came to have more interest in a variety of South Korean issues. Such interest motivated some of these churches actively to collaborate with their Korean counterparts in human rights and the reunification movement in Korea. An example of this is the Fourth Korean-German Christian Conference held in Seoul Academy House, June 8 to 10, 1981, under the overarching theme "Christian Confession in a Divided Nation" and the secondary theme "Confessing Sin and New Responsibility." In a joint resolution emerging from this conference, the conferees recommended that the KNCC establish a committee or an institute to discuss and promote Korean reunification issues and that the KNCC request the German church to support Korean-German discussion on peaceful reunification (fifth clause). Pursuant to this recommendation, on February 26, 1982, the KNCC resolved to establish an Administrative Committee for the Institute of Reunification Issues as a special committee. On September 16, this administrative committee was formed.[16]

Following the lead of the German church, U.S. churches also expressed an interest in the Korean division and owned up to whatever responsibility they might have regarding it. As a result, in 1985, the Third Korean–North American Church Conference was held; it produced a resolution whose gist was that the United States was the nation that divided Korea and that the U.S. church, along with the Korean church, must assume joint responsibility for the reunification of the Korean peninsula.[17]

These meetings between Korean Protestants and representatives of German and U.S. churches produced at least two positive results. One was that in 1985 and the following year, representatives of the U.S. church and World Council of Churches made official visits to North Korea, where they exchanged opinions with North Korean church leaders and helped to ease the tension in the Korean peninsula. The other was that the meetings stimulated the World Council of Churches to have an interest in Korea to the extent it brought about a direct meeting between churches of North and South Korea.

TOZANZO CONFERENCE

From October 29 to November 2, 1984, a meeting of Consultation on Peace and Justice in Northeast Asia was held in Tozanzo, Japan, sponsored by the World Council of Churches. Sixty-five church leaders from twenty-five countries attended it—from Asia, the Pacific, the Middle East, Latin America, Eastern and Western Europe, and North America.[18] This was the first international conference in which the churches of Korea and other countries intensively discussed issues of peace and reunification in the Korean peninsula; it constituted an important watershed in the Korean church's reunification movement.

Moreover, a product of this meeting—"Prospects for Peaceful Resolution of the Conflict: Report and Proposal" (generally known as the Tozanzo Report)—is regarded as having provided a new milestone in the Korean church's reunification movement.[19] To summarize, this statement first declared that peaceful reunification of the Korean peninsula had to be the goal and result of a concrete practice of the gospel of reconciliation; second, that peaceful reunification is not a unilateral mission of either the North or the South Korean church alone but a common task of both churches; and, third, that establishing peace and reunification in the Korean peninsula is not the responsibility of the two Korean churches alone but a common responsibility of the entire world church body.[20] The five-year period from 1985–89 saw active efforts to implement these resolutions enunciated at Tozanao.[21]

Meetings of North and South Korean Churches

From 1986 to 1990, southern and northern churches met every two years at Glion, Switzerland, three times altogether. Known as the Glion conferences, these meetings turned out to be significant turning points in the Korean church's reunification movement. The first meeting took place on September 2, 1986, sponsored by the World Council of Church's Committee on International Problems. It was held in seminar format with the topic "The Biblical and Theological Basis for Christians' Concern on Peace." Twenty-two representatives from both North and South Korean churches participated, including four representatives from the Chosŏn Christian Alliance.[22]

The Second Glion Conference took place November 23 to 25, 1988. It came on the heels of the Declaration on National Reunification and Peace of the Korean Christian Church (issued by the KNCC in February 1988) and the World Council of Church's Consultation on Peaceful Reunification of the Korean Peninsula, held in Inch'ŏn (April 1988). It took place under the banner of the Second Consultation on the Peaceful Reunification of the Korean Peninsula.

The participants worshiped and experienced fellowship together, participated in Bible study, took Communion together, and discussed a variety of issues related to peaceful reunification.[23] The conference endorsed the KNCC's declaration on peaceful reunification, proclaimed 1995 as the jubilee year for reunification, decided on the Sunday immediately preceding August 15 as Peaceful Reunification Sunday, and adopted a common prayer.[24]

In the year following the Second Glion Conference, churches of the North and the South met to discuss peace and reunification of the Korean peninsula and continued their relations with churches of the world. From April 23 to 26, 1989, the two churches met for the Washington Consultation on Peace and Reunification of the Korean Peninsula, sponsored by the U.S. National Council of Churches.[25] In the same year, from September 29 to 30, they met again for the Consultation on East Asian Peace and the Church's Mission, sponsored by the Japanese National Council of Churches.[26] In the latter, it was decided that North Korean representatives would be invited to KNCC's Seoul assembly in February 2000 and, if that proved infeasible, once again to meet overseas in June of the same year.

From July 10 to 13, 1990, the two churches met again at Tokyo's Korean YMCA, for the Tokyo Christian Conference on Peaceful Reunification and Mission of the Fatherland, sponsored by the Assembly of Christian Churches of Korean Residents in Japan (Chaeil taehan kidokkyohoe ch'onghoe).[27]

From December 2 to 4, 1990, a third Glion conference was held. And of all the meetings held between North and South Korean Christians up until then, this one proved to be the most progressive and also the most abundant and specific in content.[28] The two churches agreed on nine clauses of a Five-Year Jubilee Plan for Cooperative Work, which included mutual visitation, urging North and South Korean authorities to adopt a mutual nonaggression declaration, and installing an operational apparatus to pursue the project.

That these series of meetings resulted in selecting 1995 as the jubilee year for reunification—thereby affixing concrete goals toward reconciliation and harmony—should be seen as extremely meaningful in the history of Korean reunification movement.

The Declaration of the Korean [Protestant] Church on National Reunification and Peace: The KNCC's Declaration on Reunification

DEVELOPMENTS LEADING TO THE KNCC'S DECLARATION ON REUNIFICATION

Upon the recommendation of the Fourth General Assembly of the Korean-German Church Association, the Korean National Council of

Churches organized the Administrative Committee for the Institute of Reunification Issues on September 16, 1982, and, in the next year, sought numerous times to hold conferences but failed because of interference from the government.[29] Consequently, on June 16, it issued a Declaration on the Interference on Holding Conferences regarding Reunification Issues. Such pronouncement was unavailing, and for four years the Korean church could not hold meetings in Korea to discuss reunification issues. This situation perforce channeled the church's energies into strengthening its relations with other national churches and the World Council of Churches.

It was only in 1985 that study and discussion on reunification issues became possible in Korea. From March 27 to 28 of that year, the KNCC held its Thirty-Fourth General Assembly at Onyang, a city in southern Ch'ung-ch'ŏng province, and adopted and declared the Korean Church's Declaration on Peaceful Reunification. Significantly, this declaration set forth that the reunification movement should, in principle, be people-centered and peaceful. It also advocated peaceful exchanges thoroughly grounded on humanitarian principles and stated the ultimate goal of reunification as the realization of democracy and social justice. It included a confession addressed to God and the nation for the church's connivance in or justification of the division. This declaration, formally speaking, was the Korean church's first official declaration on reunification, and is significant in that it preceded the KNCC reunification declaration (1988) in clarifying the Korean church's determination for peaceful reunification.[30]

After the Korean Church's Declaration on Peaceful Reunification was issued, the First KNCC Consultation on Reunification Issues was held on May 24 of the same year, sponsored by KNCC's Institute of Reunification Issues, with the theme "Justice, Peace, and Church." The institute was able to continue the consultation series, such that between January 21 and 23, 1988, up to five consultations had been held. After those five consultations, the KNCC, on February 29, 1988, at the Thirty-Seventh General Assembly, presented the Christian Church's Declaration on National Reunification and Peace, which was met with a standing ovation and unanimously passed.

This declaration, divided into three parts, begins with a confession of faith regarding the triune God and the mission of the people of the land, proffering faith-based reasons for the Korean Protestant church's need to eliminate the division. In the first part, the declaration proposes a theological basis for a "confession of sin regarding the division and hatred." In the second, it proposes five principles of reunification, by adding the principles of "humanitarianism" and "the democratic participation of all members of the nation" to the three—autonomy, peace, and pan-national solidarity—already stated in the July 4 joint declaration. It also called upon the governments of North and South Korea to institute measures implementing these principles. Finally, in the third part, the declaration includes "The Korean

Christian Church's Task for Peace and Reconciliation," setting forth recommendations such as declaring 1995 as the year of reunification jubilee,
exchanging visits between North and South Korean churches, and holding
educational activities related to peace, reunification, and other similar concerns relative to the formation of a national community.

THE PLACE OF THE KNCC REUNIFICATION DECLARATION

The KNCC reunification declaration is a milestone in the history of the
Korean national reunification movement in that it "opened the sluice gates
of reunification discussion at the civilian level."[31] The reunification principles proposed in this declaration "accommodated and synthesized the reunification principles advocated by progressive elements in the South Korean
Protestant church since the 1960s."[32] Moreover, this declaration influenced
not only the Korean Protestant community, but the Korean reunification
movement in general and the entire world Christian church as well.

It is partly because of this declaration that President Roh Tae Woo's
government was compelled to issue the July 7 Declaration, aimed at furthering a reconciliatory approach to reunification with the North. Later
almost all of KNCC's points were incorporated in the North–South Korean Agreement on Reconciliation and Nonaggression and Exchange and
Cooperation, adopted by both Koreas on December 13, 1991, and in the
Joint Declaration on De-Nuclearization of the Korean Peninsula, provi-
sionally signed on December 31 of the same year.

Such inclusion indicated that both North and South Korean governments accepted the declaration's expressed concern for the good of the entire national community. The declaration also had an ecumenical dimension
as well, as it provided opportunities for churches of various countries to
work closely together on a common set of issues, thereby adding specificity
to their global ministries.

The 1990s: Diversification of the Reunification Movement in the Protestant Church

SOUTH KOREANS' VISIT TO NORTH KOREA

After the KNCC reunification declaration was issued, the Reverend
Moon Ikhwan was emboldened to visit North Korea in 1989 in response
to an invitation from Kim Il Sung. He was accompanied by fellow Protestant Yu Wŏnho. This visit precipitated a spell of intensive "security rule"
surveillance. Nonetheless, Moon's visit provided an opportunity for dis-
seminating the reunification discussion, which had to date been confined
within the Protestant church, out into the public at large, and enhancing
its spread. His visit also opened the way for Catholic college student Im

Sukyŏng and a Catholic priest, the Reverend Mun Kyuhyŏn, to visit North Korea. Their visit, in turn, encouraged the Catholics—who until then had been comparatively passive in the movement—to embrace reunification as an important agenda item. Moon's visit, in short, struck a blow against the South Korean government's monopoly over reunification discussion with the North Korean government.

PROGRESSIVE-CONSERVATIVE PROTESTANT SOLIDARITY IN THE REUNIFICATION MOVEMENT: THE NORTH-SOUTH SHARING MOVEMENT AND THE KOREAN CHRISTIAN COUNCIL FOR PROMOTING PEACEFUL REUNIFICATION

In the 1990s, with the collapse of the Soviet Union and the Eastern bloc, North-South relations entered a new phase on the Korean peninsula, with high-level meetings taking place between the two sides.

The Protestant reunification movement at the time was being carried out through a variety of channels: the first channel was that of the Peaceful Reunification and Jubilee Movement, centered on the KNCC; the second, that of the Coalition of Christian Social Movement, a group whose chief agenda included promoting peace and armament reduction in the peninsula; the third, that of pan-Korean conferences, participated in by North and South as well as overseas Koreans, in which Protestants also participated; the fourth, the women's movement; and, finally, that of Evangelical, conservative Protestants who, in the 1990s, emerged as a new force in the movement.[33]

Until the 1990s, the Evangelicals evinced little interest in reunification as a religious issue. What religious interest they had in North Korea was evangelistic, in finding ways to evangelize there and recoup the losses they had suffered in the Korean War. Since 1990, however, without giving up their evangelistic concerns, the Evangelicals also developed an interest in helping to solve North Korea's social ills.

Much of this shift came about in the 1980s, as the Evangelicals embraced a Kingdom of God movement that had its theological grounding in the Lausanne Covenant of 1974, a faith statement that expressed "penitence both for our neglect and for having sometimes regarded evangelism and social concern as mutually exclusive."[34]

At about the time the Evangelicals began to explore ways to participate in the reunification movement, the progressive Protestants, who had been unrivaled in their leadership in various social movements in South Korea, had become burned out with regard to them and were in the doldrums. Consequently, when the Evangelicals brought their fresh passion and deep coffers into social ministry, the ministry was reinvigorated. The progressives needed the Evangelicals' energy and material resources, and the Evangelicals

needed the progressives' expertise; consequently, they cooperated. Concrete manifestations of their cooperation included the Citizens' Association
for Practicing Economic Justice (Kyŏngjae chŏngŭi silch'ŏn simin yŏnhap),
which was formed at the end of the 1980s, and the Christian Committee for
Effecting Fair Elections (Kongmyŏng sŏn'gŏ silch'ŏn kidokkyo taech'aek
wiwŏnhoe) and Citizens' Action Council for a More Just Society (Chŏngsa
hyŏp), which were formed later.

In the reunification movement, as well, cooperation took place between these two groups, resulting, on April 27, 1993, in the South-North
Movement for Sharing for Peace and Reunification (Nam-Buk nanum
undong) and on December 5, 1994, in the Korean Christian Council to
Promote Peaceful Reunification (Han'guk kidokkyo p'yŏnghwa t'ongil
ch'ujin hyŏpŭi hoe).

The South-North Movement for Sharing is the Protestants' united organ for the reunification movement, with the Evangelicals constituting the
main element, working closely with the progressives. This organization has
thus far been discreet in its operation and has led the way in helping North
Koreans. It has also formed a research committee composed of fifteen or
so Protestant scholars, publishing their research and holding numerous
seminars.[35]

The Korean Christian Council for Promotion of Peaceful Reunification is a huge umbrella organization consisting of 116 Protestant groups;
the South-North Movement for Sharing is its core member. In the council's mission statement, intent is stated to pursue comprehensive measures
in solidarity with others to achieve peaceful reunification by promoting
cooperation aimed at furthering mutual understanding. There is also the
intent to engage in consultation and research for policy formulation, to prepare for the 1995 jubilee, and to promote efforts toward a sense of common
national identity among Koreans on both sides of the thirty-eighth parallel.

CONTINUOUS MEETING BETWEEN THE CHURCHES OF THE NORTH AND THE SOUTH

Outside Korea, progressive Protestants continued their meetings with
Christians from other countries in promoting unification. The Christian
Conference on the Peaceful Reconciliation and Missions of the Fatherland
was held from July 10 to 13, 1990, in Tokyo. The participants adopted an
Agreement of Tokyo Meeting for the Jubilee of Peaceful Reconciliation.
This agreement's main points consisted of the following: urging mutual
reconciliation and maintaining a position for coexistence between the two
Koreas, abolishing all obstacles that stood in the way to expanding the exchange, and reducing armaments and invigorating peace negotiations; the
agreement also called for withdrawal of U.S. troops and nuclear arms, adop-

tion of a nonaggression pact, and mutual visits of northern and southern churches to further their various ministries.

Meetings outside Korea between North and South Korean Christians also continued apace. A symposium of Christian scholars from the North and the South was held at Los Angeles from March 14 to 19, 1991, under the theme "Prospects for Peaceful Reconciliation in Korea." The Twenty-Fifth Annual Meeting of North American Christian Scholars was held from May 28 to 30, 1991, at Stony Point, New York. At that gathering, from the North came Ko Kijun, Yi Sŏngbong, Choe Okhwi, Kim Haesuk, Han Sihae, Pak Sŭngdŏk, Kim Kusik, Ro Ch'ŏlsu. From the South came Chi Myŏnggwan, Pak Sugyŏng, Song Kŏnho, No Myŏngsik, Han Wansang, Pyŏn Honggyu, Yi Mahnyŏl, and others. Under the theme "Our Mission in the Formation of a New National Community," the participants engaged in a lively exchange of opinions. In the same year, from July 9 to 12, under the sponsorship of the Association of National Missionary Studies, a Christian Conference of Evangelism and Peaceful Reunification took place in Tokyo with the topic "Christians' Role in Peaceful Reunification and Evangelism of the Fatherland."

A working-level consultation on the five-year jubilee joint project was held October 11 to 12, 1991, in Toronto, Canada. Among those gathered there were the South's Kwŏn Hogyŏng and the North's Kang Yŏngsŏp, who was central committee chairman of the Chosŏn Christian Alliance, both of them discussing the "Direction of the 1995 Jubilee Project and Preparation for Agreement and Solidarity." For working-level consultation on this matter, on January 7, 1992, Kwon Hogyŏng visited North Korea. On February14, Ko Kijun, secretary of the Chosŏn Christian Alliance, was scheduled to visit KNCC's Forty-First General Assembly, but his visit was aborted at the last moment. Later that year, on October 21, the Korean Christian Laymen's Conference convened in Tokyo, and October 20–22, the Third Christian Conference of Tokyo convened. But inasmuch as the North Korean nuclear problem loomed on the international scene at the time, it became almost impossible for North-South dialogue to proceed.

THE FOURTH INTERNATIONAL CHRISTIAN CONSULTATION AND THE MEETING OF NORTHERN AND SOUTHERN CHURCHES

The Fourth International Christian Consultation was held from March 28 to 31, 1995, at Kyoto Kansai Seminar House in Japan. Participants included twenty-two representatives from the South and four from the North. Dr. Feliciano Carino and thirty-one other representatives from outside Korea also participated. The event was partly supported by the World Council of Churches, with the National Council of Churches of Japan providing all the logistic needs. At the conference, the participants agreed on a five-clause action list, such as holding the August 15, 1995, joint jubilee worship at Panmunjŏm, the neutral village near the thirty-eighth parallel. They urged working-level representatives from both sides to hold a preparatory meeting.[36]

Moreover, a declaration adopted by the World Council of Churches in this consultation contained specific steps the churches of the North and South should take. They included holding the jubilee together, eliminating legal obstacles to reunification in the Korean peninsula, denuclearizing Korea, formulating a strategy for arms reduction, and solving humanitarian problems. The conference participants agreed that in keeping with the liberating spirit of the jubilee, if anyone on either side of the peninsula suffered from unjust imprisonment due to the division, the churches should work together for their speedy release and repatriation. These agreements, however, were undermined by the tense political situation that prevailed in the peninsula: on August 15, 1995, the planned jubilee joint worship failed to take place at Panmunjŏm, and the other agreed-upon actions also failed to materialize.

Nevertheless, meetings of northern and southern churches continued afterward. In 1997, as almost ten years had passed since the U.S. National Council of Churches had formulated Peace and Reconciliation in the Korean Peninsula, the U.S. National Council of Churches organized a conference participated in by North and South Korea and the United States. This conference was held from March 17 to 19 in New York City. It reaffirmed the basic direction and spirit of the 1986 policy conference and the promise of the July 4, 1972, North-South Joint Declaration on Peaceful Reunification. During the twenty-seventh German Church's Day event June 17 to 22, 1997, in Leipzig, North and South Korean representatives met. Near the end of September and early October that year, Secretary Kim Tonghwan and Director Kim Yŏngju of the KNCC visited North Korea upon the invitation of Kang Yŏngsŏp, chairman of the Chosŏn Christian Alliance.

Protestant Food Aid to North Korea

In the 1990s, North Koreans suffered from extreme food shortages. These food shortages were caused by a variety of internal and external factors, in addition to years of flooding. The more important factors include the collapse of the Communist bloc, making it impossible for the North any longer to depend on its "socialist brothers." The lack of arable land and the inefficiency of the socialist system were also factors. That the authorities rejected professional opinion while implementing a self-sufficiency policy in agriculture is also seen as a decisive cause for the problem.

Among South Korean civilian organizations, the church was the first to extend a helping hand to the North. In the early 1990s, before an immense flood devastated the North, some in the church learned that North Korea's food situation was dire, and took the initiative "secretly" to help North Koreans. Mindful of the legal restrictions of the time, they took the approach of helping North Korea through a third country.

From the middle of the 1990s, the Protestant church went all-out in aiding North Korea, irrespective of denominational background as either progressive or conservative. Earlier, to escape the government's restraints, the churches had no choice but to form an interdenominational cooperative organization. But by the mid-1990s, various denominations engaged independently in fund-raising or forming aid mechanisms for North Korean relief purposes, or they gave aid as presbyteries or conferences within particular denominations. Christian organizations outside the church (or denomination) also actively participated. Previously, leery of North Korea, many were reluctant to aid the North openly or to be known to be doing so by the media. Eventually, however, that stage was overcome. By the late 1990s, various Christian media, including the Christian Broadcasting Service, appealed for North Korean aid and gave coverage to the processes and situations of the aid.

Protestant organizations that collected funds to help the North did so independently by affiliating with the National Civilian Organizations' Conference for Aiding North Koreans (Pukhan tongp'o topki mingan tanch'e chŏn'guk hoeŭi). Based on 1997 sources, the following Protestant organizations may be identified by name as having taken part in this kind of work: the National Association of Methodist Youths, Salvation Army Headquarters, 97 Holy Assembly, Korean Christian Methodist Conference, Korean Christian Full Gospel Church, Christian Youth and College Reunification Peace Corps, Christian Assemblies of God, the Christian Holiness Church, the Christian Baptist Church, Korean Episcopal Church, Korean Jesus Presbyterian Church (Kaehyŏk), Korean Jesus Presbyterian Church (Kaehyŏk-hapsin), Korean Jesus Presbyterian Church (Kosin), Korean Jesus Presbyterian Church (Taesin), Korean Jesus Presbyterian Church (T'onghap), Korean Jesus Presbyterian Church (Hapdong), Korean Jesus Presbyterian Church Youth Association, Korean YWCA Federation, the Movement to Share Food and Share Love with North Korean Women, Campus Crusade for Christ, the Ecumenical Youth Council in Korea, the National Association of Ministers for the Realization of Justice and Peace, Chinju Christian Federation for Supporting North Korean Brethren, the Movement for North-South Sharing for Peaceful Reconciliation, Korean Church Women's Federation (Peaceful Reunification Committee), Korean International Organization for Countering Hunger, the KNCC (Emergency Measure Headquarters for Helping North Korean Brethren), Korean

Christian Social Service Association, Korean Christian Elders Association, Korean Christian Confederation (Committee for Aiding North Korean Brethren), Korean Christian Student Confederation, Korean Christian Youth Conference, Korean Evangelical Conference, World Vision Korea, Association of Korean Women's Organizations, Korean Women Theologians Association, the National Alliance of Korean YMCA. In addition to these, individual churches occasionally collected funds for North Korean people and children. In local areas, too, Christian churches, organizations, and individuals either formed aid agencies and actively ran them or supported such agencies from behind the scenes.

In July 1997, Korean Protestants who had hitherto strived separately to aid North Korea formed the Association of the Korean Christian Churches for the Support of North Korea (Han'guk kidokkyo Pukhan tongp'o huwŏn yŏnhaphoe). The intent behind this organization was not only to smooth the exchange of information and streamline the aid efforts, but also to overcome the government's monopolization of the route to North Korea. This federation's services became invaluable for those with collected funds but lacking means to transmit them to North Korea through appropriate channels. According to information released by this federation, from April 3, 1997, to November 7, 2002, it sent aid worth 29 billion 260 thousand wŏn, or approximately $24,330,000.[37]

What is noteworthy is that since receiving aid worth more than 1 billion wŏn ($740,740) on April 3, 1997, the central committee of North Korea's Christian Federation assumed independent control over both the fax and mail transmission of messages checking on the receipt of the materials. This can be seen as a small achievement that came about because of the southern church's continuing efforts to designate the federation as its northern partner. Hitherto, the federation's activities in the North were scarcely noticeable, as the federation could not wield any influence. But as a result of the continuous attention and aid it had received from the South, its stature had risen near the end of the 1990s. Granted that the federation might merely have been exploited, this development still bears attention.

NOTES

1. On issues discussed in this section on reunification, I have learned much from Kim Yangsŏn, *Han'guk kidokkyo haebang simnyŏnsa* [A History of the Korean Protestant Church during the Ten Years following Liberation] (Seoul: Taehan Yesugyo Changnohoe T'onghoe Chongyo Pu, 1956); and Kim Hŭngsu, "Hanguk kyohoe ŭi t'ongil undong yŏksa e taehan chegŏmt'o" [A Reconsideration of the Korean Protestant Church's Participation in the Reunification Movement], *Kisayŏn*

mugŭ [The Book-Magazine of Kisayŏn], 3 (Seoul: Han'guk Kidokkyo Sahoe Munjae Yŏn'guwŏn, 1991).

2. Kang Inchŏl, "Han'guk kaesinyo ŭi chŏngchi sahoe chŏk kinŭng e kwanhan yŏn'gu: 1945–1960" [A Study of Korean Protestant Churches' Sociopolitical Function: 1945–1960] (Ph.D. diss., Seoul National University), 224–235.

3. Chang Pyŏnguk, *6.25 Kongsan namch'im kwa kyohoe* [Communists' Southern Invasion on June 25 and the Protestant Church] (Seoul: Han'guk Kyoyuk Kongsa, 1983), 184.

4. Kim Yangsŏn, *Han'guk kidokkyo haebang simnyŏnsa*, 90.

5. Ibid., 140.

6. On this point, see Kim Hŭngsu, "Han'guk kyohoe ŭi t'ongil undong yŏksa e taehan chegŏmt'o," 111–112. Particularly helpful is his discussion on how Mun Ikhwan and Kim Kwansŏk contributed to integrate the democratization and reunification movements.

7. No Chungsŏn, ed., *Minjok kwa t'ongil I: Ch'aryo* [The Nation and Reunification 1: Sources] (Seoul: Sakyejŏl, 1985).

8. Kim Sang'gŭn, "Minjok ŭi t'ongil kwa saegye P'yŏnghwa rul wihan han'guk kyohoe ŭi konghŏn" [Korean Protestant Church's Contribution to National Reunification and World Peace], in *Han'guk kidokkyo kyohoe hyŏpŭihoe ch'angnip 70 chunyŏn* [The 70th Anniversary of the Korean National Council of Churches], ed. KNCC (Seoul: KNCC, 1994), 43.

9. Ibid.

10. Ibid., 43–44.

11. No Chungsŏn, *Minjok kwa t'ongil I: Ch'aryo*.

12. Kim Sang'gŭn, "Minjok ŭi t'ongil kwa segye," 44.

13. T'ongil sinhak tongji hoe, ed., *T'ongil kwa minjok kyohoe ŭi sinhak* [A Theology for Reunification and National Church] (Seoul: Hanul, 1990), 299.

14. T'ongil sinhak tongji hoe [Reunification Theology Fellowship], ed., "Che 2ch'a 'choguk t'ongil ur wihan puk kwa haewoe tongp'o kidok sinja kan ŭi taehwa" [The Second Dialogue between North Korean and Overseas Protestants on the Reunification of the Fatherland], in *Tongil kwa minjok kyohoe ŭi sinhak* [A Theology of Reunification and the National Church] (Seoul: Hanul, 1990), 304.

15. Ibid., 299.

16. Pak Chonghwa, "Hanbando t'ongil rul wihan nambuk kyohoe ŭi silch'ŏn—charyo mojip" [Acts of North-South Korean Churches Regarding the Reunification of the Korean Peninsula—a Source Collection], in *Nambuk kyohoe ŭi mannam kwa p'yŏnghwa t'ongil sinhak—kidokyyo t'ongil sinhak charyo mit p'yŏnghwa sinhak nonmun moŭm chip* [A meeting between Churches of the North and the South and a Theology of Peaceful Reconciliation—A Collection of Sources on a Christian Theology of Reunification and Writings on a Theology of Peace], ed. Hanguk kidokkyo kyohoe hyŏpŭihoe t'ongil wiwŏnhoe (Seoul: KNCC, 1990), 2.

17. Kim Sang'gŭn, "Minjok ŭi t'ongil kwa segye," 44.

18. Pak Chonghwa, "Hanbando t'ongil rul wihan nambuk kyohoe ŭi silch'ŏn," 13.

19. Pak Sŏngjun, *1980nyŏndae Han'guk kidokkyo t'ongil undong e taehan koch'al*

[A Reflection on Korean Protestants' Reunificaton Movement in the 1980s], in *Sinhak sasang* [Korea Theological Study], no. 71 (Winter 1990).

20. Pak Chonghwa, "Hanbando t'ongil rul wihan nambuk kyohoe ŭi sil-ch'ŏn"; Pak Sŏngjun, *1980nyŏndae Han'guk kidokkyo t'ongil undong e taehan koch'al*, 962. The entire text of the Tozanzo Report is in *Nambuk kyohoe ŭi mannam kwa p'yŏnghwa t'ongil sinhak*, 12–19.

21. Pak Sŏngjun, *1980nyŏndae Han'guk kidokkyo t'ongil undong e taehan koch'al*, 962.

22. See *Nambuk kyohoe ŭi mannam kwa p'yŏnghow t'ongil sinhak*, 34–35. Southern participants of this meeting included Kang Munkyu, Kim Pongnok, and Kim Soyŏng; among the northern participants were Ko Kijun (head of Chosŏn kidokkyo yŏnmaeng), Kim Namhyŏk (a member of Chosŏn kidokkyo yŏnmaeng's central committee), Kim Unbong (committee chair of the peace committee of Chosŏn kidokkyo yŏnmaeng), and Kim Hyesuk (translator).

23. Kang Munkyu, "Nambuk kyohoe sangbongi 2: che 2 ch'a kŭlion hoe ŭi ch'amgwangi" [A Meeting of Northern and Southern Churches 2: Observations on the Second Glion Conference], in *Nambuk kyohoe ŭi mannam kwa p'yŏnghow t'ongil sinhak*, 38–45.

24. Pak Sŏngjun, *1980nyŏndae Han'guk kidokkyo t'ongil undong e taehan koch'al*, 963.

25. On this conference, see Pak Chonghwa, "Nambuk kyohoe sangbonggi 3: hanbando ŭi p'yŏnghwa t'ongil rul wihan wŏsingt'ŏn hyŏpŭihoe Paekyŏng" [A Meeting of Northern and Southern Churches 3: The Background of the Washington Conference on Peace and Reunification in the Korean Peninsula], in *Nambuk kyohoe ŭi mannam kwa p'yŏnghow t'ongil sinhak*, 45–46. Northern participants for this meeting were Ko Kijun, Kim Unbong, Kim Namhyŏk, and Kim Hyesuk.

26. On this meeting, see "Nambuk kyohoe sangbonggi 4: 'Tong asia ŭi pyŏnghwa e kwanhan kyohoe ŭi samyŏng' hoeŭi ch'amga pogo" [A Meeting of Northern and Southern Churches 4: A Participant's Report on "Consultation on East Asian Peace and the Church's Mission"], in *Nambuk kyohoe ŭi mannam kwa p'yŏnghow t'ongil sinhak*, 51–53. For this meeting, northern representatives included Yi Ch'ŏl (vice-chair of Chosŏn kidokkyo yŏnmaeng), Kim Unbong, Kim Namhyŏk, and Yang Suung (translator).

27. Northern representatives for this meeting consisted of Ko Kijun, Kim Unbong, Cho Kilnam, Kim Namhyŏk, and Ŏm Yŏngson.

28. See Pak Sŏngjun, *1980-nyŏndae Han'guk kidokkyo t'ongil undong e taehan koch'al*, 963.

29. See Yi Manyŏl, "Minjok ŭi t'ongil kwa p'yŏnghwa e taehan han'guk kidokkyohoe ŭi sŏnŏn ŭi ŭiŭi" [The Significance of the Declaration of the Korean (Protestant) Church on National Reunification and Peace], *Kidokkyo sasang* [Christian Thought] (January 1995).

30. Pak Chonghwa, "Haesŏl: Hanbando T'ongil ŭl wihan nambuk kyohoe ŭi silch'ŏn—charyo moŭm" [Commentary: Northern and Southern Churches' Practical Actions for Reunification in the Korean Peninsula—Source Collection], in *Nambuk kyohoe ŭi mannam kwa p'yŏnghow t'ongil sinhak*, 3.

31. Pak Sŏngjun, *1980nyŏndae Han'guk kidokkyo t'ongil undong e taehan koch'al*, 964.

32. Kim Hŭngsu, "Han'guk kyohoe ŭi t'ongil undong yŏksa e taehan chegŏmt'o."

33. Pak Sangjŭng et al., "T'ŭkpyŏl taejwadam: Kidokkyo t'ongil undong e taehan ch'onggwal p'yŏngga wa ch'ŏnmang" [Special Roundtable Conversation: Comprehensive Evaluation and Perspectives on Christian Reunification Movement], in *Kisayŏn mugŭ* 3 (1991): 21.

34. Posted on the Web page of Evangelicals for Social Action: http://www.esa-online.org/about/lausanne.html.

35. The committee's publications include *Minjok t'ongil kwa Han'guk kidokkyo* [National Unification and Korean Protestantism], ed. Kidokkyo hakmun yŏnguhoe [Korea Christian Studies Institute] (Seoul: Han'guk kidok haksaenghoe ch'ŭlp'anbu, 1994).

36. KNCC, "Hanbando p'yŏnghwa wa t'ongil rul wihan che 4 ch'a kidokkyo kukchehyŏpŭihoe pogosŏ" [A Report on the Fourth International Christian Council on Peace and Reunification on the Korean Peninsula] (KNCC, 1995).

37. Han'guk kidokkyo Pukhan tongp'o huwŏn yŏnhaphoe; see their Web page: http://www.sharing.net/Board/zboard.phd?id=Accomplishment.

CHAPTER 12

The Division and Reunification of a Nation
Theological Reflections on the Destiny of the Korean People

Anselm Kyongsuk Min

As we speak of reunification, North and South, as we Koreans have been increasingly doing in recent years, it is crucial to approach the issue comprehensively by considering as many dimensions of its challenge as we can, rather than narrowly focusing on immediate political issues. Reunification requires more than the establishment of a single government on the peninsula; it demands a long period of preparation and adjustment as well. It demands not only the unification of political, military, and economic systems and institutions but also the elimination of those elements of national consciousness that militate against reunification in many areas of life.

The question is not only how to reunify the nation but also to understand how the nation came to be divided in the first place so as to require reunification. Does the blame for the division lie solely on foreign powers such as the United States and the Soviet Union, or does it also fall on ourselves as a nation? Reunification raises not only the political question of the reunification of North and South but also the larger human question of the meaning of love and hate, unity and division, solidarity and alienation, and of how to build love, unity, and solidarity in history and society. It also raises, for those religiously inclined, the theological question of the ultimate significance of successes and failures in building solidarity.

From this comprehensive perspective, I propose to provide a Christian theological reflection on the significance of the division and reunification of a nation in the context of the two Koreas. First, I will consider the trinitarian, theological significance of unity and division, solidarity and alienation, love and hate. Second, I will reflect on the role of the national community in the history of salvation. Third, I will call attention to our own responsibility as a nation for the internal divisions characteristic of modern Korean history that ultimately led to the division of the nation in 1945. Fourth, I will analyze the closed, exclusive system of identity so typical of human relations in Korean society, a system I consider the ultimate source of the many divisions and fragmentations we suffer as a nation. Finally, in the fifth section I will locate the historic mission of the Christian churches during the *kairos* of reunification in helping the nation to overcome the tyranny of the many exclusive systems of identity and preparing the nation for the long-term challenges and responsibilities of reunification.

Division and Solidarity in the Trinitarian History of Humanity

From the theological perspective, the history of humanity is part of the history of the triune God, a history of creation, redemption, and recreation, a history of sin and grace, the story of love and hate, solidarity and division, reconciliation and alienation in their eschatological significance. This saving history of the triune God is the most profound and universal horizon and context for all theological reflections on national division and reunification. We need not only a politics, an economics, or a psychology of reunification but also a theology of reunification that brings a sense of perspective and balance to all of these approaches.

Christian faith teaches that God is a triune community of the Father, the Son, and the Holy Spirit. As the source of all divinity and existence, the Father, from all eternity, empties himself and shares the totality of his divinity with an Other, whom we call the Son, who responds to the love of the Father by returning all his being to him. The mutual love of the Father and the Son, the love that inspires the Father to share himself with the Son and the Son to return that love with the totality of his being—this love is called the Holy Spirit. The Father, Son, and Holy Spirit constitute three "persons" but only one God because they share the totality of their own being with one another. Theirs is a totally relational existence marked by complete sharing, mutual immanence, and perfect love. The difference between God and finite beings lies here: a finite being can never share the totality of its being with another and still be itself, while it is the privilege of an infinite being to be truly itself precisely by sharing the totality of its divine being with an Other. The triune God is a community of three persons each of whom shares the totality of his own being with the others while remaining different from them, a primordial solidarity of Others.

Creation, redemption, and the eschatological re-creation of all things is the work of this triune God, who seeks beings other than himself who can share in the glory of his love. The Father creates all things, both humanity and nature, in the likeness of his Son, the perfect image and self-expression of the Father, and invites them to share in the mutual love of the Father and the Son by sharing in the likeness and solidarity of the Son. When humanity refused that invitation through sin, he sent his own Son, completing the work of redemption through his life, teaching, passion, death, and resurrection as the model and source of a redeemed humanity reconciled with the Father and with one another.

While the Son is the exemplary source of all creation, redemption, and recreation, the Holy Spirit, the mutual love of the Father and the Son, constitutes their efficient and teleological source creating nature and humanity in the likeness of the Son, making possible his incarnation, life, ministry, death, and resurrection, liberating all creation from selfishness, reconciling and unifying them with God and with one another in the Son, and bringing them to share in the mutual love of the Father and the Son, the ultimate divine purpose of creation.[1]

The Son became a human being in Jesus of Nazareth and taught us in concrete historical terms what God's love for us is like. God's love is universal and unrestricted to any closed system of identity such as a particular family, clan, region, race, culture, language, religion, or class. It is a preferential love for the poor and oppressed who need greater compassion than the rich and free. It is an excessive love in the sense of embracing even one's own enemies. It is a practical love, expressing itself in deed, not only in word. It is also a political love in the sense of struggling for the liberation of all dehumanizing and alienating systems. It is, finally, a self-transcending love, a love that concretizes God's love for humanity in the here and now yet also always remains open to God's all-embracing, universal love. Jesus taught us to love in these ways, for which he paid the price by being murdered on the cross, bearing the sins and sufferings of all. His life, however, did not end with his death on the cross. Raised by the power of the Holy Spirit, Jesus opened the possibility of salvation—by virtue of solidarity with himself—to all who suffer the burden of sin and mortality.

Jesus became a model of completely redeemed humanity insofar as he practiced love for his Father and his Father's human children to the point of death on the cross and was raised to a new, eschatological mode of life through the resurrection that confirmed his inseparable union with his Father. As such, Jesus' life, death, and resurrection express the Father's definitive will for the salvation and liberation of all things and possess a cosmic, universal significance. Salvation henceforth depends on participation in and solidarity with his life, death, and resurrection. What counts for this fellowship with Jesus Christ, however, is not so much a personal encounter with him and a response of faith, which applies only to Christians, as "works of love" (Matthew 25) and a life of the beatitudes (Matthew 5) in accord with his life and message, which is open to all including those who have never met him personally.[2]

It is the role of the Holy Spirit, the bond of love between the Father and the Son, to give life to all things and enable them to enter into solidarity with the Son, the model of all solidarity and into his fellowship with the Father by promoting their mutual interdependence and solidarity, not only among human beings but also between human beings and all creation.[3] Wherever the Spirit blows, there is no more alienation between man and woman, old and young, slave and free, nation and nation. The Spirit produces love and peace by forming all into one in Christ. "I will pour out my spirit on all flesh; your sons and your daughters shall prophesy, your old men shall dream dreams, and your young men shall see visions. Even on the male and female slaves, in those days, I will pour out my spirit" (Joel 2:28–29). For those who are born again in Christ by the Holy Spirit, "there is no longer Jew or Greek, there is no longer slave or free, there is no longer male and female; for all of you are one in Christ Jesus" (Galatians 3:28). The Spirit indeed calls us to freedom but not to "gratify the desires of the flesh" but to "become slaves to one another" (Galatians 5:13) and "bear one another's burdens" (Galatians 6:2).

The Holy Spirit is essentially the Spirit of relation and solidarity that reunites and reconnects all that have been alienated and separated. Those who live by the Spirit do not alienate one another through the "works of the flesh," enmities, jealousy, anger, quarrels, dissensions, and factions, and instead enjoy the fruit of the reconciling Spirit, love, joy, peace, patience, generosity, gentleness, and self-control. Just as Christ became the model of all solidarity by breaking down in his flesh the "dividing wall" of hostility that separates human beings from one another and bringing all human beings together in "one body" into the same household of God where they are "no longer strangers and aliens" (Ephesians 2:14–19), so the Holy Spirit actually creates this "solidarity of strangers" on the model of Christ whose Spirit it is and actualizes this christological potential of all reality.[4]

From the Christian perspective, then, the division and reunion of humanity, their alienation and reconciliation, their isolation and solidarity, have not only a biological, sociological, political, or psychological but also a theological significance directly related to their ultimate destiny as created by the triune God. Human beings, like other creatures, have been created as interdependent beings. Our lives are thoroughly interdependent in every way, politically, economically, and culturally, at every level of existence, as individuals, societies, nations, and now increasingly as a world. There is not a single being that is sufficient unto itself.

And yet we also do live with illusions of self-sufficiency and with temptations to self-absolutization, which necessarily entails, in an inter-dependent world, exploitation of others and self-alienation from them, in-volving us in a spiral of division, domination, and struggle against domina-tion, a spiral that in turn generates suffering, death, and sadness. On the other hand, an honest recognition of our mutual interdependence and a willingness to cooperate with one another in creating the basic conditions of life will lead to the joy of love, beauty of harmony, and meaningfulness of life, with intimations of an eternal life in the arms of the triune God. Human beings are faced with the choice between fulfilling their destiny by recognizing their essential interdependence through love and solidarity and sharing in the fellowship of the triune God and frustrating that trinitar-ian destiny by exploiting others and isolating themselves from one another in a refusal of solidarity.

From the perspective of the love of the triune God and from the hori-zon of the order created by God, human alienations and hatreds are not only matters of psychological tensions or social crimes but also "sins" that violate God's love and contradict the order of creation. Our exploitation of other human beings is not only a political problem of the struggle for power but also a theological problem of sin before God. Our actions may be transient and human in duration and origin, but they are eternal and di-vine in significance.

Sin, of course, is not all there is to life. There is also the "grace" of God, greater and stronger than sin, the love of the Father that creates, redeems, and re-creates all things in the likeness of his Son in the movement of the Spirit, leading them to share in his glory through love and solidarity. This grace of God who has created all things for solidarity and self-transcendence precedes all human actions, liberates them from their natural inertia and self-imprisonment, and empowers them to transcend themselves toward solidarity with others and the love of the triune God. Human life thus con-sists of the dialectic of alienation and reunion, of sin and grace.

The Role of the National Community in the History of Salvation

Like all things human, salvation of humanity is not an event of the isolated individual but a product of mediation through a concrete, historically given community of interdependence. We are interdependent with others not only in this-worldly affairs but also in eschatological salvation. In this sense we generally recognize the necessity of a church. More important than a church in some sense, however, is the "nation" in the sense of *minjok* or a community characterized by a unity of ethnic origin with its own cultural, political, and linguistic history.[5]

This is quite evident in the Hebrew scriptures. The destiny of an individual Israelite is thoroughly intertwined with that of the Israelite nation. The will of God is revealed in and through events decisive of the destiny of the Israelite people such as the election of Abraham, the liberation from Egyptian slavery, the covenant on Mt. Sinai and the reception of the Mosaic Law, the conquest of Canaan, the division of the Davidic kingdom into north and south, the proclamations of the prophets in critical times, the Assyrian and Babylonian captivities, and the conquest by the Hellenistic and Roman empires. It is through these national events and experiences that the Jewish people came to learn the will of God, received their Torah, and acquired their sense of identity and vocation.[6]

What is true of the Jews is also true of all peoples. Human beings are social by nature, and the historically most influential form of human sociality is our ties to the nation to which we belong by virtue of our ethnic identity. All our fundamental conditions of life—such as our language, culture, politics, and economics—are through and through mediated by the nation. We receive our life itself through our ancestors. (This does not contradict the fact that human life today is increasingly dominated by multiethnic, multicultural, global realities, which only means that particular ethnicity is not ultimate by itself.)

The destiny of the Koreans is inseparably the destiny of the Korean nation. We find our collective joys and sorrows in the traditional poems, folk songs, and folklore from hundreds of years ago. We dream of the mountains and rivers back home in Korea even while living in the United States. We work with other ethnic groups by day but immerse ourselves by night in the serial dramas from our homeland. While living in the twenty-first century, we enjoy reliving the joys and sorrows of our ancestors by watching videos of Korean historical dramas. Though we live in a democracy, our hearts yet resonate with life during monarchical times. Living as we do in an egalitarian age, we get indignant as Koreans at the murder of Empress Min by Japanese assassins. Savior generals from long ago, such as Ulchimundok, Kang Kamchan, and Yi Sunsin, are revered as our heroes. Despite differences of religion, contemporary Koreans identify with the profound religiosity of their ancestors who built great monasteries such as Pulguksa, Haeinsa, and Pŏpchusa, and honor the great monks and thinkers of the past such as Wŏnhyo, Ŭisang, T'oegye, Yulgok, and Tasan as common teachers of the nation. We also find echoes of our own contemporary realities in the destructive factionalisms, sheer partisanships, and countless political murders perpetrated by our forebears throughout our national history, and indulge in collective self-pity at the many miseries that seem to have been the common lot of the nation.

The nation is no less significant than the family in the history of salvation. As all our religious and ethnic sensibilities are mediated through our families, our family perspectives, concepts, and images of God are themselves mediated through the history of the nation, its traditions and sensibilities. Even the faith of Korean Christians is itself mediated by the national religious sensibilities already in them and remains permanently marked by the surviving presence of Confucianism, Buddhism, and shamanism.[7] No Korean Christian is free from the familism, sense of loyalty, and authoritarianism of the Confucian tradition. The same, of course, is true of the Jewish faith in God, which was thoroughly mediated by their national experiences. This, one can say, is precisely how divine providence works. From a purely historical point of view it is quite accidental that I received my life from particular parents. From the perspective of saving providence, however, it was quite necessary that I come into the world and come to know God in a certain way through them. Without them I simply could not have been, as I could not be the same I that I actually have been. Likewise, our ethnic national ties are not just historical accidents; they express God's saving will for us and possess theological significance as providential necessities.

It is both remarkable and regrettable that for all its theological importance there really has been no substantive theological reflection on the providential significance of the nation in the sense of an ethnic community. Perhaps this is not unrelated to the traditional Christian teaching that there is no salvation outside Christian faith, which seems to imply that there is nothing of salvific value not only in other religions but also in other nations and cultures. If, however, we accept Karl Rahner's logic, which argues that God wills the salvation of *all* humanity, who as social beings can concretely know of God only through the mediation of their own religions and that their salvation through Christ, therefore, is necessarily mediated by their own religions, we can conclude, just as logically, that our salvation is mediated through the history and culture of our own nation, which are just as essential to our existence as social beings as is our religion.[8]

In this sense it is theologically necessary to say that the history of a nation is also a history of salvation for members of that nation. God the Father, who wills the salvation of all nations, has been sowing the seeds of his Word or Son, the model and source of salvation, in the history of nations through the activity of the Holy Spirit. God is the creator of all things, all humanity and all creation, not only of the small tribe of Christians. Christ lived, died, and was raised for the salvation of all. The Holy Spirit, the Spirit of both the Father and the Son, gives life to all nations, not only Christians, endowing them with the power of self-transcendence and inspiring them with the grace of solidarity and love. It is an urgent theological task to discover the traces and signs of both the Word and the Spirit in the histories of all nations and therefore also in the history of the Korean nation. It is crucial to discover the theological meaning of Korean history.

It goes without saying that the value of ethnic national identity, from the Christian perspective, is not absolute but relative. Beyond the ethnic community there is the universal human community to be recognized. It is God's eschatological will and mystery that all nations, as children of the same Father, will practice universal human love and solidarity and form "one body" as brothers and sisters in the Son in the enabling power of the Holy Spirit while also preserving their ethnic diversity (Ephesians 2). It is their ultimate theological destiny that humanity, divided into hostile groups thus far, overcome their division and achieve mutual reconciliation or unity in diversity. Christian faith, therefore, can neither absolutize any one nation nor degrade itself to the tribal religion of a particular nation. An openness to others remains absolutely essential. Christianity can recognize the importance of the nation in the history of salvation and even show a preferential, political love for a particular nation suffering oppression by another, but firmly rejects all exclusivistic, imperialist nationalism that absolutizes the importance of a particular nation at the expense of others.

The Division and Reunification of the Korean Nation in Modern History

Reunification presupposes division. It is essential, therefore, to ask why the nation was divided in the first place before we ask how to go about reunifying the nation. So many discussions of reunification simply assume that the division of the nation was imposed by foreign powers, which is unquestionably true. It is remarkable, however, that most discussions do not even bother to ask whether Koreans themselves may not also bear a responsibility for their own division, not in the sense of some prominent politicians cooperating with imperialist foreign powers in dividing the nation but in the sense of creating or allowing a substantial internal division and polarization of the nation antecedent and in fact leading to the actual political separation imposed by foreign powers. I do think that we Koreans also bear a collective responsibility and that it is critical to ask about this responsibility as an essential part of the discussion of reunification. Without a national awareness of what internal factors led to the division of the nation in the first place, we are likely to confine our discussion to external political conditions for reunification, which are important enough but also inadequate in themselves because they leave intact the deeper, immanent sources of national division.[9]

In tracing our own responsibility for the division of the country we may have to go at least as far back as the closing days of the Chosŏn dynasty, when the internal contradictions of traditional Korean society were becoming manifest and disabling the nation so that it could not defend itself against the beginnings of foreign invasion. We can mention the endemic nepotism, sheer partisanship, rampant corruption, and destructive quarrels among the ruling aristocratic clans, factions, and officials diverting the attention and energy of the nation away from the pressing issues of the res publica to the pursuit of partisan interests. The most divisive factor, however, was the system of class division between aristocrats and commoners and between the rich landowners and the poor masses of people that included a significant number of slaves and the political ideology that justified such political and economic division. No wonder that the entire nineteenth century was a century of successive rebellions against the ruling elite among the oppressed and suffering masses, from the Hong Kyŏngnae Rebellion of 1812 through the civil unrest on Cheju Island in 1813 to the farmers' insurrection in the three southern provinces of 1862 to the massive Tonghak Revolution of 1894.

The beginning of the twentieth century was a time in world history when workers, farmers, and poor people in general were organizing themselves in revolutionary movements all over the world in order to overthrow oppressive inherited class divisions, and it was only a matter of time before such movements could and did reach a Korean peninsula already internally ripe for them, where the Korean Communist Party was first organized in 1925.[10] We experienced the impact of such movements in the split of the nation in the immediate aftermath of liberation in 1945. There were not only clashes, often bloody, between right-wing and left-wing politicians, but also, more profoundly, unrelenting conflicts between the rich landowners and rising bourgeoisie on the one hand and poor tenant farmers, workers, day laborers, and a significant number of intellectuals on the other, of which the political clashes were but formal expressions.

Even before and even without the arrival of the occupation armies of the United States and the Soviet Union, Korea had already been an internally divided nation, with a formal division, its political, territorial expression, soon to follow necessarily. It does not seem unreasonable to think that seriously divided as it was between the few rich and the many poor, Korean society in mid-twentieth century had few historical choices—either a right-wing dictatorship repressive of all revolutionary movements or a socialist government expressive of their demands, or, as actually happened, a division into a communist North and a capitalist South. The limitation of historical choices was all too evident in the repressive social realities of much twentieth-century Korean history. There was perhaps something providential, however, about this actual division: in a situation where there was no way of reducing the conflict of rich and poor through social justice and democratic procedures, it was indeed better that the nation be divided into two rather than remain one political entity embracing the extremes of rich and poor and suffering their bloody mutual destruction.

Furthermore, since the liberation of 1945, Christianity, Catholic and Protestant alike, was seized with an anticommunist Cold War ideology and tried both to justify the extreme gap between rich and poor and reinforce the political division of the nation. Lacking a historical consciousness and blindly pro-American and anticommunist, the churches ignored the challenge of social justice in the name of the condemnation of atheism and reinforced the division of the nation by demonizing and antagonizing fellow Koreans of the North. This uncritical anticommunism of the churches in modern times must be considered a true scandal in the history of Korean Christianity.[11]

About this matter we have much to reflect on and repent for as a nation. The blame for the division of the country cannot be confined to foreign powers. Reflection on our own responsibility makes us attentive to the many fatal failings and lapses we have ourselves committed. Why were Koreans so fragmented, powerless, and shortsighted in the presence of such unmistakable and relentless foreign threats to national integrity in the second half of the nineteenth century and at the beginning of the twentieth? What were the causes of such social fragmentation and political impotence? Exhausting political infighting, rampant corruption, pathetic ignorance of the movements of contemporary world history, fateful indifference to the signs of the times, scandalous neglect of the massive problems of poverty and starvation—all these were not only crimes against the nation but also sins against God demanding national repentance and conversion. It is imperative to first examine our own national conscience and repent of the many sins we have committed in neglecting the common good of the nation in a senseless pursuit of selfish partisan interests and bringing about not only the loss of national independence at the turn of the century but also the division of the nation half a century later. We must do this before we go on to talk about how to reunify the nation.

What are we to think of the total blindness of our nation, our ancestors, and ourselves to the movements of world history and the bearing of such movements on the destiny of the Korean people? Where do we locate the blame for the division of the nation into classes, nobles and commoners, rich and poor? As long as social and economic divisions persist, can a reunified Korea remain unified, or would it not rather always find itself on the brink of destructive internal conflicts?

The 2001 ratio in the GDP of the two Koreas is about twenty to one, which means that, were they to be reunited now, the twenty-five million fellow Koreans of the North, some 35 percent of the total population of a reunified Korea, would constitute the bottom 5 percent of Korean society. Such a society can be neither an ethically just society nor a sociologically stable society. It would seem clear that the fellow Koreans of the North, poor yet used to a certain egalitarianism, would not simply acquiesce in such an extreme gap between rich and poor in a rampantly capitalist society. What guarantee would there be that we would not repeat, on a more tragic scale, the same conflict between right-wing and left-wing groups we suffered in the immediate aftermath of liberation in 1945 that ultimately led to the bloody civil war of 1950–1953? Is it too far-fetched to worry about the possibility of the emergence of a right-wing fascist regime precisely to prevent and repress the organized resistance of poor workers and farmers, as regularly happens in many Latin American countries with serious class divisions? Under these circumstances, where and on whose side would the churches stand? On the side of right-wing dictatorships again? Would this kind of reunification really be preferable to the continuing division of the country?

Exclusive Systems of Identity and the "Korean Disease"

Reflection on the causes of national division also contains clues to how we should prepare ourselves for eventual reunification. From the perspective of a comprehensive approach, it is clear that reunification involves more than unification of the political system. It involves reflection on how to remove those enduring fundamental causes of national division. And there are indeed many such causes.

Interdependence is a human destiny. We cannot receive the gift of life nor grow nor achieve any worthwhile goal except through mutual dependence. The greatest imperative for interdependent humanity, therefore, is to build ties of solidarity with others. For embodied human beings, this means building ties with those who are closest to us physically, spatially, geographically, experientially, and in terms of survival interests. We build these ties and organize systems of identity with those who belong to the same family, clan, hometown, alumni network, region, church, interest group, class, and other sources of identity. It is through these systems of identity that we find comfort, security, identity, and meaning in an otherwise cold, competitive, threatening, and dehumanizing world. Failure to find a minimum system of identity leads to loneliness, alienation, and sense of failure. One can say that this failure accounts for much of the social crisis—isolation, alienation, atomization—in contemporary U.S. society.

Here, however, is also the difficulty. A system of identity, normally a source of so much comfort, joy, and meaning, can absolutize itself and turn into a closed system exclusive of all other systems of identity, generating all sorts of social, political, and national problems. Extreme clannishness, stubborn regionalism, excessive loyalty to the alumni network, fanatical sectarianism, pretentious classism, and deep-seated patriarchy—generally admitted by the Koreans themselves to be characteristic of their own people and constitutive of what is popularly called "the Korean disease"—are products of the closed, partisan systems of identity that exclude and discriminate against all "others" who do not belong to the same system.

Systems of identity, even when somewhat exclusive, would be harmless if social conditions were simple and afforded few opportunities for tension among different groups, or if social conditions, although more complex, yet also provided such a clear demarcation between the common good of society as a whole and the private interests of different groups that systems of identity confined their operation to the sphere of the private. Today, however, the complexity of social conditions has multiplied opportunities for conflict among groups with regard to the production and distribution of wealth and power, which in turn has called for an enlargement of the role and scope of public authorities as the ultimate guardian of the common good; further, this enlargement has also increased the temptation and pressure for private groups to exploit the organs and resources of the common good for private gain. For half a century we Koreans have been witnessing the exploitation of the public power and resources of the government by various partisan systems of identity for their own selfish interests: the monopoly of governmental power by Christians in the regime of Syngman Rhee, by the military and the regional interests of Kyŏngsang provinces in the regimes of Generals Park Chung Hee, Chun Doo Hwan, and Roh Tae Woo, the monopoly of opportunities in many fields by the graduates of Seoul National University.

The Korean history of the last half millennium is a history of the tyranny of various exclusive systems of identity, monopoly of governmental power by certain aristocratic families, oppression of women by men, the bloody struggle for power among factions, repression of common people by the nobility, as witness so many historical dramas of recent years such as *Ilch'ulbong, Yongŭi Nunmul, Yŏin Ch'ŏnha,* and *Myŏngsŏng Hwanghu.* No Korean has been either safe or free from the tyranny of exclusive systems of identity of one kind or another, which has been the *han* and tragedy of the entire nation, the shame and scandal of an entire people, indeed a curse on the nation.

There are many causes for the division of a nation, but I suggest that such causes may be regarded as diverse expressions of the exclusive system of identity such as familism, regionalism, classism, sexism, and sectarianism. Fundamental to the many causes is the system of identity exclusive of all who do not belong to the same narrow system. It is also clear that the tyranny of a closed system of identity is directly proportionate to the size of wealth and power that such a system seeks to monopolize at the expense of all others. The only alternative to the tyranny of a closed system of identity, then, is to ensure justice in the production and distribution of wealth and power. The tyranny of identity embodies, reinforces, and manifests the self-justification and self-absolutization of human beings who can survive only through such collective self-identification. As such, the tyranny of identity may well constitute the "original sin" of the Korean people (and indeed of all peoples).[12]

Such an original sin contradicts in every way the love of the triune God taught by Jesus, its universality, preferentiality, excessiveness, practicality, political character, and self-transcendence. An exclusive system of identity is a particularism that rejects all others as well as an elitism that justifies the exploitation and repression of the majority. It is likewise a legalism with no mercy to one's "enemies" as well as a hypocrisy paying only lip service to love without deeds. It is antipolitical in that it regards all opposition to its own power as a threat to national security. It is, finally, an atheistic, in fact antitheistic evil that contradicts the universal, eschatological love of the triune God through all these tendencies.

I do not imply that this tyranny of identity is characteristic only of Koreans or that Koreans are the most guilty of it. It applies to all humanity, and each nation is guilty of it in its own way marked by its history. Modern Western nations are certainly also guilty, except that their most characteristic tyranny of identity is largely based on common economic interest, not on feudal, tribal interest as is the tyranny of identity characteristic of most traditional non-Western societies including Korea.

I do imply, however, that this tyranny of identity has been serious enough, in Korean history, in its negative consequences on the common good and destiny of the people, especially as an original source of national divisiveness, to deserve a focused attention in a theological reflection on the meaning of national division and reunification. I also imply that this tyranny in its Korean manifestation is too serious in its harm to be neutralized and trivialized as a Korean form of "party politics." Party politics respects the basic rules and laws of a democratic society and does not suspend the constitution, kill members of opposition parties, or monopolize the resources of the state for the sake of a particular clan, region, alumni network, and the like, all of which were perpetrated by the Korean systems of identity at one time or another.

The Mission of the Churches in the *Kairos* of Reunification

Reflection on the challenge of national reunification from these comprehensive and theological perspectives also indicates the mission of the churches in this *kairos* of reunification. An essential part of that mission would be to contribute to the healing of the wounds of national division by helping the nation to overcome the many exclusive systems of identity and thus to the long-term, comprehensive preparation of the nation for eventual reunification. This, I suggest, is the historically most compelling task of the churches. It would also be the theologically most appropriate task to the fundamental purpose of the churches as the People of God and the Body of Christ, which is to bear practical witness to and become, in history, the sacrament, both a sign and an instrument, of the eschatological will of the triune God who invites all humanity and creation, through their mutual love and solidarity, into God's eternal fellowship.[13]

For this singular mission the churches have been blessed with rich resources. The doctrine of human salvation based on divine grace, not human works, frees us from all preoccupations with ourselves that separate us from one another and frees our energies for service to God and neighbor. The universalist doctrine of human solidarity as a community of eschatological destiny provides a perspective larger than that of any historical human group and enables us to attend to the most profound theological bonds that unite us together as human beings for all our differences and to condemn all divisive imperialisms, nationalisms, and economic systems in the name of what unites yet transcends us all. The deepest human identity and destiny are not those derived from the achievements of an isolated individual or from membership in a particular clan, region, gender, class, nation, or even religion, but those derived from being the children of the same Father and brothers and sisters in the Son brought together in a solidarity of others by the Holy Spirit.

The Christian perspective in its theocentric universalism relativizes all human perspectives including Christian dogmatic formulations while also stressing, in its incarnationalist particularism, the necessity of concrete historical praxis, which varies under particular circumstances; it does not allow either the reduction of all things to history and particularity or the escape into the eternal from particular historical responsibilities.

The Christian tradition of two millennia contains a wealth of insights and inspirations for every occasion and comes to life in its worship, scripture reading, homilies, religious education, retreats, theological reflections, and other organizational activities. All these resources must be mobilized for the mission of the churches.

I would like to highlight two aspects of the task of bearing practical witness to the solidarity of others in the triune God. The first is to actively participate in the movement for social justice that seeks to abolish all structural sources of inequality and discrimination that separate and alienate human beings from one another. This is demanded by the divine love taught by Jesus, which is universal, preferential, excessive, practical, political, and transcendent. Especially pressing and even desperate is the need to abolish the extreme gap between rich and poor and the discrimination between regions; abolishing this gap is also the necessary condition for a national re-unification worth achieving. A reunification achieved without substantial reduction of class and regional divisions would be a far greater tragedy and disaster than continuing division. Just as we need to work for justice if we want peace, so we have to work toward reduction of class division and re-gionalism if we truly care for reunification. It would be sheer sentimental-ism to speak of the *han* of national division and shed tears over the human tragedy of separated families while remaining thoroughly indifferent to the ominous gap between rich and poor and the rampant regionalism that has been vitiating every recent election in South Korea.

The second aspect of solidarity is the cultivation or formation of soli-darity into a culture of the civic spirit; this cultivation requires reform of certain surviving feudalistic traits of the Korean national consciousness. There are five components to civic spirit: public-spiritedness or conscious-ness of the res publica, political consciousness, egalitarian consciousness, pluralistic consciousness, and a culture of dialogue. Here I confine myself to public-spiritedness, perhaps the most crucial of the five. A democratic so-ciety is a society in which people who are Other to one another in the sense of belonging to different systems of identity recognize their mutual depen-dence and solidarity for all the basic conditions of life and seek to determine together their common future as a community of destiny. As citizens, mem-bers of such a society are members of a political community consisting of others before they belong to their respective systems of identity based on the family, clan, region, gender, religion, and class, bearing a common re-sponsibility for the decisions affecting their common interests and the con-sequences of such decisions.

The future of a democratic society depends on how far the citizens can transcend their respective systems of identity and identify themselves in conscious solidarity with the common good of the larger political commu-nity, a community of others, and how far they can remain loyal to the com-mon interest of that community in the exercise of their collective decisions and responsibilities without either trying to discriminate against and exclude others or imposing the particular interest of a clan, region, origin, or reli-gion on the rest. As a community of Others the democratic state is not the private property of a particular group but the public property that belongs to all. The authority to make laws, impose taxes, investigate crimes, inspect products, impose penalties, authorize policies, mobilize citizens, and declare war is a public authority, not a private power to be exploited for the sake of private interests. Fundamental to the civic spirit is a sense of a larger com-munity of others beyond the particular systems of identity, the willingness to respect the integrity of the common public interest, order, and authority as belonging to all, and the readiness to assiduously respect the distinction between the private and the public.

Without this sense of the public spirit, the public authority and property of the state are likely to be exploited at will as dictated by the private interest of the system of identity that happens to be in power, which often does not mind ruthlessly sacrificing the interests of all others who do not belong to the same system of identity. The last half century of Korean history clearly witnesses the horrendous evils perpetrated by a particular system of identity when it came into power, such as a particular group (the military), particular region (the Kyŏngsang provinces), particular class (the business conglomerates), particular religion (Christianity), and particular alumni networks (Kyŏnggi High School and Seoul National University). It is clear that there can be no genuine progress in democratic politics in Korea without tearing down these closed, tyrannical systems of identity and inculcating a culture of public-spiritedness or a sense of the res publica.

Practicing the civic spirit is not easy; it requires an asceticism, a self-denial of a certain kind. It means dying to me and my group and living to others. The public spirit demands loyalty to the interest of the community as a community of others beyond my interest or that of my system of identity as well as accepting others without discrimination as members of our community and entering into practical solidarity with them. Political consciousness demands I treat all others justly; egalitarian consciousness demands that I treat others as my equal and refuse to subordinate others to my selfishness and desire to dominate or to appeal to a privileged treatment for myself or my group. Pluralistic consciousness and the culture of dialogue likewise demand that I transcend the interest and perspective of my own group, empty myself and listen to others with respect. The civic spirit thus requires renunciation of individual and collective selfishness, loyalty to a community larger than one's own system of identity, and political respect and love for others without discrimination. In short, contemporary Korean society is crying out for the concretization, in the form of the praxis and virtue of the civic spirit, of the universality, excessiveness, preferentiality, political character, and self-transcendence of Christian love or solidarity of others in the triune God.

Suffering has always been a dominant fact of human life. There is, however, an important difference between the sufferings of the past and the sufferings of the present: sufferings of the past had been predominantly, although not exclusively, due to natural disasters, while sufferings of the modern world have been predominantly, although not exclusively, due to humanly contrived disasters. Natural disasters such as flood, drought, hurricanes, and earthquakes have always taken their human toll, but it is the

peculiarity of human sufferings of the twentieth century that natural disasters are outweighed by humanly contrived disasters, especially disasters
brought about by the exploitation of the public powers and resources of
the state, the organ of the common good, for the sake of private interests.
Consider the two great World Wars; the Korean War; the Vietnam War; the
many conflicts in Somalia, Bosnia, Sri Lanka, Kashmir, Rwanda, the Congo,
Palestine, Northern Ireland, Iraq; and the many legalized genocides, exploi-
tations, and discriminations against women, minorities, workers, refugees,
and "illegal aliens" throughout the world including the United States and
Western Europe.

These sufferings are social, structural evils deliberately caused and supported by the full official powers of the states. These are due to the abuses
of the public authorities of the state, and by the same token, there can only
be political responses (i.e., collective actions) to such abuses. Such colossal
evils can be prevented only by the massive praxis of the civic spirit vitally
interested in preventing the privatization of the public powers of the state
and making sure, through vigilance and criticism, that such powers be used
only for the sake of the common good, which always includes the preferential option for the marginalized excluded from that good. The power of the
state remains a principal source of both great good and great evil in the
modern world, and no love indifferent to how this power is used can be
genuine love. In this sense it is safe to say that the praxis of the civic spirit
is the most effective way of practicing Christian love in the contemporary
world and that no true contemporary Christian can remain indifferent to
the praxis of the civic spirit.[14]

It is evident that the era of reunification cries out for the praxis of the
civic spirit on a massive scale. A reunification of Korea, without the culture
of the civic spirit, would only mean extension to the North of the divisive
materialism, regionalism, sectarianism, and other tyrannical forms of identity already rampant in the South and reduction of the public resources of
the state to an instrument in the hands of a closed system of identity. It
would not be too difficult to imagine the depth of alienation and wrath,
under such circumstances, on the part of our fellow Koreans of the North,
who would find themselves excluded from the ruling systems of identity.

By emphasizing the political translation of the solidarity of others in the
triune God into the virtue and praxis of the civic spirit as the historically
most compelling and theologically most appropriate task and mission of
the churches, which belongs to what might be called indirect, long-term
preparation, I do not mean to exclude projects of a more direct kind from
the tasks of the churches: relief work for the starving compatriots of the
North, efforts to counteract prejudices and distortions about the North,
various forms of consciousness raising of congregations, presentation of

Christian perspectives on current reunification issues, and any activity that would reduce tensions and alienations between North and South and bring them closer together. The churches should engage in these activities and even use them as opportunities to cultivate the solidarity of others and the civic spirit as concrete ways of practicing Christian charity.

What about the "mission" to the North, a topic most dominantly on the minds of Korean Christians when they discuss reunification? I think there are two kinds of mission: mission in the broad and the narrow senses of the term. Mission in the broad and ultimate sense is to participate in the mission of God—the *missio Dei*—already operating in history to liberate and save human beings through reconciliation and communion. What I am claiming is that contributing to the elimination of the causes of division and laying the long-term foundation for reunification by focusing on the solidarity of others in the triune God and its political expression, the praxis of social justice and the cultivation of the civic spirit, is not only the historically most relevant task of the churches but also the most effective way of participating in the mission of God in the context of contemporary Korea.

What about the mission of the churches in the narrow sense of explicitly proclaiming the Good News of Christ, baptizing people, and organizing communities of faith? In principle, the need for this sort of mission will always remain. Much, however, depends on the circumstances and approaches.

In terms of circumstances, I am not sure whether the churches in the South are in a morally credible position to proclaim the Good News of Jesus Christ to other people. As many people have been pointing out, South Korean Christianity has been tainted beyond measure by ecclesiocentrism, clerical authoritarianism, concentration on personal fortune, addiction to purely quantitative growth, sectarianism, constant feuding, retreat from social concerns, collective self-preoccupation, and numerous scandals and abuses. Establishing churches in the North under these circumstances would mean transplanting the prevalent southern form of church life and extending the scandal of corruption and divisiveness to the North, which in turn would only exacerbate the existing national division and social corruption and further discredit Christianity.

In terms of approaches, we live in an era when it is more important and convincing to practice the words of Jesus than merely to preach his words or preach about his words. Evangelizing by words more often invites suspicion and the charge of hypocrisy. True evangelization also requires respect for the dignity and conscience of others. Threatening them with eternal damnation and maligning their religions as works of the devil, as many Protestant street preachers do, is not the way of proclaiming the Good News; it alienates non-Christians from Christianity. For these and other reasons I propose that we place a moratorium on all missionary work to the North in the narrow sense for the first twenty years after political reunification and confine ourselves instead to the mission in the broad sense by focusing on concrete signs of love and solidarity, social work, medical service, education, job training, and the like. When a sufficient number of Christians dedicate themselves to this mission of God in a truly selfless way and convince their northern compatriots that they are not interested in seeking power for themselves or for their own denominations but only in manifesting the love of the triune God and serving their northern brothers and sisters, they are not only setting good examples of Christian love but also inviting questions about the source of their dedication, which can naturally lead to a dialogue on the Good News.

NOTES

This is a revised version in English translation of a paper originally presented in Korean at the "Conference on Healing and Reunification on the Korean Peninsula," July 9, 2001, in Los Angeles.

1. This is not a technical paper in theology as such but a theological reflection on a current issue. I have, therefore, refrained from going into the technical questions of theology, contenting myself with presenting in broad outlines those aspects of Christian faith directly relevant to the theological dimensions of the various issues involved in the reunification of Korea. For a technical elaboration of the doctrine of the Trinity, see my "Solidarity of Others in the Power of the Holy Spirit: Pneumatology in a Divided World," in *Advents of the Spirit: An Introduction to the Current Study of Pneumatology*, ed. Bradford Hinze and D. Lyle Dabney (Milwaukee, Wisc.: Marquette University Press, 2001), 416–443; my *Solidarity of Others in a Divided World: A Postmodern Theology after Postmodernism* (New York: T & T Clark International, 2004), chap. 6; my *Paths to the Triune God: An Encounter between Aquinas and Recent Theologies* (Notre Dame, Ind.: University of Notre Dame Press, 2005); see also Jurgen Moltmann, *The Church in the Power of the Spirit* (London: SCM Press, 1977; San Francisco: HarperSanFrancisco, 1991), 50–65.

2. Wolfhart Pannenberg, *Systematic Theology* (Grand Rapids, Mich.: Eerdmans, 1998), 3:615.

3. On Jesus Christ as the model of solidarity, see my "Solidarity of Others in the Body of Christ," *Toronto Journal of Theology* 12, no. 2 (Fall 1998): 239–254; and my *Solidarity of Others*, chap. 7.

4. On the Holy Spirit as the Spirit of solidarity, see my "Solidarity of Others in the Power of the Holy Spirit" and my *Solidarity of Others*, chaps. 5, 6, and 10.

5. The term "nation" has many connotations and a complicated history. It may mean a community based on the unity of ethnic or racial origin such as the Polish or Korean nation or a community based on the identity of political structure and authority such as the American nation, which is "one nation, under God" according

to the pledge of allegiance. These two meanings, ethnic and political, are not separable. The ethnic nation always seeks to embody itself in forms of political and cultural organization appropriate to its collective self-consciousness and even to assert its political identity and independence against foreign aggression, while political and cultural unification also reinforces the sense of ethnic unity. The political nation contains at least one ethnic community—and increasingly many ethnic communities in the modern world—and has to cope with the politics of race and ethnicity. I am using the term "nation" in the ethnic sense along with its own political and cultural dialectic throughout this paper. For the history and variations in the concept of "nation," see Benjamin Akzin, *States and Nations* (London: Hutchinson, 1964), 9–52; and Anthony D. Smith, *Theories of Nationalism* (New York: Harper & Row, 1971), 153–191.

Against the traditional claims of racial or ethnic purity for the Korean nation often made by Korean nationalists, in recent decades younger historians have objected that the Korean *minjok* is not as homogeneous as it has been asserted to be. I agree with this objection. There may be no single ancestor from which all present-day Koreans have descended without admixture of foreign ethnic blood. There has always been a degree of migration and intermarriage throughout Korean history. The Tan'gun myth is significant not as a fact but as a myth, an ideology that has been historically used to strengthen the sense of ethnic identity among Koreans.

Does this mean that it is meaningless to speak of the Korean people as one nation? Unless one demands proof that all seventy million contemporary Koreans are descended from the same original ancestors as a condition for saying that Koreans constitute one ethnic nation (a historically impossible and unrealistic condition), there is a meaningful sense in referring to the Koreans as one nation, as there is in referring to the Irish or Polish or Japanese as one nation, insofar as Koreans have achieved, over at least two thousand years of historical developments that include integrating many heterogeneous factors such as foreign religions, cultures, and immigrants, a degree of ethnic unification and integration sufficient to distinguish them from other ethnic groups such as the Japanese, Vietnamese, etcetera and in identifying them as a distinct group with its own coherent characteristics.

The Korean language does not cease to be one language because it has been integrating many foreign words and expressions, as long as it retains its basic grammar and distinctive vocabulary. In fact, the strength of any living entity is its ability to take in foreign elements and integrate them into its own identity. The same is true, I think, of ethnic identities. Expressions such as "sharing the same blood" may seem too strong if taken in the impossible sense of descent from the one common ancestor but may not be if taken in the historically realistic sense of an ethnic unity achieved over a long time out of integrating foreign elements including foreign blood. Throughout this chapter I assume that the Koreans are one nation in this historical sense of development and integration.

For an interesting and informative historical study of the origin of the consciousness of identity as a nation among the Koreans, see John Duncan, "Proto-nationalism in Premodern Korea," in *Perspectives on Korea*, ed. Sang-Oak Lee and Duk-Soo Park (Sydney, Australia: Wild Peony, 1998), 198–221. Others point out that it was toward the end of the Chosŏn dynasty, in 1904, that the word *minjok* was first used; see *Han'guk Ilbo* (May 28, 2004), A17, which features a conversation with Professor Im Ji-hyŏn of Hanyang University. My historical, developmental view of national identity also assumes that the consciousness of national identity is itself a product of historical development and that it did not have to exist from the very beginning. Part of such development involves the history of interpretation by later generations. A human being or society can be many things, at least in an incipient way, without always being conscious of them. We are fully justified in interpreting our ancestors of the Koryŏ dynasty and the Three Kingdoms as constituting part of the Korean *minjok* on the ground of their ethnic continuity with us even though they may not have had an explicit consciousness of themselves as belonging to the same *minjok*. Many poor people are members of the working class even though they may not yet have developed a class consciousness. Sometimes people may never become conscious of what they are, while later generations may still be fully justified in interpreting them in certain ways. Augustine, for example, was never, and could not have been, conscious of being the greatest theologian of the Western Church, but many historians of theology feel fully justified in interpreting him to be so. People of the Neolithic Age never thought of themselves as living in the Neolithic Age, which is what they did although they were not conscious of doing do. We are not always conscious of all the constitutive social conditions that make us what we are, and it is part of the task of the historian to disclose and interpret such conditions for whole groups, societies, and civilizations.

6. On the role of the national community in the formation of Hebrew identity, see Paul D. Hanson, *The People Called: The Growth of Community in the Bible* (San Francisco: Harper & Row, 1986).

7. I show this in my *Spiritual Ethos of Korean Catholicism* (Seoul: Sŏgang University Social Research Institute, 1971).

8. See Karl Rahner, "Christianity and the Non-Christian Religions," in *Theological Investigations* (Baltimore: Helicon, 1966), 5:115–134; also my *Solidarity of Others*, chap. 9, and *Paths to the Triune God*, chaps. 2 and 3.

9. Typical recent discussions of reunification fail to reflect on the collective responsibility of the Koreans themselves for the division of Korea and the state of the internal division of Korean society during the first half of the twentieth century and to integrate these into a systematic reflection on appropriate national preparation for the eventual reunification of the peninsula. Examples of such failure include most essays in the following collection as well as monographs: The Center for Pacific and Asian American Ministries (CPAAM), ed., *The Christian Conference on Healing, Reconciliation, and Unification: July 9–10, 2001* (Claremont, Calif.: CPAAM, 2001); *P'yŏnghwa wa t'ongil sinhak* [Theology of Peace and Unification], vol. 1 (2001); Pak Sun'gyŏng, *Minjok t'ongil kwa Kidokkyo* [Reunification of the Nation and Christianity] (Seoul: Han'gilsa, 1986); Mun Kyuhyŏn, *Pundan ŭi Changp'yŏk ŭl nŏmŏsŏ* [Beyond the Wall of Division] (Seoul: Turi, 1990).

10. For a history of the Communist movement in Korea, see Dae-Sook Suh, *The Korean Communist Movement, 1918–1948* (Princeton, N.J.: Princeton University Press, 1967).

11. On the uncritical pro-Americanism and anticommunism of the churches, see Mun Kyuhyŏn, *Minjok kwa hamkke ssŭnŭn Han'guk Ch'ŏnchugyohoesa* [History of the Korean Catholic Church from the National Perspective] (Seoul: Pitture, 1994), 2:13–114.

12. On the exclusivistic tendencies of the Koreans, see my "From Tribal Identity to Solidarity of Others: Theological Challenges of a Divided Korea," *Missiology* 27, no. 3 (July 1999): 333–345. There are many Korean-language monographs dealing with the issue: Hwang T'aeyŏn, *Chiyŏk p'aekwŏn ŭi nara* [A Nation of Hegemonic Regionalism] (Seoul: Mudang Midia, 1997); Yi Kyut'ae, *Han'gugin ŭi ŭisik kujo* [The Structure of the Korean Consciousness] (Seoul: Sinwŏn Ch'ulp'ansa, 1995); Kukchehakhoe, *Han'guk munhwa wa Han'gugin* [Korean Culture and the Koreans] (Seoul: Sagyejŏl Ch'ulp'ansa, 1998); Ch'oe Chunsik, *Han'gugin ege munhwa ka innŭnga?* [Do Koreans Have a Culture?] (Seoul: Sagyejŏl Ch'ulp'ansa, 1997).

13. I provide a more detailed discussion of the nature and mission of the church as a sacrament of the "solidarity of Others" in the triune God in my *Han'guk kyohoe 2000* [The Korean Church 2000: Beyond Authoritarianism and Ecclesiocentrism: Theology and Recommendations for a Servant Church] (Seoul: Benedict Press, 2000), 162–176 and 292–296.

14. For a further discussion of the constitutive components of the civic spirit, see ibid., 299–308. For a book-length discussion of the concept of the "solidarity of Others" so central to this essay as well as to my recent thinking, see my *Solidarity of Others in a Divided World*.

PART FIVE

Growth and Challenges

CHAPTER 13

Sibling Rivalry in Twentieth-Century Korea

Comparative Growth Rates of Catholic and Protestant Communities

Donald Baker

At the end of the twentieth century, according to figures supplied to South Korea's Ministry of Culture and Tourism by seventeen of Korea's nearly one hundred different Protestant denominations and subdenominations, there were an estimated 12,260,321 Protestant Christians in the Republic of Korea.[1] At that same time, Korea's Catholic Church reported a membership of 4,071,560. Those are remarkable figures. One hundred years earlier, at the beginning of the twentieth century, there were fewer than 20,000 Protestants in all of Korea. There were also approximately 42,000 Korean Catholics at that time, for a total of little more than 60,000 Christians in Korea in 1900. Yet a hundred years later, if those figures are to be believed, that small Christian community had grown 266 times larger, to more than 16 million. Once greatly outnumbered by clients of shamans and patrons of Buddhist temples, Christians claimed that in 2001 their community embraced over one-third of the entire South Korean population of 47 million plus. Moreover, most of that increase had occurred since the early 1960s.

This story is not quite as remarkable as those figures would indicate. The number of Protestants is somewhat exaggerated. The South Korean government found only 8,760,336 Protestant Christians in its national census of 1995. This is a substantial increase over the 6,489,282 Protestants it found a decade earlier, in 1985. This increase of 2,271,054, or 35 percent, over just one decade, is impressive, but it also raises doubts that in the following six years, from 1995 to 2001, the Korean Protestant community could have grown even faster, adding another 3,499,985 members, a 40 percent jump in a little more than half as much time.

Our suspicions are confirmed by Gallup surveys taken in 1984, 1989, and 1997. Gallup estimated, based on face-to-face interviews with a representative sampling of 1,613 South Koreans, that 20.3 percent of the population was Protestant in 1997, approximately 9.3 million, compared with 19.2 percent in 1989 (8.2 million) and 17.2 percent in 1984 (6.9 million). That would give a more believable rate of increase, 35 percent between 1984 and 1997, including 13 percent in the eight years after 1989. Inasmuch as the Gallup margin of error is 2.4 percent, the Gallup figures can be read as confirming the national census figures as well as challenging the figures Protestant organizations have reported for themselves.[2] Protestant churches claimed a total of 10.3 million members in 1989 (24.3 percent of the population), 9 million in 1986 (22 percent of the population), and 7.6 million in 1981 (19.8 percent), millions more than either the government or Gallup found.[3]

The figures for the number of Catholics in Korea in recent years are more reliable. The Korean Catholic Church claimed to have more than two million members in 1985, slightly more than the 1,865,397 Catholics found by government census takers that same year. By 1992, the Korean Catholic Church was claiming to have grown more than 50 percent in seven years, to more than 3 million.[4] Such a high growth rate would be suspicious were it not for the fact that Gallup confirmed that Catholics made up 5.7 percent of the population in 1984, which would be a little more than 2 million and 7 percent of the population in 1989, close to three million. By 1997, Gallup found that Catholics made up 7.4 percent of the population, which would give South Korea more than 3.4 million Catholics, slightly above the 1995 census figures of 2.9 million.[5] This relatively close fit between the number of Catholics estimated by Gallup, found by government census takers, and reported by the Korean Catholic Church for earlier years makes the Catholic Church's claim to have reached the 4 million mark by the end of 2000 plausible.

If we can trust the membership figures the Korean Catholic Church reports for itself, that makes the Catholic Church an unusual religious organization in South Korea today. When we compare the membership figures reported by various religious organizations with the figures on religious affiliation obtained by government census takers, we can't help but notice that there usually are large discrepancies between the two sets of figures.

For example, the government found 8 million Buddhists (19.9 percent) in 1985 and 10.3 million Buddhists in 1995 (23.2 percent). However, Buddhist organizations themselves reported 20.6 million Buddhists in 1989 and 28.9 million Buddhists in 1992. As we have already seen, the government found 6.4 Protestant Christians in 1985 and 8.7 million in 1995, but Protestant organizations reported a total of 14.4 million members in 1992 (when you add up the figures for all the various Protestant denominations and subdenominations).

When we look beyond the "big three" religions (Buddhist, Protestant, and Catholic), the discrepancies are even greater. The government found only 483,000 Confucians in 1985 (1.2 percent) and 211,000 (0.8 percent) a decade later, although the national Confucian organization claimed in both 1989 and again in 1992 to have 10 million followers. Ch'ŏndo-kyo claimed to have a million followers in 1989 and 1.1 million in 1992, but government census takers could find only 27,000 believers in Ch'ŏndo-kyo in 1985 (0.07 percent) and 28,000 in 1995. Won Buddhism fared almost as badly. The government found only 95,000 Won Buddhists in 1985 (0.23 percent) and 87,000 in 1995, although Won Buddhists claimed 1.1 million in 1989 and 1.2 million in 1992.

The total number of members reported by various South Korean religious organizations in 1992 was in excess of 66 million, at a time when there were fewer than 42 million people living in South Korea. Furthermore, according to both Gallup and the government, half of that 42 million laid claim to no religious affiliation.[6]

If the statistics on who believes what in South Korea are so wildly at odds, how can we compare growth rates of Korea's Catholic and Protestant communities over the years of the twentieth century? We can't, if we expect any measure of exactitude. However, before the 1960s, when intradenominational rivalry in Protestant circles began to fuel both rapid church growth and even more rapid growth in reported conversion rates and congregation sizes, the figures reported for the number of Catholics and Protestants on the peninsula appear to be fairly reliable.

Be that as it may, even if those numbers are not completely accurate, we can at least use them to surmise the relative sizes of the Catholic and Protestant populations. Moreover, after 1980, we begin to have access to numbers independent of those religious organizations themselves report, thanks to Gallup polls and the government census. That allows us to move beyond vague generalizations in determining how successful Catholic and Protestants have been at bringing more Koreans into their churches.

Comparing the size of the Catholic and Protestant communities on the Korean peninsula over the last century and comparing the different rates at which they have grown at different times should shed some light on why there are so many more Protestants than Catholics in South Korea today, although there were Catholics in Korea a full century before there were any Protestants. Those same comparison figures may assist in assessing why, since the mid-1980s, the Korean Catholic Church has begun to grow at a faster rate at the same time as the Protestant growth rate slowed.

Waging a Lonely Battle

Economic historians often talk of the advantages of being a follower rather
then a leader when they discuss comparative rates of industrialization and
modernization. What they mean is that late-industrializing countries are
able to take advantage of technology developed by others right away without having to spend many years and a lot of money developing that technology themselves. Their insight might be applicable to the history of religion as well.

When Protestant missionaries first arrived in Korea in the 1880s, the
Korea Catholic Church was already a century old. Significantly, the Catholic Church had fought vigorously over the course of that century to topple
the walls of religious intolerance, putting the Chosŏn dynasty on notice that
Christian missionaries could call upon the support of foreign governments if
their lives were threatened. In addition, the monotheistic message of Christianity, so strange to Korean ears in the eighteenth century, was no longer
so unfamiliar after a century of Catholic preaching. Presbyterian and Methodist missionaries inherited a credibility they probably would not have enjoyed if the Korean Catholic Church had not paved the way.

Because of the barriers to government persecution erected by Catholics
and also because of the Catholic interjection of monotheism into Korean
religious culture, Protestants were able to preach more widely and gain
converts more quickly than Catholics had ever been able to do during their
first century in Korea. This advantage gave the Protestant proselytizing a
momentum it has never lost.

The Korean Catholic Church was born in 1784, before there were
any Catholic missionaries on Korean soil preaching to Koreans.[7] It was organized by Confucian literati who had become convinced by Jesuit missionary publications from China that Catholicism complemented rather
than challenged Confucianism.

Those Catholic Confucians were forced to reevaluate their initial im-
pressions when they learned, thanks to a 1790 letter from the French bishop
in Beijing, that Catholics were not permitted to honor their deceased parents or grandparents with the standard Confucian mourning ritual. That
ritual, known as *chesa*, involved bowing before a wooden tablet on which
was inscribed the name of the deceased. Church authorities in Rome had
ruled that bowing before such a tablet was an act of idolatry. That ruling
placed Korea's new Catholics in a difficult position. They were required
by their government to honor their dearly departed with appropriate Confucian rituals, but their new religious beliefs required them to modify those
rituals.

The government of premodern Korea, like many other premodern governments in East Asia, exercised ritual hegemony over its population. That means that, in addition to the traditional monopoly over the legitimate use of force that normally defines a government, premodern Korean governments also claimed a monopoly over the legitimate use of ritual. This was especially so in the case of the Confucian Chosŏn kingdom, which learned from ancient Confucian tradition that force and ritual were the two primary governing tools of the state. In Chosŏn Korea, the central government determined which spirits were worshiped, by whom they were worshiped, and when and where they could be worshiped. Korea's first Catholics challenged that ritual hegemony in two ways. First, they refused to perform the mourning ritual in the prescribed manner. Second, they performed their own rituals, such as the Mass, without government authorization.

This challenge to the Chosŏn government's authority led to the execution of two Catholics in 1791 for destroying the ancestral tablets they were supposed to treasure and bow before. Their blood spilled on the ground outside the provincial capital of Chŏnju made it clear to those who had not realized it before that Catholicism and Confucianism were not totally compatible, at least as long as Confucianism demanded ritual hegemony.

Individuals, such as the famous scholar Tasan Chŏng Yagyong, who had become Catholics out of the belief that the Catholic God would help them become better Confucians found that they had arrived at an unexpected fork in the road. They could either remain faithful Catholics and leave the Confucian path, or they could stay on the Confucian Way and distance themselves from Catholicism. Many made the safer decision and abandoned Catholicism. Others, particularly those who were not members of the Confucian scholarly elite, went underground in an effort to practice their new faith hidden from the sight of government officials.

A large enough percentage of the membership of this infant Korean Catholic Church chose Catholicism over Confucianism to enable Zhou Wenmo, a missionary priest from China who reached Korea early in 1795, to report back to his superiors that there were already more than four thousand Catholic believers on the peninsula. Six years later, that figure is said to have climbed to ten thousand.

Then growth came to a dead halt in 1801. "A dead halt" is the correct term, because when a more tolerant king died and a new, underage king with more intolerant in-laws assumed the throne, the Catholic Church was hit with its first major persecution. Not only was the Chinese priest captured and executed, but hundreds from his flock were executed as well.

The first executions in 1801 were for violations of the ritual hegemony of the Confucian state. However, in the course of its brutal interrogations of Catholics, the government discovered that more than ritual hegemony was at stake. The state's monopoly of the legitimate use of force was being threatened as well. Desperate for the freedom to perform those rituals they believed were essential to their salvation, Korean Catholics had begun trying to enlist foreign military assistance, namely the French navy, to force the Chosŏn kingdom to grant ritual autonomy to the small Catholic community. Catholics thus became in government eyes more than ritual perverts. They became subversives as well.

Korean Catholics who survived the persecution of 1801 had to wait more than three decades for a priest to replace the martyred Father Zhou. When a French priest arrived in 1836, he reported back to his superior that there were more than six thousand Catholics in Korea, a somewhat smaller community than before persecution broke out in 1801. That priest was soon joined by two others, but it wasn't long before news of their presence and their activities reached government ears. In 1839 another major persecution broke out, and again the Korean Catholic church was deprived of the priestly leadership it needed so badly.

The Catholic Church did not give up, either inside Korea or outside. More French priests were smuggled into Korea, as was the first ordained Korean, Father Andrew Kim Taegŏn. The Catholic community again began to grow, surpassing twelve thousand by 1854, and possibly as many as twenty-three thousand by 1865. That latter number, reported by those French priests, includes many babies who were baptized shortly before their deaths, so the actual functioning Catholic community was smaller than that.

By this time, the Korean Catholic Church had even established a printing facility and seminary at Paeron in Ch'ungch'ŏng province. Such increased activity could not long escape government notice. Another major wave of persecution, the largest one ever, broke out in 1866. By the time it wound down three years later, thousands of Korean Catholics had been killed, and Korea had to go another ten years without a single priest. When a new contingent of priests finally arrived in 1876, they estimated that there were only ten thousand Catholics left alive.[8]

However, at almost Catholicism's darkest hour, a ray of sunlight appeared—in the form of imperialism. First Japan and then Western countries such as the United States, England, and France began forcing their way onto Korean territory. France, in particular, was determined to put an end to the persecution and execution of its subjects. In 1886 France forced Chosŏn to agree to modify the treaties it had already signed with Japan, the United States, and the United Kingdom to include a guarantee that foreigners could "engage in educational activities"—in other words, proselytize and minister to their flock—without government interference.[9] With that clause, Chosŏn Korea relinquished the ritual hegemony that had been a bulwark of its power and legitimacy for centuries. Soon not only French priests but other Christians as well were able to openly preach to and convert Koreans on Korean soil.

Koreans Encounter Another Form of Christianity

When the first Protestant missionaries arrived in 1884, the freedom to proselytize had not yet been formally recognized, so they entered the peninsula under the guise of providing medical and educational services. Soon, however, they began preaching publicly and converting Koreans to their version of Christianity.

In the late nineteenth century, not only in Korea but elsewhere around the globe, the relationship between Protestant Christianity and Catholic Christianity was not as friendly as it is today. As far as Protestants back then were concerned, Catholics were no closer to salvation than Buddhists or other non-Christians were. Catholics felt the same way about Protestants. The depth of the rivalry between the two can be seen in a note Horace G. Underwood sent back to North America soon after he arrived. Underwood wrote that Catholic missionaries in Korea were teaching "Romanism," not Christianity.[10]

The rivalry between Catholics and Protestants was probably exacerbated by cultural differences between the two groups of missionaries. Catholic missionaries were predominantly French priests. The Protestant missionaries, however, were mostly men and women from North America who looked down on the French and all other non-English-speaking Europeans as old-fashioned and undemocratic. Moreover, the Protestants felt it imperative that they distinguish themselves from Catholics so that they would not face the same official animosity the Catholics still suffered from after a century of persecution.

One device the Protestants used to distinguish their version of Christianity from that of Roman Catholicism was to use a different term for God. Catholics referred to God as "Ch'ŏnju," a Sino-Korean term that can be literally translated as "the Lord of Heaven." After toying for a while with the idea of using that term, since it was the only name Koreans knew at that time for a God who in any way resembled the Christian God, the North American Protestant missionaries decided instead to coin a term that sounded more indigenous than "Ch'ŏnju" did.

They decided to name the Protestant God "Hananim," a name that they claimed was an indigenous term for the One God. They were also willing to accept the term "Hanŭnim," which they claimed was another indigenous term for the Creator and Ruler of the Cosmos, arguing against linguistic evidence that Hananim and Hanŭnim were simply variant pronunciations of the same term. Even though their reasoning was flawed, in that there is no evidence of an indigenous Korean monotheism or of the term "Hanŭnim" being used before the nineteenth century to refer to the Creator and Ruler of the Cosmos, they made a brilliant choice.[11] By using what sounded like an indigenous Korean name for God, they not only distinguished themselves from the Catholics with their foreign-sounding name for God; they also made it possible for Koreans to convert to Christianity without feeling that by doing so they were rejecting the beliefs and values of their ancestors. In other words, they created a form of Christianity that felt more familiar to most Koreans than the Christianity of Catholicism did, giving Protestants an advantage in the competition to persuade Koreans to attend their churches.

Their strategy to make monotheism appear indigenous was aided by the previous century of Catholic efforts to introduce the notion of one and only one God to the Korean people. Although the vast majority of Koreans had not been won over to Catholicism by the 1880s, the notion of one God had spread far enough beyond the small Catholic community to stimulate the birth of Korea's first indigenous organized religion.

The Tonghak religion, which preceded Protestantism in Korea by a couple of decades, preached one God, whom followers tended to refer to as Ch'ŏnju in the nineteenth century. With both Catholics and then Tonghak already talking of One God before the Protestants arrived, the Protestant message did not sound as strange as it might otherwise have.

The founders of Korean Protestantism made another decision that helped distinguish their form of Christianity from Catholicism by drawing Protestant Christianity closer to Korean culture. More out of financial necessity than strategic thinking, they adopted the Nevius method of proselytizing.

John Nevius had been a missionary to China who argued that, for the Christian church to plant sturdy roots in foreign soil, it should not be too dependent on foreign missionaries or foreign financial support. Applied in Korea, the Nevius doctrine meant the establishment of a seminary to train Korean pastors less than two decades after the first Protestant missionaries arrived in Korea. The Nevius doctrine also facilitated the erection of an independent presbytery of the Presbyterian Church in Korea in 1907, led by thirty-three foreign missionaries and thirty-six Korean elders, which quickly ordained seven Korean ministers.[12] With Korean elders and Korean pastors, the Protestant community seemed much more Korean than the Catholic community in which foreign priests still greatly outnumbered Korean priests.

A third factor that helped the Protestant churches in Korea gain an edge over the Catholics was their promotion of modern education and health facilities. The Korean Catholic Church did not devote nearly as much time or energy to building modern hospitals or educational institutions as the Protestant community did, partially because persecution had driven Catholics into remote mountain valleys, where they grew tobacco and produced earthenware pottery, and partially because their French leadership represented a side of Catholic thinking that tended to downplay concern for matters of this world. This situation allowed Protestants to establish themselves, rather than Catholics, as representatives of the modern civilization of the Western world.

Yonsei University and its affiliated Severance Hospital and Medical School as well as Sungsil University all have their origins in the early years of the Protestant missions in Korea. It wasn't until 1936 that the first Catholic-run general hospital was opened, and not until the 1950s did a Catholic institution of higher education for the general public, rather than for training future priests, open its doors. The result was that Protestant Christianity quickly began to be identified with modernity, an identification that eluded the Korean Catholic Church until the 1960s at the earliest.

One last factor that gave the Protestant Christianity an advantage over the Catholic version when competing for Korean converts can be found in the differences between Catholic and Protestant forms of worship. Until the late 1960s the most important Catholic ritual, the Mass, was said in Latin, a language few Koreans understood. Moreover, for most of the Mass, the priest-celebrant stood with his back to his congregation, and that congregation acted more as witnesses to the Mass than as active participants in that sacred ritual. Most Protestant services, on the other hand, were conducted in Korean. Moreover, not only did the pastor face his congregation, he encouraged his congregation to join with him in worshiping God through communal prayer and the singing of hymns. In addition, even though those hymns were borrowed from Western hymnals, they were translated into Korean and used language that must have felt more comfortable to Koreans than the Catholic hymns of praise to a distant "Lord of Heaven." Protestants sang instead "What a friend we have in Jesus," "Father, I stretch my hands to thee," and "Praise be to Father and to Son."[13] The Protestant participatory style of worship, especially when that participation took the form of communal singing of hymns filled with language reminiscent of the familiar Confucian virtues of filial piety and trust between friends, drew Koreans into Protestant pews.

Thanks to appearing more Korean and more modern and providing more participatory forms of worship than the Catholic Church, the Protestant community grew much faster than the Catholic community. In 1885, the first year Protestant proselytizing began in Korea, there were approximately 14,000 Korean Catholics. Protestants at that time could be numbered only in the dozens, or possibly the hundreds. Fifteen years later, long-sought religious freedom had allowed the Catholic community to triple in size, to 42,411. Protestant churches were growing fast but, with a total membership at only 20,914, there were still only half as many Protestants as Catholics.

That gap closed only slightly by 1905, when there were approximately 64,000 Catholics in contrast to 37,407 Protestants. Remarkably, just two years later, in 1907, there were more Protestants, almost 73,000, than Catholics, who had dropped back slightly to 63,340. The Protestant lead over the Catholics grew even wider over the next three years. By 1910 the Protestant community numbered 144,242, almost double the size of the Catholic community of 73,517.

What had happened? Why did Korean converts to Christianity suddenly begin choosing the Protestant variety of Christianity so much more often than they chose the Catholic version? One reason often given is the adrenaline surge Protestant Christianity received from the Great Revival of 1907, which began in P'yŏngyang and inspired the Convert a Million Koreans to Christianity movement in 1909–1910. But that begs the question. We still need to seek an explanation for the gains garnered during that evangelical drive. Why was it so successful that the number of Protestant Christians in Korea doubled from 1905 to 1910?

Some seek to explain the surge of interest in Christianity at this time as a search for solace in the face of the loss of Korean independence to Japanese imperialism or as a search for meaning in the face of the challenge the collapse of the Chosŏn dynasty posed to traditional values and the traditional way of life.[14] But that doesn't explain why so many Koreans turned to Christianity rather than to Buddhism and why more turned to Protestant Christianity than to Catholic Christianity.

We have suggested a couple of explanations above. Protestant Christianity was identified with modernity, and it offered worship services that were more attractive than those its competitors offered. At the beginning of the twentieth century, Protestant worship services were the only religious rituals in Korea that included communal singing and also were the only communal religious rituals, outside of those associated with shamanism and folk religion, that were conducted primarily in the language of everyday life. An additional explanation may be found in traditional Korean beliefs and religious practices. Koreans have long been torn between a belief in human perfectibility and a recognition that not only are human beings not perfect; they are morally frail.[15] Both forms of Christianity offered an explanation for this moral frailty. The doctrine of original sin allowed Korean converts to Christianity to escape the conundrum of trying to reconcile belief in human perfectibility with the experience of moral failure by abandoning the traditional belief that human beings could reach moral perfection through their own efforts. Instead, Christianity in both its forms offered what was to Koreans a relatively novel solution—supernatural assistance from God above.

Protestantism also offered something Catholicism did not: an emotional release from guilt through cathartic outbursts of confessions of guilt. Catholicism had its sacrament of confession, but a quiet recitation of sins to a priest in the privacy of the confessional was too restrained and too disciplined for typical Korean religiosity. Many Koreans preferred the individual variations and the personal emotional release allowed in revival meetings because that was the sort of religiosity they had grown accustomed to in shaman rituals. Priests perhaps reminded them too much of *yangban* scholars, urging them to restrain their emotions rather than encouraging them to channel their emotions in a new and more appropriate direction.

It is in the first two decades of the twentieth century, when Catholics were fighting against intrusions onto what had been their turf and defending their exclusive claim to the small Christian community of Korea and Protestants were fighting to overcome the Catholics' century-long head start that rivalry between Catholics and Protestants was the most intense and the most overt.[16] Catholics and Protestants alike began publishing tracts condemning the other's form of Christianity as dangerous heresy. Catholics started first, in 1907, the same year the Great Revival began. *Yesu chin'gyo sapae* (Four Conditions a True Religion of Jesus Must Meet) insisted that Protestant churches represented a heretical distortion of the true Christian tradition by rejecting the apostolic succession represented by the pope and all the bishops and priests under his authority and by undermining the unity of Christendom with a multitude of autonomous denominations. Protestants responded the next year with titles such as *Yesu Ch'ŏnju nyanggyo pyŏnnon* (A Discussion of the Doctrinal Differences Separating Catholics from Protestants), which condemned Roman Catholicism for relying on non-biblical sources such as the writings of early Catholic leaders and for placing the pope and priests between God and his people, blocking direct communication between a believer and God above.[17]

The battles between Catholics and Protestants in the first decades of competition were not confined to publications. There were also more serious disputes, beginning with a complaint that in 1894 Korean Catholics had physically attacked some Korean Protestants who came to watch those Catholics constructing what became Myŏngdong Cathedral. There was also an incident in 1899 when a few Catholics stormed the editorial offices of the *Hwangsŏng sinmun* (Capital Report) newspaper to protest what they felt was an anti-Catholic tone in an article that had appeared in that newspaper.

The most serious disputes arose in Hwanghae province, where the rivalry between Catholics and Protestants was the most intense. In 1901, Catholics complained that their local official, who happened to be a Protestant, was corrupt. When the government ruled that the Protestant official should be allowed to stay in his post, the French priest in that region complained to authorities in Seoul, prompting a countercomplaint from the Protestant missionary, Horace G. Underwood.

In 1902, in that same general area, Protestant villagers complained that Catholics were forcing them to pay for the construction of a Catholic church for their village. Another dispute arose when a Catholic farmer's cow died soon after his Protestant neighbor's cow died of a fatal infection: the bereaved Catholic complained that the Protestant farmer should compensate him for the spread of the infection that caused the loss of his valued bovine.[18]

Usually, however, the competition between Catholics and Protestants was more indirect, less between individuals identified with one of the two competing religious traditions than between the beliefs and practices distinguishing those siblings. Nevertheless, even that indirect competition occasionally strayed beyond doctrinal differences to the more public arena of politics.

From the very beginning of Japanese colonial rule over Korea, Protestants enhanced their image at the expense of Catholics by playing a much more active role in the nationalist struggle than Catholics did. This was not a deliberate tactic but more likely the result of differences between their respective communities. Because Protestant missionaries pioneered the introduction of modern education into Korea, many of those they converted were among the few Koreans with the sort of modern education that leads to modern beliefs such as pride in national independence.

Catholic missionaries, for their part, appeared to prefer to keep their flock isolated from the temptations of the secular world and therefore did not have as many followers with modern ideas such as nationalism. Evidence of the Catholic fear of the effects of modern education is found in Catholic nationalist An Chung-gŭn's account of the reaction to his suggestion that French missionaries establish a Catholic university. He claims that the French priest he talked to rejected his proposal with the excuse that "too much education would weaken the faith of Korea's Catholics."[19]

Over the course of the thirty-five years Japan ruled Korea, there were several incidents in which Catholics sat on the sidelines while Protestants stepped into the front ranks of the forces fighting against Japanese attempts to force Koreans to act the way the Japanese wanted them to act.

The first such incident occurred in the second year of colonial rule. In an apparent attempt to forestall possible acts of resistance to their rule by Korean Christians, in 1911 the colonial government claimed that a plot to assassinate the Japanese governor-general had been uncovered. Then the colonial government arrested hundreds asserted to having been involved in that conspiracy. The vast majority of those arrested were Protestants. Most were released without facing a trial; of those who were put on trial, the vast majority were acquitted. Consequently, this Japanese attempt to accuse Christians of being terrorists served primarily to enhance the image of Protestant Christianity as promoting the best interests of the Korean nation.[20]

The next incident, one in which Protestant activists gained a significant public relations advantage over passive Catholics, was the famous March First Incident, named after the day nationwide proindependence demonstrations broke out in 1919. Of the more than 15,000 Koreans picked up by the police for questioning about their involvement in that nationalistic movement, only 54 (0.3 percent) were Catholic. In contrast, 2,254 Presbyterians (14.8 percent) and 518 Methodists (3.4 percent) were singled out by the police as possible leaders and brought in for questioning.[21]

A dispute over participation in Shinto ceremonies honoring the Japanese emperor put the spotlight on Protestants as nationalists concerned about the fate of their nation, as opposed to Catholics who appeared to be more concerned about avoiding conflict with secular authority, legitimate or illegitimate.

The Vatican had ruled in 1933 that such Shinto ceremonies were civic rather than religious, so when the Japanese government-general in 1935 ordered students at all schools, including religious schools, to participate in those ceremonies, Catholic-run schools had no qualms about complying. Protestants resisted, however, and closed some schools rather than organize student participation in what they considered an idolatrous ritual. Even though Methodists in 1937 and Presbyterians in 1938 succumbed to government pressure and agreed to officially consider such ceremonies as expressions of patriotic rather than religious sentiment, enough individual Protestant leaders continued to resist and to suffer for their resistance that the nationalist image of Korean Protestantism was further enhanced.[22]

Despite its indigenous, nationalistic, and modern image, Protestant Christianity was not able to bring more than a small percentage of the total Korean population into churches during the colonial period. Catholics, despite the fact that they had been on the peninsula for well over a century at that point, were even less successful. According to figures the churches themselves reported, there were fewer than 90,000 Catholics in all of Korea in 1920 and only 167,435 Protestants. By 1930, that figure had supposedly risen to slightly more than 110,000 Catholics and 260,000 Protestants, a sizable increase for both camps in terms of percentage growth but still less than 2 percent of the total population of more than 20 million.[23] Despite a further increase by 1940, Christians remained a small minority. The Japanese government reported in 1940 that it found only 113,401 Korean Catholics on the peninsula, and 382,718 Protestants.[24]

The Era of Rapid Growth

It was not until the 1960s that both the Protestant and Catholic communities began to experience rapid growth, attracting much attention outside Korea and radically altering the religious landscape of Korea. To do so, they first had to overcome the shock of the division of the Korean peninsula after liberation from Japanese rule into an anti-Christian Communist North and an anticommunist South.

There are no reliable figures on the religious population of South Korea in the years immediately following the establishment of the Republic of Korea. South Koreans were too busy fighting poverty and Communist soldiers to count how many of them were Catholic or Protestant. It is known, however, that according to the figures collected by the Japanese in 1940, 30 percent of Korea's Catholics (34,885) lived in Hwanghae and P'yŏngan provinces, which were cut off from South Korea in 1948. For Protestants the figures were much more alarming inasmuch as 61 percent of Protestant Koreans located by the Japanese in 1940 were in those northern provinces. That is 234,159 out of a total population of only 382,718.[25]

Most of those Christians must have moved south to escape Communist persecution. They also must have preached their religion fervently to their new neighbors in the South. By the time relatively reliable figures were available again, the Christian community south of the demilitarized zone had more than doubled in size despite the loss of the northern provinces.

In 1960 the various Christian denominations in South Korea reported to the government that there were 623,072 Protestants and 451,808 Catholics. The loss of so much territory in which Protestants were dominant had given Catholics a chance to almost catch up. Catholics had quadrupled their numbers since 1940, while the Protestant community had not even doubled in size. However, that was the last time Catholic and Protestant figures were to be that close.

According to figures reported by religious organizations themselves in 1970, the Catholic growth rate had slowed somewhat in the 1960s, giving South Korea about 788,082 Catholics. Protestant Churches, however, reported that their combined membership had increased 500 percent, to 3,192,621. That dramatic difference in reported growth rates continued for another couple of decades. By 1980, the Korean Catholic Church claimed to have 1,321,293 members, contrasted with a total of 7,180,627 claimed by the various Protestant denominations and subdenominations. Government surveys showed that the gap was not quite that large, with 6,489,282

Protestants to 1,590,624 Catholics in the 1985 census. Nevertheless, according to that census, there were still four times as many Protestants as Catholics in South Korea.[26]

There had been less than twice as many Protestants as Catholics in 1960, so clearly something had happened from the 1960s through the 1980s to give Protestant churches an even greater comparative advantage over Catholic churches than they had been before 1960. Even though that intra-Christian gap had narrowed to only three times as many Protestants (8,760,336) as Catholics (2,950,730) in the 1995 census, nevertheless that three-decade-long Protestant surge cries out for an explanation.

One explanation, ironically enough, may be found in the fragmentation within Protestant denominations that devout Protestants often decry. The difference between a unified Roman Catholic Church and a Protestant community divided by Presbyterian, Methodist, Holiness, Assemblies of God, Pentecostal, and Baptist labels is of relatively little significance. Instead, it is the fragmentation within denominations, which has led to at least fifty-eight different Presbyterian subdenominations today, as well as five Methodist subdenominations, nine Pentecostal subdenominations and four Baptist subdenominations, that has spurred rapid church growth.[27]

In the immediate postliberation period, those internal divisions first arose from criticism against those who had given in to Japanese pressure and participated in state-mandated Shintō ceremonies by those who had refused to do so and had ended up in prison as a result. Later divisions were over such issues as whether or not to affiliate with the World Council of Churches, which some Korean Christians felt was procommunist. Theological hairsplitting also led to further divisions of subdenominations into subsubdenominations. Whatever the reason, this fragmenting and fragmenting again of Protestant bodies fueled rapid church growth because it led to increasing competition, which was expressed through more proselytizing and a resultant higher conversion rate.[28]

One reason increasing competition led to more proselytizing and therefore a higher rate of conversions is that each new subdenomination built new churches and trained its own group of ministers to staff them. The result was an extraordinary surge in the material and personnel infrastructure of the Korean Protestant community. By 1960, over half of all halls of worship and 45 percent of all clergy in Korea were Protestant. The 5,011 Protestant churches and 10,964 Protestant clergy that year gave the Protestant community a significant advantage over the Catholic Church, which had only 1,858 churches and 1,394 priests and therefore could not reach as many potential converts.[29]

The Protestant advantage in numbers of salespeople and retail outlets should not be interpreted as merely a reflection of rapid Protestant church growth. It is also a cause, since this Protestant lead over the Catholic Church in infrastructure precedes the Protestant lead in membership. As early as 1901, there were already 216 Protestant churches in Korea, compared to only 42 Catholic churches. By 1907 that ratio had risen to 642 to 47.[30] The same imbalance in the number of clergy available for Protestant and Catholic proselytizing existed in the early stages of the rivalry between them. In 1916, according to Japanese figures, there were 49 Catholic priests in Korea, compared to 1,909 Presbyterian and Methodist pastors.[31] At that time, the number of Presbyterians and Methodists in Korea outnumbered the number of Catholics by less than two to one, yet there were thirty-eight times as many Protestant pastors.

The Catholic Church in Korea was aware of its competitive disadvantage. In the 1920s, Catholic missionaries complained that "[a Protestant pastor's] budget for one year was at least two million yen, but the Catholic missionary's budget for one year was only about thirty thousand yen.... The Protestant side had 500 foreign missionaries and 2,000 Korean pastors and evangelists, whereas the Catholic side had only 60 missionaries."[32] That disparity grew larger in absolute terms in the second half of the twentieth century.

In 1970, Protestant churches reported a total of 12,866 churches and 16,982 clergy, compared to only 2,299 Catholic churches (including 1,884 missionary stations) and 883 Catholic priests. Eighty percent of all houses of worship and ninety-five percent of all clergy in South Korea were now Protestant, and that ratio has remained relatively steady ever since. Moreover, in 2001, the last year for which figures were available when this chapter was written, there were thirty times as many Protestant churches as Catholic churches (37,662 to 1,228) and twenty-three times as many Protestant ministers as Catholic priests (71,678 to 3,116). This difference in resources is much greater than the difference in the actual size of the two communities. According to the Gallup poll of 1997, the last year for which reliable membership figures are available, Protestants outnumbered Catholics by only three to one in South Korea (9.3 million to 3.4 million).[33]

Deciphering Rapid Rates of Growth

There are three key questions a historian of religion should ask in trying to understand rapid church growth in South Korea in the second half of the twentieth century: First, why have so many Koreans suddenly adopted a specific religious affiliation? (The number of self-proclaimed Buddhists has risen as fast as the number of self-proclaimed Christians, giving South Korea a Buddhist population of 8–10 million at the start of the twenty-first century.) Second, why have Protestant churches grown so much faster than the

Catholic Church? Finally, how has the Korean Catholic Church managed to begin narrowing the membership gap between Protestants and Catholics over the last couple of decades?

The answer to the first question comes in two distinct parts.[34]

It should be noted first that the rapid urbanization of South Korea since 1960 has prompted Koreans to turn to churches, temples, and other halls of worship to replace the rural social networks in which they were once enmeshed. In 1960, slightly more than one out of four South Koreans lived in towns and cities with fifty thousand or more inhabitants. The urbanization rate soared to 78.5 percent by 1995. As Koreans streamed out of their villages into ballooning cities, such as Seoul, they left the familiar world of kin and friend behind. Thrown into a sea of anonymity, they searched for new communities to replace the community that had comforted them through the ups and downs of village life. For many, churches and other religious organizations provided that community.

The second part of the answer to the first question is that for many Koreans, urbanization has meant modernization, which means some degree of Westernization. Among Western ideas that modernizing Koreans have adopted is the concept of religious affiliation, of membership in a specific religious organization. In premodern times, Koreans moved from Confucian school to Buddhist temple to shaman shrine without necessarily feeling that they were exclusively Confucian or Buddhist or a follower of shamanism.

That fluidity began to change when Catholics and Protestants introduced the notion of a public commitment to a specific religious community. Since Christianity, especially Protestant Christianity, became identified with modernity in twentieth-century Korea, Koreans who wanted to appear modern began to do what Christians did: they increasingly came to identify themselves as members of a specific religious community. Buddhist imitation of this Christian practice explains the rise in the number of self-proclaimed Buddhists that has accompanied the rise in the number of those who call themselves Catholics or Protestants. Evidence for this hypothesis of a linkage between urbanization and religious affiliation can be found in census figures. Those figures show not only that religious affiliation has risen with the rate of urbanization but also show that religious affiliation is much more common among city dwellers than it is among the few remaining village residents.[35]

As for the second key question posed above, given that religious affiliation is a mark of a modern, urban Korean, why have so many more urban Koreans chosen Protestant Christianity for their affiliation rather than Catholicism or even Buddhism?

For an explanation for that phenomenon, it is necessary to return to a

variety of factors mentioned earlier: Protestant Christianity has had a positive image as both modern and nationalistic. Protestant churches offer worshipers a more joyous and participatory form of worship. And Protestant
Christianity managed to appear less foreign than Catholicism by creating
an indigenous-sounding name for the Christian God and by ensuring almost from the start that the vast majority of Protestant church leaders were
Koreans rather than foreign missionaries.

Those are all important reasons for the success of Protestant Christianity
in Korea. But the most important reason of all may be the proselytizing zeal
of Korea's Christians, particularly zeal fueled by an oversupply of pastors
with an abundance of church pews needing to be filled. In other words,
Protestant Christianity may have outsold Catholicism and other religious
competitors primarily because it has had more salespeople and more retail
outlets.

If that is the case, why has the difference in size between Catholic and
Protestant communities narrowed in percentage terms over the last decade
and a half? In 1974, there were 1 million Catholics in Korea, compared
to Protestant claims of 3.4 million. By 1985, the number of Catholics had
doubled to 2 million. (The government census found only 1,865,397 Catholics that year, but the Gallup poll the previous year estimated that Catholics were 5.7 percent of the population, or 2.3 million.) Protestants had
almost doubled their numbers as well, to 6.4 million. However, it took
Catholics only seven more years to add another million followers, passing
the 3 million mark at the end of 1992. (Census figures show that the Catholic community did not reach that size until 1995.) The Protestant community had grown as well, to about 8 million, according to a government survey. However, there were now slightly fewer than 3 Protestants for every
Catholic in South Korea, a smaller lead than had existed the previous couple of decades.[36]

The Korean Catholic Church claimed to have reached the 4 million
mark at the end of 2000. There are no reliable figures for the Protestant
community, but if we extrapolate from the most recent Gallup poll, that
of 1997, it can be assumed that there are now between 9 and 10 million
Protestants in South Korea. That would mean that the Korean Catholic
community has been growing faster in percentage terms, though not in absolute numbers, than has the Protestant community. There are now only
about two and a half Protestants for every Catholic. For the first time, Korea's Catholics make up more than 8 percent of the entire South Korean
population.

If the figures calculated by both the government and Gallup for the respective sizes of the Catholic and Protestant communities in South Korea
between 1983 and 1997 are examined, the trend becomes clear (table 1).

TABLE 1. Comparative Catholic and Protestant membership figures

Year	Catholics	Protestants
1983	1,590,624	5,337,308
1985	1,865,397	6,489,282
1991	2,443,533	7,973,634
1995	2,950,730	8,760,336
1997 (Gallup)	3.4 million	9.3 million

Sources: Gallup Korea, ed., *Han'gugin ŭi chonggyo wa chonggyo ŭisik: '84 nyŏn, '94 nyŏn, '97 nyŏn chosa kyŏlgwa wa pigyohan chonggyo yŏn'guso* [The religions and religious consciousness of the Korean people: A comparative study of the results of religious surveys taken in 1984, 1989, and 1997] (Seoul: Gallup Korea, 1998); Han'guk chonggyo sahoe yŏn'guso, ed., *Han'guk chonggyo yŏn'gam* [Yearbook of Korean religion] (Seoul: Korean Scholar Press, various years).

TABLE 2. Comparative growth rate figures

1983–1985	Catholics gain: 274,773	Protestants gain: 1,151,974
	Catholics grew 17%	Protestants grew 21%
1985–1991	Catholics gain: 578,136	Protestants gain: 1,484,352
	Catholics grew 30%	Protestants grew 22%
1991–1995	Catholics gain: 507,197	Protestants gain: 786,702
	Catholics grew 20%	Protestants grew 10%
1995–1997 (Gallup figures)	Catholics gain: 450,000	Protestants gain: 539,664
	Catholics grew 15%	Protestants grew 6%

Source: Yi Yonghun, *Sullye ŭi kilmogo-e sŏsŏ: Han'guk kyohoe ŭi onŭl, kŭ chindan kwa chŏnmang* [At the start of a journey: The Korean church today, problems and prospects] (Suwŏn: Catholic Press, 2004).

Obviously, there are still many more Protestants than Catholics in South Korea. However, a look at comparative rates of growth reveals that the Protestant community is no longer growing faster than the Catholic community. Between 1985 and 1995, the Korean Catholic population grew 58.2 percent, while the Protestant population grew only 35 percent (table 2).[37]

Table 2 brings us back to the third question posed above: How have Korea's Catholics regained the lead in growth rates they lost after 1907? The most likely explanation is that they have begun to imitate the Protestant formula for success.

First of all, in the 1970s the leadership of the Korean Catholic Church became solidly Korean. Until 1941, there had been more foreign priests than Korean priests in Korea. The expulsion of many foreign missionaries by the Japanese changed that, but with the return of many of those missionaries in the 1950s, there were still almost as many Western priests as Korean priests. It wasn't until 1973 that there were enough Korean priests to outnumber foreign priests in Korea two to one (639 Korean priests to 285 foreign priests).[38]

The Korean Catholic Church received another boost when the Korean head of the hierarchy, Kim Suhwan, was made Cardinal Kim, becoming an internationally respected prince of the church, in 1969. Three years later, in 1972, for the first time in Korean Catholic history, all major Korean dioceses came into Korean hands.[39]

In another sign of the Koreanization of Korean Catholicism, Korean Catholics began saying Mass in Korean rather than in Latin at the end of 1969. Not long afterward, in 1972, they began using a new translation of the Bible that they shared with the Protestant community. Catholics could now call God Hanŭnim instead of relying solely on the awkward Sino-Korean term Ch'ŏnju.[40]

Another indication of the Koreanization of Korean Catholicism was the increasing Catholic involvement in Korean political issues, especially human rights issues and the fight for democracy. In 1966, the Korean Catholic Church finally replaced its catechism, which had been in use since 1831 and had fostered a theology that assigned little spiritual merit to involvement in secular matters.[41]

Encouraged by the new activist spirit of the Vatican Council of 1962 and supported by a new catechism that saw the secular and the sacred as more intertwined than separate, priests began joining Protestant ministers in the battle for social justice. By the 1980s, Myŏngdong Cathedral had become well known as a site for political protests. Priests and nuns were frequently on the front lines of demonstrations and on the front pages of Seoul's newspapers. What had once been a passive church, identified with producers of earthenware pottery, was becoming increasingly identified with the more activist and progressive forces in Korean society.[42]

One more indication that the Catholic Church was learning from Protestants how to succeed is that the number of Catholic priests on the peninsula increased sharply. In 1984, there had been only 1,080 Korean Catholic priests. By 1994, that number had almost doubled.[43] In only a decade, more than a thousand more young Korean men had taken vows of celibacy and dedicated their lives to the Church.

In 2001, the Korean Catholic Church reported it had 3,116 priests. That is still far behind the more than 70,000 Protestant ministers in the Republic of Korea, but it is three times as many priests as Korea had only twenty years ago. With that many additional proselytizers on the streets, it is not surprising that the Catholic Church is attracting more people into its churches every year.

There is one more area in which Korea's Catholics have learned from Korea's Protestants. Catholics have become much more vigorous propagandists of the faith, and they also have adopted Protestant techniques for keeping converts in the church.[44] Catholic parishes are now beginning to do as Protestant churches have long done. They are dividing their congregations into small neighborhood-based groups that meet regularly, encouraging each other in their shared faith and identifying other members of the neighborhood who might be interested in joining them at church on Sunday.

Despite all the changes they have adopted, Catholics cannot take all the credit for the slight closing of the gap between the size of the Protestant and Catholic communities. Part of that credit should go to the Protestants themselves. Probably because of the emotional intensity of much Protestant proselytizing and because the search for higher numbers had led some pastors to enroll some whose commitment to, or even knowledge of, Christianity was weak, the Protestant community has the highest dropout rate of any major religious community in Korea.

Brakes on Protestant Growth Rates

As the number of Protestants has grown in Korea, so has the number of former Protestants. Figures Gallup compiled in 1997 reveal that 44 percent of the South Korean population either are now or have once been Protestant Christians. That breaks down to 20.3 percent who now say they are Protestant and an additional 23.7 percent who say they were once Protestants but now are Buddhist, Catholic, or without any religious affiliation.

About three-fourths of those who once had a religious affiliation, but no longer do, told Gallup they were Protestants in the past. In excess of 87 percent of those who have switched their religious affiliation to Buddhism were once Protestant, as were 70 percent of those who have switched their religious affiliation to the Catholic Church. As a result of this high defection rate, there are now more former Protestants than current Protestants in South Korea today.[45]

To be fair, it should be pointed out that Catholics, at 34.5 percent, and Buddhists, at 32.3 percent, have high defection rates as well, although not nearly as high as Protestants. Interestingly, the Protestant community has consistently shown a defection rate above 50 percent since 1984. That would indicate that the Korean Protestant community is not the rock-solid stable force it is usually depicted as being.[46] If Protestant churches did a better job of keeping members of their congregations from leaving, they would not only stay far ahead of their Catholic competitors; they could probably claim a larger share of the overall South Korean population than Catholics and Buddhists combined.

That is unlikely to happen, however. Few still believe what many even just a decade ago believed, that within a few years over half of the South Korean population would attend a Protestant Church on Sunday. Instead, it is probable that the Protestant community will continue to grow, but at a somewhat slower pace. The Catholic community will also continue to grow, probably at a somewhat faster pace than the Protestant community, but not fast enough to catch up with Protestants anytime soon.[47] Moreover, they will each to try to grow at the other's expense. Catholics will continue to entice people from Protestant pews into Catholic churches, which is where they find almost three-quarters of their converts who once frequented a non-Catholic house of worship. Protestants will continue to try the same tactic in regard to Catholics, with less success. Only 12 percent of Protestants who converted from another religion came from the Catholic community.[48]

Conclusion

This continuing competition within the Christian community will probably fuel further church growth, as Catholic gains inspire Protestants to even more vigorous outreach efforts and Protestant gains inspire the same for Catholics. However, this competition may also ensure that Catholics and Protestants continue to see themselves more as rivals than as fellow worshipers of the same God.

Don Clark, one of North America's most astute observers of Christianity in Korea, recently wrote, "Korean Catholics and Protestants do not normally see themselves as belonging to the same tradition or even the same religion."[49] His observation is confirmed by public opinion polls, which reveal that more Protestants feel cool toward Catholics (45.5 percent) than feel warm toward them (33.8 percent) and that Catholics feel friendlier toward Buddhists (34.46 percent) than toward Protestants (14 percent). Even more surprising, almost twice as many Catholics think highly of Buddhist teachings (36.6 percent) than are favorably impressed with Protestant teachings (19.6 percent). Moreover, more Catholics have a good impression of Buddhist teachings than have a bad impression of them, but the reverse is true of their attitude toward Protestant teachings. Figures show that 43.8 percent of Catholics gave a negative evaluation of Protestant teachings in contrast to only 19.6 percent who gave a positive evaluation.[50]

Given the long history of competition between the Catholic and Protestant communities in Korea and the scant goodwill between them, it is unlikely that their sibling rivalry will end anytime soon. That is good for Korea, if one wishes to see more rapid church growth. However, it is bad for Korea, if one would wish to see less bickering and more mutual understanding and cooperation. Meanwhile, on the sidelines, Buddhists will enjoy watching the continuing competition between those two Christian groups while their community grows as well, ensuring that a substantial

proportion of the religion-oriented population of the Republic of Korea
remains non-Christian.

NOTES

1. Donald Clark, "History and Religion in Modern Korea: The Case of Protestant Christianity," in *Religion and Society in Contemporary Korea,* ed. Lewis R. Lancaster and Richard K. Payne (Berkeley: Institute of East Asian Studies, University of
California, 1997), 196–202, has a list of ninety-six Protestant denominations and
subdenominations.

2. Gallup Korea, ed., *Han'gugin ŭi chonggyo wa chonggyo ŭisik: '84 nyŏn, '94
nyŏn, '97 nyŏn chosa kyŏlgwa wa pigyohan chonggyo yŏn'guso* [The religions and religious consciousness of the Korean people: A comparative study of the results of religious surveys taken in 1984, 1989, and 1997], (Seoul: Gallup Korea, 1998), 13,
17.

3. The figures reported by Christian organizations themselves are found in
Andrew Kim, "Protestant Christianity in South Korea: A Historical Sociology of
Its Cultural Reception and Social Impact, 1910–1989" (Ph.D. diss., University of
Toronto, 1996), 247.

4. Han'guk chonggyo sahoe yŏn'guso, ed., *Han'guk chonggyo yŏn'gam, 1994*
[Yearbook of Korean religion] (Seoul: Korean Scholar Press, 1994), 63.

5. Gallup Korea, *Han'gugin ŭi chonggyo wa chonggyo ŭisik,* 218.

6. Ibid., 198.

7. There had been Catholic missionaries in Korea in the 1590s, but they were
chaplains to invading Japanese forces and did not focus much of their proselytizing
energy on the Koreans on the peninsula. Only later, when they encountered Koreans who had been kidnaped to Japan, did they begin to preach to Koreans as well.
There is no credible evidence that the few Koreans who were converted to Catholicism in Japan had any impact on the religious history of the Korean peninsula.

8. The figures for the number of Catholics during the period of persecution
are taken from Joseph Chang-mun Kim and John Jae-sun Chung, *Catholic Korea*
(Seoul: Catholic Korea Publishing Company, 1964), 877–881; *Han'guk chonggyo
yŏn'gam, 1993,* 122; and Pae Se-yŏn, "Han'guk-esŏ ŭi P'ali woebang chŏn'gyohoe
ŭi sŏn'gyo pangch'im" [The strategy adopted by the Paris Foreign Mission Society
for proselytizing in Korea], in *Han'guk kyohoesa nonmunjip 1* [A collection of articles
on the history of the Korean Church, volume 1], ed. Han'guk kyohoesa yŏn'guso
(Seoul: Han'guk Kyohoesa Yŏn'guso, 1984), 743–767.

9. Ch'oe Chang-go, *Kukka wa chonggyo* [Church and State] (Seoul: Hyŏndae
Sasangsa, 1983), 74.

10. Yun Kyŏngno, "Ch'ogi Han'guk kaesin-gyo ch'ŭk ŭi Ch'ŏnjugyo-gwan:
kaesin'gyo sŏn'gyosadŭl ŭi kyŏnhaerŭl chungshimŭro" [Early Korean Protestant attitudes toward Catholicism: The opinions of Protestant missionaries], in *Han'guk
kyohoesa nonch'ong* [A collection of articles on the history of the Church in Korea],
ed. Han'guk kyohoesa yŏn'guso (Seoul: Han'guk Kyohoesa Yŏn'guso, 1982), 367.

11. For more on the Protestant invention of an indigenous Korean monotheism, see my "Hananim, Hanŭnim, Hanullim and Hanŏllim: The Construction of Terminology for Korean Monotheism," *Review of Korean Studies* 5, no. 1 (June 2000): 105–131. Most scholars of Korean Christianity have not been convinced by the evidence I present in that article that Koreans had no indigenous term for a monotheistic deity until Protestants coined a term for them.

12. Lak-Geoon George Paik, *The History of Protestant Missions in Korea, 1832–1910* (Seoul: Yonsei University Press, 1929), 389.

13. See, for example, Horace G. Underwood, ed., *Hymns of Praise* (Seoul: Trilingual Press, 1894), and *Chan Mi Ka: A Selection of Hymns for the Korean Church* (Seoul: Methodist Episcopal Church, 1895).

14. See, for example, Paik, *History of Protestant Missions*, 367–378, and Chu Ch'ae-yong, "A History of the Protestant Church in Korea from a New Perspective," in *Korea and Christianity*, ed. Chai-Shin Yu (Seoul: Korean Scholar Press, 1996), 150–151.

15. See my "Danger Within: Guilt and Moral Frailty in Korean Religion," *Acta Koreana* 4 (July 2000): 1–25.

16. George Paik discusses the Protestant hostility to Catholicism in his *History of Protestant Missions in Korea*. For example, on page 257, he cites a missionary listing "the perverted teachings of Roman Catholicism" as one of the primary obstacles to the spread of Protestant Christianity in Korea.

17. Sin Kwangch'ŏl, *Ch'ŏnjugyo wa Kaesin'gyo* [Catholicism and Protestantism] (Seoul: Han'guk Kidokkyo Yŏksa Yŏn'guso, 1998), 108–169; Yun Kyŏngno, "The Relationship between Korean Catholics and Korean Protestants in the Early Mission Period," in *Korea and Christianity* (Seoul: Korean Scholar Press, 1996), 7–37.

18. Sin, *Ch'ŏnjugyo wa Kaesin'gyo*, 89–108; Yun, "Relationship," 12–21.

19. Yi Chuho, "Sinang'in An Chunggŭn non" [The Catholic An Chunggŭn], *Han'guk kyohoesa nonch'ong*, 391.

20. Kang Wi Jo, *Christ and Caesar in Modern Korea: A History of Christianity and Politics* (Albany: State University of New York Press, 1997), 44–47; Andrew Kim, "Protestant Christianity," 23–24; Kim In-su, *Han'guk Kidokkyohoe-sa* [The history of Korean Protestantism] (Seoul: Korean Presbyterian Press, 1994), 200–206.

21. *Han'guk chonggyo yŏn'gam 1993*, 128.

22. Kang Wi Jo, *Christ and Caesar*, 61–69; Kim Yangsŏn, "Compulsory Shinto Shrine Worship and Persecution," *Korea and Christianity*, 87–120.

23. Figures for the Catholic population are taken from Han'guk Kat'ollik Taesajŏn p'yŏnch'an wiwŏnhoe, ed., *Han'guk Kat'ollik taesajŏn, purok* [The dictionary of Korean Catholicism, appendix] (Seoul: Han'guk Kyohoesa Yŏn'guso, 1992), 322–327. Figures for the Protestant population are taken from *Han'guk chonggyo yŏn'gam, 1993*, 190–191.

24. Japanese figures for 1940 are taken from *Chōsen no shūkyo oyobi kyoshi yōran* [Survey of religions and shrines in Korea] (Keijō: Government-General of Chōsen, Gakumukyoku, Shakai Kyoikuka, 1941), 80–81.

25. *Chōsen no shūkyo oyobi kyōshi yōran*, 75.

26. Korean Overseas Information Service, *Statistical Data on Korea, 1983* (Seoul: Korean Overseas Information Service, 1983); Yun Sŭng'yong, *Hyŏndae Han'guk chonggyo munhwa ŭi ihae* [Understanding the contemporary religious culture of Korea] (Seoul: Hanul Ak'ademi, 1997), 206.

27. Clark, "History and Religion."

28. Here I am stealing shamelessly from the University of Washington sociologist Rodney Stark, who has argued that the more retailers there are in a religious marketplace, the larger the crowd that will come to shop there.

29. Korean Overseas Information Service, *Statistical Data on Korea.*

30. *Han'guk chonggyo yŏn'gam, 1993*, 122; *Han'guk Kat'ollik taesajŏn*, 322.

31. *Han'guk chonggyo yŏn'gam, 1993*, 130.

32. Paris Foreign Mission Society, *Le Catholicisme en Corée* (Hong Kong: MEP, 1924), 103–107, as cited in Yun Kyŏngno, "Relationship," 32. There is an English translation of this French text, but the American priest who translated that work left out those complaints about the superior resources available to Protestants. Patrick Byrne, *The Catholic Church in Korea* (Seoul: Maryknoll Fathers, 1926).

33. These figures are courtesy of the Ministry of Culture and Tourism and are drawn from only the seventeen largest Protestant denominations, except for the Gallup figures, which came from Gallup Korea, *Han'gugin ŭi chonggyo wa chonggyo ŭisik.*

34. In 1965, all religious organizations in South Korea, both Christian and non-Christian, reported a total of 3.5 million followers at a time when the total population of South Korea was 28.7 million. See Yun Sŭng'yong, *Hyŏndae Han'guk*, 206. Also see Yu Tong-sik, *Han'guk chonggyo wa kidokkyo* [Christianity and Korean religion] (Seoul: Taehan Kidokkyo Sŏhoe, 1965), 185.

35. See, for example, the government figures for 1985 and 1991 in *Han'guk chonggyo yŏn'gam, 1993*, 296; and Gallup, *Han'gugin ŭi chonggyo wa chonggyo ŭisik*, 238. Andrew Eung-gi Kim, "The Rise of Protestantism in Contemporary South Korea: Non-Religious Factors in Conversion," *Review of Korean Studies* 5, no. 1 (June 2002): 11–29, presents a similar argument for the rapid growth of Protestant Christianity, although he does not discuss why Protestant Christianity benefited more from rapid urbanization and dramatic social change than Catholicism did.

36. The Catholic figures here come from *Han'guk chonggyo yŏn'gam, 1994*, 66.

37. Yi Yonghun, *Sullye ŭi kilmog-e sŏsŏ: Han'guk kyohoe ŭi onŭl, kŭ chindan kwa chŏnmang* [At the start of a journey: The Korean church today, problems and prospects] (Suwŏn: Catholic Press, 2004).

38. *Han'guk Kat'ollik taesajŏn, purok*, 326.

39. Yun Sŭng'yong, *Hyŏndae Han'guk*, 136, 149.

40. Ibid., 136, 151.

41. Ibid., 122.

42. For more on the Catholic turn toward politics, see my "From Pottery to Politics: The Transformation of Korean Catholicism," in *Religion and Society in Contemporary Korea*, ed. Lewis R. Lancaster and Richard K. Payne (Berkeley: Institute of East Asian Studies, University of California, 1997), 127–168.

43. *Han'guk chonggyo yŏn'gam, 1995*, 84.

44. James Grayson, "Cultural Encounter: Korean Protestantism and Other Religious Traditions," *International Bulletin of Missionary Research* 25, no. 2 (April 2001): 66–72, makes a similar point.

45. Gallup, *Han'gugin ŭi chonggyo wa chonggyo ŭisik*, 245–252.

46. Sŏ Usŏk, "Han'guk chonggyo ŭi sŏngjang kwa wigi" [A turning point in the growth of Korean religious organizations], in Gallup, *Han'gugin ŭi chonggyo wa chonggyo ŭisik*, 224–225.

47. The Catholic growth rate has already begun to slow down. Moreover, as the number of people enrolled as Catholics continues to grow, the number of those Catholics who are no longer active members of their local church has grown even faster. Yi Yonghun, *Sullye ŭi kilmog-e sŏsŏ*, 204–206.

48. Gallup, *Han'gugin ŭi chonggyo wa chonggyo ŭisik*, 246.

49. Don Clark, "Protestant Christianity and the State: Religious Organizations as Civil Society," in *Korean Society: Civil Society, Democracy, and the State*, ed. Charles Armstrong (New York: Routledge, 2002), 188.

50. Sin Kwangch'ŏl, *Ch'ŏnjugyo wa Kaesin'gyo*, 12–13.

CHAPTER 14

Modernization and the Explosive Growth and Decline of Korean Protestant Religiosity

Byong-suh Kim

S ociological studies have often found that institutional disorganization and the loss of the social function of religion may occur
when society becomes modernized. Peter Berger summed it up thus: "The
impact of modernity on religion is commonly seen in terms of the process
of secularization, which can be described as one in which religion loses
its hold on the level both of institutions and of human consciousness."[1]
Berger's harsh assessment may well describe the state of the Korean Protestant church today. For the last forty years, a startling wave of modernization
accompanied by industrialization, urbanization, and rapid social mobility
have swept Korea. Religions in Korea have been profoundly influenced by
onrushing modernization to the point of losing traditional preeminence and
social function.

Modernization in Korea began earlier, at the beginning of the twentieth century and during the final years of the Chosŏn dynasty, when Catholic pioneers, Protestant missionaries, and patriotic Korean Christian leaders
were hard at work. Elements of modernization were found during the era
of Japanese colonial domination. But the recent modernization under the
"economy first" policy of the military regimes of Generals Park Chung
Hee and Chun Doo Hwan occurred at a much faster pace and greater depth
than was seen at the tail end of the Chosŏn dynasty and the Japanese period.
Modernization of more recent years resulted in great social change accompanied by industrialization, urbanization, and rapid cultural and social mobility. This has been unlike the earlier modernization trends. Modernization invading the Protestant church in the 1960s led to explosive growth
up to the 1980s. Recent years have witnessed a sharp downward decline,

occurring as modernization was tapering off and various other factors affected church attendance.

Of course, modernity cannot be blamed for all the ills and conflicts existing in the Korean Protestant church today. Nor can modernity be isolated as the single factor responsible for the rapid rise and growth decline of the membership of the Korean Protestant church today. Modernization has not only invaded Korean Protestantism, but has also created various other conflicts within the church. Church conflicts linked to modernization may have seriously damaged the established church, yet as viewed from the conflict perspectives of modern sociology, such conflicts might also have contributed to church growth.[2] That indeed was what happened in the Korean Protestant church during recent modernization, especially from 1970 through 2001.

According to Korean statistical reports, the Korean Protestant church population (excluding cultist groups) was 5,859,000 in 1980. The same sources reported 4,870,000 in 1979 and 3,760,000 in 1978. The annual growth rate of church population was about 1,000,000 during the period from 1978 through 1984, the year of the Korean Protestant church's centennial celebration. The church population at that time hit the 10,000,000 mark, almost 20 percent of the total population of South Korea. The growth pattern of church membership is shown in table 1. In 1950 Protestant church membership was 500,198; ten years later it was about 24.6 percent more, with 623,072 members reported. At the peak of the 1960–1970 modernization period, church membership grew explosively, to 3,192,621 in 1970, a 412.4 percent increase. The growth rate began slowing from 1985, with 28.7 percent that year, 23.9 percent in 1991, and only 9.0 percent in 1995. The two largest denominational churches, Presbyterian and Methodist, during 1996 through 1997 had only a 1.9 percent membership

TABLE 1. Trend of growth in church membership

Year	Members (N)	Growth (%)
1950	500,198	
1960	623,072	24.6
1970	3,192,621	412.4
1977	5,501,491	56.7
1985	6,489,242	28.7
1991	8,037,464	23.9
1995	8,760,336	9.0

Sources: Research Institute for Korean Religion and Society, *Yearbook on Religions* (1993); Ministry of Culture and Information, ROK Government, *Authorized Religions and Religious Organizations* (1987); ROK Government, *Population and Housing Census* (1991). The figures were compiled by Lee Won Kyu based on these statistical data.

increase.[3] The remarkable growth of the church population in Korea during the modernization period is rare in the history of the Protestant mission in the world. Naturally, the Korean church is proud of such a success in church expansion. However, the growth in size alone may not necessarily be a success. An examination of the process of such a rapid growth and its ecclesiological consequences is required.

First, the historical process through which the Korean Protestant church grew so strongly will be examined. Next will be an analysis of how recent modernization has taken place as related to conflicts within the Korean church. Third to be addressed is how the Korean church grew so explosively in spite of, or because of, such conflicts in the church. Finally, an attempt will be made to explore the reasons for the growth decline in recent years along with modernization trends, all posing troubles in Korea today. Emile Durkeim, one of the founding fathers of modern sociology, once wrote, "A social fact is every way of acting, fixed or not, capable of exercising on the individual; or again, every way of acting which is general through a given society, while at the same time existing in its own right independent of its individual manifestations."[4] Durkeim thus suggests that a person's life experience, such as religious conversion, is partly influenced by the social and historical situation that exists externally to the individual. This social determinism of Durkheim ignores the capacity of an individual as a self-willed actor, yet the social, political, and economic factors of the structural setting should be considered important as they all influence the motivational aspect of the individual converts. What happened in the Korean Protestant church may well be explained by external factors found in Korean society.

Historical Background of Early Modernization and the Church Growth in Korea

When the first American Protestant missionary, Dr. Horace Allen, arrived on the Korean peninsula in 1884, the social structure was beginning to change with a new consciousness toward a more egalitarian society. This was indeed a first experience of modernization for the Korean people. At about this same period of early Christian missionary activities, there were numerous peasant revolts. The Tonghak peasants' revolt and reform movements by Sirhak (practical learning) adherents and radical young reformists who were engaged in a failed coup d'etat all shook the hierarchical system of the Chosŏn dynasty. In addition, the impact of the Japanese victory over China in the Sino-Japanese war of 1894–1895 shocked the Confucian rulers who had relied on the power of China for centuries. They saw Japan's victory with its Westernized military system and weaponry and

began to question the Confucian value systems that had been the fundamental basis for the consciousness of the Korean people.

At this juncture, Protestant missionaries introduced the gospel of Christianity, providing significant impetus for changing Korean social structure
toward a more egalitarian society. Christianity as a belief system for human-
ization and liberation of the oppressed was welcome to the commoners and
slaves at the same time as it was a threat to the status of the nobility. Korean
women who had been deprived of their basic human rights began to be
emancipated, especially through modern education introduced by the missionaries. Because of these emancipation movements, the population of the
early Korean church began to increase, mostly with commoners, slaves, and
women.

Historically, the roots of Korean Christianity go back to the Chosŏn
dynasty of the seventeenth and eighteenth centuries. When Roman Catholic Christianity was first introduced to the Korean people through China,
Catholic Christianity was at first regarded as a curious Western philosophy
and later as a subversive and evil teaching, harmful to Korea's Chosŏn dynasty. Christian philosophy, which advocated the equality of all men and
women under one God, was considered a threat to the basic class structure
of the Chosŏn dynasty.

The Chosŏn dynasty under the influence of Confucianism had a strict
system of four classes: the *yangban* (nobility), the *chungin* (middle people),
the *sangmin* (commoners), and the *ch'ŏnmin* (lowest class). The *yangban*
were at the top of the Chosŏn dynasty stratification system. The designa-
tion *yangban*, which originated in the Koryŏ dynasty, means two ranks: the
eastern group (*tongban*), who were civil officers; and the western group
(*sŏban*), who were military people. Among the *yangban* class, the highest
people were sons of a legitimate marriage (*chŏkcha*); the lower level was
held by sons of a concubine (*sŏja*). The *chungin* were the professionals and
technicians, who usually lived in the center of the capital city. They were
educated and passed the government examination (*kwagŏ*), but they were
restricted to serving the government as accountants, interpreters, judicial
officers, and clerks. The *sangmin* were the people who engaged in farming,
commerce, and trade. They were the majority of the total population; they
could never become *yangban*. *Yangban* called them *ssangnom*, a derogatory
expression used even today for those who rudely misbehave. The *ch'ŏnmin*,
the lowest class, were the slaves, slaughterers, butchers, sorcerers, and
convicts. They were not allowed to live in the villages. They had their
communities outside village boundaries. The *ch'ŏnmin* were born to slave
mothers and were property of *yangban*. Christianity was introduced to Koreans who lived under the strict rules of the *ban*, *sang*, and *ch'ŏn* system of
social stratification.

Emancipation of the Oppressed by Roman Catholic Christianity

Chosŏn-dynasty Korea was a "hermit kingdom" until 1876, when Japan forced the Korean government to open its ports. It was, however, possible for some reform-minded Confucian scholars belonging to the Sirhak school who were critical of the orthodox Neo-Confucianism espoused by Zhu Xi to begin studying the texts of Western learning (biblical texts in Chinese). In those days, there was a politically alienated group of *yangban*, the *namin*, who joined with some reform-minded *chungin* and were greatly interested in Western learning. So when Yi Sŭng-hun was going to China as an envoy in 1784, Yi Pyŏk, the *namin yangban* who headed the Catholic study group, asked Yi to get in touch with Catholic missionaries. Yi contacted a French missionary, Jean Joseph de Grammont. He became so impressed by the Christian theology that he was converted to Christianity, baptized by Father Grammont, and became Pierre (Peter) Yi Sŭng-hun, the first baptized Korean. Now the Korean Catholic Church calls him the father of Korean Catholic Christianity.[5]

When Yi Sŭng-hun returned to Korea with some biblical texts and other Christian literature written in Chinese characters, some *namin* and *chungin* scholars started to study them and became Christian as well. They started proselytizing in secret among the *chungin* and *namin*. They had secret meetings for the study of Western learning and worship services. Internally, the three groups in this early Catholic community were tightly knit: *chungin* family members, Sirhak sympathizers, some politically alienated *yangban* (*namin*). They had strong bonding among themselves by sharing the secret of their Christian identity. The secret activities of *namin yangban* and *chungin* Catholics were finally revealed, and massive persecutions started. When secret meetings, which were held at the house of Kim Pŏm'u (Thomas), a *chungin* and leader of the Bible study group, were revealed, he was arrested and sent into exile; he died two years later. The Zhu Xi conservatives and Sŏnggyun'gwan Confucian scholars were actively involved in the persecution of Christians. Some ten thousand Catholic Christians were martyred, including Kim Taegŏn, the first Korean priest. A total of 103 Catholic martyrs in Korea were canonized by Pope Paul when he visited Seoul in 1984 to commemorate two hundred years of the Korean Catholic Church.

Thus, during the seventeenth and eighteenth centuries, Catholic Christianity played a significant role in undermining the system of stratification of *ban*, *sang*, and *ch'ŏn* by advocating that God created human beings equal. This ideology of equality seriously threatened the structure and stratification of the Chosŏn dynasty. Furthermore, the unity of the *namin* faction and the reform-oriented *chungin* group became a formidable force for opposition against the establishment. Already, the number of *ch'ŏnmin* classes was dwindling, mostly because escaping slaves joined with the *sangmin* group. In the early period, the Korean Catholic Church was made up mostly of *chungin*, the *namin* faction of *yangban*, and their slaves. They had difficulty in proselytizing among the lower classes of *sangmin* and *ch'ŏnmin* because of the government's persecution. It was a hardship for the lower classes to read the Chinese biblical tests and literature. Consequently, Korean Catholic Christianity grew slowly. Nevertheless, the spirit of emancipation for the oppressed underclass, *sangmin* and *ch'ŏnmin*, was clearly having an impact on the rigid system of stratification in the latter period of the Chosŏn dynasty and thus provided a road for the successful activities of the Protestant missions.

Emancipation of the Oppressed by Protestant Missionaries

The spirit of emancipation for the oppressed continued when the first formal American Protestant missionaries arrived at Inch'ŏn harbor on Easter Sunday in April 1885; Canadian and Australian missionaries followed in 1888 and in 1889. They divided the mission territory into four regions. The northwestern region was designated for the Northern Presbyterian Mission, U.S.A.; the southwestern Chŏlla area was for the Southern Presbyterian Mission, U.S.A.; the northeastern Hamgyŏngdo was for the Canadian Mission; the southeastern was for the Australian Mission and the Northern Presbyterian Mission, U.S.A.; and the central area, including Seoul, was for the Methodist Mission. This division has a profound implication for the various theological orientations of Korean church leaders. Korean Protestant Christianity (Korean Protestantism, hereafter) was regarded as mediator of the modern democratic idealism to Korean society at first, then as a patriotic religion for national independence, and as a religion of messianic hope for the oppressed people, especially *sangmin, ch'ŏnim,* and women. Two Koreans, Yi Ŭngch'an and Sŏ Sangyun, were baptized in 1879 and 1882, respectively, by Scottish Presbyterian missionaries in Manchuria. They were *sangmin* merchants and Korean-language instructors for missionaries John MacIntyre and John Ross. Together they embarked on an effort in the fall of 1882 to translate the Bible, first the Gospels of Luke and John, and later the Acts of the Apostles. Unlike the translation of the Bible into Chinese, their work was done in hangul, which was the written language of the commoners and women. The translated booklets were smuggled into Korea and spread among the underclass people, commoners and women. Many of them were converted to Christianity, laying foundations for their church on their own before the missionaries arrived. The hangul Bible was simple and easy to learn, and the biblical message became the hope of the oppressed *sangmin, ch'ŏnmin,* and women.[6]

How the early Korean Christianity could emancipate the oppressed people in Korea was well expressed by a famous writer, Yi Kwangsu, as follows:

> Christianity introduced Western civilization to Korea for the first time and pioneered social and cultural reform. Korean churches enhanced new moral standards based on the idea of individual freedom along with the Gospel of Christian faith brought to the oppressed people. Korean Christianity made great contributions to Korean society through various programs of mission schools, hospitals, and welfare organizations. By training national leaders, the churches have lifted up the spirit of the people, removed illiteracy, and engaged in reform movements in Korea, especially in the farm areas.[7]

Thus, Protestants during the first century of their mission activities beginning in 1884 and throughout the latter part of the Chosŏn dynasty made great contributions to the early modernization process that took place in Korea. However, up to this point, Catholics and Protestants had only limited effect on Korean religion and education.

Accordingly, the modernization engendered by mission activities could not create significant increases in membership. The rapid church growth came later, during the Japanese colonial domination, when Koreans were deprived of their native culture and national identity. In recent years explosive church growth has been possible through modernization in company with industrialization, urbanization, and cultural and social mobility.

Church Growth under Japanese Colonial Domination

There was a stirring of the Korean national independence movement while Korea was still under Japanese control. During this time many national leaders shaped their nascent movements, centering on the churches. Churches in turn worked hard to cultivate a national spirit for independence and to promote human dignity despite the Japanese presence. Thus, a considerable number of religious leaders participated directly in the struggle for national independence dating from the final years of the Chosŏn dynasty when Korea was seriously threatened by big powers such as China, Japan, Russia, the United States, England, and France.

After the failed coup d'etat by the radical young reformists of the *yangban* class in 1884, some escaped and learned democratic idealism abroad, mainly in Japan and the United States. Upon their return to Korea, they launched a variety of freedom movements—the Independence Club and People's Assembly, for example. Independence Club leaders, among them Seo Jaepil (Sŏ Chaep'il), Yun Ch'iho, Nam Kungŏk, and Yi Sangjae, were all educated Christians. Most of these leaders were from the *yangban* social class, but as they became Christian they all adopted the Christian doctrine of equality for all. They worked diligently for national independence with an ideology of liberty and humanity. Conservative government officials of a pro-Russian bloc finally urged the king to dissolve the club by arresting its leaders.

At this juncture, the People's Assembly (Manmin Kongdong Hoeŭi) was organized throughout the nation, fueled by the outrage of the people. Night demonstrations took place for forty-two days.[8] The king ultimately released the leaders of the Independence Club, but on December 25, 1898, conservatives pressured the king to arrest 430 leaders of the Independence Club and of the People's Assembly. This signaled the end of those reform movements, mostly initiated and led by Christian leaders. After the collapse of the Independence Club and the People's Assembly movement, those who had been actively involved split into two groups. One group engaged in an evangelical revival movement, which resulted in the Great Revival of 1907. The other group engaged in a secret movement of the New People's Association (Sinminhoe), which was organized in 1906 and led by educated Christian leaders such as Yun Ch'iho, An Ch'angho, Yi Sŭnghun, Yi Sangjae, and others. Some young students also organized the Christian Youth Independent Association in the Sangdong Methodist Church under the leadership of the Reverend Chŏn Tŏggi and Yi Chun.

Japan's victories in the Sino-Japanese War (1894–1995) and the Russo-Japanese War (1904–1905) spurred the Japanese to speed up the colonization of Korea, and the national reform movements were transformed into anti-Japanese struggle. During this critical period of Korean history, an era of political modernization, Koreans were massively converted to Christianity as the Christian churches became the centers for the independence movements. For the first time, democratic ideals were widely introduced by Christian leaders such as U.S.-educated Yun Ch'iho, An Ch'ang Ho, and Cho Mansik. These church leaders were in the vanguard of nationwide independence movements as well as educational and economic reform activities imbued with patriotic zeal.

Because of the severe suppression by the Japanese colonial government, these patriotic leaders went inside the church to continue fighting for independence alongside spiritual leaders. The result was the Great Revival of 1907. That revival was led by the Reverend Kil Sŏnju of the Central Presbyterian Church in P'yŏngyang, the largest Korean church at that time (and the subject of Chong Bum Kim's chapter in this volume) Kil's method of ministry was focused on an early-morning prayer meeting, influenced by Buddhist rituals, and disciplined Bible studies (*sagyŏng hoe*). Kil was also influenced by the Nevius method of mission, which advocated self-propagation, self-government, self-support, and organized Bible studies.

The Great Revival of 1907 and the New People's Association movement were partly the result of the emancipation of the *sangmin* and the *ch'ŏnmin* classes. The Japanese colonial government saw the threat of the Christian forces led by the New People's Association and arrested 220 leaders and members on an alleged plot to assassinate Terauchi, the Japanese colonial governor-general. Of those seized, 105 were eventually indicted and served many years in prison.[9] While they were imprisoned, missionaries helped them as best they could, and many prisoners became Christians.

At this juncture the Japanese colonial government began to implement the policy of "Japanization of Korea." The Japanization drive sought to force Koreans to change their names to Japanese style, to use only Japanese at all schools, and to abolish songs, hymns, and literature that were seen as even remotely subversive.

Japanization finally forced all Koreans, including Christians, to participate in Shintō worship. Shintō worship was a clear example of ideological and religious control over Korean Christianity. Small Shintō shrines were distributed to families of Korean students, who were instructed to worship every day. This was a dark period for Korean Christianity. Many Korean Christians who refused to worship the gods of Shintōism were arrested, tortured, and suffered death in prison.

The church's participation in the struggle for national independence engendered a level of credibility and support for Christianity in non-Christian communities. This public support and the cultural pioneering activities resulted in the massive increase of membership that was later called the Great Revival. The March First Independence Movement arose in 1919, the most important single political event at this juncture in the Korean church. A Declaration of Independence was prepared and signed by a group of thirty-three leaders of the movement. Sixteen of these were Christians who spearheaded a nonviolent movement for national independence from Japanese rule. This event became historically significant to church growth as the non-Christian public began to look up to the church for its selfless and sacrificial participation in the national political efforts.[10]

The rapid growth of the Korean Protestant church was followed by tyrannical oppression exerted by Japanese colonial forces. Many Korean Christian leaders were made to surrender to the Japanese, casting a dark shadow over church growth efforts. Curiously, the Japanese engaged in a modernization drive in Korea during the occupation. Japan invested heavily in agricultural as well as manufacturing sectors, renovating the Korean infrastructure while keeping the landlord system intact. A "rationalized" landlord relationship was established by way of property rights, putting the old landlords under the colonial government. Thus, the Korean landlords had to adapt to the Japanese policy. The reform policy increased Japan's ability to extract food surpluses from Korea. The Japanese also developed some heavy industries in Korea, but they were mostly for Japanese interests. Korea became a supply and production line for Japanese expansion into Manchuria and China.[11]

The Effects of Modernization, Industrialization, and Urbanization on Church Growth

At the end of World War II, Korea was freed of Japanese domination, but Koreans were presented with a country divided north and south. Not long after liberation, in 1950, a war broke out between the people of north and south. During the Korean conflict, a massive number of Christians from North Korea took refuge in the South. Many of those Christian refugees built churches and spread the Gospel wherever they settled all over South Korea.

Sects of Protestant orientation sprang up rapidly, spawning more than two hundred sectarian and cult groups in South Korea.[12] The churches and denominations were split, often with ugly scenes, fistfights, and court battles, over property rights. Many of the bigger churches became wealthy as a result of the increase of membership, and some built prayer temples in the mountains. Some small churches experienced a break off of sects or cults. Strangely, this factionalism within the church spurred an explosive increase in total church population. How can such a strange spurt in church growth be explained?

First, the political, military, and social structure during this period provided a favorable setting for rapid church membership growth. Right after liberation from Japan, many Christians participated in political activities under President Syngman Rhee, a Christian, and his Liberal Party. The Syngman Rhee government established a reinforcing relationship with the church hierarchy. Churches under Rhee enjoyed maximum freedom, except for those bristling at his dictatorial rule. Moreover, the South Korean people as a whole considered the United States a reliable ally who had helped Korea in the struggle for liberation from Japan and in the battle against Communist aggression from the North. Koreans in general identified the United States as the nation that had brought the Christian religion to Korea and thus looked at Christianity in a favorable light. Under such favorable social conditions, the Korean church leaders skillfully utilized the pro-Christian regime of Rhee and the favorable sentiment of the Korean people in their effort for church expansion and other evangelical activities. It should be noted that while the image of the Korean church as "pro–Syngman Rhee" or "pro-American" was helpful for building church membership, many thoughtful people, especially intellectuals and university students, were highly critical of the church's alliance with the dictatorial regime and of U.S. influence over Korean politics and the military buildup in the country.

Second, this period of rapid growth of church and sect may also be psychologically related to the anomie confronting Korean society after liberation and during the Korean War. During occupation, Koreans had been deprived by the Japanese in countless ways. Their national identity had been taken away. Moreover, during the Korean War, massive population mobility produced rootlessness and anomie. Many refugees, especially those from the North, felt a keen sense of frustration and alienation, wishing to belong to a community where they could find comfort and direction for life. Third, for those who were alienated and lived on the margin, the sects and cults were more appealing than the established churches, as they could hear there a ready-made remedy for their social "ills." They could look for otherworldly rewards as well as promise for material blessings in the present world. Even the established churches were split into many sectarian factions in order to meet the needs of wandering refugees who, in large numbers, had become Christian converts during the Korean War.

These three historical factors that led to Korean church growth and the increase of sectarian groups all prepared the way for the extremely rapid rise of religiosity during the period of modernization. Because of these unique historical processes and experiences of the Korean churches and sects, the impact of modernization has made the churches and sects grow even more rapidly in recent years.

The Unique Nature of Contemporary Modernization and Church Growth in Korea

Modernization may be viewed in terms of what Reinhart Bendix has defined as "all those social and political changes that accompanied industrialization."[13] As discussed earlier, modernization in Korea started at the beginning of the twentieth century, thanks to the activities of such young reformists as Kim Okkyun, Sŏ Chaep'il, Pak Hyŏnhyo, and others and by Protestant missionaries and workers in mission schools. The Japanese colonial government, amid industrialization and urbanization, achieved a limited modernization exclusively for Japan's own economic interests. Modernization in recent years, however, is quite different from the earlier modernization in scope, pace, and depth and consequently has resulted in revolutionary changes in all areas of social institutions and social structure.

Evidence of rapid industrialization may be found in the GDP growth trend in Korea. The Korean economy has achieved high growth since the early 1960s through a series of five-year economic plans. During the twenty-one years from 1962 to 1983, the average annual growth rate was

TABLE 2. Change in annual growth rate by industry (percentage)

Industry	1954–1961	1962–1970	1971–1978	1979–1983
Agriculture, forestry, fisheries	3.4	3.5	3.3	2.9
Mining and manufacturing	11.1	17.1	17.7	5.9
Social overhead capital and other services	3.3	10.6	9.8	4.1
GDP average growth rate	3.9	8.7	9.9	4.4

Source: Bank of Korea, *National Income Accounts* (1983).

about 8.3 percent, and the per capita GDP for 1983 drastically increased to $1,884.00 from only $82.00 in 1961. This extraordinary spurt in economic growth was largely achieved through industrialization and export-first trading in the international market. Certainly, there was no such economic development in the past, one accompanied by industrialization, massive urbanization, and cultural and social mobility.

In the recent modernization period, Korean industrialization drastically reshaped the industrial and employment structure (table 2). Up to the early 1960s, agriculture, forestry, and fisheries dominated the Korean economy, accounting for about 45 percent of GDP. But by 1976 the manufacturing and mining sectors had surpassed agriculture, forestry, and fisheries. Fast growth in mining and manufacturing industries brought about a significant transformation of the industrial structure along with expansion of the nation's economy.

Change of industrial structure brought about corresponding changes in the employment sector. The employment ratio of the mining and manufacturing sector increased to 23.3 percent in 1983 from 8.8 percent in 1964. The employment ratio of agriculture, forestry, and fisheries, on the other hand, decreased to 29.7 percent in 1983 from 61.9 percent in 1964. Such changes in industrial and employment structure created a mass rural-urban migration. In the early 1960s the rural population was 58.4 percent of the national population; it shrank to 45.9 percent in 1970 and 28.9 percent in 1979 (table 3).[14] The mass rural-urban migration created large slum areas where rural migrants often lived in absolute poverty, as they could not find jobs easily. But once they found jobs, mostly in the manual-labor sector, their aspirations grew.

TABLE 3. Decline of the Korean farm population (unit: 1,000)

Year	National population	Farm population	Farm population as percentage of total
1953	21,546	13,151	61.0
1960	24,989	14,559	58.3
1970	31,435	14,422	45.9
1979	37,605	10,883	28.8

Source: Korean Economic Planning Board, *Annual Statistical Report* (1980).

The mass rural-urban migration created by industrialization also nearly destroyed the traditional extended family structure that was the backbone of rural societal stability and communal life. Although the nuclear family system is convenient for young couples who leave their home bases and live in the region where their jobs are, they may easily feel rootless, longing for intimate communal support. Of course, many families could achieve relatively high social status in the newly established occupational areas, managing a middle-class life. Yet they continued to strive for even higher social status while experiencing a keen sense of relative deprivation.

In sum, despite rapid economic improvement, the gap between the haves and the have nots became greater. The shaky economic condition persisted, even though GDP grew rapidly, primarily engendered by ever-increasing foreign debts (about $43 billion in 1981).

In the political area, the economy-first policy of the Park Chung Hee government stressed rapid economic development at any cost. Such a tightly controlled policy for development created a serious retardation in democratization and fostered political apathy among the Korean people. The bureaucratic authoritarianism of the Park regime did not permit any free discussion on issues related to national goals, the concept of the state, or even national ideology. The government often labeled individuals as Communists if they demanded any reform of the political, economic, or any other institutional structures and practices.

Traditionally, there has been a reverence among the Korean people for government bureaucrats. Becoming a high-ranking government official had symbolic significance for family status. The military government skillfully used this knowledge to build a system of political authority for industrial development in Korea. The authoritarian bureaucracy bred a new group of power elite, and those who were of marginal social status felt a keen sense of political alienation and apathy. The hypothesis that industrialization was bound to lead to the democratic process based on rationality did not prove true in the recent modernization of Korea.

Korean development depended heavily on foreign loans, primarily from the United States and Japan. Such economic dependency on the United States and Japan made it difficult for the Korean government to maintain a broad base for international relations and people's support. The defeat of the United States in Vietnam, the growing anti-American sentiment in the Third World countries, and anti-Japanese feeling throughout Asia all made it difficult for the Korean government to carry out effective diplomatic strategies. Moreover, South Koreans had to live constantly under the threat of a North Korean invasion as their government constantly reminded them. The situation of a divided Korea has made Koreans extremely uncomfortable and often frightened as the military government used the continuing threat of a North Korean invasion as a weapon to suppress dissidents.

The nature and problems of modernization in contemporary Korea may be summarized in terms of the never-ending gap between the haves and the have-nots resulting from industrialization and unequal distribution, the frequent fluctuations in economic growth and the resulting economic instability, and the authoritarian bureaucratic control of economic development, all of which retarded the democratic process. Human rights and individual freedom have been curtailed, and industrialization and urbanization have resulted in mass rural-urban migration, rooting out the basis of communality and destroying the close family ties of the extended family. In sum, the modernization that has brought about certain material comforts has nevertheless made the Korean people pay tremendous costs in noneconomic institutional life, including religion.

The impact of such rapid social change through modernization created a social-psychological condition of anomie. A significant number of Koreans lost a clear direction in life and were burdened with strain and stress and loss of communality. They felt a sense of powerlessness and political apathy under the tight military government control and were often confused by the plurality of values embraced by the modernization process. It was under such chaotic conditions that Korean Protestant churches grew explosively. Why?

Influence of Recent Modernity on the Rise of Religiosity

Religion as a social institution has many distinct social functions as it gives answer to people's ultimate concern or ultimate inquiries. When an individual faces a situation of tension and confusion, that individual needs to have a clear self-identity and definition of the situation. Thus, a person can construct an identity through interaction with others in a setting of reference groups or communities. The person can see meanings by defining a situation through the understanding of the intersectional relationships with the generalized others. Religion gives self-identity for an inward common order and definition of situation for meaning in social life.

Church or sect is indeed a reference group for these needs of individuals. In a Korean context, when one confronts the situation of unrest, chaos, tension, and instability in the process of modernization, one can look at the church for the construction of self-identity and the social meaning of reality. In Korea, when the trends of industrialization were combined with the social characteristics of the Korean churches and sects, a unique social context developed. Thus, people en masse knocked on the doors of the church searching for selfhood and meaning in life. How these two trends—modernization and development of religiosity—worked together in Korea in the midst of rapid social change may be explained as follows.

The military government in 1961–1980 encouraged economic development above all other institutional advancements. The developmental motif of the economy-first policy has a philosophy of material success at any cost. A sense of fierce competition often made individuals self-centered, egoistic, and selfish. A dog-eat-dog competition, particularly over land and space in the congested cities, may be observed. Such a self-centered motif has influenced the Korean churches, which have become highly stratified.

The gap between the wealthy churches and the poor churches has become so wide that a pastor of a big church in 1981 received more than $2,000 in monthly salary, with all sorts of fringe benefits such as a free parsonage, auto services, education for children, and a discretionary account for parish activities. At the same time, a small, rural church pastor barely survived on about $90 a month without any fringe benefits or pension arrangement. The development psychology, along with industrialization, brought about a "bigness syndrome": the size of an institution was understood as a measure of success. Korean churches and some sectarian groups experienced the same syndrome. Many developed budgets and engaged in church building using highly technological systems. Emphasis came to be placed on the size of the congregation. When rapid urbanization took place in the recent modernization process, the Korean church expansion was realized mostly in urban settings. Rapidly expanding churches were invaded by urbanism as a way of life.

Louis Wirth long ago pointed out that urbanization might be explained in terms of human ecology, social organizational structure, and personality structure.[15] From a human ecological point of view, urban life is greatly influenced by the ecological setting, locality, environmental condition, and values and norms attached to them for creating a lifestyle. In Korea, heterogeneous cultic and sectarian groups developed in various parts of big cities. They often appealed to the poor and the social dropouts with promises of material blessings and prosperity in their life here and now. The cultic groups, in particular, start off on the fringes of big cities and slowly move into the heart of them (e.g., the Unification Church).[16]

As a society is rapidly industrialized and urbanized in the process of modernization with the capitalistic developmental motif, the money economy system inevitably dominates the society. Personality structure and lifestyles developed by human interaction based on the money economy and the calculability of cold cash have spread among the people in religious organizations. As a result, they have weakened the traditional sense of sharing as well as the communal life of sharing. Exact calculability and impersonal, blasé attitudes are perhaps necessary in city living, but they have also invaded the religious community.

Social Disorganization and Money Economy

Rapid economic development and urbanization often bring about social disorganization, as discussed earlier. When a society is so rapidly urbanized, a strong bureaucratic system is often needed to maintain law and order. Such a tight bureaucratic control, however, tends to erode basic human rights and alienate those not in power. The explosively growing churches and sects also had to be highly organized, centering on charismatic leaders who often became wealthy and powerful in the church or sect establishment. But modernization, industrialization, and urbanization occurred not only in Korea but also all over the rest of Asia. Why then uniquely in Korea has modernization influenced religiosity so strongly, when other newly industrialized countries in Asia (e.g., Hong Kong, Taiwan, Singapore) have not experienced it in this manner? And why has the Protestant church alone experienced such an explosive growth in Korea?

Here we need to note the traditional characteristics of the Korean Protestant church and sectarian movements. Traditionally, most of the Korean Protestant churches have had a shamanistic tendency, following the indigenous belief system—totemism, shamanistic fetishism, and other kinds of nature worship. Korean shamanism is the belief system of this-worldly blessing—material wealth, good health, and other personal and familial well-being.

This emphasis on worldly personal blessing became a significant part of congregational life, especially in sectarian groups. In the industrial process, encouraged by the New Village movement of the government, the Korean masses wanted to achieve a better life through whatever means were available to them. They came to the church or sects for a better life here and now, as some religious leaders stressed, and even promised. For example, attractive messages by the Reverend Cho Yonggi of Yŏido Full Gospel Church in Seoul are for the so-called "three beats blessings," namely, the blessings of health, material, prosperity and going to heaven after death, all promised to those who attend the church regularly. Such promises appealed strongly not only to the poor but also to the middle class, who have a strong sense of deprivation relative to the upper class.

As discussed earlier, unlike Christian churches in other Asian states, and the Catholic Church and Buddhism in Korea, the Korean Protestant church has had a long tradition of human liberation, dating from the early years of its mission. Therefore, those who long for basic human rights and individual freedom tend to look to the Korean church tradition for human liberation. This tradition of human rights activities has continued in various Protestant organizations such as the National Council of Churches (NCC), Urban Industrial Mission, Korean Christian Student Federation (KCSF), and YMCA, and more. Such human rights activities initiated by the church organizations have increased the institutional credibility and public support among a wide range of people—intellectuals, university students, and common people, especially factory workers, laborers, and women, who had been oppressed under the patriarchic system. Now, nearly 70 percent of the total church population is female, and the majority of adherents are from poor family backgrounds. These people have been at the fringe of the rapidly industrializing society.

Finally, it should be pointed out that Korean church people themselves are the source of church expansion as they are extremely drawn to evangelical proselytization. Moreover, the Protestant church, alone among all the religions in Korea, adopted the Nevius method, which stressed a self-propagandizing, self-governing, and self-supporting mission. This mission policy led the Korean Protestant church to become independent from the Western missionaries from the early period of its development.[17]

As we have seen, the Korean Protestant church is no longer growing as it used to, although its membership was still increasing by about 1.4 percent in 1994 (see table 1).[18] What are the reasons for such a decline in church membership growth? Discussed below are three specific factors as related to improvement in economic life, political stability with democratization of Korean society, and disenchantment toward churches in general.

Decline of Church Membership Growth in Recent Years

As Korea has economically developed through modernization, the leisure industry has been rapidly growing. No longer is church the place where people come to spend their leisure hours as great varieties of leisure opportunities are available during the weekends. From the 1980s, a drastic increase of the leisure facilities was developed in such sports as tennis, golf, swimming, bowling, and others. There were only twenty-six golf courses in 1995. Now, close to a thousand golf courses are operating. Golfers increased in numbers from 710,000 in 1980 to 8,970,000 in 1996. Skiers numbered only 4,600 back then, but in 1995 there were 2,270,000 active skiers. Privately owned automobiles have rapidly increased in numbers since 1970. There were only 29,000 privately owned cars in 1970; that number soared to 179,000 cars in 1980, to 1,900,000 in 1990, and finally, in 1996, to 6,650,000. Most of the cars are used for leisure activities during weekends.[19]

Many who do not go out for leisure habitually stay home to watch weekend programs on television instead of going to the church on Sundays. Only 30.2 percent of the total population had television in 1970, but in 1990, 97.2 percent owned a television set. The hours of television watching increased dramatically from 14.3 hours per week just a few years earlier to 21.4 hours per week in 1996. Eight of those television-viewing hours were during the weekends with focus on popular programs such as sports and drama during the prime-time hours.[20]

Today, few people are starving and in desperate straits. Psychologically, people are much more content with their situation and do not rely on religion to enrich their lives. Instead, they pursue secular activities for enjoyment and relaxation, going out for mountain climbing, fishing, and other leisure activities. Moreover, the Korean church has lost its traditional preeminence as an institution for human rights and social reform. Korean Protestant churches adapted too much to the secular aspects of modernization. The Korean church is now too big and too rich. It became overly materialistic, oriented to the accumulation of wealth and expansion of church properties. Nonbelievers no longer look up to the church as the institution they can resort to for solutions to their problems. They consider big organizations to be self-serving, guilty of collective selfishness.

As discussed earlier, the explosive growth of the Korean Protestant church was partly due to the political instability and social unrest during the period of the military regimes of Park Chung Hee and Chun Doo Hwan. When a society is politically unstable, oppressed by the government, people being deprived of their basic human rights tend to knock on the doors of religious or sectarian groups. But as society becomes politically stable and the economic condition comfortable, people tend to engage in pleasure-oriented activities.

Korean society, after nearly forty years of struggle for democracy, has now finally achieved democratic order. The political condition is relatively stable. The so-called IMF (International Monetary Fund) crisis is successfully controlled, and the Korean economy is maintaining a stable course. There is a sufficient dollar reserve to pay off external debts, including what the Republic of Korea had to borrow from the IMF.

People leave church for many reasons, including negative factors within the church. When society becomes democratized, with the freedom to criticize, people tend to look at church more critically. Blind conformity no longer prevails among church members. Many former churchgoers no longer attend. A recent study conducted by H. B. Koh found this breakdown among respondents who no longer attend church: 45 percent had "no particular reasons"; 25 percent were "disappointed"; 21 percent had "moved"; and 7 percent "changed churches."[21] Koh's study suggests that those who leave church are mostly those suffering from a sense of disappointment, a lack of caring, and the indifference they felt from their church.

Understanding of the attitudes held by Koreans today helps explain the decline in the growth of the Protestant church. In response to a Gallup survey, 91.9 percent of the respondents said that there are too many pseudoreligious churches, 87.9 percent blamed church splits, 84.7 percent blamed the fights among members over the church budget and finance, 79.6 percent complained about the low quality of the pastors, 79.6 percent indicated that the church pursues expansion instead of a search for truth. Others made the following complaints: overemphasis on church offerings (68 percent), no help for life problems (62.9 percent), no action on the love the churches preach (48.8 percent), too many churches (41.9 percent), overinfluence of religion on society (39.6 percent). The Korea Gallup study clearly indicates that Koreans in large measure have a negative attitude toward the Protestant church today.[22]

Conclusion

The Korean church has a tradition of human liberation from the time Koreans learned about the Gospel of Christianity. During the latter years of the Chosŏn dynasty, many church leaders were devoted to reforming the feudalistic nation and later fought for the independence of the nation from the Japanese colonial domination. Many missionaries and leaders of the early Korean church struggled for pioneering goals in education and social welfare. Efforts for social and political reforms, national independence, and human liberation brought about the earlier modernization in Korea. In recent years, this tradition of human liberation persisted in the form of the struggle for human rights, individual freedom, and democracy. This tradition of human liberation increased the institutional credibility and public support among a wide range of people. This tradition for human liberation in the Korean church is, however, threatened by the wave of recent modernization accompanied by industrialization, commercialization, and urban decay. The church has been invaded by elements of secularization, materialism, and a monetary economy and has developed bureaucratic structures similar to those of large industrial complexes.

The development motif under the economy-first policy of the military government greatly influenced the church. In highly "successful" megachurches in Korea, there is no longer an intimate interaction of the Christian community—koinonia—by means of which a true communion of saints is possible. While the Korean masses in the midst of rapid social change gather around the church searching for self-identity, a sense of belonging, and meaning in life, the churches are caught up in the self-centered development of expanding the size of the congregation, collecting lots of money, and constructing fancy buildings. In consequence, the Korean church in the midst of modernization is losing its preeminent role as a salvific institution.

As a negative result of this accelerated modernization process, Korea has experienced social disorganization, economic crises, and sociopolitical instability. The traditional fabric of social values based on family, education, religion, and welfare has crumbled as society becomes increasingly oriented toward consumer-driven capitalism. The Korean church today is experiencing serious problems, and the decline in its growth rate is a direct influence of the secularization processes taking place in conjunction with modernization, commercialism, and capitalistic development. Now, the Korean church has a real challenge ahead in recovering its place as a center of human liberation.

NOTES

1. Peter Berger, *The Heretical Imperative* (Garden City, N.J.: Doubleday, 1979), 26.

2. For a clear explanation of the conflict school of sociology, see Georgi Simmel, *Conflict and Web of Group Affiliation* (New York: Free Press, 1955), and Lewis Coser, *The Functions of Social Conflict* (New York: Free Press, 1956).

3. This statistical analysis was made by Yi Wŏn'gyu, based on various government reports on religions in Korea. The figures can be found in Yi's "Han'guk kyohoe ŭi sŏngjang kwa kŭ tunhwa yoin e Taehan sahoehakchŏk koch'al" [A Sociological Study of the Factors Contributing to the Growth and Decline of the Korean (Protesant) Church], in *Sinhak kwa segye* [Theology and the World], no. 34 (1997): 145–187.

4. Emile Durkheim, *The Rules of Sociological Method* (New York: Free Press, 1950), 13.

5. Han'guk Kidokkyo yŏksa yŏn'guso [The Institute of Korean Church History Studies], *Han'guk Kidokkyo ŭi yŏksa, 1* [A History of the Korean Church, 1] (Seoul: Christian Literature Press, 1989), 55–115; Timothy S. Lee, "A Political Factor in the Rise of Protestantism in Korea: Protestantism and the 1919 May First Movement," *Church History* 69, no. 1 (March 2000): 116–142.

6. Han'guk Kidokkyo yŏksa yŏn'guso, *Han'guk Kidokkyo ŭi yŏksa, 1*, 242–243.

7. Yi Kwangsu, "Kŭmil Chosŏn yasokyohoe ŭi kyŏlch'ŏm" [Shortcomings of Today's Christian Church], *Ch'ŏngch'un* [Youth], November 1917, quoted in An Pyŏnguk, "Kidokkyo wa minjok sasang" [Christianity and National Thought], in *Han'guk ŭi kŭndaehwa wa Kidokkyo* [Modernization of Korea and Christianity], ed. Han'guk kidokkyo munhwa yŏnguso (Seoul: Sungjŏn Taehak Ch'ulpansa, 1983), 77–78.

8. Han'guk Kidokkyo yŏksa yŏn'guso, *Han'guk Kidokkyo ŭi yŏksa, 1*, 62–265; Lee, "Political Factor," 127–128.

9. Korean historians now call it "the 105-man incident" (*paegoin sagŏn*); it was a frame-up by the Japanese colonial government.

10. A detailed analysis of church growth as related to Korean nationalism, especially expressed during the March First Independence Movement, was succinctly made by Timothy Lee; see Lee, "Political Factor," 130–141.

11. Japan's modernization efforts in Korea during the colonial domination was explained in detail by Stephan Haggard and Chung-in Moon, "The State, Politics, and Economic Development in Postwar South Korea," *State and Society in Contemporary Korea*, ed. Hagen Koo (Ithaca, N.Y.: Cornell University Press, 1993), 57–59.

12. Tak Myŏnghwan, *Han'guk ŭi sinhŭng chonggyo* [New Religions of Korea] (Seoul: Sŏngch'ŏngsa, 1972), 55.

13. Reinhart Bendix, *Nation Building and Citizenship* (New York: Wiley, 1964), 6.

14. Kim Sugon, *Nodong konggŭp kwa sirŭp kujo* [Labor Supply and Unemployment Structure] (Seoul: Han'guk Kaebal Yŏn'guwŏn, 1976), 63.

15. Louis Wirth, "Urbanism as a Way of Life," *American Journal of Sociology* 44 (July 1938).

16. Byong-suh Kim, "Ideology, Conversion, and Faith Maintenance in a Korean Sect: The Case of the Unified Family of Rev. Sun Myung Moon," in *Koreans in America*, ed. Association of Korean Christian Scholars in America (Memphis, Tenn.: KCS Press, 1977), 6–59.

17. Han'guk Kidokkyo yŏksa yŏn'guso, *Han'guk Kidokkyo ŭi yŏksa, 1*, 222–225.

18. Yi Wŏn'gyu, "Han'gul kyohoe ŭi sŏngjang," 17.

19. Ibid., 18.

20. Ibid.

21. H. B. Koh, "Factors to Influence the Church Growth Based on the Leadership Training of New Believers" (Ph.D. diss., Methodist Seminary, Seoul, 1993), 76.

22. Han'guk kaellŏp [Gallup Korea], *Han'gugin ŭi chonggyo wa chonggyo ŭisik* [Koreans' Religions and Religious Consciousness] (Seoul: Han'guk kaellŏp, 1998), 148.

CHAPTER 15

Beleaguered Success
Korean Evangelicalism in the Last Decade of the Twentieth Century

Timothy S. Lee

At the beginning of the twentieth century, Christians constituted less than 1 percent of the Korean population.[1] By the end of the century, according to a 1995 survey by the South Korean Statistics Office, Christians constituted 26.3 percent of the South Korean population, surpassing Buddhists, the next largest religious group, at 23.3 percent. In 1997, according to another major study, Christianity's numerical edge over Buddhism was even larger—27.4 percent versus 18.3 percent. In both these studies, Protestants constitute the vast majority of Korean Christians: 75 percent of the Christian population (or 19.7 percent of the entire population) in the 1995 survey (with the remaining 6.6 percent Catholic) and 73 percent of the Christian population (20.3 percent of the entire population) in the 1997 survey (with the remaining 7.4 percent Catholics).[2] What these statistics obscure, however, is that within Korean Protestantism itself there exist two main subgroups—Evangelicals and, for lack of a better term, non-Evangelicals—and that between them, Evangelicals predominate by a margin even larger than that between Protestants and Catholics.

Throughout Korean Christian history, non-Evangelical Protestants have played and continue to play vital roles. This was the case especially during the 1970s and 1980s, when liberal Protestants created the Minjung Theology[3] and took the lead in opposing political dictatorships. Even so, in terms of numbers and church influence, Evangelicals overshadow their non-Evangelical counterparts. In fact, Evangelicalism so predominates the Korean church, its success or growth so influences Korean Protestantism as a whole, that Evangelicalism and Protestantism are more or less synonymous in Korea.

That Evangelicalism grew phenomenally in (South) Korea from the early 1960s to the end of the 1980s is well known. And in the face of statistics like the above, one might suppose that such a success persisted all the way through the end of the century—that the 1990s, no less than the previous decades, was an unqualifiedly triumphant one for Korean Evangelicalism. Such a hypothesis, however, would scarcely be supported by the actual history of the period. For in the 1990s, Korean Evangelicalism underwent a much more ambiguous and troubling development. Indeed, in the last decade of the twentieth century, Korean Evangelicalism—in spite of significant successes it enjoyed in areas such as civil society, politics, and economy—was a beleaguered religion, beleaguered by a stalemated growth, scandals involving its prominent members, and challenges posed by other religions of Korea. Substantiating this thesis is the object of this chapter.

Evangelical Predominance in Korean Protestantism

Evangelicalism is broadly defined here to include movements more specifically known as Fundamentalism and Pentecostalism—as a species of Protestantism characterized by a literalist bent in biblical interpretation, a soteriology that values the individual over society, fervent advocacy of evangelism, and a piety that emphasizes conversion experience and personal relationship between God and believer, relegating rituals such as baptism and communion to a secondary place. In Evangelicalism, salvation is typically achieved through conversion, wherein one accepts Jesus Christ as personal savior and resolves to live in accordance with the Gospel.[4]

It is well known among students of Korean Christianity that Evangelicalism predominates in Korean Protestantism, so much so that it is often simply taken as axiomatic, with very little discussion as to why that is the case. Therefore, for the sake of clarity, as well as to illustrate the validity of the axiom, I will start the discussion by demonstrating that Korean Protestantism is indeed predominantly Evangelical.

There are a number of ways to make this point. One is by examining the piety of the first missionaries who laid the foundations for the Protestant faith in Korea. Numerous authors—such as L. George Paik, Min Kyoungbae, and Everett N. Hunt Jr.—have already researched this issue and have found the missionaries to be decidedly Evangelical.[5] Here, it suffices merely to cite the following oft-quoted remark by Arthur J. Brown, who, at the beginning of the twentieth century, frequented Korea as secretary of the Foreign Mission Board of the Northern Presbyterian Church:

> The typical missionary of the first quarter century after the opening of the country was a man of the Puritan type. He kept the Sabbath as our New

England forefathers did a century ago. He looked upon dancing, smoking, and card-playing as sins in which no true follower of Christ should indulge. In theology and biblical criticism he was strongly conservative, and he held as a vital truth the premillenarian view of the Second Coming of Christ. The higher criticism and liberal theology were deemed dangerous heresies.[6]

The prominence of revivalism—a hallmark of Evangelical faith everywhere—serves as further evidence that Evangelicalism has predominated in Korean Protestant history, an understandable development given that the missionaries themselves were from revivalist tradition and sought to replicate that tradition in Korea. Indeed, ever since Korea's Great Revival in 1907, revival meetings have thrived and come to characterize Korean Protestantism, leading some historians to mistake them as a unique trait of the Korean church.[7] Eventually a distinct tradition of Korean revivalism emerged, with the likes of Kil Sŏnju, Yi Yongdo, and Kim Iktu paralleling American Evangelists Charles Finney, Dwight Moody, and Billy Sunday in the ways they set the tone of the church. Moreover, since the 1960s, the Korean church has ceased to be an epigone of American Evangelicalism and has become a leader of international revivalism in its own right, holding some of the largest revival gatherings ever held in Christian history—including the mammoth World Evangelization Crusade of 1980, which reportedly recorded more than seventeen million in attendance.[8]

Another kind of evidence relevant to this discussion are surveys that seek to determine where Korean Protestants stand with respect to several key beliefs in Evangelicalism, such as the conversion experience, the inerrancy of the Bible, and the attitude toward other religions. In doing this, we are fortunate to have two major studies: *Han'guk kyohoe 100-nyŏn chonghap chosa yŏn'gu* (Centennial Comprehensive Study of the Korean [Protestant] Church) (*CCSKC* hereafter), by the Christian Institute for the Study of Justice and Development, and *Hyŏndae kyohoe sŏngjang kwa sinang yangt'ae e kwanhan chosa yŏn'gu* (An Investigation into the Growth and Religiosity of the Korean [Protestant] Church) (*IGRKC*), by the Institute for the Study of Modern Society.[9] Both surveys, published in 1982, directed questions to two sample populations—the South Korean clergy and the laity. Their results indicate that an Evangelical ethos suffused the Korean Protestant church.

In one question, for example, the *IGRKC* asked whether having the experience of the Holy Spirit was essential for salvation, which was in reality another way of asking if the conversion experience was necessary for salvation since a Holy Spirit experience either entails or presupposes a conversion experience.[10] To this question, the response was overwhelmingly in the affirmative. Of the 160 sampled clergy, 73 percent affirmed the absolute necessity of conversion experience; 26.4 percent, its desirability; and only .06 percent (1 minister), its superfluity. Of the 1,257 sampled laypersons, 58.5 percent affirmed its absolute necessity; 35.9 percent, its desirability; and only 5.5 percent, its superfluity or their uncertainty about the answer. Thus, it stands to reason that in the early 1980s, the majority of the laity and even larger majority of the clergy in Korean Protestantism regarded the Holy Spirit experience (conversion experience) to be absolutely necessary, and almost all of them regarding it as desirable. The *CCSKC* corroborated these findings. When asked whether they had felt the certainty of salvation, participants in the survey responded overwhelming in the affirmative: 773 (98.2 percent) of the 787 clergy and 1,854 (93.1 percent) of the 1,991 laity.[11] Since it is the certainty of salvation that is sought in conversion experience, the evidential value of this result is clear.

Another essential doctrine in Evangelicalism pertains to the inerrancy of the Bible. Missionaries and Korean church leaders alike have held fast to, and vigorously disseminated, this doctrine. In 1914, for example, a missionary wrote the following:

> The missionary body of Korea has as a whole been characterized by an unreserved acceptance of the Bible as the truth of God, believing the poetical parts are divinely inspired songs; the historical parts are accurate accounts of what happened to actual persons, not relegating Adam to the myths and Abraham to the shades, nor putting Job and Jonah in a class with Jack and Jill.... In spite of the strong tide of destructive criticism there has been little wavering in the teaching of the Word in Korea. The Korea missions consider that the Bible is to be accepted as a whole, and is not like a moth-eaten bolt of cloth, from which may be cut, according to human will and judgment, here and there, a usable remnant.[12]

Largely because of the influence of missionaries such as this author and the Korean church leaders who shared his sentiments, biblical inerrancy has reigned supreme in Korean Protestantism.[13] This was reflected in the *CCSKC*, where 84.9 percent of the clergy and 92.3 percent of the laity affirmed that they believed every word of the Bible to be God-inspired and, hence, unerring. A belief in the inerrancy of the Bible also means believing in the corollaries that accompany that principle. Thus on the issue of the veracity of the virgin birth of Christ, according to the *CCSKC*, 97.0 percent of the clergy and 95.6 percent of the laity answered affirmatively. On their acceptance of biblical miracles, 94.5 percent of the *CCSKC* clergy and 95.6 percent of the laity gave positive responses. Similarly, the *IGRKC* found 89.3 percent of the clergy and 84.5 percent of the laity responding in the affirmative on the same issue.

On the existence of afterlife, the *CCSKC* found 98.4 percent of the clergy and 91.6 percent of the laity believing in it. On the resurrection of Jesus, according to the *CCSKC*, 91.5 percent of the clergy and 70.5 percent of the laity held it to mean that Jesus' dead body had come back to life (as opposed to holding a more allegorical meaning of it). As to eschatology, the *CCSKC* showed that 98.3 percent of the clergy and 94.8 percent of the laity affirmed their belief in Christ's return; finally, of the clergy and laity, 95.4 percent and 89.1 percent, respectively, believed Jesus' return to be imminent.

Another well-known trait of Evangelicalism is its exclusivist soteriology, the belief that there is no salvation outside Christianity, if not Evangelicalism. This trait was borne out by the *CCSKC*. To the question "What do you think of other religions?" the pluralist response—that the truth of other religions was just as valid as that of Christianity—received the least percentage: 4.7 percent of the clergy and 8.8 percent of the laity. The percentage was higher for a somewhat more inclusive response—that Christianity's truth is superior—20.7 percent for the clergy and 25.0 percent for the laity. The exclusivist response that only Christianity's truth is valid received the highest percentages: 70.9 percent for the clergy and 62.6 percent for the laity. Unfortunately, the *CCSKC* and the *IGRKC* did not conduct similar surveys during the 1990s. There is, however, another major study on Korean Protestant religiosity that was conducted in 1997: *Han'guk kaesin'gyoin ŭi kyohoe hwaltong kwa sinang ŭisik* (Korean Protestants' Churchly Activities and Religious Consciousness) by Gallup Korea.[14] This survey, concerned with broader issues than those of the *CCSKC* and the *IGRKC*, did not ask some of the significant questions posed in the earlier studies, such as those concerning the inerrancy of the Bible or the essentiality of the Holy Spirit (born-again) experience. Still, some of its questions were revealing: such as whether the respondents had accepted Jesus Christ as their personal savior (73.2 percent said yes), had experienced the Holy Spirit (52 percent, yes), were certain of their salvation (67.9 percent, yes), believed in the end of the world (68.9 percent, yes), believed in the return of Jesus (80.7 percent, yes), and believed in the possibility of salvation in other religions (24.5 percent, yes).[15]

These findings, when compared with those of the 1980s studies, suggest that Korean Evangelicalism had lost some ground in the 1990s. Granted, one should not read too much into some of these figures, such as those relating to the Holy Spirit experience and the certainty of salvation, since even a respondent who had not experienced them may nonetheless consider them essential, in which case the respondent (methodologically speaking) would still qualify as an Evangelical. Overall, it is clear that even while Evangelical religiosity diminished somewhat in the 1990s, the Evangelical ethos for the most part continued to predominate in the Korean Protestant church.

With that point granted, one faces a specific question: what percentage of Korean Protestants and their churches is Evangelical? Since, to my knowledge, there is no survey that directly addresses this issue,[16] an answer must be estimated, for example, by determining the percentage of respondents in similar surveys who embrace attributes deemed Evangelical. Extrapolating from the results of the *IGRKC* and the *CCSKC*, one can estimate that in the early 1980s, well over 90 percent of Korean Protestants were solidly Evangelical; and an extrapolation from the Gallup Korea survey would indicate that near the end of the 1990s at least 75 percent of all Korean Protestants were solidly Evangelical.[17]

The question of what percentage of Korean Protestant churches are Evangelical also has to be answered in an estimate, for there appears to be no published survey that directly addresses this question, either. However, if these churches' individual religious orientation is difficult to determine, the religious orientation of the denominations most of them belong to is well known, making it possible to surmise how many of the churches are Evangelical or non-Evangelical. In South Korea, there are three non-Evangelical Protestant denominations—the Episcopal Church, the Lutheran Church, and the openly liberal Presbyterian denomination known as Taehan Kijang Changno Kyohoe (the Presbyterian Church in the Republic of Korea). It is more or less safe to say that all the other Protestant denominations are Evangelical. According to *The Christian Yearbook of Korea: 1991*, these three non-Evangelical churches possessed 1,359 churches in 1990—about 4 percent of the total.[18] This figure concurs with the minimum 90 percent estimate for the Evangelicals based on the findings of the *IGRKC* and the *CCSKC* in the 1980s.

The Christian Yearbook ceased publication after the 1991 edition, but according to a figure cited in the Gallup Korea survey mentioned above, there were 1,565 churches from these three denominations in 1997, or about 5 percent of all the Protestant churches in Korea.[19] Conversely, this indicates that toward the end of the 1990s, 95 percent of all Korean Protestant churches were Evangelical. This figure appears to conflict with the estimate based on the Gallup Korea survey that suggests as low as 75 percent for the proportion of Evangelicals in the Korean Protestant church in the 1990s. In actuality, however, there is no conflict here since a church as an institution may hold to a certain orientation even if some of its members do not. Either way, the point that clearly emerges from this estimation is that institutionally, as well as individually, Korean Protestantism in the 1990s was predominantly Evangelical. For this reason, I will use "Evangelical" and "Protestant" interchangeably in the rest of this chapter.

Evangelicalism as South Korea's Most Successful Religion in the 1990s

South Korea is a religiously pluralistic society, in which no single religion absolutely dominates. Still, if success is defined as "the attainment of wealth, position, honors, or the like," there is no denying that some religions succeed more than others.[20] In 1990s South Korea, Evangelicalism was that religion. An initial case for this claim can be made on the basis of a finding by the 1997 Gallup Korea survey: 53.2 percent of the nonbelievers surveyed stated that the Protestant church's influence in the society was on the increase, whereas similar figures for the Buddhist church and the Catholic Church were 40.6 percent and 43.0 percent, respectively.[21] Of course, such a finding alone is not persuasive enough. Nevertheless, a much stronger, even indisputable, case can be made for this claim if we examine how much influence the Protestant church, or Evangelicalism, wielded in some key areas of the Korean society during the decade—namely, civil society, politics, and economy—especially in comparison with other religions.

Civil society as a historical category has been used to mean a series of societal developments that occurred in the West, accompanying the rise of capitalism and the bourgeoisie. As a substantive category, the term has little applicability outside the West; the term, however, has also been used analytically, to mean, for instance, "realms of organized social life that is voluntary, self-generating, (largely) self-supporting, autonomous from the state, and bound by a legal order or set of shared rules."[22] In this sense, the concept is very much applicable to South Korea—and to Evangelicalism—and admits of the claim that a significant portion of the South Korean civil society of the 1990s consisted of Evangelicalism and that of all the religions, Evangelicalism had the most effect on this realm.

This claim can be attested in part by the sheer size and extent of the Evangelical church, which undeniably is "organized social life that is voluntary, self-generating, (largely) self-supporting, and autonomous from the state." As already noted, according to the Gallup Korea study, by 1997 the percentage of Korean Protestants in proportion to the general population surpassed that of Buddhists, the next largest group, by 20.3 percent to 18.3 percent, and of Catholics, which registered 7.4 percent. When it comes to the number of churches, however, the Protestants were ahead much earlier: in 1990, they were reported to have 34,407 churches to 9,231 of the Buddhists, and 844 of the Catholics. The number of the clergy reported for that year was 58,288 for the Protestants; 25,205 for the Buddhists; and 7,640 for the Catholics.[23] Six years later, the gap widened, with Protestant churches numbering 58,046, to the Buddhists' 11,561 and the Catholics' 1,019.

Protestant clergy was numbered at 98,905, compared to the Buddhists' 26,037 and the Catholics' 10,151.[24]

The Protestant predominance was noticeable in less churchly institutions as well. In 1995, the Protestants counted 174 incorporated foundations and associations, to the Buddhists' 75 and the Catholics' 70.[25] In 1996, sixty-nine institutions of higher education (colleges, junior colleges, universities, and seminaries) belonged to the Protestants, as opposed to a mere two for the Buddhists, and twelve for the Catholics. In the same year, the Protestants published 111 periodicals, to the Buddhists' 27 and the Catholics' 71.[26] A 1985 study found that 391 (61 percent) of 637 faith-based welfare agencies—homes for the elderly, orphanages, medical centers, vocational centers, and the like—were Protestant; a 2001 study found that 225 out of 440 such agencies (66 percent) were Protestant.[27] Evangelicals, therefore, must have operated 61 to 66 percent of all faith-based social welfare agencies in the 1990s. More specifically, a movement to donate organs began in South Korea in 1991. Ten years and 570 transplants later, it was reported that 65.4 percent of the donors were Protestants, compared with 7.8 percent for the Buddhists and 7.3 percent for the Catholics.[28] Finally, as Professor Yi Mahnyŏl notes in his chapter in this volume, when the North Korean famine began in the 1990s, Protestants constituted the first South Korean civilian group to initiate relief efforts, sending, between April 3, 1997, and November 7, 2002, aid in the amount of 29 billion 260 thousand won, or approximately $24,330,000.[29]

Politics was also an arena where South Korean Evangelicals exerted a disproportionately large share of influence during the 1990s. In fact, the 1990s saw a rise in the political influence of the entire Korean Christian community, for Catholics also garnered considerable political clout during that decade, attested by the presidency of Kim Dae Jung (1998–2003), a devout Catholic. Even so, the lion's share of political influence lay with the Protestants. This was in part due to their strong presence in the South Korean government in the 1990s, most notably Kim Young Sam, a Presbyterian elder who served as president of South Korea from 1993 to 1998. Protestants also dominated his administration: out of 175 ministers and vice-ministers, seventy-six (about 43 percent) were Protestants. By comparison, the number of Buddhists in the administration was twenty-seven (15 percent); of Catholics, forty-seven (29 percent); and of nonbelievers, twenty-five (about 14 percent).[30]

It was not only in the executive branch that the Protestants enjoyed plurality; the same situation prevailed in the National Assembly, where they constituted about half the members.[31] In the first half of Kim Dae Jung's administration, too, Protestants were well represented. For example, although Kim himself is a Catholic, his influential wife, Lee Hee Ho, is a Methodist. Moreover, according to a Buddhist study conducted in 2000, of the top hundred governmental positions that year, including the presidency, Protestants occupied 42; Buddhists, 9; Catholics, 20; members of other religions, 3; and nonbelievers, 26.[32] Another study found that in the National Assembly that same year, 207 of 273 members professed a religion, and of these 107 (39 percent of the entire assembly) were Protestants; 30 (11 percent) were Buddhists; and 69 (25 percent) were Catholics.[33] A 1998 nationwide election of regional officials—governors, mayors, and similar offices—countered the trend of a Protestant ascendance in politics, as more Buddhists (82 out of a total of 228, or about 36 percent) were elected than Protestants (58 or 25 percent), Catholics (28 or 12 percent), or nonbelievers (60 or about 26 percent).[34] This result qualifies overall Evangelical influence in South Korean politics, but not enough to undermine their preponderance.

All in all, these figures alone are sufficient to make the point that Evangelicals were the most influential religious group in 1990s' South Korean politics. But that point becomes even more apparent when we examine the influence they displayed in the presidential elections of 1992 and 1997. In the 1992 election, none of the three top candidates—Kim Young Sam, Kim Dae Jung, and Chung Ju Yung (the founder of Hyundai)—received a majority of the votes.[35] Considering that regionalism was a factor in this election as in all elections in South Korea and that Kim Young Sam's home base, Kyŏngsang province, is one of the least Christianized provinces in the country, there is little doubt that his being an elder of Ch'unghyŏn Presbyterian Church, the flagship church of the largest Presbyterian denomination (Hapdong) in Korea, was a decisive factor in his attracting Evangelical votes from all over the country and winning the election.[36] Indeed, during this election, the Evangelicals mobilized on behalf of their favorite son. Ch'unghyŏn Presbyterian Church, for example, formed a group of elders specifically to canvass for Kim, and Evangelical churches all over the country held gatherings to pray for the election of an Elder for president.[37] In response, Kim promised that if elected, he would see to it that "hymns would continuously ring out from the Blue House."[38] Consequently, according to *K'ŭrisch'an sinmun*, South Korea's leading Protestant weekly, over 90 percent of the Evangelicals voted for Kim Young Sam in that election.[39]

The Evangelical prowess displayed in the 1992 election was not lost on the candidates running in the 1997 presidential election. Among the contenders was Kim Jong Pil, an archconservative and a Methodist deacon. In his case, though, religious affiliation was of little help: his infamous political opportunism and sordid ties with past dictators repulsed even the Evangelicals. The two main contenders were Kim Dae Jung and Yi Hoech'ang, both Catholics. Given these choices, the Evangelicals, unlike in the previous election, did not heap special attention on any particular candidate.[40] The reverse, however, was not the case: Yi, both Kims, and other candidates made a point of courting the Evangelicals by canvassing churches and visiting with the pastors. They paid special attention to so-called kingmakers such as Cho "David" Yonggi, minister of Yŏido Full Gospel Church, the world's largest single church, and Kim "Billy" Chang-hwan, president of Kŭkdong Pangsong, an influential Evangelical broadcast network.[41] At their interviews on the Kŭkdong Pangsong, for example, the candidates took care to comment about their faith. Kim Jong Pil, in his interview, said, "There aren't many countries that are more earnest than ours in believing in God and seeking to share the Gospel. I hope we will live out this spirit and faith in all our lives"; Yi Hoech'ang recited his favorite biblical verses, Isaiah 43:1–3, from memory, and stated that whenever faced with difficulties, he had depended on God; Kim Dae Jung trumped them both by saying that in his life thus far he had experienced five near-death incidents, six years of imprisonment, and ten years of exile, and in the midst of it all he had personally experienced and seen God twice.[42] In the end, it is more likely that the Asian currency crisis had more to do with Kim Dae Jung's election than his ability to play to Protestant sensibilities. Nevertheless, that Kim continued to hold the Protestants in high regard was displayed at a prayer gathering he attended before he left for the Blue House, with three hundred or so Protestant leaders in attendance, in which he asked for Christians to pray for the nation and to "display the Puritan spirit in particular so as to overcome the collapsed economy."[43]

Aside from politics and civil society, economy is another crucial realm of society. In this realm, Evangelicalism's influence in the 1990s appears to have been less pronounced than in the others; nevertheless, it was still strong enough to surpass that of the other religions. A prima facie case for this claim can be made this way: South Korea is an urban society, with most of the wealth concentrated in the cities, where Protestants tend to live. According to the South Korean National Statistics Office, in 1995 Protestants constituted over 25 percent of the population in the Seoul metropolitan region. Moreover, they constituted over 30 percent of the population in the wealthiest districts of Seoul, Kangnam-gu and Sŏch'o-gu.[44] Thus, it is plausible to assume that in the 1990s, Protestants possessed more wealth and wielded more influence in the economy than any other religionists in Korea.

Buttressing this argument are the following, more concrete, pieces of evidence. A 1995 study by a research affiliate of the leading daily *Joong ang ilbo* analyzed the religions of 4,903 chief executive officers of 4,076 private enterprises in South Korea and found that 34 percent (1,667) professed a religion. Of these religious CEOs, about 42.8 percent (713) were Protestant; 38.3 percent (638), Buddhists; 17 percent (280), Catholic; and the remaining about 2 percent (36), believers of other religions.[45] This study also reported that of the top ten *chaebŏls* (presidents of conglomerates) in 1995, three were Protestants (one of them an Episcopalian), another three Buddhists, one Confucian, and three nonbelievers.[46] Another study found that of the presidents of the top hundred Korean businesses in 1999, thirty-one were Protestants, twenty-three Buddhists, eleven Catholics, and twenty-nine nonbelievers.[47]

A Beleaguered Evangelicalism

The picture should now be clear: Evangelicalism was South Korea's most successful religion in the 1990s. This picture, however, tells only half the story, and the other half is not very pretty—at least for Evangelicals. For if the 1990s was a decade of preponderant (though not quite hegemonic) sway for the Evangelicals, the decade was also a one of beleaguerment for them: the period when the growth of their churches slowed, scandals involving some of their high-profile members shocked the public, and open conflict arose between them and other religious groups.

Analyzing census figures collected by the National Statistics Office, sociologist of religion Lee Won Gue observed that between 1991 and 1995, membership in the Korean Protestant church increased from 8,037,464 to 8,760,336—a gain of 9 percent.[48] No Ch'ichun, another leading sociologist of religion, estimates a 4 percent growth rate between 1990 and 1995.[49] He also notes that growth rates in 1994 and 1995 for the two largest denominations, Yejang Hapdong and Yejang T'onghap, whose combined memberships constitute about half of the total Protestant membership, was less than 1 percent.

Had this kind of development been noted with regard to the Protestant churches in Europe or the United States, where church memberships have been sliding for decades, not much alarm would have been sounded. However, it did arouse concern in South Korea—home to twenty-three of the fifty largest churches in the world, including five out of the top ten largest churches.[50] The slowdown represented a departure from earlier trends: between 1960 and 1970 the membership in Evangelical churches grew by 412.4 percent (from 623,072 to 3,192,621); by 56.7 percent between 1970 and 1977; by 29.7 percent between 1977 and 1985; and by 23.9 percent between 1985 and 1991.[51] As far as I am aware, there has not yet been a thorough statistical study of this decline in the 1990s to determine, in particular, if this decline actually dipped to negative numbers. Nevertheless, it is clear that there is now widespread concern among Korean Evangelical leaders over the possibility, if not the probability, that no more growth lies ahead in the near future.[52]

This decline has exacerbated some long-standing problems in Korean Evangelicalism. One such problem has been the diminishment of respect for Evangelical ministers, especially new seminary graduates in search of pastorates. This diminishment of respect has been due, in part, to the seminaries' producing too many graduates, many of whom were ill prepared for the role of church leader—many of whom in any case could not be absorbed by either existing congregations or newly established churches. Even well-established seminaries, such as those belonging to the two largest Presbyterian denominations, tended to recruit more students than actually needed by their congregations—partly for financial reasons, since student tuition was their main source of revenue. But the more serious reason lay with the overabundance of nonaccredited and poorly equipped theological institutions that produced a slew of poorly trained graduates annually. In 1995, for example, there were more than 310 theological institutions in Korea, of which the Ministry of Education accredited only 38.[53] In total, these theological institutions produced about eight thousand graduates every year in the 1990s, and since only about a thousand of them graduated from the seminaries of the six well-established denominations, the majority were the products of accredited but poorly equipped seminaries or, worse, of unaccredited institutions—in either case, ill equipped to minister to a highly educated society.

Much of the church growth in South Korea before 1990 resulted from new seminary graduates striking out on their own and founding new congregations in unevangelized areas. By the 1990s, however, churches saturated the country, and it became increasingly difficult for new ministers to found pastorates. Many seminarians, as a result, opted for overseas work as missionaries, swelling the number of their ranks to more than ten thousand at the end of the decade, putting the Korean church second only to its United States counterpart in the number of missionaries it sent abroad.[54] Those seminarians who did not go overseas had no choice but to compete in the domestic religious marketplace, jostling with those already ensconced in churches for members.[55] The demeanor the clergy exuded in such competitions undoubtedly smacked more often of hucksterism than sacrificial devotion. Such behavior is a likely reason that the 1997 Gallup Korea study found that of all its respondents, 71.1 percent thought the Protestant church to be more interested in increasing its size and influence than in seeking truth, as opposed to 33.8 percent for the Buddhists and 32.1 percent for the Catholics. It may also be the reason that in a 1995 Gallup Korea poll on the "honesty and professional ethics of Korean professionals," 1,564

Korean men and women aged twenty or older rated the minister fifth. Ahead of the minister were the Catholic priest (first), the university professor (second), the Buddhist monk (third), and the television reporter/ announcer (fourth). In a similar survey conducted in 1993, the minister was not even in the top five.[56]

The ministers' lack of proper theological education and their preoccupation with membership numbers were not the only problems to face the Evangelical church in the 1990s. It was also bedeviled by a series of scandals involving some of its high-profile members. The first of these involved a millenarian, or rapture, controversy that reached its height in late 1992. At the center of it was the Reverend Yi Changnim, who since the 1980s had been predicting an end to the world on October 28, 1992, and who maintained that only those who adhered to his teachings would be saved, lifted up to heaven, and met by a returning Christ. To the utter bewilderment of most Koreans, including the Evangelicals, fifteen hundred or so of his followers prepared to abandon the world, selling their property and severing ties with unbelieving families. Most Evangelical leaders promptly dissociated themselves from Yi and branded him a heretic, but it is questionable whether the public was as quick to dissociate them from Yi, since between the two, theologically speaking, much more was alike than different. The rapture, of course, never came, and Yi was arrested for committing fraud: the police discovered that he had been collecting money from his followers—resorting to extortion in some cases—and investing some of it in a bond that would not mature until well after October 28, 1992.[57]

Other scandals followed. On June 29, 1995, the upscale, five-story Sampoong Department Store in Seoul's posh Kangnam district collapsed, killing 501 and injuring 937. Seoul residents had witnessed the collapse of shoddily constructed buildings before, but never one of this magnitude.[58] Residents later became angry upon learning that the building's owner—a deacon at Youngnak Presbyterian Church, Korea's most prestigious Presbyterian church—had allowed it to stand despite obvious signs of imminent collapse.

In another instance, after Hanbo Steel filed for bankruptcy in January 1997, it became known that the company had been bribing numerous public officials in an attempt to remain solvent. In the course of the subsequent investigation, President Kim Young Sam's son Hyŏnch'ŏl was implicated. Soon after, it came to light that even though he had no official authority, the son had been deeply involved in policy decisions at the Blue House and in peddling influence. This abuse of power at the highest level of government enraged the public, which supported the judge who sentenced the president's Evangelical son to three years' imprisonment.[59] The "Hanbo incident" proved to be a nightmare for Kim Young Sam in other ways as well, for it was followed by a series of developments that ultimately resulted in what Koreans call the IMF crisis. And the president's inability to handle this economic crisis completely undermined his reputation, such that in the last year of his term, even his own church did not welcome him.[60]

Then there was the "Northern Wind Operation" or the "Amalek Strategy." This refers to a scheme concocted by Kwŏn Yŏnghae, Kim Young Sam's appointed director of the Agency for National Security Planning (NSP) (formerly the Korean Central Intelligence Agency). He loathed Kim Dae Jung's politics and, during the 1997 election, sought to taint Kim by portraying him as being under the influence of the North.[61] When the scheme was found out, Kwŏn attempted to commit hara-kiri. Although the Korean public knows of this conspiracy as the Northern Wind Operation (*pukp'ung chakchŏn*), Kwŏn himself preferred to call it the Amalek Strategy, seeing himself as the Moses who would vanquish the evil Amalekites that stood in the way of God's people. It was not surprising that he would pick a reference from the Hebrew scriptures: he, like the president, was an Evangelical elder and avid Bible reader.[62]

Finally there came the "Dress Lobby" (*ot lobi*), a bribery scandal involving three self-avowed Evangelical women who attended Bible study at the same church, and their clothier. Two of the women were wives of high government officials; a third was wife of a *chaebŏl*—known as a devout Evangelical himself—in trouble with the law for illegally hoarding wealth outside the country. The controversy swirled around mutual accusations between the women as to who was guilty in initiating a bribe in the form of expensive dress purchased from the clothier's shop. Although the court eventually found the wife of the *chaebŏl* guilty, in the course of the investigation the case evolved into something much more complicated and weighty—provoking accusations of a prosecutorial cover-up, exposing problems in the judiciary system, and compelling the government to introduce, for the first time in South Korean history, the office of special prosecutor. The case deeply embarrassed the government and the Evangelicals, but especially the latter, as the women came across as pious hypocrites, mouthing pieties and lies in the same breath—directly contradicting each other in public hearings, even as they swore on the Bible.

These scandals were disconcerting and conflictive enough, but in the 1990s, the Evangelicals also experienced another kind of conflict—between them and other religionists. Although the Evangelicals themselves provoked most of the friction, especially vis-à-vis the Buddhists, by the end of the decade, they found themselves at the other end of the provocation as well.

There is no question that much of this conflict stemmed from Evangelicalism's exclusivist soteriology and the way it demonizes the traditional religions of Korea. The Korean churchman who most starkly expressed such antagonism was perhaps Pak Hyŏngnyong, an influential Fundamentalist theologian who studied under J. Gresham Machen, the paragon of American Fundamentalism. Pak had once asserted, "Christianity's most appropriate relation to other religions is not compromise but conquest.... The attitude of the religion that bears the name of Jesus Christ [to other religions] is not compromise but clash and conquest."[63]

Apparently, some Evangelicals took Pak's message literally. In June 1998, for example, an Evangelical man broke into a Zen center in Cheju Island, decapitated 750 granite Buddha statues, and destroyed other religious objects. When under arrest, he confessed to attempting to convert the temple into a church. Disturbing as it was, this was not an isolated incident, nor was it the most heinous: on several occasions antagonistic Evangelicals burned entire Buddhist temples to the ground.[64]

It is to the Buddhists' credit that none of them have been reported to have retaliated in kind, at least not yet. However, incivility breeds incivility; and if not the Buddhists, then other religious or semireligious groups were quick to learn from the Evangelicals' unilateral, uncivil tactics. A prime example is the conduct of the Hanmunhwa undonghoe (Korean Cultural Campaigns Association; KCCA), a coalition of religious and semireligious organizations that erected a statue of Tan'gun, Korea's mythical founder, in 369 Korean public schools in 1998 and 1999 and declared its determination to erect one in every other public school in Korea.[65] The KCCA's rationale is that since all Koreans recognize—or should recognize—Tan'gun as their national founder, if children grew up paying honor to his statues in the schools, national unity would be enhanced.

In reality, however, the Tan'gun statues have engendered divisiveness. The statues infuriated the Evangelicals, who condemned them as idols, pointing correctly to the fact that a number of indigenous religions worship Tan'gun as a deity.[66] They also questioned the constitutionality of the KCCA's action, since they believed that requiring students to pay obeisance to the statues amounted to infringing on their religious freedom. To the Tan'gunists' contention that inasmuch as the statues were set in place with the principals' permission, due process was observed, the Evangelicals retorted that an endeavor as grave as the KCCA's should not have been left to the discretion of the principals. The Evangelicals called on the government to remove the statutes immediately. Not getting satisfaction, some of them took matters into their own hands, assaulting and damaging many of the statues, thereby provoking an accusation from the Tan'gunists that they were less than true patriots.[67]

Although they denounced the Tan'gunists, in the end the Evangelicals oddly mirrored them. Like the Evangelicals, the Tan'gunists were on a quest, although theirs was carried out in the name of Korean nationalism, and aimed at solidifying a national identity that they alleged had become diluted as a result of alien influences such as Evangelicalism. Moreover, the Tan'gunists are similarly convinced of the rightness of their quest, and are unwilling to relent. Hence, the Evangelicals' beleaguerment in this regard persists.

Afterword

Conflict with other religionists, scandals that besmirched the church, apparent stagnation in the growth of the membership—these problems as well as the successes of the 1990s—such as being the numerically largest religious institution and wielding preponderant influence in the civil society, politics, and economy of the land—indicate that Korean Evangelicalism started the twenty-first century in a very different mode than it started the twentieth. Then, Korean society was in shambles, and the church was barely in society, and was not yet of it. A great many Koreans expected that the church would be leavening for the common good. A hundred years later, the Korean Evangelicals have to decide whether that expectation has been met. However they decide, this much is clear: in the twenty-first century, Evangelicalism is not only in Korean society but also of it.[68]

NOTES

1. David B. Barrett et al., *World Christian Encyclopedia,* 2nd ed. (Oxford and New York: Oxford University Press, 2002), vol. 1, p. 682.

2. Gallup Korea, *Han'gugin ŭi chonggyo wa chonggyo ŭisik* [Koreans' Religion and Religious Consciousness] (Seoul: Gallup Korea, 1998). According to this study, in 1997, 20.3 percent of Koreans professed to be Protestant, 18.3 percent Buddhist, and 7.4 percent Roman Catholic. On the other hand, a 1995 census report by the South Korean National Statistics Office found 23.2 percent of South Koreans to be Buddhists, 19.7 percent Protestant, and 6.6 percent Roman Catholic (*1995 In'gu chut'aek ch'ongjosa: ch'oejong chŏnsujipkye kyŏlgwa* [Seoul: T'onggye ch'ŏng, 1995]). There are also two to three thousand who belong to Korean Orthodox Church, but that number was apparently too small to be detected by the census.

3. See Andrew Sung Park, "*Minjung* and *Pungryu* Theologies in Contemporary Korea: A Critical and Comparative Examination" (Ph.D. diss., Graduate Theological Union, 1985). Also see the chapters in this volume by Paul Chang and Wonil Kim.

4. On the general characteristics of Evangelicalism, see George Marsden, *The Encyclopedia of Religion,* ed. Mircea Eliade (New York: Macmillan, 1985), s.v. "Evangelicalism."

5. L. George Paik, *The History of Protestant Missions in Korea, 1832–1910* (1927; repr, Seoul: Yonsei University Press, 1971); Everett N. Hunt Jr., *Protestant Pioneers in Korea* (Maryknoll, N.Y.: Orbis, 1980); Min Kyoung Bae, *Han'guk kidokkyo kyohoesa* [A History of the Korean Christian Church], rev. ed. (Seoul: Yonsei University Press, 1993). Also see my "Born-Again in Korea: The Rise and Character of Revivalism in (South) Korea, 1885–1988" (Ph.D. diss., University of Chicago, 1996).

6. Arthur Judson Brown, *The Mastery of the Far East* (New York: Charles Scribner's Sons, 1919), 540.

7. Ryu Tong-shik [Yu Tong-sik], *Han'guk sinhak ŭi kwangmaek* [Veins in Korean Theology] (Seoul: Chŏnmangsa, 1982), 56.

8. "Two Aspects of an Evangelical Quest to Christianize Korea: Mammoth Crusades and Sectarian Incivility," *Acta Koreana* (July 2002); Kim Chinhwan, *Han'guk kyohoe puhŭng undongsa* [A History of Revival Movements in the Korean Church], rev. ed. (Seoul: Seoul Sŏjŏk, 1993).

9. Han'guk Kidokkyo Sahoe Munje Yŏn'guwŏn [Christian Institute for the Study of Justice and Development], ed., *Han'guk kyohoe 100-nyŏn chonghap chosa yŏn'gu* [Centennial Comprehensive Study of the Korean (Protestant) Church] (Seoul: Han'guk Kidokkyo Sahoe Munje Yŏn'guwŏn, 1982); Hyŏndae Sahoe Yŏn'guso [Institute for the Study of Modern Society], ed., *Han'guk kyohoe sŏngjang kwa sinang yangt'ae e kwan han chosa yŏn'gu* [Investigation into the Growth and Religiosity of the Korean [Protestant] Church] (Seoul: Hyŏndae Sahoe Yŏn'guso, 1982).

10. Hyŏndae Sahoe Yŏn'guso [Institute for the Study of Modern Society], *IGRKC* (Seoul: Hyŏndae Sahoe Yŏn'guso, 1982), 77ff.

11. Han'guk Kidokkyo Sahoe Munje Yŏn'guwŏn [Christian Institute for the Study of Justice and Development], *CCSKC*, 63. As to what constitutes salvation, 74.6 percent of the ministers accepted the definition of it as each individual's going to heaven after death, 17.5 percent as the establishment of the kingdom of God on earth; 7.9 percent failed to respond. The breakdown on the same question for laymen was as follows; 66.9 percent, 29.4 percent, 3.8 percent (*CCSKC*, 64).

12. J. U. Selwyn Toms, *Korea Mission Field* (February 1914). *Korea Mission Field* was a missionary journal published in Korea in the first half of the twentieth century.

13. This, of course, is not to say that no Korean Protestants disputed the doctrine. The most famous disputer in this regard was the Reverend Kim Chae Choon, who in 1953 founded a new denomination, the Presbyterian Church in the Republic of Korea, on liberal principles.

14. On commission by Hanmijun, an organization of Korean Protestant ministers.

15. (Seoul: Durano, 1999), 57.

16. That this question is not addressed may be puzzling to an American scholar of religion, since it seems so basic to understanding Protestantism in the United States, but this may also say something about the nature of Protestantism, or for that matter, Christianity, in (South) Korea: that is, because of the prevalence of an

Evangelical ethos, and the lack of a strong "mainline" tradition, there is little occasion for such a question to arise as a serious issue. Furthermore, given the Evangelicals' numerical superiority over the Catholics and non-Evangelicals, and given their exclusionist theology, there is a much stronger distinction between them in Korea than in the West. A telling example of this is the fact that because of the monopolization by Evangelicals of the standard Korean translation for Christianity, *kidokkyo*, Catholics do not normally use the term to refer to themselves, preferring instead *ch'ŏnjugyo*. The word *kaesin'gyo* specifically means Protestantism, but the Evangelicals do not ordinarily use it as commonly as *kidokkyo* to refer to themselves.

17. This may mean that in the late 1990s, there were more non-Evangelicals in the church than in the 1980s; it could also mean that a higher percentage of Koreans attended the churches primarily for social, rather than normally religious, reasons, or both.

18. This point is supported by the fact that these denominations had 347,977 members, about 3 percent of the total Korean Protestant population for that year. Han Yongje, ed., *The Christian Yearbook of Korea: 1991* (Seoul: Christian Literature Press, 1991), 6:215–216. In 2001 Korean Computer Missions conducted an informal Internet study, based on its Web site visitors' response to the question "Have you had a Holy Spirit experience?" Of the 1,440 visitors, 77 percent (1,110) responded yes. Since 2001 was not far from the 1990s, this finding, albeit ad hoc, corroborates the point that Evangelicals constituted at least 75 percent of Korean Protestants in the 1990s. *Kookmin ilbo*, August 2, 2001.

19. Gallup Korea, *Han'gugin ŭi chonggyo wa chonggyo ŭisik*, 147.

20. *Random House Webster's Unabridged Dictionary*, s.v. "success."

21. Gallup Korea, *Han'gugin ŭi chonggyo wa chonggyo ŭisik*, 462.

22. Larry Diamond, "Rethinking Civil Society: Toward Democratic Consolidation," *Journal of Democracy* 5, no. 3 (1994): 6; quoted by Sunhyuk Kim, "Civil Society in South Korea: From Grand Democracy Movements to Petty Interest Groups?" *Journal of Northeast Asian Studies*, Summer 1996:82–83.

23. Munhwabu (Ministry of Culture), *Han'guk ŭi chongyo hyŏnhwang* [The State of Korean Religions], 1990; cited in *Han'guk chonggyo yŏn'gam, 1993* [A Yearbook of Korean Religions, 1993] (Seoul: Han'guk chonggyosahoe yŏn'guso, 1993), 208.

24. These were figures reported by these religions' denomination as of December 31, 1996. Cited in Gallup Korea, *Hangukin ŭi chonggyowa chonggyo ŭisik*, 198.

25. Munhwa Kwan'gwangbu, Chongmusil [Ministry of Culture and Tourism, Religious Affairs], *Han'guk ŭi chonggyo hyŏnhwang, 1999* [State of Korean Religions, 1999] (Seoul: Munhwa Kwan'gwangbu, 2000).

26. Figures from *Han'guk chonggyo hyŏnhwang*, quoted in *Kŭrisch'an sinmun*, November 30, 1996.

27. Buddhists had 9; Wŏn Buddhists, 57; and Catholics, 180. Kwŏn O'hyŏn, "Han'guk chonggyo hyŏnhwang pogo" [A Report on the State of Korean Religion], in *Midŭm kwa silch'ŏn—onul ŭi chwap'yo* (Faith and Practice—Coordinates for Today) (Seoul: Taewonjŏnsa, 1985), cited in No Ch'i Chun, *Han'guk ŭi kyohoe*

chojik [The Organization of Korean Churches] (Seoul: Minyŏngsa, 1995), 124. *Kookmin ilbo*, July 25, 2001.

28. *Kookmin ilbo*, July 25, 2001.

29. Han'guk Kidokkyo pukhan tongp'o huwŏn yŏnhaphoe; see their Web page: http://www.sharing.net/Board/zboard.phd?id=Accomplishment.

30. *Pulgyo sinmun*, March 21, 2000.

31. *Kŭrisch'an sinmun*, January 11, 1997.

32. *Pulgyo sinmun*, March 21, 2000.

33. *Joong ang ilbo* (U.S. edition), August 4, 2000.

34. *Pulgyo sinmun*, June 16, 1998.

35. In that election, 81.9 percent of the 29,422,658 registered voters cast their ballots. Of these, 9,977,332 (41 percent) voted for Kim Young Sam; 8,041,285 (33 percent), for Kim Dae Jung; and 3,880,067 (16 percent), for Chung Ju Yung, who professed no religion. Andrew C. Nahm, *Introduction to Korean History and Culture* (Seoul and Elizabeth, N.J.: Hollym, 1993), 318.

36. This should not be taken to mean that the Evangelicals were narrow-minded politically, that they voted for Kim Young Sam simply because he was an Evangelical himself. Given his records as a pro-democracy leader in the 1970s and 1980s, he would have been a strong candidate regardless; but then, Kim Dae Jung was just as well known for his pro-democracy leadership during those decades, if not more so, and had an even tighter lock on his region, the Chŏlla provinces, than Kim Young Sam had on his. That the former was a Catholic and the other an Evangelical must have been a decisive factor among the Evangelical voters outside the Chŏlla provinces.

37. *K'ŭrisch'an sinmun*, February 2, 1998.

38. By saying this, Kim meant that if elected, he would make the presidential residence available for regular Evangelical services. When elected, he attempted to live up to this promise, only to encounter a fierce Buddhist protest, which caused him to backpedal; this waffling, in turn, soured his relationship with many of his Evangelical supporters.

39. *K'ŭrisch'an sinmun*, February 2, 1998.

40. In contrast, non-Evangelical Protestants came out in full support of Kim Dae Jung, and some of them ended up in high positions in Kim's administration. Consequently, from 1998 onward, it would be more accurate to say that Protestants, rather than Evangelicals, stood out in South Korean politics. It is difficult to tell how many of the Protestants in Kim's administration were Evangelical or non-Evangelical. Even so, if the full spectrum of South Korean politics in considered, including the national assemblymen and women, there is no question that the Evangelicals predominated.

41. *K'ŭrisch'an sinmun*, May 31, 1997 and August 4, 1997; *Joong ang ilbo*, December 8, 1997.

42. *K'ŭrisch'an sinmun*, August 25, 1997 and September 1, 1997.

43. Ibid., March 2, 1998.

44. By 1990, nearly 75 percent of South Koreans were urban dwellers. T'onggye-ch'ŏng [National Statistics Office], *Chiyŏkkgan in'gu pulgyunhyŏng punp'o*

ŭi wŏnin kwa kyŏlgwa [Causes and Effects of Uneven Distribution of Population in Regions], vol. 4-2 of *1990 In'gu chut'aek ch'ong chosa chonghap punsŏk* [Comprehensive Analysis of 1990 Population Census], 5. The 1995 census study result can be found in *Kookmin ilbo*, May 27, 1997; also see *K'ŭrisch'an sinmun*, March 4, 1995.

45. These were adherents of Confucianism (17), Wŏn Buddhism (15), the Unification Church (2), Ch'ŏlligyo (1), and Ch'ŏgogyo (1).

46. *Weekly Economist* (Seoul), March 29, 1995, 17.

47. *Pulgyo sinmun*, May 9, 2000.

48. Lee Won Gue, "A Sociological Study on the Factors of Church Growth and Decline in Korea," *Korea Journal*, Winter 1999:238.

49. *K'ŭrisch'an sinmun*, March 1, 1997.

50. This was the finding for 1992. *Christian World*, cited in *Choson ilbo*, February 8, 1993. The five churches were Yŏido Full Gospel Church (Seoul), the largest with 600,000; Nambu Full Gospel Church (Anyang), the second-largest with 105,000; Kumnan Methodist Church (Seoul), the seventh-largest with 56,000; Sungŭi Methodist Church (Inch'ŏn), the ninth-largest with 48,000; and Chuan Presbyterian Church (Inch'ŏn), the tenth-largest with 42,000.

51. Lee, "Sociological Study," 238.

52. See "Chŏsŏngjang sidae, mokhoe chŏllyak ŭi saeroun paerŏdaim yoch'ŏng" [Low Growth Period, a New Paradigm for Ministerial Strategy Requested], *K'ŭrisch'an sinmun*, March 2, 1998.

53. *WEF-Theological News* (Seoul), January–March 1995, 6.

54. http://www.kwma.org/2000/200102/2001mission.html. See *Operation World, 21st Century Edition*, ed. Patrick Johnstone and Jason Mandryk (Harrisonburg, Va.: Paternoster Publishing, 2001), 388.

55. See No Ch'ichun's incisive article "Mokhoeja Kwa'ing Paech'ul" [Overproduction of Ministers], *K'ŭrisch'an sinmun*, March 1, 1997. Also see "Mokhoejadul ŭi kyŏngjaeng sidaega watta" [The Age of Competition Has Come for the Ministers], *K'ŭrisch'an sinmun*, February 9, 1998.

56. Cited by Korea Computer Missions: http://kcm.co.kr/statistics/5/s013.html.

57. *Han'guk ilbo*, September 25, 1992.

58. "Sampoong paekhwajŏon punggwoe" [The Collapse of Sampoong Department Store]; http://www.cn.co.kr/data1/Fm174-01/s174-13-a01.htm.

59. *Kukmin ilbo*, "Hyŏnch'ŏl ssi 3-nyŏn hyŏng Sŏn'go/piri Sagŏn Kongpan" [Mr. Hyŏn Ch'ŏl (Kim) sentenced to three years/A Public Hearing on the Corruption Case]; http://desk.kmib.co.kr/cgi-bin/txtview?f=1997101303010004.txt.

60. *K'ŭrisch'an sinmun*, February 2, 1998.

61. http://www.donga.com/fbin/news_plus?d=news127&f=np127aa020.html.

62. *K'ŭrisch'an sinmun*, April 6, 1998.

63. Park Hyŏngnyong, "Igyo e taehan t'ahyŏp munje" [The Problem of Compromising with Other Religions]," *Sinhak chinam*, quoted in *Han'guk chonggyo sasangsa* [A History of Korean Religious Thought], ed. Kim Ch'angt'ae and Ryu Tong Shik (Seoul: Yonsei University Press, 1986), 247.

64. "Buddhism under Siege in Korea," http://www.buddhapia.com/eng/tedesco/3.html.

65. "Nuga Tan'gun ŭi mok ŭl paenun ka?" [Who is decapitating Tan'gun?], *Sunday Seoul*, April 29, 2000, E-26.

66. An excellent work on this issue is Yi Mahnyol, "Tan'gun'gyodo wa Han'guk kidokkyoin sai ŭi kaltŭng munje" [Issues in Conflict between Tan'gunists and Korean Christians] (UCLA Henry Luce colloquium paper, delivered February 8, 2002).

67. By April 2000, thirty-seven Tan'gun statues were either removed or damaged, with some of the culprits being identified as Evangelicals. See "Nuga Tan'gun ŭi mok ŭl paenun ka?"; *Sunday Seoul*.

68. For a historical study of Korean Evangelicalism during this century, see my "Born-Again in Korea."

CHAPTER 16

In Search of Healing
Evangelical Conversion of Women in Contemporary South Korea

Kelly H. Chong

South Korea has been receiving increasing recognition in recent years for the spectacular growth and success of Protestantism on its soil. Not surprisingly, this comes amid intensified interest on the part of both the Western academy and the public in the revitalization and expansion of religious "fundamentalisms" around the globe, including that of traditionalist Islam, evangelical and fundamentalist Protestantism in the United States, and Pentecostalism in various parts of Latin America.

In Korean academic circles, a great deal of research has already been undertaken to explain the phenomenon of evangelical expansion in South Korea, an effort that has resulted in a solid body of scholarship across various fields.[1] As can be expected, this has been a highly complicated subject matter that has invited a variety of approaches and interpretations.[2] Despite much intense discussion however, there has been surprisingly little attention to one extremely important subject matter—the experience of women.

In Korea, women have long constituted the overwhelming majority of evangelical church membership.[3] Beyond their numerical predominance, what has been particularly remarkable about Korean women's evangelical involvement has been the fervent spirituality and dedication with which they have approached the religion since the beginning and the pivotal role they have played in the growth and maintenance of the churches. Given the centrality of women to the survival and development of evangelicalism over the course of the last century in Korea, their experiences and stories demand serious attention.

This chapter presents some of the findings and analyses of research I conducted on South Korean evangelical women between 1996 and 1999. During that period, I carried out an in-depth ethnographic study of two evangelical churches in Seoul, one Presbyterian and the other Methodist, focusing on the nature and meaning of women's religiosity and institutional participation.[4] By exploring closely the experiences and narratives of women, this chapter seeks to further the understanding of the nature, role, and significance of women's evangelical involvement in contemporary South Korea and their contribution to the success of Korean evangelicalism in the post–World War II era.

In this chapter, I suggest that a useful place from which to understand Korean women's evangelical involvement is to view it within the context of dramatic social and cultural changes experienced by South Korea since the 1960s, particularly those affecting gender and family relations. More specifically, in South Korea, women's enthusiastic conversion to evangelicalism can be most meaningfully understood as a part of women's response to the contradictions of the contemporary patriarchal family, which has posed particular dilemmas for them.

In this context, the evangelical church plays two central roles for women: first, as a vehicle—both spiritual and institutional—for coping with and seeking liberation from domestic or marital distress and suffering, and second, as a resource for negotiating gender and family relations, particularly through accommodation to traditionalist ideology of gender and family as interpreted by the church. The impact of women's faiths and religiosity, in the Korean evangelical context, is a highly contradictory one, characterized by powerful tensions between "liberating" and "oppressive" forces.

Women's Conversion and the Crisis of Family and Gender in Contemporary South Korea

Since embarking upon a program of "late-late" export-led industrialization in the early 1960s, South Korea has undergone an extraordinary process of social and economic transformations. Within a single generation, South Korea has successfully emerged from the rubble of war and the socioeconomic distortions from thirty-five years of colonial rule to become an ostensibly prosperous and modern nation. But despite such achievements, the single-minded pursuit of economic development has also had its costs. It has fostered a society faced with enormous cultural contradictions, characterized by ongoing tensions between forces of "modernity" and "tradition."

These contradictions, though cutting through various levels of society, are nowhere more evident than in the realm of family and gender relations. In recent years, the Korean family has undergone some major modernizing changes, including a decline in fertility rates, a trend toward nuclearization of the family, and the spread of Western values. The contemporary Korean family, however, is an arena characterized by an enormous degree of internal tension, as modern forces clash intensely with the powerful ideals and values of the traditional family.

While such a situation generates conflicts for everyone involved, it has become a particular source of dilemmas for women. In the past few decades, Korean women's unprecedented participation in both mass and higher education has produced some significant changes in their basic status and outlook. Because women are caught, however, in a family system that, though modernized in various respects, still subjects women to a remarkably traditional set of ideals, norms, and demands, the lives of many of them have come to be characterized by a range of acute contradictions and conflicts, particularly in the domestic and marital sphere. Conversion narratives offered by two church members offer insight.

The first response is from Yŏng-sin, a forty-three-year-old housewife with three children. I had asked her to tell me how she became a Christian.

My family was Buddhist, and my husband's family didn't have any religion. They were very against the church. I was brought to church by my sister-in-law, who was the only believer in the family. I never particularly had any desire to go to church, but when my sister-in-law was trying to convert me, I didn't refuse because I am not the type of person who can refuse other people that easily or could assert my thoughts. So I went to the church with her in the beginning, but it never did much for me, and I never wanted to go. And I found the Bible and sermons very hard to understand too. I knew God existed and Jesus saved us and loved us and all that but I found it all rather hard to relate to my life.

My first turning point came when I got into a car accident, when, because of my mistake, I drove myself and my kids off a bridge. But when none of us were seriously hurt, I knew that God loved me and that I wasn't trying to obey him for nothing; from then, I found God entering my mind. But my biggest turning point came through a family seminar I attended. . . . I think I was transformed through the family seminar because it spoke directly to my problems at the time.

You see, the reason I was in such a bad mental shape was that I was very unhappy, stressed, and depressed at home. My married life hadn't been easy. My in-laws ran a cake-making business, which required a lot of work, a lot of which I ended up doing. And I had to do all the housework too. See, I was the last child in my family, and didn't know how to work like that. So getting married and living with parents-in-law was a shock. My mother-in-law wasn't a horrible person inside, but the work was too hard. I felt like she was making me do everything, and I was bad at refusing. I used to go home to my mother and cry all the time. And I fought with my husband a lot about it. It was

*really, really hard for me, mentally, physically, so I came to gradually hate
and resent my husband.*

    *On top of it, it was unbearable because they didn't treat me with respect.
You see, my husband's family is a very conservative family. Their attitude
was, you don't have any right to speak—they totally ran over and ignored
(*muksal hada*) me. It was maddening and unbearable. So I was thinking why
do I have to live with this disrespect (*musi*)? I wasn't treated this way at
home. But if I didn't obey, I felt I was insulting my own mother and father,
that they would think they hadn't raised me properly. So I couldn't rebel. But
it wasn't real obedience (*sunjong*) as far as I was concerned; it was just
enduring, on the outside, just not to give my parents a bad name.*

    *And my husband, I suppose that he thinks I am this inside person who
doesn't know anything about life so he doesn't bother discussing anything with
me. If I talk about politics and stuff, he says like, What do you know about
it? He does watch out for me but that's just because he's afraid I would be
"tainted" by the world. So he sees me as this totally ignorant-of-the-world
woman of the house, not knowing anything, just raising kids and doing
housework. He still does that. He's always telling me not to do this or that,
but I'm over forty! He was two-faced, too, I felt. He went around and did all
these bad things and told me and the kids not to do this and that. He just
wants to imprison me at home.*

    *At first, I was so angry that I had to put up with this kind of person,
and I told God I won't put up with it. I said it was unfair that he can do
whatever he wants and I have to be this good, pious, Christian woman. I
wanted to live a worldly existence too a little. It felt really unjust, that as a
Christian, I had to put up with this kind of existence. I felt such hatred for my
husband. When his business started failing, he started to go wayward. He
drank, he gambled, played instead of trying to save it because he was
despondent about the business. . . . With all this hatred for him, I would refuse
to pray for him. I just watched him, to see what he would do. That's probably
why his business failed in the end. But God helped me be patient. If he
hadn't, I don't know what would have happened by now.*

The second response is from Chang-mi, a forty-four-year-old housewife with three children.

*I didn't come from a Christian family, although actually, my husband's family
was. At first, I started going to church with my husband's family, but I really
couldn't say that that I was a Christian. I didn't have any faith. But then, in
my marriage, there developed a lot of problems and conflicts. I became really
lonely and I really needed to find something. . . . You see, my husband, even
though he's supposed to be a Christian, there was this big conflict between his*

Christian life and worldly life. See, my husband's a military man, and well, he always put his work and duty ahead of his family, do you know what I mean? It seems that that's the main difference with women and men; with men, there is always this discrepancy between how they're supposed to be as Christians and how they really live. Men are not like women, who find heavenly refuge in blessings and just go wild for God.

And there were other problems too. First of all, I must say that I wasn't quite prepared for what I encountered in marriage. I didn't really know what I was in for. . . . When I first got married, you know, we just dated, I didn't really know him. Then I was married to this man. I didn't know much about his character, his thoughts. I had really distinct ideas about how I wanted to live and I found out that they were so different from my husband's. I also married my husband because he was the first who seemed to be able to "lead" me. I thought him very manly. But he "led" me to the extent that he disregarded everything I said, and being the soldier that he is, he would just bulldoze over me, and I just ended up following. Of course I realized only later that this was not a good trait when you are trying to be married to the person. I had no idea how much I had to sacrifice once I got married.

Well, after a few years of marriage, I began to feel cheated out of my life. When I got married, I was really into my studies, especially studying French. But when I got married, I had to give all that up. . . . I asked myself, is this what I married my husband for? To cook food for him? I saw that my life wasn't developing. . . . I used to be idealistic and thought I didn't want money and stuff and that the most important thing was to struggle together with someone I loved. And I married my husband because he was from a Christian family and I thought he couldn't be that bad. I also thought he had potential, career-wise. But I felt like my life was at a standstill. So then I changed. I became obsessed with materialistic things, getting a big house, money, status. Then I started pushing my husband to continue his studies, trying to make a scholar out of him. But his grades were bad. And he became really hard to deal with. He developed a really bad temper, getting angry all the time. Things got so bad that it came to a point where I felt like I couldn't live with him any more. This is when I started to really seek God.

A fruitful way to comprehend the evangelical participation of South Korean women is to view it as a form of their response to a crisis of gender and family in contemporary South Korean society, more specifically, the contradictions confronting the modern Korean patriarchal family. While conversions can by no means be reduced to a single cause, my findings strongly suggest that for many women, evangelical participation serves first and foremost as a means for dealing with problems and conflicts arising from the arena of gender and family relations.

As revealed above, acute domestic crises often emerge as a key motivating factor behind women's church participation or conversion. This is a theme that is embedded in and emerges ubiquitously in the conversion narratives of evangelical women. Although the particular trajectories of conversion may vary for each individual, the theme of domestic distress—revolving around the pain of loveless marriages, intense conflicts with husbands and mothers-in-law, unmanageable domestic burdens, and frustrations from unfulfilled individual aspirations—forms a unifying element across an overwhelming number of narratives.

In many ways, it is clear that a major part of the domestic conflicts of women are rooted in the highly oppressive dimensions of the Korean family system that continue to inflict enormous psychic injuries on women. The crux of contemporary women's dilemmas, however, does not lie simply in the effects of lingering patriarchal oppression, but in the discrepancy between the still-powerful elements of the traditional family and gender system and the changes generated in the lives of women by the forces of contemporary culture and values.[5] To put it another way, the clash between the traditional norms, values, and practices of the traditional family and gender system, and the transformed expectations on the part of modern, well-educated women—particularly for better, more egalitarian domestic and marital relations that most women, unfortunately, find difficult to attain—serves as a major source of domestic conflicts.[6]

Important support for this thesis is provided by another striking aspect of the conversion stories of Korean evangelical women: surprisingly frequent accounts of serious physical illness or breakdown that are recalled as events preceding church participation or "genuine" conversion.[7] While very few women admitted that attending church was motivated directly by the goal of attaining a cure for their ailments, conversion for many was often precipitated by experiences of short- and long-term illness or trauma that they interpreted as symptoms of domestic anguish. As one church member related:

> My parents were Christians, but as I remember it, I just went back and forth to church, didn't have much deep faith before marriage. Then what happened after I got married was that I had to live with my husband's parents and his three siblings. I didn't expect this at all; my husband just up and announced a week before our wedding that we'd have to live with them. Well, when he announced it, I was surprised but accepted it, not thinking much of it, because I had no idea how hard it was going to be. I thought it'd be all right; everyone else does it. But things weren't so easy it turned out. It was so much more difficult than I ever expected. I took care of two of his siblings for five years, then the youngest one, for eight years. Those were the hardest years of

*my life. Then when I was pregnant with my second child, I contracted bad
tuberculosis. I was so sick. I was always healthy but this happened toward the
end of my pregnancy. This totally shocked me. But that's when I started to
really ask why. Why did I get sick like that? I realized then that it must have
been from all the stress and had to do with something about my domestic
situation. Then through counseling with a Christian I came to realize that it
was because I was a sinner. So that's when I decided to think seriously about
my faith, God, and gained conviction about my salvation.*

Many women showed no observable physical causes for which they
could get help. In such cases, doctors usually chalked up women's illnesses
to "nervous disorder" and were unable to help them. One woman related:

*Because of all the stress at home, my health began to really deteriorate. It got
so bad that when I was sitting in the church, I was hardly aware of where I
was, and I would break out into a cold sweat, become dizzy, and couldn't
walk. I had massive headaches all the time and couldn't even walk without my
husband's support. When I went to the hospital, they said there was nothing
especially wrong with me, just that my stomach was bad, and that it just
seemed like a psychological problem. I realized perhaps that this was because I
didn't try to develop my faith further, and so God was "hitting" me. So I
went to my cell leader. She prayed very hard for me and said to me, you just
have to do what the church asks you to do and you will be all right.*

In the Korean context, women's experience of domestic distress appears
to be further exacerbated by another pivotal factor: the relative paucity of
other legitimate channels within society through which women can air
their grievances and seek help for their problems. Living in a society in
which it is still deemed improper and embarrassing to air one's domestic
problems to anyone outside, even to professional counselors or psychiatrists,
women are often left feeling alone, isolated, and helpless, without a place to
turn. As one woman put it, "Things were so piled up inside me that if anyone even touched me, I would just break into a river of tears. There was no
one to console me, no one to talk to."

In the following sections, I examine two central aspects of women's
religiosity—spirituality and institutional participation—and explore the
role evangelical religion plays in women's domestic struggles.

Spirituality and Conversion: The Path toward Healing

The first place to turn to in understanding the central role evangelicalism
plays as a resource in women's efforts to cope with their domestic situations

is the realm of spirituality. In recent social science studies of women and traditionalist religion, the aspect of spirituality as an emotional and psychological resource for women has been relatively neglected.[8] For Korean evangelical women however, my evidence overwhelmingly indicates that spirituality, the heart of evangelical women's religiosity, lies at the center of their efforts to deal with domestic anguish and suffering, especially by helping to foster experiences of profound psychic release, healing, and empowerment.

In general, conversion is understood as a transformation, a turnaround, implying radical change in the nature of the person undergoing religious conversion.[9] At the most basic level, it is a fundamental change in self-identity, change of a worldview and even an entire emotional world.[10] In evangelical terms, conversion means self-transformation as it occurs through "rebirth" and salvation in Jesus Christ. Conversion, however, is not necessarily a uniform, predictably patterned process. Even within the same religious tradition, conversion can be experienced by different people in different ways.

For Korean evangelical women, the first and most important step in conversion begins with a process I refer to as "opening up." As a believer begins to forge an individual relationship with God, opening up is a process in which one learns, often for the first time, to reveal and articulate one's inner self and concerns to God, seeking God's help in dealing with them. For many women, this step often constitutes a significant part of their efforts to attain internal healing. As one woman stated, "Before I didn't have anyone to tell my problems to. Now when I have pain in my heart, I just pray to God and he takes my worries away. God comforts me, consoles me, and makes everything better." Another woman confessed, "I found a God who responds to all my cries, however small, a God that watches over me, who consoles me when things are difficult and painful. I was always so oppressed (*nullida*) and had no means to express myself, but now I can because I know I am a child of God."

In this endeavor, prayer is one of the central vehicles through which such intimate communication with God is pursued. Emphasized repeatedly by the church as one of the most important activities of the believer, prayer in Korean churches is seen as more than a channel for approaching and conversing with the divine; it is also a vehicle for regularized self-revelation, fervent spiritual release, and spiritual and bodily experience of the divine.

Opening up occurs not only individually, but collectively as well, in venues such as cell meetings.[11] Weekly female cell meetings, a combination of guided small-group Bible study and intensive fellowship, are in practice vehicles for fostering openness and sharing of personal lives and problems, with the ultimate aim of facilitating conversion. One member described her experiences in the group this way: "When I went to a cell meeting for the first time, I experienced an indescribably peaceful feeling. What I realized was that other people are not different from me, in their lives, problems, and feelings. Until then, I thought my life was peculiar, but that was not the case. And I received consolation from that, before anything else."

In the process of conversion, another central way by which women are moved toward healing and in their ability to cope with domestic situations is through the act of self-surrender. In evangelicalism in general, the act of surrender is considered a crucial turning point in the conversion process; for Korean evangelical women, surrender has particularly important implications for facilitating the healing process by serving as a major source of psychic relief.

One of the notable aspects of the concept of surrender in the Korean evangelical context is the pronounced emphasis on the notion of self-abandonment, that is, the idea of a total relinquishment of the self and will to divine control. In the act of "entrusting" everything to God and unconditionally obeying his will, surrendering appears to serve as an important means of attaining profound psychic unburdening that frees women from day-to-day burdens.

The third aspect of the conversion process that is crucial to the healing and coping efforts of Korean evangelical women is the experience of divine love. In evangelicalism, to be reborn signifies a reconstitution of identity, most important, as someone who learns to live in the knowledge and experience of God's love. Although the experience of divine love can be meaningful for any believer, it has, in the Korean context, particularly profound significance for women, especially by fostering a sense of empowerment and deep internal transformation that promotes the healing process.

I have found that in South Korea, one of the major sources of psychic injury for women is the problem of emotional deprivation in marriage, especially the felt absence of conjugal love, intimacy, and spousal respect that over time seems to contribute to a decline in the sense of self-worth and self-esteem in many women. The experience of divine love and rebirth as "God's child" enables many believers to reconstitute their inner confidence and self-worth, making up for love that is often missing in their lives. As one woman remarked, "I never felt like I received much love from anyone. But all this was compensated for by God. For the first time in my life, I felt loved, blessed and special."

Not surprisingly, God's love sometimes becomes so central to a woman's life that God/Jesus replaces the husband as the primary intimate companion and the locus of male authority in a woman's life. Needless to say, this displacement often incurs the envy of the husband. Indeed, in the evangelical rhetoric among women, Jesus is often seen not only as a father, but also as a lover who can provide for all of the woman's needs that the husband cannot. In extreme cases, a woman's devotion to God becomes so intense that she "abandons" her family, her husband, and her domestic duties to become "Jesus-crazy," generating severe domestic conflicts.

Although religious faith does not lead most women to such extreme measures, it can be seen here how women's religiosity and faith can serve as an instrument of resistance, particularly against male domination and control. Even in cases where women do not neglect their homes, the force of divine presence and love offers women a means of internal resistance, a sense of psychic autonomy against their "tormentors," especially husbands and mothers-in-law. As one woman remarked in regard to dealing with her husband, "Before, when my husband would say hurtful things to me, I would get really hurt, but with my faith, it doesn't hurt me anymore. So I say to my husband, you can try all you want to torment me, but I won't get mad, and I am not tormented. If you want to know why, I wish you can experience this yourself."

God's Work: Negotiating Autonomy and Empowerment

Another major aspect of Korean women's religiosity that functions as a critical resource for domestic coping is institutional participation. In most Korean churches, women unquestionably have been, and in many cases still are, subordinated within the church hierarchy and authority structure. Women, for the most part, are not only kept from positions of power but are relegated in general to support-level tasks within the church, where they are regarded primarily as "helpers" (*toum paep'il*) and "service-workers" (*pojoja*).[12] Nevertheless, for many women, church involvement functions as a crucial means for attaining a measure of social autonomy and empowerment, particularly by enabling women to forge autonomous spheres and make use of nondomestic talents and abilities.

First of all, churches are important as a sphere of extradomestic, female-centered community, in which women get together and create a separate space of their own away from their families. The vehicles for these activities may range from cell meetings to weekday dawn or evening prayer meetings and Bible classes to activities related to women's missionary societies, which require women to meet several times a week to carry out service-oriented tasks.

Although most women sincerely believed that they were going to church to carry out their duties as Christians, it was also clear that these frequent gatherings often come to serve a focal point of their social lives, a crucial social outlet that was acceptable in the eyes of their families and societies. Indeed, numerous women actually described the church as a temporary "escape" from home. For others, church participation clearly becomes a means of internal resistance against the constraints of their lives and male domination as they seize upon the church as a "resting" place from the sufferings and oppressiveness in the home.

One woman, a small-business owner, persuaded her husband, for instance, that the only way she could remain sane was for him to let her faithfully attend church. She was thus using her sickness and church as both an instrument of resistance against his oppression and a tool for gender negotiation:

> Yes, people tell me I'm "hanging" too much onto God. But my husband knows that if I don't go to church like I do, I'd be a sick person! So he says to me, for you, work is not the most important thing. What's the point if you have money but get sick so we have to pay the hospital bills? My husband knows this, so going to church is one thing he doesn't say anything about. For me, church comes before everything else. Even if I'm with nonchurch friends, I leave and go to church if a church matter comes up. But everyone knows what God means to me, so that I can't live without him.

Despite the fact that women are generally put in charge of carrying out the subordinate and the most menial of tasks in the church, from administrative support work to "dirty" kitchen and cleaning duties, the church, ironically, also serves as a place where women can exercise nondomestic talents and abilities, offering them a chance to experience a sense of achievement outside the domestic arena, even to "exercise the brain."[13] Indeed, in many churches, there were, in addition to the usual menial female responsibilities, other tasks women could pursue as part of church service, such as those related to teaching (of other women, rarely men) and community service. It was obvious that these opportunities—which ranged from the position of cell leader, deaconess, or Sunday school teacher to numerous church service groups and women's missionary societies—gave women a legitimate outlet for their talents and energies and for pursuing individual achievement in a society where there were few other such avenues available for women outside the domestic arena.

Although some women express resentment of the often heavy burdens placed on them by the church, for many others, church participation can also lead to a visible enhancement of self-esteem and confidence, as the women discover hidden talents and abilities long suppressed, resulting sometimes in dramatic internal transformations. Numerous women reported, for instance, of having undergone personality transformations, usually from being "meek" and "shy" to becoming more confident, bold, and outspoken, ready to carry out any task and battle for God. As one woman professed:

By going to church, my personality changed 180 degrees. In one corner of my mind, I hated being left behind and being left in the background of things, but I didn't have the courage to take the front line in anything. But through going to church and believing in Jesus, these impulses in my insides became expressed outwardly, and I became so outgoing, a person who can speak out anywhere, can talk well and a lot. From being this demure and introverted person, I became this outgoing, bright, and cheerful person.

Achieving the position of leadership, such as being appointed a cell leader or a deaconess, seemed to offer many women a particularly rewarding sense of achievement and esteem.[14]

What my study has also uncovered is that for many women, gaining public recognition for their accomplishments and contributions also serves as a major source of self-satisfaction, esteem, and fulfillment—especially if it comes from the pastor. Such feelings reflect the deep need many women seem to have for social recognition. That these forms of external recognition (*injŏng*) occupy a central place in many women's motivation for church involvement is testified to clearly by the following observations by one woman: "I think in a lot of cases, doing church service is for self-fulfillment, satisfaction of ego (*chasin ch'ungman*). It's not for Jesus, to pay back for him for what he's done for us. It's to receive recognition from others, for others to think you are good (*ch'ak hada*). That's a good feeling, so you try even harder, to look good to other people."

In sum, institutional participation is, along with spirituality and faith, an important resource for improved domestic coping and for achieving a measure of emancipation from patriarchal oppression for women. Through faith, women find in institutional involvement a means for acquiring a measure of personal space as well as empowerment, both of which help them better deal with the difficulties of their daily lives. Church participation is also important for women because by forming friendships or networks with other believers, women can gain practical help in dealing with domestic difficulties as well as enhancing the well-being of their households. Church participation is not without its difficulties, however, as women must deal with the demands of home and church, both of which can be overwhelming.

The Meaning of Accommodation

One of the most perplexing aspects of women's religiosity in the Korean evangelical setting is that, while women appropriate evangelical beliefs and practices as an instrument of gender emancipation and resistance, many of them come to support and embrace, often with profound sincerity, the principles of the traditional patriarchal family as a solution to their domestic problems. Indeed, several churches that I investigated often functioned as important resources for helping women deal with their domestic problems, advocating the ways of the Confucian-patriarchal family—through such programs as marriage seminars as well as advice meted out in cell meetings and other gatherings—as a solution to women's dilemmas.

In this section, I examine the puzzling question of women's turn to religious patriarchy as a domestic solution within the Korean evangelical context. What is suggested here is that women's accommodation to patriarchy is a highly complex and contradictory process that cannot be seen as a simple act of acquiescence, but one that is also expressive of women's efforts to actively negotiate the domestic situation. In this respect, accommodation can be most usefully seen, in many respects, as a strategy, a strategy by Korean women to negotiate their domestic and marital relations. However, insofar as accommodation leads to the reaffirmation of traditional family relations and female gender identity, it is a move that serves to further women's subordination, especially through the preservation of the current patriarchal family system.

One of the most ironic dimensions of women's religious engagement and conversion in the Korean evangelical context is the support women apparently come to develop for a set of ideologies that they see as lying at the root of their predicament, those that buttress the legitimacy of the very family system that is the source of so much of their suffering. This ideology of gender, asserted as a divinely sanctioned set of Christian beliefs, unequivocally embodies and expresses the basic principles of the Confucian family and gender relations, including the belief in the inherent superiority of men, strict traditional separation of inside/outside gender roles, and the necessity of women's "docile obedience" (*sunjong hada*) and "endurance" (*ch'amda*) as the fundamental principle of conjugal relations and the basis for maintaining family harmony and peace.[15] One cell leader described her church's belief this way:

> *I really believe sincerely that for any woman, obedience is something she has to deal with and accept. Without the wife obeying the husband, God will not use that home. We think the husband has to treat the wife well for the wife to obey, but that's not the case. A wife has to obey first, unconditionally. . . . A wife obeying, raising her husband continuously and making him the leader, that is the most essential aspect of marriage, the most important part from which everything else will follow.*

While at first glance it may appear perplexing that so many women come to embrace a set of ideologies that lie at the very root of their subordination, what is suggested by my findings is that for many evangelical women, the act of accommodation to church-supported ideology is best understood not simply as a capitulation to male domination, but also as a rational strategy for dealing with their domestic situations, more particularly, for renegotiating gender relations.

Although "true" evangelical conversion is usually seen to signify a person's sincere commitment to and belief in traditionalist ideas, such views for many women are not always initially appealing. In fact, what I have found is that many women at first struggle considerably with such patriarchal views. They question, for instance, the validity of such beliefs in light of current feminist ideas, wondering, for instance, why it is that the wife must obey the husband. But many women decide to try out these ideas and practices because they often come to see that such ideas and practices can be employed as an instrument in gender bargaining and in achieving improved domestic relations.[16]

The first way that women come to see accommodation as a means for domestic negotiation is as a tool for reforming the behavior of others, especially the husband. The belief is that through their own perfect adherence to all the rules of virtuous feminine conduct as advised by the church, the wives can "inspire" the husbands to change and behave better. Indeed, numerous women professed to having transformed their husbands by their own diligent effort to become more ideal wives; some said, for instance, that they were able to change their stubbornly Confucian (Yugyo *chŏk*) husbands to become more respectful, loving, or affectionate. According to one woman:

> You see, my husband is extremely traditional, he just wanted a real traditional wife. He used to give no respect to me, because I'm just a woman and a wife, but now, he thinks he must give women respect, too. He never used to listen to me or my opinions, didn't give me the time of day. But now, he listens; if anything, I have more to say now. Of course, my husband still has his traditional aspects. He doesn't like for women to be forward, or to be progressive. Like when I praise with my hands raised in church, he doesn't like that.

Another way the wives can change their husbands is to make them more communicative. One of the common complaints Korean women have of their husbands is that the husbands do not like to talk. The behavior of "silent" and "close-mouthed" husbands may in part reflect men's attempts to live up to the ideal image of the traditional Korean male, but it frequently also expresses the husbands' resentment of "aggressive" and "nagging" wives. Many women said, however, that when they began to behave in a more gentle, submissive, and less assertive manner, their husbands began to "soften up," becoming more "open-hearted." Various women reported a more long-lasting character change in their husbands as well, such as when husbands were transformed from being "domineering" and "selfish" to being more considerate and understanding.

Finally, many respondents talked about their husbands becoming more "domestic" or "family oriented," changes that signified not only the husbands' willingness to be more attentive to the home and children but also the taking on of more moral responsibility for domestic matters, instead of holding the wife responsible for everything. This change, in particular, represented an effective way for Korean women to redefine the boundary of traditional gender roles. One woman commented:

> One of the ways my husband changed through the church is that all those things he used to blame me for—he stopped doing that and started taking responsibility for everything himself. He saw himself as my helper, to take that seriously. Before when kids were bad, he used to just hit them out of anger; now he repents for all those things he used to blame me for, and for pushing all the responsibility on me. And when I look at his workbook, I see dried tears on the pages. So what he learned in church is what a husband and a father is supposed to be within Jesus Christ.

Of course, when the wife's efforts result in the conversion of the husband, this is considered the ultimate victory.

It is important to note, however, that reformations of husbands do not come about easily, may take a long time, and in some cases do not happen at all. Furthermore, these endeavors, insofar as they require a great deal of effort, accommodation, and often unwanted self-transformations on the part of women, sometimes involve serious psychological costs for them. Nevertheless, there is little doubt that for the majority of women, reembracing the traditional family ideology is seen as an appealing option because it is viewed as a possible strategy of improving the domestic situation and renegotiating the terms of gender relations.

Another fascinating aspect of female submission in the Korean context is that it is appropriated by women not only as a means of gender bargaining, but also as a weapon of passive resistance. For instance, my research revealed that women often employ a strategy of radical subservience—what I call "obeying with a vengeance"—as a subversive means of enforcing upon others, such as husbands or mothers-in-law, the obligations and moral compulsions of long-term gratitude. As one woman put it, "You know, if I didn't obey, and just ran off like I wanted to, would my husband have the gratitude he now has for me, for what I have endured in the past?" Such strategies of virtuous submission can also become a powerful weapon of internal resistance and defense by women, especially when they acquire a sense of inner moral superiority.

Another way in which women are able to achieve inner resistance against male domination is by replacing the authority of the husband with that of God. Through their own exemplary conduct, women can use the strategy of perfect submission as a means of acquiring more power and status within the household.

However, despite the complexity in the meaning of women's accommodation, this strategy, insofar as it results in the reinforcement of the very set of behaviors and attitudes that are responsible for women's subordination—namely that of "docile" obedience, endurance, and self-sacrifice—has highly conservative consequences for women. Furthermore, insofar as conversion involves and results ultimately in normative consent for women—that is, a genuine belief in and commitment to the ideals of the traditional family and gender relations—evangelical faith becomes for women an effective medium through which the integrity of the family system and the status of women within it are preserved and maintained.

In many ways, this strategy reflects the successful attempt on the part of the church in re-domesticating contemporary women for the family system. Through a program whose aim is to reform what it views as overly "aggressive" or "willful" (ŏkseda) females who have become undisciplined in the modern age, the church is often successful in deepening women's commitment to the family by persuading them to re-embrace traditional gender roles and identity and to accept primary responsibility for domestic conflicts. One of the goals of the Korean church, it would seem, is redefining women's consciousness and identity in ways that will ensure their dedication to the goals, harmony, and perpetuation of the traditional family system.

Conclusion

Understanding women's role in and contribution to Korean evangelicalism is critical to understanding the overall success of Christianity in South Korea. However, this chapter has illustrated Korean evangelicalism is a religion that has a highly complex set of meanings for Korean women.

It has been argued here that women's turn to evangelicalism can in large part be seen as their efforts to deal with the stresses and contradictions of the modern Korean family, rooted especially in the tension between the changed expectations of women and the continuing norms and practices of the traditional family. In this regard, one of the first attractions and roles of evangelical faith for Korean women is as a means of coping with and seeking relief from domestic problems, especially by way of healing and empowerment provided through spirituality and institutional participation.

In spite of such a liberating function, evangelical faith also possesses highly contradictory implications for Korean women, giving rise to consequences that are as much oppressive as liberating. Most significant is that, in successfully reshaping women's fundamental self-conceptions, identities and goals through conversion, evangelical faith serves as an effective medium for women's re-domestication, resecuring women's allegiance and commitment to the family system. In other words, the nature of women's evangelical beliefs and practices, as matters stand now, undercuts the emancipation possibilities inherent in their faiths; instead it serves as a vehicle for maintaining existing social arrangements.

This is not to say, however, that, evangelical beliefs do not bring about positive transformations. As has been seen, evangelical beliefs can have a real impact on the quality of women's lives, by improving the capacity of women to negotiate their everyday situations and even producing some practical improvements in domestic relations. Women can reform or convert their husbands, for example, and make use of their newfound spiritual power to achieve significant internal empowerment that helps them better cope with their environment. However, insofar as these changes do not signify or add up to any notable transformations of the fundamental structures or politics of domestic and religious patriarchy, women's current situations, and their dilemmas within them, will most likely be perpetuated. Indeed, it is perhaps this double role of evangelicalism as both a vehicle for helping women negotiate the challenges and frustrations of the patriarchal family and a vehicle for re-domesticating women to that very family system that has rendered it, for now, such a uniquely effective instrument for maintaining the integrity of current family and gender relations.

NOTES

1. In this chapter, I use the term "evangelicalism" to refer to the majority of Protestant churches in South Korea. Although Korean Protestantism encompasses almost all known Protestant denominations, I would strongly argue that most of them could be categorized as "evangelical" because the beliefs and practices of most of these denominations and their churches display the distinctive and salient characteristics of what we currently understand by this term. See Timothy S. Lee, "Born Again in Korea: The Rise and Character of Revivalism in (South) Korea, 1885–1988" (Ph.D. diss., University of Chicago, 1996). For definitions of evangelicalism, see James D. Hunter, *American Evangelicalism: Conservative Religion and the Quandary of Modernity* (New Brunswick, N.J.: Rutgers State University Press,

1983); and David H. C. Read, "The Evangelical Protestant Understanding of Conversion," in *Handbook of Religious Conversion*, ed. H. Newton Malony and Samuel Southard (Birmingham, Ala.: Religious Education Press, 1992), 137–146.

2. See Gil Soo Han, *Social Sources of Church Growth: Korean Churches in the Homeland and Overseas* (New Brunswick, N.J.: Rutgers State University Press, 1994); Byong-Suh Kim, "The Explosive Growth of the Korean Churches Today: A Sociological Analysis," *International Review of Mission* 74 (1985): 61–74; John T. Kim, *Protestant Church Growth in Korea* (Belleville, Ontario, Canada: Essence Publishing, 1996); Lee, "Born Again in Korea"; Hyung-Kyu Park, "The Search for Self-Identity and Liberation," *International Review of Mission* 74 (1985): 51–60; Bong Rin Ro, "The Korean Church: God's Chosen People for Evangelism," in *Korean Church Growth Explosion*, ed. Bong Rin Ro and Marlin L. Nelson (Seoul: Word of Life Press, 1998), 11–44; Kon-Ho Song, "A History of the Christian Movement in Korea," *International Review of Mission* 74 (1985): 20–37; and David Kwang-Sun Suh, "American Missionaries and a Hundred Years of Korean Protestantism," *International Review of Mission* 74 (1985): 6–19.

3. The proportion of female membership in Korean Protestant churches is estimated to range from 60 to 75 percent. See Hyo-Jae Yi, "Christian Mission and the Liberation of Korean Women," *International Review of Mission* 74 (1985): 93–102; and Gallup Korea, *Han'guk Kaesin'gyoin ŭi kyohoe hwaltong mit sinang ŭisik* [Korean Protestants' Church Activities and Religious Consciousness] (Seoul: Turano, 1999).

4. My research consisted primarily of intensive participation observation and in-depth interviewing of close to a hundred women and men in the two churches. Although I cannot claim that these churches were representative of all evangelical churches in South Korea, they were, I argue, typical in many senses. Not only did the two churches represent the two largest Protestant denominations in South Korea, they were also representative of the theologically and culturally conservative mainstream middle-class evangelical churches that constitute the majority of churches in South Korea. Most of my interviews, both semistructured and open-ended, were with married women between the ages of thirty-five and fifty-five, although interviews were conducted with women of other age categories, and with men as well. Numerous interviews were also carried out with pastors, church leaders, and specialists in Korean Christianity.

5. Powerful evidence for the contradictory position of contemporary South Korean women is provided by the following structural factor: the acute discrepancy between Korean women's level of education and their rates of labor participation. South Korean women comprise one of the most highly educated populations in the world; as of 1990, some 24.4 percent of Korean women were enrolled in institutions of higher education. The figure for women in neighboring Taiwan was only 19.6 percent. However, compared to Taiwan, South Korean women have a much lower overall rate of workforce participation at every age (accompanied by a pattern of postmarital exit); in the age category 25–29, the prime childbearing age, South Korean women's workforce participation was only a little more than half the rate of their Taiwanese counterparts—27.1 percent compared to 43.9 percent. Furthermore, in Taiwan, higher levels of female education lead uniformly to a higher

probability of employment. In South Korea, the opposite occurs; among married women, more education leads to a lower probability of employment. See Mary C. Brinton, Yean-Ju Lee, and William L. Parish, "Married Women's Employment in Rapidly Industrializing Societies: Examples from East Asia," *American Journal of Sociology* 100, no. 2 (1995): 1099–1130.

6. It is important to point out that for most of the women I interviewed, changes in their expectations related mostly to improvements in family life and marital relations; they were not so much about aspirations beyond the domestic sphere, in the feminist sense, though for some women, this was an important concern. Most women I talked to still held to beliefs about the importance and sanctity of marriage and their roles within it.

7. Conversion is by no means necessarily a sudden or a one-time affair, or an event motivated simply by psychological or emotional factors. For Korean evangelical women, however, crises related to domestic suffering, events so severe as to result in real or psychosomatic illnesses in an overwhelming number of women, are too ubiquitous to ignore as a factor in female church involvement and conversion. For different perspectives on conversion, see William Sims Bainbridge, "The Sociology of Conversion," in *Handbook of Religious Conversion*, ed. H. Newton Malony and Samuel Southard (Birmingham, Ala.: Religious Education Press, 1992), 178–191; John Lofland and Rodney Stark, "Becoming a World-Saver," *American Sociological Review* 30 (1966): 862–875; Lewis R. Rambo, "The Psychology of Conversion," in *Handbook of Religious Conversion*, ed. H. Newton Malony and Samuel Southard (Birmingham, Ala.: Religious Education Press, 1992), 159–177; James T. Richardson, "The Active vs. Passive Convert: Paradigm Conflict in Conversion/ Recruitment Research," *Journal for the Scientific Study of Religion* 4, no. 2 (1985): 119–236; and Roger A. Straus, "Religious Conversion as a Personal and Collective Accomplishment," *Sociological Analysis* 40, no. 2 (1979): 158–165.

8. One notable exception is R. Marie Griffith, *God's Daughters: Evangelical Women and the Power of Submission* (Berkeley: University of California Press, 1997).

9. Bainbridge, "The Sociology of Conversion," 178–191.

10. See Hans Mol, *Identity and the Sacred: A Sketch for a New Social-Scientific Theory of Religion* (New York: Free Press, 1976); and Rambo, "Psychology of Conversion," 159–177.

11. Cell meetings are small (5–10 people), weekly, usually sex-segregated Bible-study or fellowship meetings held in the homes of the members. All members of a given church are hooked up to a cell group in their residential area. Cell groups have now become the central organizational core of most Korean Protestant churches and serve as the churches' most important social, monitoring, and evangelizing unit.

12. Female ordination is still not allowed by the majority of Protestant denominations and most of the top lay leadership positions, such as church elderships, are held by men in most denominations.

13. Many women I talked to were indeed resentful about their status within the church, complaining not only about how menial their tasks were but also about the excessive demands made on them by the leadership. Several women I talked to

sarcastically referred to themselves as the "kitchen herd" (*puŏk ttegi*) and "army of laborers" for the church (*kyohoe ŭi nodonggun*).

14. In one of the churches, becoming a cell leader was a rigorous process requiring an intensive period of training; it was thus a highly prestigious position for women.

15. It should be noted that Korean evangelical gender ideology is by no means monolithic. There are some variations or reinterpretations of the fundamental Confucian positions on gender, some of which even reveal efforts at accommodation to the contemporary ideological climate. Some churches, for instance, tone down the harshly patriarchal character of the traditional principles by enjoining husbands to love their wives in return for obedience, a position similar to that espoused by many American evangelicals. However, the common stress on such matters as the unquestionable necessity of female obedience as a prerequisite for harmonious marital relations reflects clearly the ways in which biblical principles have been interpreted through a Korean cultural lens.

16. As has been observed in various marriage and family seminars, the church itself, in its rhetoric, also presents many of these ideas as a strategy, a strategy for "clever women" to improve their domestic situations, especially by manipulating the attitudes and behavior of husbands. These injunctions for domestic improvement are also often clearly designed to appeal to the self-interest of women.

CHAPTER 17

The Christian-Buddhist Encounter in Korea

Kang-nam Oh

Buddhism and Christianity are currently the two dominant religions in South Korea, with approximately one-half of the country's population of forty-five million as their adherents. Of these adherents, approximately one-half are Buddhists and the other half Christians.[1] Under such circumstances, it seems obvious that a dialogical and cooperative relationship between these two religions in Korea is both a prerequisite and an imperative for the peaceful and harmonious future of Korean society.

The main purpose of this chapter is to survey briefly the historical background of these two religions in Korea, to analyze the current situation of the Buddhist-Christian relationship in Korea, and to explore possible ways of improving the encounter between these two religions in the future. I will argue that Korean Buddhism and Christianity, realizing the important historical and religious functions they perform in Korean society, should work together, think together and wake up together for the socio-ethical welfare, philosophico-theological depth, and interior and spiritual well-being of the Korean people. This chapter proposes that such a congenial relationship and cooperation between Buddhism and Christianity on the Korean peninsula is a step toward fulfilling their global responsibility as world religions.

Historical Background

KOREAN BUDDHISM

It is traditionally believed that Buddhism was introduced into Korea in 372 C.E. during the reign of King Sosurim of Koguryŏ, one of the three kingdoms that comprised Korea at that time. Although some scholars plausibly claim that Buddhism must have been in the country earlier than that date, the traditional records say that Buddhism was first officially accepted when the king enthusiastically welcomed a monk called Sundo (Xundao), who was dispatched as a member of the delegation from northern China, and built a monastery to house him. Although there is no knowing the exact actual date of Buddhism's entry into Korea, it is safe to say that by the middle of the fourth century C.E. it had firmly established itself on the peninsula.

The other two kingdoms, Paekche and Silla, also officially accepted Buddhism in 384 and 534, respectively. It is well known that Paekche played the major role of introducing Buddhism to Japan.[2] The golden age of Buddhism in Korea came during the Unified Silla period (668–935). During this period, Buddhism was the main force unifying the nation and developed many advanced cultural and artistic achievements. The full blossoming of Buddhism produced such great spiritual thinkers as Wŏnhyo (617–686) and Ŭisang (625–702), whose academic reputations and influence were felt in China and Japan as well as in Korea.[3]

Buddhism also thrived under royal patronage in the succeeding Koryŏ dynasty (935–1392). During this period, many memorable achievements appeared, including the carving of more than eighty thousand woodblocks and later inventing the world's first movable type to print the Buddhist canon. There were also some eminent Buddhist monks such as Ŭich'ŏn (1055–1101), a son of King Munjong, and Chinul (1158–1210), one of the most influential Buddhist thinkers in the history of Korean thought.[4]

During most of this period, however, Buddhism was an active participant in political power struggles. Especially around the end of the period, Buddhism with its tremendous holdings of land, wealth, and serfs, as well as its other privileges, such as exemption from taxation, military service, corvée labor, and the like, effectively became a state within a state.[5] This situation gradually led the Buddhist *saṅgha* (monastic order) into corruption, stagnation, and decline.

The decline of Buddhism accelerated with the establishment of the new Chosŏn dynasty (1392–1910). "Partly out of conviction, partly out of desire to emphasize a break with the past, and partly to curb the divisive influence of the Sangha," King T'aejo, the founder, "declared himself and the new dynasty Confucian."[6] Soon after the first several sovereigns, the suppression of Buddhism intensified until the religion reached its nadir at the dawn of the twentieth century. During this predominantly Confucian period, although there were some eminent monks and Buddhist thinkers, they were overshadowed by the great Neo-Confucian scholars of the age, and Buddhism became almost exclusively the religion of women and old people in the countryside and mountains.[7]

During Japanese colonial rule over Korea (1919–1945), Japan, which remained a largely Buddhist country, tried to help Korean Buddhism "revive" itself. This "revival," however, meant mainly "Japanizing" Korean Buddhism. Among other things, Japan forced Korean Buddhist monks to model themselves after their Japanese counterparts and required that they marry in order to hold monastic office. This and other policies to revive Buddhism in Korea did the religion more harm than good.

After the liberation of Korea in 1945, one of the harms caused by the Japanese control of Korean Buddhism emerged in the form of a power struggle between married and celibate monks.[8] This battle was a legacy of Japanese policy toward Buddhism and was one of the most prominent reasons why Buddhism, even in religiously pluralistic Korean society, was not very appealing to the general Korean public for some time. But as the chaos in the Korean *sangha* has diminished, the religion seems to have a vibrant future ahead of itself. For example, the Chogye Order, the largest sect of Korean Buddhism, has undergone dramatic reforms since 1994, and these changes have kindled among the lay members of the Buddhist community new hope for a true revival of Korean Buddhism.

In terms of its relationship to Christianity, Buddhism, which has been severely suppressed for so long in Korean history, was in no position to compete with Christianity, let alone to attack it. Despite some serious factional struggles within their own tradition, Buddhism was by far the more passive and pacifist of the two religions.

KOREAN CHRISTIANITY

Christianity in its Catholic form became known to Koreans during the early part of the seventeenth century through the diplomatic envoys dispatched to China and the Catholic literature they brought with them. These books written by the Jesuit missionaries in China were studied by some Korean scholars belonging to the Practical Learning (Sirhak) school as part of what they termed "Western Learning." By the middle of the eighteenth century, this initial intellectual curiosity about Western Learning had turned into an enthusiastic interest in Catholicism.

The rapid spread of Catholicism caused conflict with the Chosŏn government, which had adopted Neo-Confucianism as its state religio-political ideology. No matter the deeper reasons behind this conflict, it brought waves of persecutions against the Catholic church in Korea.[9]

The official persecution of Christianity ended in 1884. Around that time, Protestant missionaries began to enter Korea in great numbers. Since then, the number of Catholic and Protestant Christians in Korea has increased at such a tremendous speed that the mission work in Korea became known as "one of wonders of modern mission."[10] At the present time, Korean Protestant Christianity has more than thirty-nine thousand churches, including the world's largest churches in Seoul. Korean Catholicism had its one hundred heroes and heroines of the faith canonized when Pope John Paul II visited Korea in 1984 to commemorate the 200th anniversary of the official foundation of the Korean Catholic church, thereby making Korea the world's fourth-largest country in terms of the number of Catholic saints. As James H. Grayson says, "Moving into the final decade of the twentieth century, the Christian churches, especially the Protestant churches, are the dominant religious fact of modern Korean history."[11] It is also true, however, that most recently Christian churches have stopped growing and have even begun to decline in terms of the number of their adherents, as Byong-suh Kim notes in his chapter in this volume.

Present Monological Relationship

It is therefore no exaggeration to say that in recent times there has been no direct contact or meaningful encounter between Buddhism and Christianity in Korea. Both religions have been busy concentrating on their own survival and separate development in relative isolation from each other. There has been, so to speak, only monologue within their own territories, and no constructive and mutually enriching dialogue.

Most recently, however, these two hitherto independent and mutually indifferent religions in Korea have come into closer contact with each other. One of the main reasons seems to be the rapid urbanization of Korean society, which gives people more chances to mingle with people with other religious persuasions. Another reason might be found in the explosion of mass media, an explosion that has tremendously increased people's exposure to religious beliefs other than their own.

Whatever the reasons may be, these increasing contacts between Buddhism and Christianity have, unfortunately, proved to be more a cause of conflict than an opportunity for mutual understanding and acceptance. There have been, of course, some encouraging events fostered through these closer contacts. For example, in 1986 I was privileged to participate in the Buddhist-Christian Dialogue meeting sponsored by the Academy House in Seoul; there Buddhist scholars and monks and Christian theologians and ministers gathered together to discuss issues of mutual concern, with Professor Heinrich Ott from Basel as a guest speaker. Some conscientious theologians, represented by Dr. Pyŏn Sŏn-hwan, the former president of Methodist College in Seoul, have expressed genuine interest in Buddhist-Christian dialogue as a means of fostering mutual understanding and transformation. His most recent Festschrift on religious pluralism is a good example of the budding interest among some Christian theologians in religious pluralism in general and Buddhist-Christian dialogue in particular.[12]

In recent years, some nuns from the Catholic church, the Buddhist *sangha*, and the Wŏn Buddhist organization got together to discuss possibilities for future cooperation in the areas of social work and meditative life. In February 1995, representatives of Buddhism, Catholicism, and Protestantism agreed that they would work together for the nationwide human organ donation campaign.[13]

Notwithstanding these few rays of light, the general picture of the Buddhist-Christian relationship in Korean society today is gloomy and, more often than not, even ugly. To give just a few examples, a number of Buddha statues that were standing outside had red signs of the cross painted on the foreheads, and some of the stone statues were partially destroyed. One army officer closed a Buddhist dharma hall in his compound and disposed of the Buddha image somewhere in the mountains. Groups of Christians have marched carrying placards and shouting "Jesus Heaven; Buddha Hell" or "Buddhist temples are headquarters of devils" and the like. There have even been cases of Buddhist temples burned down by Christian arsonists. In June 1998 a Christian called Kim Sujin cut off the heads of 750 statues of the buddhas at Wŏnmyŏng Sŏnwŏn in Cheju Island.[14]

This type of exclusivism is found not only among ignorant laypeople but also among some learned leaders of Protestant churches. Several years ago, Dr. Pyŏn Sŏn-hwan, the above-mentioned former president of Methodist College in Seoul, was deprived not only of his position as the president of the college but also of his professorship and ministerial privileges—effectively excommunicating him from the order—primarily because of his sympathetic attitude toward other religions, and particularly Buddhism. When Pyŏn made a statement to the effect that salvation was possible outside the church, he was severely criticized by fellow Christians from almost every denomination in Korea.

Such a list of negative results of the Buddhist-Christian encounter in Korea could go on and on.[15] But even these few examples are enough to give us some sense of the strained contacts between Christianity and Buddhism. To give an even clearer picture, however, let me summarize a Buddhist monk's analysis of some of the general misconceptions Christian adherents have regarding the Buddhist religion. According to this monk, many Christians in Korea have the following wrong notions about Buddhism:

Buddhism is a superstition.
Buddhism is idolatry.
Buddhism believes in a man, the Buddha, while Christianity believes
    in God, Jesus.
Buddhism is mere enigmatic philosophy, while Christianity is a
    religion accessible to everyone.

Buddhism is responsible for all the wrongdoings of some Buddhist monks.
Buddhism is the devil's teaching, which should be wiped from the face of the world.[16]

The increasingly uncomfortable and sometimes antagonistic encounters between Buddhism and Christianity are caused, in most cases, by exclusivistic religious attitudes held by the vast majority of Korean Christians.[17] Traditionally, grassroots Koreans were generally flexible toward different religious faiths. This eclectic or pluralistic attitude was aptly observed by Homer B. Hulbert, an early missionary who went to Korea in 1886:

> The reader must ever bear in mind that in every Korean mind there is a jumble of the whole, that there is no antagonism between the different cults.... As a general thing, we may say that the all-round Korean will be a Confucian when in society, a Buddhist when he philosophises and a spirit worshipper when he is in trouble.[18]

It is not my goal to argue here whether or not this type of tolerant attitude was widespread among all Koreans, including Confucian scholars of the Chosŏn dynasty,[19] nor is it to discuss whether or not this kind of syncretic tendency is a positive and ideal paradigm for one's relationship to other religions.[20] The point here is that such an open and adaptable attitude toward religions found at least among the common people previously is now hardly seen among Koreans, even among Korean Christian lay followers, let alone their leaders. As a matter of fact, Korean Christianity as a whole is characterized by its extreme exclusivism against other religions.[21]

It is sad to observe, likewise, that Buddhism and Christianity in Korea have gone their separate ways with tight monologic mind-sets. The few serious contacts, even those that were initiated by some Christians, have often ended up being irritating and obnoxious. How might Korean religions move from monologue to dialogue?

Future Dialogical Partnership

With regard to our need to move from a monologic and antipathetic relationship to dialogical and amicable reciprocity, Leonard Swidler of Temple University once said, "It is only by struggling out of the self-centered monologic mindsets into dialogue with 'the others' as they really are, and not as we have projected them in our monologues, that we can avoid such cataclysmic disasters. In brief, we must move from the Age of Monologue to the Age of Dialogue." To emphasize the urgency of dialogical partnership among the religions of the world, he stated graphically, or almost bluntly, "The future offers two alternatives: death or dialogue."[22]

Paul Mojzes argues that the relation between religions can range from war to antagonism, indifference, dialogue, cooperation, and synthesis.[23] In the face of the grave consequences that might result from destructive interreligious relationships, Korean Buddhists and Christians should make a conscious decision to move toward reconciliation. Korean Buddhists and Christians must choose dialogue rather than death, dialogue and cooperation rather than war and antagonism. How then to move from the age of monologue to the age of dialogue? How then to change a relationship of indifference and antagonism to one of dialogue and cooperation?

Some time ago, while discussing the future possibility of Confucian-Christian dialogue in Korea, I made several suggestions that I believed would help foster a dialogical and cooperative relationship between the two religious traditions.[24] In this previous discussion, I recommended that Korean Confucians and Christians cultivate a pluralistic perspective and thus learn to see the other religion as complementary rather than as competitive or threatening to their own religion. I also proposed that, from this basic perspective, they develop a cooperative relationship or partnership of working together and thinking together. I would like to expand on these suggestions in this discussion of Buddhist-Christian relationship.

First of all, I believe that both Buddhists and Christians should realize that their dialogical relationship would enable them to embark upon what John S. Dunne calls "the spiritual adventure of our time," that is, "passing over to the standpoint of another culture, another way of life, another religion" and "coming back with new insight to one's own culture, one's own way of life, one's own religion."[25] Through this productive and mutually advantageous interaction, Korean Buddhists and Christians can bring about what is called "the fusion of horizons" that surely will vivify the religious vision and activate the socio-ethical life in Korea. It also seems to me that this process of passing over and coming back between Buddhism and Christianity can be most effectively carried out through what I call working together and thinking together.

A similar idea is expressed by Paul Knitter when he says, "The future will require with ever greater urgency that those of us who choose to live our lives religiously, will have to do so interreligiously." According to him, this means that "the task of understanding ourselves religiously ... will have to be carried out together with persons of other religious traditions."[26] Buddhism is of course not an entirely "other" religious tradition to Korean Christians, and neither is Korean Christianity a completely "other" religious faith to Korean Buddhists, for both of them are spiritualities shared by half of the Korean population. For Koreans, both religions are in a sense "our religions" shared by "our" people for the spiritual enrichment of "our" people. What could be more important for Korean Buddhists and Christians than trying to understand each other not only to bring about religious mutuality but also to come to their own religious maturity?

WORKING TOGETHER

In such a complex society as Korea's, no one religion can claim that it alone can answer all the questions the country faces now. All religions should cooperate in meeting the challenges of the time. In this sense, it is necessary that both Buddhists and Christians, as well as people belonging to any other religion, leave behind the old paradigms that see everything only in terms of right or wrong, true or false, superior or inferior, and other similar false dichotomies and dualistic categories. Instead of spending their time and energy in arguing to prove themselves to be the only superior, right, and true religion, they should unite themselves as partners in helping to save the Korean people from all kinds of social, economic, political, ethical, and religious ills and injustices. Furthermore, they should collaborate in the alleviation of the suffering resulting from the ecological problems that are so rampant in Korea now. They should join together in what Paul Knitter describes as "soterio-centric" concern.

In more concrete terms in the context of Korean society, this means that Buddhists and Christians in particular should put their ideals of compassion (*karuṇā*) and love (*agape*) together to take tender care of the underprivileged, the alienated, the marginalized, and the dehumanized strata of people in Korea. This also means that they must put their time and energy together in putting their ideal of being-for-others into practice and be concerned to solve the problems caused by Korea's rapid urbanization, industrialization, and commercialization. This means again that they should unite under the common endeavor of tackling the growing individualism, materialism, and fierce competition found in the newly modernized society of Korea. This of course means above all that they should work hand in hand to bring permanent peace in the Korean peninsula by realizing the reunification of their homeland.[27]

Korean Buddhists and Christians have a good historical precedent for such joint efforts among the religions in Korea. During the March First Independence Movement against Japanese colonial rule in 1919, Buddhists and Christians, together with Koreans of other religious persuasions, were willing together to risk even their lives to bring about the common goal of national independence. Buddhists and Christians should reenact this historical example and work together to help bring about a more peaceful, just, fair, and humane society in Korea.

THINKING TOGETHER

Although cooperative work in constructive socio-ethical projects between Buddhism and Christianity is extremely important, it should be pointed out that this "soterio-centric" concern on the socio-ethical dimension is not enough. I firmly believe that there should be thinking together as well: Buddhists and Christians should join together in discussing and sharing the fundamental issues in the realms of philosophy and theology, as other scholars have suggested.

To take a few examples, Professor Masao Abe and his friends propose that the comparison of the Buddhist concept of *sūnyatā* (emptiness) and the Christian idea of *kenosis* (emptying) would be a good topic for Buddhist-Christian conversation; Professor John Keenan suggests that Christian Christology should be reexamined in the light of Mahayana soteriology; and Professor Seiichi Yagi of Japan and his colleagues try to show that they can build a bridge between Buddhism and Christianity through various theological and conceptual frameworks.[28]

It seems to me that Korean theologians and Buddhist scholars can also have a fruitful dialogue by engaging themselves in exploring the concepts of *minjung* and sentient beings (*chungsaeng*). It is interesting to note that in recent years there have appeared some theologians and Buddhist scholars who are interested in "Minjung Theology" and "Minjung Buddhism," both of which are concerned with the people (*minjung*), especially suffering and marginalized people.[29]

I believe these and other attempts to develop Buddhist-Christian dialogue at the level of basic metaphysical and theoretical concerns are important in building up mutual understanding and congeniality between Buddhism and Christianity.[30] Such attempts will bring great merit to both religions, as well as to Korean society as a whole. It seems to me, however, that dialogue at a mere conceptual level is not enough. Dialogue ultimately must be carried out at the deepest level of spirituality.

WAKING UP TOGETHER

What is this deepest level? I believe that it is the level of ultimate transformation, which is called *kkaech'im* in Korean Buddhism and *metanoia* in Christianity. I am convinced that Buddhist-Christian dialogue, as well as any meaningful dialogues between any other religions, should be carried out on this ultimate level of consciousness-transformation. This type of dialogue is what I call a "metanoio-centric" approach, *metanoia* literally meaning "change of consciousness."

As is well known, Buddhism is a religion dedicated to *bodhi*, which means wisdom, awakening, enlightenment, and the like. This is what the

Buddha experienced under the bodhi tree in Bodhgaya at the moment of his awakening. This enlightenment experience is what all subsequent followers of the Buddha have sought in their religious pursuits. For most Buddhists this awakening experience—*kkaech'im* in Korean, *wu* in Chinese, and satori in Japanese—means the ultimate transformation of consciousness, which they believe makes them truly free and authentically human. This experience is what they call alpha and omega, heart and womb, the raison d'etre of Buddhism. Buddhism without this experience, according to many Buddhists, is "a sun without its light and heat."[31]

What about in Christianity? As I argued elsewhere, the central teaching of Jesus' ministry is his idea of *metanoia*, which he proclaimed in his first preaching: "Repent [*metanoiete*], for the kingdom of heaven is at hand."[32] As Hans Küng says, this is "a radical change in man's thinking and a conversion (Greek, *metanoia*), away from all forms of selfishness, toward God and his fellow men," which brings about "a changed awareness, a new way of thinking, a new scale of values." It is "a radical rethinking and re-turning on the part of the whole man, a completely new attitude to life." I agree with Küng when he concludes that this ultimate transformation of the whole being is "of central importance" in Christianity.[33]

What I would argue is that Buddhist-Christian dialogue should include, and ultimately center upon, this fundamentally crucial question of the ultimate transformation of consciousness. If Buddhists and Christians are engaged in a dialogue to confirm this experience as *a* (if not *the*) common goal of their religious endeavor and discuss various methods that might facilitate this transformation among a greater number of Korean Buddhists and Christians,[34] then their dialogical waking up together, I believe, would be significant and fruitful for both of these religions.

Conclusion

Hans Küng says, "No survival without world ethic. No world peace without peace between the religions. No peace between the religions without dialogue between the religions."[35] Where else can this be more relevant than in the contemporary Korean religious scene and society in general? At the present time Korea is one of the most religiously pluralistic societies. Many people in Korea, believers and nonbelievers alike, are now worried about the interreligious tension found in Korea.

I believe that both Buddhists and Christians should learn from Wŏnhyo, the great seventh-century Korean Buddhist thinker. In his famous *hwajaeng* (harmonization of disputes) theory, he encouraged a pluralistic perspective toward religious beliefs. With regard to reality, Wŏnhyo says, we cannot avoid facing many categorically opposing views such as being and nonbeing, emptiness and essence, that is, "eternalist and noneternalist views." According to him, "if we cling to either one of these two views," we fail to do justice to reality; instead, we should not absolutize any one side of the pair but accept each side as complementary to the other.[36] It seems to me that this type of pluralistic perspective so powerfully advocated by Wŏnhyo should be reactivated as a base for future Buddhist-Christian dialogue.

Thomas Merton, the great twentieth-century American thinker, says, "If the West continues to underestimate and neglect the spiritual heritage of the East, it may hasten the tragedy that threatens man and his civilization."[37] Korean Buddhists should know that even though they are Buddhists they too can underestimate and neglect the deepest level of spirituality in their own tradition and thus should learn to appreciate it again; and Korean Christians should realize that, even if they find a great deal of meaning in their newly adopted religious tradition, that does not mean that they should underestimate or neglect the traditional religions of the East.

It is a well-known fact that many aspects of Buddhism in contemporary Korea have been influenced by its encounter with Christianity.[38] As John Cobb Jr. also notes, it is true that "Christian theology is deeply affected by the encounter with Buddhism."[39] Regardless of what these two religions think, the age of monologue and separate development is already at an end. If such encounter and mutual influence is inevitable, it is indeed better for Korean Buddhism and Christianity to consciously engage in a more methodical and meaningful dialogue.[40] As Thich Nhat Hahn, a Vietnamese Buddhist monk, says, Jesus and Buddha must be brothers.[41] There is no reason that the followers of Jesus and those of the Buddha cannot have brotherly and sisterly dialogue. This type of congenial dialogue between Buddhism and Christianity is not only for their own mutual renewal and transformation but also, as Küng suggests, for the peaceful future of Korean society as a whole, which is essential at the same time for world peace as well. A truly amicable dialogue between these two religions in Korea, in this sense, must be considered as a prerequisite for their being globally responsible in bringing peace to this war-stricken world.

NOTES

I would like to thank professors Anselm Kyongsuk Min, Timothy S. Lee, and Robert Buswell for their comments and suggestions on early drafts of my chapter.

1. According to 1995 census figures released by the South Korean government, Christians, as a whole, comprise 8,354,000 people, constituting 26.3 percent of the total population. Roman Catholics comprise 6.6 percent of this figure, and

Protestants the remaining 19.7 percent. Republic of Korea, *1995 In'gujut'aek ch'ongjosa ch'oejong chonsujipkye kyŏlgwa* [The Final Results of the Census for Population and Housing in 1955]; see http://www.nso.go.kr/report/data/census5.htm. By comparison, Buddhism claims 8,060,000 adherents, or 23.2 percent.

2. For more detail, see James H. Grayson, *Korea: A Religious History* (Oxford: Clarendon, 1989), 46ff.

3. See Yukio Sakamoto, *Kegon-gaku Kyogaku no Kenkyū* [A Study of Huayan Doctrines] (Kyoto: Heirakuji Shoten, 1956, 1973), 421ff. and 233ff.

4. Robert E. Buswell, *The Korean Approach to Zen: The Collected Works of Chinul* (Honolulu: University of Hawai'i Press, 1983), and his more recent work, *Tracing Back the Radiance: Chinul's Korean Way of Zen* (Honolulu: University of Hawai'i Press, 1992). See also Hee Sung Keel, *Chinul: Founder of the Korean Sŏn Tradition* (Berkeley: Center for South and Southeast Asia Studies, University of California, 1984).

5. Noble Ross Reat, *Buddhism: A History* (Berkeley: Asian Humanities Press, 1994), 179.

6. Ibid., 182.

7. During the latter part of this period, Buddhist temples were not allowed to be built within the boundary of the capital city of Seoul. Moreover, Buddhist monks were denied access to the city.

8. See Lewis R. Lancaster, "Buddhism in Korea Survives Suppression and Change," in *Buddhism: A Modern Perspective*, ed. Charles S. Prebish (University Park: Pennsylvania State University Press, 1975), 216.

9. For some of these deeper reasons, see Kang-nam Oh, "Sagehood and Metanoia: The Confucian-Christian Encounter in Korea," *Journal of the American Academy of Religion* 61, no. 2 (1993): 305–308.

10. For the historical context of the early Christianity in Korea, see David Chung, *Syncretism: The Religious Context of Christian Beginnings in Korea*, ed. Kang-nam Oh (Albany: State University of New York Press, 2001).

11. Grayson, *Korea*, 206.

12. Pyŏn Sŏn-hwan et al., *Chonggyo Tawŏnjuŭi wa Han'guk-chŏk Sinhak* [Religious Pluralism and Korean Theology] (Seoul: Han'guk Sinhak Yŏn'guso, 1992).

13. *Vancouver Korean Press*, February 24, 1995, A-14. Recently a similar group has been formed with younger scholars such as Dr. Jin Kim, a Christian pastor and scholar, and Dr. Jin-wol, a Buddhist monk and scholar.

14. For a detailed report of similar incidents, see *Kidokkyo sasang* [Christian Thought], no. 479 (November 1998): 56–64. The cover story of this issue deals with the Buddhist-Christian encounter in Korea. For an excellent discussion of the so-called Christian incivility, see Timothy S. Lee, "Two Aspects of an Evangelical Quest to Christianize Korea: Mammoth Crusades and Sectarian Incivility," *Acta Koreana* 5, no. 2 (2002).

15. See also Pyŏn Sŏnhwan, "I ttang esŏ Chonggyo kaltŭng munje" [The Question of Religious Conflicts in this Land), *Tabo* 13 (Spring 1995): 49–51.

16. Ibid., 50ff. See also a personal witness given by Hyon Gak Sunim, an

American-born Buddhist monk in Korea, in his recent best-seller, *Manhaeng: Habadŭ esŏ Hwagyesa kkaji* [Buddhist Practice: From Harvard to the Hwagye Temple], 2 vols. (Seoul: Yŏllimwŏn, 1999).

17. Timothy S. Lee assumes that 95 percent of Korean Protestants are fundamentalists and evangelicals. To avoid giving the misleading impression that this chapter is an apologetic for Buddhism carried out on Buddhist terms, I tried to find some information regarding any Buddhist attacks on or critiques of Christianity. I have so far found no documented instances of Buddhists attacking Christian churches or cathedrals. When I visited Korea in June 2002, I asked the monk Jinwol, a proponent of interfaith dialogue in Korea, whether he was aware of any incidents in which Korean Buddhists attacked Christians verbally or physically in recent years, and he said he was not. I asked the same question of my Christian friends in Korea, and they gave the same answer. This question needs further investigation and research.

18. Homer B. Hulbert, *The Passing of Korea* (1906; repr., Seoul: Yonsei University, 1969), 403–404.

19. It should be noted that Confucian scholars of the Chosŏn dynasty were as exclusivistic as any group of people in the world. For more discussion, see John Isaac Goulde, "Anti-Buddhist Polemic in Fourteenth and Fifteenth Century Korea: The Emergence of Confucian Exclusivism" (Ph.D. diss., Harvard University, 1985); and Anselm Kyongsuk Min, *The Spiritual Ethos of Korean Catholicism* (Seoul: Sogang University Research Institute, 1971).

20. Prof. Anselm Kyongsuk Min, in his comments on this chapter, aptly pointed out that this "jumble of the whole" can be "an epitome of incoherence" if it is not based on "the principled ground of genuine respect for all religions."

21. See Kang-nam Oh, "Christianity and Religious Pluralism in Korea," *Religious Studies and Theology*, September 1986, 27–38. My personal experience since the publication of my book *Yesu-nŭn ŏpda* [No Such Jesus] (Seoul: Hyŏnamsa, 2001) testifies to this type of extreme exclusivism, especially among some ministers.

22. Leonard Swidler, John B. Cobb Jr., Paul F. Knitter, and Honica K. Hellwig, *Death or Dialogue: From the Age of Monologue to the Age of Dialogue* (London: SCM, 1990), viii.

23. "Types of Encounter Between Religions," in *Attitudes of Religions and Ideologies toward the Outsider*, ed. Leonard Swidler and Paul Mojzes (Lewiston, N.Y.: Edwin Mellen, 1990), 1.

24. Kang-nam Oh, "Sagehood and Metanoia: The Confucian-Christian Encounter in Korea," *Journal of the American Academy of Religion* 61, no. 2 (Summer 1993): 308–315.

25. John S. Dunne, *The Way of All the Earth* (New York: Macmillan, 1972), ix.

26. "Christian Salvation: Its Nature and Uniqueness: An Interreligious Proposal," paper sent to me in January 1995, 1.

27. See the most recent book by Francis Cardinal Arinze, *Religions for Peace: A Call for Solidarity to the Religions of the World* (New York: Doubleday, 2002).

28. See John B. Cobb Jr. and Christopher Ives, eds., *The Emptying God: A Buddhist-Jewish-Christian Conversation* (Maryknoll, N.Y.: Orbis, 1990); John Keenan,

The Meaning of Christ: A Mahayana Theology (Maryknoll, N.Y.: Orbis, 1989); and Seiichi Yagi and Leonard Swidler, *A Bridge to Buddhist-Christian Dialogue* (Mahwah, N.J.: Paulist Press, 1990). For more detail on the other possible topics for Buddhist-Christian dialogue, see Leonard Swidler's chapter, "Topics in the Dialogue," ibid., 11–37; Paul Ingram, *The Modern Buddhist-Christian Dialogue: Two Universalistic Religions in Transformation* (Lewiston, N.Y.: Edwin Mellen, 1987); Roger Corless and Paul F. Knitter, eds. *Buddhist Emptiness and Christian Trinity: Essays and Explorations* (Mahwah, N.J.: Paulist Press, 1990); Donald W. Mitchell, *Spirituality and Emptiness: The Dynamics of Spiritual Life in Buddhism and Christianity* (Mahwah, N.J.: Paulist Press, 1991); and Sallie B. King and Paul O. Ingram, eds., *The Sound of Liberating Truth: Buddhist-Christian Dialogues* (Surrey, England: Curzon, 1999), esp., David Chappell, "Buddhist Interreligious Dialogue: To Build a Global Community," 3–35. In addition, Prof. Robert Buswell suggested in his correspondence to me that the Buddhist concept of *upāya* (skillful means) and the traditional East Asian doctrine of three-teachings-are-one could be considered as contact points for Buddhist-Christian dialogue. I dealt with the idea of *upāya* in my paper "Christianity and Religious Pluralism in Korea," *Religious Studies and Theology* 6, no. 3 (September 1986): 27–38. For the import of the three-teachings-are-one doctrine for interreligious relationship, see Chung, *Syncretism*.

29. See Jung Young Lee, ed., *An Emerging Theology in World Perspective* (Mystic, Conn.: Twenty-Third Publications, 1988); and Pŏpsŏng et al., eds., *Minjung Pulgyo ŭi t'amgu* [In Search of Minjung Buddhism] (Seoul: Minjoksa, 1989), and *Arŭm ŭi haebang* [Liberation of Knowledge] (Seoul: Hanmadang, 1989).

30. For the other various theoretical frameworks, see Paul O. Ingram and Frederick J. Streng, eds., *Buddhist-Christian Dialogue: Mutual Renewal and Transformation* (Honolulu: University of Hawai'i Press, 1986).

31. See D. T. Suzuki: "In all events there is no Zen without satori, which is indeed the Alpha and Omega of Zen Buddhism. Zen devoid of satori is like a sun without its light and heat." In William Barrett, ed., *Zen Buddhism: Selected Writings of D. T. Suzuki* (Garden City, N.Y.: Doubleday, 1956), 84.

32. Oh, "Sagehood and Metanoia," 314; Matthew 4:17 and parallels.

33. Hans Küng, *On Being a Christian* (London: Collins, 1977), 191, 250.

34. Recently I found an interesting article written by Paul O. Ingram in which he suggested that there should be three forms of dialogue: conceptual, socially engaged, and interior. It seems that the third one, which "concentrates on spiritual techniques and their resulting experience," may be comparable to my "metanoiocentric" dialogue. See his "'Fruit Salad Can Be Delicious': The Practice of Buddhist-Christian Dialogue," *Cross Currents* 50, no. 4 (2001): 541–549.

35. *Global Responsibility in Search of a New World Ethic* (New York: Crossroad, 1991), xv.

36. For Wŏnhyo's idea on this point, see K. Oh, "Wŏnhyo's Buddhist Thought for Today," *Korean Studies in Canada* 2 (1994): 90–97. See also C. G. Jung's statement: "Only the paradoxical comes anywhere near to comprehending the fullness of life. Non-ambiguity and non-contradiction are one-sided and thus unsuited to express the incomprehensible." "Psychology and Alchemy," trans.

R. R. C. Hull, in *The Collected Works of C. G. Jung*, ed. Herbert Read et al. (Princeton, N.J.: Princeton University Press, 1977), 15.

37. Thomas Merton, *Mystics and Zen Masters* (New York: Farrar, Straus & Giroux, 1986), 46.

38. Some examples of the Christian influence on the Buddhist community *sangha* in Korea include more active recruiting of new members, reorganization of the ecclesiastical structure, popularization of Buddhist teachings through the so-called Buddhist training college (*kyoyang taehak*); regular meetings on Sundays, and so on.

39. Ingram and Streng, *Buddhist-Christian Dialogue*, 231.

40. One of the reviewers of this chapter suggested that although the responsibility of this type of dialogue on the Christian side must lie heavily on the mainline Christians, a continued attempt should be made to include more fundamentalist and evangelical Christians in this dialogue. I appreciate these comments.

41. See Thich Nhat Hahn's *Going Home: Jesus and Buddha as Brothers* (New York: Riverhead, 1999), and *Living Buddha and Living Christ* (New York: Riverhead, 1995). I have translated both books into Korean.

A Select Bibliography for the Study of Korean Christianity

Baker, Donald. "A Different Thread: Orthodoxy, Heterodoxy, and Catholicism in a Confucian World." In *Culture and the State in Late Chosŏn Korea*, edited by JaHyun Kim Haboush and Martina Deuchler, 199–281. Cambridge, Mass.: Harvard University Asia Center, 1999.

———. "The Martyrdom of Paul Yun: Western Religion and Eastern Ritual in 18th Century Korea." *Transactions of the Royal Asiatic Society, Korea Branch*, 54 (1979): 33–58.

———. "Tasan and His Brothers: How Religion Divided a Korean Confucian Family." In *Perspective in Korea*, edited by Sang Oak Lee and Duk Soo Park, 172–197. Sydney: Peony, 1998.

Biernatzki, S. J.; William E. Luke Jin-Chang Im; and Anselm K. Min. *Korean Catholicism in the 1970s*. Maryknoll, N.Y.: Orbis, 1975.

Billings, Peggy. *Fire Beneath the Frost: The Struggles of the Korean People and Church*. New York: Friendship Press, 1984.

Blair, William N., and Bruce Hunt. *The Korean Pentecost and the Suffering Which Followed*. Carlisle, Penn.: Banner of Trust, 1977.

Brown, G. Thompson. *Not by Might: A Century of Presbyterians in Korea*. Atlanta: Presbyterian Church in U.S.A., 1984.

Cho, Wha Soon. *Let the Weak Be Strong: A Woman's Struggle for Justice*. Edited by Lee Sun Ai and Ahn Sang Nim. Bloomington, Ind.: Meyer-Stone Books, 1988.

Ch'oe, Yongho. "Christian Background in the Early Life of Kim Il-Sŏng." *Asian Survey* 26, no. 10 (October 1986): 1082–1099.

Choi, Jaikeun. "Doctrinal and Institutional Development of Catholicism in 19th Century Korea: An Analysis Based on a Comparative Study of the Great Persecutions of 1801 and 1866." Ph.D. diss., Harvard University, 1997.

Christian Conference of Asia, ed. *Minjung Theology: People as the Subjects of History*. Singapore: Christian Conference of Asia, Commission on Theological Concerns, 1981.

Chryssides, George D. *The Advent of Sun Myung Moon: The Origins, Beliefs, and Practices of the Unification Church*. New York: Palgrave MacMillan, 1991.

Chung, Chaisik. *Korea: The Encounter between the Gospel and Neo-Confucian Culture*. Geneva: WCC Publications, 1997.

Chun, Sung C. *Schism and Unity in the Protestant Churches of Korea*. Seoul: Christian Literature Society of Korea, 1979.

Chung, David. *Syncretism: The Religious Context of Christian Beginnings in Korea*. Albany: State University of New York Press, 2001.

Chung, Jun Ki. *Social Criticism of Uchimura Kanzō and Kim Kyo-shin*. Seoul: UBF, 1988.

Clark, Allen. *A History of the Church in Korea*. 1961. Rev. ed., Seoul: Christian Literature Society of Korea, 1971.

———. *The Nevius Plan for Mission Work: Illustrated in Korea*. Seoul: Christian Literature Society, 1937.

Clark, Donald N. *Christianity in Modern Korea*. Asian Agenda Report, no. 5. Lanham, Md.; and London: University Press of America, 1986.

———. "Growth and Limitation of Minjung Christianity in South Korea." In *South Korea's Minjung Movement: The Culture and Politics of Dissidence*, edited by Kenneth M. Wells, 87–103. Honolulu: University of Hawai'i Press, 1995.

———. *Living Dangerously in Korea: The Western Experience 1900–1950*. Norwalk, Conn.: Eastbridge, 2003.

Corfe, C. J. *The Anglican Church in Corea*. Seoul: Seoul Press, 1905.

Dallet, Charles. *Histoire de l'Église de Coreé*. 2 vols. 1874. Reprint, Seoul: Royal Asiatic Society, Korea Branch, 1975.

Davis, Daniel M. *The Life and Thought of Henry Gerhard Appenzeller (1858–1902), Missionary to Korea*. Lewiston, N.Y.: Edwin Mellen, 1988.

Diaz, Hector. *A Korean Theology: Chu-gyo Yo-Ji: Essentials of the Lord's Teaching by Chŏng Yak-jong Augustine (1760–1801)*. Friebourg: Neue Zeitschrift für Missionswissenschaft, 1986.

Fisher, J. E. *Democracy and Mission Education in Korea*. New York: Teachers' College, Columbia University, 1928.

Grayson, James Huntley. "Cultural Encounter: Korean Protestantism and Other Religious Traditions." *International Bulletin of Missionary Research* 25, no. 2 (2001).

———. *Early Buddhism and Christianity in Korea: A Study in the Emplantation of Religion*. Leiden: E. J. Brill, 1985.

———. *Korea: A Religious History*. Rev. ed. London: RoutledgeCurzon, 2002.

Harrington, Fred Harvey. *God, Mammon, and the Japanese: Dr. Horace Allen and Korean-American Relations, 1884–1905*. Madison: University of Wisconsin Press, 1944.

Harvey, Youngsook Kim. "The Korean Shaman and the Deaconess: Sisters in Different Guises." In *Religion and Ritual in Korean Society*, edited by Laurel Kendall and Griffin Dix, 149–170. Korea Research Monograph, no. 12. Berkeley: Institute of East Asian Studies, University of California, 1987.

Hunt, Everett N. *Protestant Pioneers in Korea*. Maryknoll, N.Y.: Orbis, 1980.

Huntley, Martha. *Caring, Growing, Changing: A History of the Protestant Mission in Korea*. New York: Friendship Press, 1984.

Hurston, Karen. *Growing the World's Largest Church*. Springfield, Mo.: Chrism, 1994.

International Review of Mission. Special issue titled "Han'guk kyohoe: sŏn'gyo 100 chu'nyŏn [Korean Church: 100th Anniversary of the Mission]. Vol. 74, no. 293 (January 1985).

Kang, Wi Jo. *Christ and Caesar in Modern Korea: A History of Christianity and Politics*. Albany: State University of New York Press, 1997.

———. *Religion and Politics in Korea under Japanese Rule*. Studies in Asian Thought and Religion, vol. 5. Lewiston, N.Y.: Edwin Mellen, 1987.

Kerr, Edith A., and George Anderson. *The Austrian Presbyterian Mission in Korea, 1889–1941*. [Sydney?]: Australian Presbyterian Board of Missions, 1970.

Kim, Changseok Thaddeus. *Holy Places of the Korean Martyrs*. Seoul: Lay Apostolate Council of Korea, 1986.

———. *Lives of 103 Martyr Saints of Korea*. Seoul: Catholic Publishing House, 1984.

Kim, Helen. *Grace Sufficient: The Story of Helen Kim*. Nashville, Tenn.: The Upper Room, 1964.

Kim, Joseph Changmun, and Chung John Jaesun, eds. *Catholic Korea Yesterday and Today*. Seoul: Catholic Press, 1964.

Kim, Nyung. "The Politics of Religion in South Korea, 1974–1989: The Catholic Church's Political Opposition to the Authoritarian State." Ph.D. diss., University of Washington, 1993.

Kim, Sung-gun. "Korean Christianity and the Shinto Shrine Issue in the War Period, 1931–1945: A Sociological Study of Religion and Politics." Ph.D. diss., University of Hull, 1989.

Kim, Yong-bock, ed. *Minjung Theology: People as the Subjects of History*. Singapore: Christian Conference of Asia, 1981.

Korea Journal. Special issue titled "200 Years of Korean Catholicism." August 1984.

Lancaster, Lewis R., and Richard K. Payne. *Religion and Society in Contemporary Korea*. Korea Research Monograph, no. 24. Berkeley: Institute of East Asian Studies, University of California, Berkeley, 1997.

Lee, Chull. "Social Sources of the Rapid Growth of the Christian Church in Northwest Korea, 1895–1910." Ph.D. diss., Boston University, 1997.

Lee, Jong Hyeong. "Samuel Austin Moffett: His Life and Work in the Development of the Presbyterian Church of Korea, 1890–1936." Ph.D. diss., Union Theological Seminary in Virginia, 1983.

Lee, Jung Young, ed. *Ancestor Worship and Christianity in Korea*. Vol. 8: *Studies in Asian Thought and Religion*. Lewiston, N.Y.: Edwin Mellen, 1988.

Lee, Kun Sam. *The Christian Confrontation with Shinto Nationalism*. Philadelphia: Presbyterian and Reformed Publishing Co., 1966.

Lee, Peter H., ed. *Sourcebook of Korean Civilization*. Vol. 2: *From the Seventeenth Century to the Modern Period*. New York: Columbia University Press, 1996. (Translated primary sources on Korean history, culture, and religion.)

Lee, Timothy S. "Born-Again in Korea: The Rise and Character of Revivalism in (South) Korea, 1885–1988." Ph.D. diss., University of Chicago, 1996.

———. "A Political Factor in the Rise of Protestantism in Korea: Protestantism and the 1919 March First Movement." *Church History* 69, no. 1 (March 2000): 116–142.

Moffett, Samuel H. *The Christians of Korea*. New York: Friendship Press, 1962.

Moon, Steve S. C. "The Recent Korean Missionary Movement: A Record of Growth, and More Growth Needed." *International Bulletin* 27, no. 1 (January 2003): 11–16.

Mortmann, Jürgen, et al., eds. *Minjung: Theologie des Volkes Gottes in Südkorea.* Neukirchen-Vylun: Neukirchener Verlag, 1984.

Mullins, Mark R., and Richard Fox Young, eds. *Perspectives on Christianity in Korea and Japan: The Gospel and Culture in East Asia.* Lewiston, N.Y.: Edwin Mellen, 1995.

Oak, Sung Deuk. "The Indigenization of Christianity in Korea: North American Missionaries' Attitudes towards Korean Religions, 1884–1910." Th.D. diss., Boston University, 2002.

———. ed. *Sources of Korean Christianity, 1832–1945.* Seoul: Institute for Korean Church History, 2004.

Ogle, George E. *How Long, O Lord: Stories of Twentieth-Century Korea.* Philadelphia: Xlibris, 2002.

———. *Liberty to the Captives.* Atlanta: John Knox Press, 1977.

Omenyo, Cephas N., and David Choi. "Korean Missionary Enterprise in West Africa 1979–1999: A Preliminary Study." *Exchange* 29, no. 3: 213–239.

Pak, Ung Kyu. "From Fear to Hope: The Shaping of Premillennialism in Korea, 1884–1945." Ph.D. diss., Westminster Theological Seminary, 1998.

Paik, Jong Koe. *Constructing Christian Faith in Korea: The Earliest Protestant Mission and Ch'oe Pyŏng-hŏn.* Zoetermeer: Uitgeverij Boekencentrum, 1998.

Paik, L. George. *The History of Protestant Missions in Korea, 1832–1910.* 1927. Reprint, Seoul: Yonsei University Press, 1987.

Palmer, Spencer. *Korea and Christianity: The Problem of Identification with Tradition.* Seoul: Hollym, 1967.

Park, Andrew Sung. *The Wounded Heart of God: The Asian Concept of Han and the Christian Doctrine of Sin.* Nashville, Tenn.: Abingdon, 1993.

Park, Chung-shin. *Protestantism and Politics in Korea.* Seattle: University of Washington Press, 2003.

Park, Seong-won. *Worship in the Presbyterian Church in Korea: Its History and Implications.* Frankfurt am Main: Peter Lang, 1999.

Rha, Young Bok. "An Analysis of the Terms Used for God in Korea in the Context of Indigenization." Th.D. diss., Boston University, 1977.

Ruiz de Medina, Juan G. *The Catholic Church in Korea: Its Origins, 1566–1784.* Translated by John Bridges. Rome: Instituto Storico, 1991.

Sauer, Charles August. *Methodists in Korea, 1930–1960.* Seoul: Christian Literature Society, 1970.

Sayer, Robert. "Potters and Christians: New Light on Korea's First Catholics." *Korean Culture* 6, no. 2: 26–39.

Scott, William. *Canadians in Korea: Brief Historical Sketch of Canadian Mission Work in Korea.* N.p.: 1975.

Shearer, Roy E. *Wildfire, Church Growth in Korea.* Grand Rapids, Mich.: Eerdmans, 1966.

Sunoo, Harold Hakwon. *Repressive State and Resisting Church: The Politics of the CIA in South Korea.* Fayette, Mo.: Korean American Cultural Association, 1976.

Underwood, Horace G. *The Call of Korea.* New York: Fleming H. Revell, 1908.

Underwood, Lillias H. *Underwood of Korea.* 1918. Reprint, Seoul: Yonsei University, 1983.

Wangerin, Theodora S. *God Sent Me to Korea.* Washington, D.C.: Review and Herald Publishing Association, 1968.

Wasson, Alfred W. *Church Growth in Korea.* New York: International Missionary Council, 1934.

Wells, Kenneth M. *New God, New Nation: Protestants and Self-Reconstruction Nationalism in Korea, 1896–1937.* Honolulu: University of Hawai'i Press, 1990.

Won, Yong Ji. *A History of Lutheranism in Korea: A Personal Account.* St. Louis, Mo.: Concordia Seminary, 1988.

Yi, Young-suk. "Liberal Protestant Leaders Working for Social Change: South Korea, 1957–1984." Ph.D. diss., University of Oregon, 1990.

Yu Chai-shin, ed. *The Founding of Catholic Tradition in Korea.* Mississauga, Ontario: University of Toronto, 1996.

———. *Korea and Christianity.* Seoul: Korean Scholar Press, 1996.

Contributors

Donald Baker teaches Korean history and religion in the Department of Asian Studies at the University of British Columbia in Vancouver, Canada, where he is also director of the university's Centre for Korean Research. He served as Luce Distinguished Professor of Korean Christianity at the University of California, Los Angeles, in 2004.

Robert E. Buswell Jr. is professor of Buddhist Studies in the Department of Asian Languages and Cultures at the University of California, Los Angeles, and founding director of UCLA's Center for Korean Studies and Center for Buddhist Studies. He is principal investigator for the Luce Program in Korean Christianity.

Paul Yunsik Chang received his MA in Theological Studies from Harvard Divinity School and his MA in sociology from the University of California, Los Angeles, where he was a Luce Predoctoral Fellow in the study of Korean Christianity. He is currently a Ph.D. candidate in the Sociology Department at Stanford University.

Cho Kwang is professor of Korean history at Korea University. His research focuses on the social and political history of the late Chosŏn dynasty. He is the author of, among many other publications, *Chosŏn hugi Ch'ŏnjukyosa yŏn'gu* (A Study of Late-Chosŏn Catholic History) (Seoul: Koryŏ Taehakkyo Minjok Munhwa Yŏn'guso, 1988).

Donald N. Clark is professor of history at Trinity University, San Antonio, Texas, where he also serves as director of its International Studies Program. His many publications include *Christianity in Modern Korea* (Lanham, Md.; and London: University Press of America, 1986); *Culture and Customs of Korea* (Westport, Conn.: Greenwood Press, 2000); and *Living Dangerously in Korea: The Western Experience 1900–1950* (Norwalk, Conn.: EastBridge, 2002).

Kelly H. Chong received her doctorate in sociology from the University of Chicago and is currently a research associate and visiting lecturer in the Women's Studies in Religion program at the Harvard Divinity School. She has published articles in *Sociology of Religion* and the *Journal of Women's History* and is currently working on a project dealing with women, religion, and the politics of gender in South Korea.

James Huntley Grayson, an anthropologist with an interest in the historical transmission of religions, is professor of Modern Korean Studies and director of the Centre for Korean Studies, School of East Asian Studies, at the University of Sheffield, England.

Wi Jo Kang is Wilhelm Loehe Professor Emeritus at Wartburg Theological Seminary in Dubuque, Iowa. After receiving his Ph.D. from the University of Chicago, he taught for thirty-five years, holding positions at Columbia University, Seoul National University, Yonsei University, and the University of California, Los Angeles (as Luce Distinguished Professor of Korean Christianity in 2003). His publications include *Religion and Politics in Korea under the Japanese Rule* (Lewiston, N.Y.: Edwin Mellen, 1987) and *Christ and Caesar in Modern Korea: A History of Christianity and Politics* (Albany: State University of New York Press, 1997).

Byong-suh Kim is professor emeritus of sociology at Ewha Woman's University (Seoul). In 2001 he served as the first Luce Distinguished Professor of Korean Christianity at the University of California, Los Angeles. His recent research includes work on social stratification and Christianity in Korea.

Chong Bum Kim received his B.A. in history from Cornell University, M.Div. from the Harvard Divinity School, and M.A. and Ph.D. from Harvard University. He has taught at Harvard University; the University of Massachusetts, Boston; and Bentley College.

Wonil Kim is assistant professor of Old Testament Studies at La Sierra University. He is a co-editor of *Reading the Hebrew Bible for a New Millennium: Form, Concept, and Theological Perspective* (Harrisburg, Pa.: Trinity Press International, 2000).

Gari Ledyard has been associated with the study of Korean history and culture for more than fifty years. He taught at Columbia University in

New York for most of that time, retiring in 2000 as King Sejong Professor of Korean Studies Emeritus. He continues to be active in research and writing.

Timothy S. Lee received his Ph.D. from the University of Chicago Divinity School and is assistant professor of the history of Christianity and director of the Asian Studies Program at Brite Divinity School, Texas Christian University. In 2002 he served as the Luce Postdoctoral Fellow in Korean Christianity at the University of California, Los Angeles.

Sung-Deuk Oak is visiting assistant professor of Korean Christianity at the University of California, Los Angeles, and was previously a Luce Postdoctoral Fellow at UCLA. His publications include *Sources of Korean Christianity, 1832–1945* (Seoul: Institute for Korean Church History, 2004), *Horace G. Underwood Papers*, vol. I (2004), *Correspondence of John Ross and Henry Loomis* (2004), and *The Rise of Korean Protestant Christianity: North American Missionaries' Attitudes towards Korean Religions, 1884–1910* (forthcoming).

Kang-nam Oh received his B.A. and M.A. from Seoul National University and his Ph.D. from McMaster University in Canada. He is professor of Religious Studies at the University of Regina, Canada, where he teaches Buddhism, mysticism, and religious pluralism.

Anselm Kyongsuk Min is professor of philosophy of religion and theology at Claremont Graduate University. His many books include *Dialectic of Salvation: Issues in the Theology of Liberation; Korean Christianity 2000: Beyond Authoritarianism and Ecclesiocentrism* (in Korean); *The Solidarity of Others in a Divided World: A Postmodern Theology after Postmodernism*; and *Paths to the Triune God: An Encounter between Aquinas and Recent Theologies.*

Jacqueline Pak is a visiting professor of Korean Studies at the University of Pennsylvania. As a Luce Postdoctoral Fellow in 2001, she taught the history of Korean Christianity at the University of California, Los Angeles. Her forthcoming book, *The Founding Father: Ahn Changho and the Origins of Korean Democracy,* is based on archival research on An Ch'angho and Sŏ Chaep'il. She is also the editor of *Famine or Feast: North and South— Democracy, Division, and Diaspora* (New York: Asia Society with M. E. Sharpe, 2005).

Yi Mahn-yol has taught for more than three decades at Sookmyung Women's University in Seoul. He is currently chairman of the Institute of Korean History and served for ten years as director of the Institute of Korean Church History Studies. His many publications include *Han'guk Kidokkyo wa minjok ŭisik* (Korean Protestantism and National Consciousness) and *Han'guk Kidokkyo ŭiryosa* (A History of Christian Medical Practices in Korea).

Index

In this index the use of *t* indicates a table found in the text.